Grow Rich while Walking into the Golden Aged World (with Meditation Commentaries)

Written by:

Brahma Kumari Pari,

LL.B. (Hons.)(London), LL.M (Wol.), Ph.D.

Edited by:

Sivaneswary Laws, BA (Hons.) English and Philosophy

Table of Contents

Figure 4

Other Books by Brahma Kumari Pari

About the Author

The author of this book is in the process of walking into the Golden Aged world. Through this book, based on her experiences and the knowledge which she has acquired, she is:

1. guiding others to walk into the Golden Aged World.

2. teaching on how one could come out of financial and other difficulties.

The author was writing articles on her Golden Aged experiences before she began to write books. She has also been writing articles and books on:

1. the Holographic Universe,

2. her various kinds of spiritual experiences,

3. the quantum energies which are involved with providing the world, including the Golden Aged world.

4. the various ancient religious knowledge,

5. Brahma Kumaris Raja Yoga, meditation practices, history etc.

The author has been widely reading on the Hindu scriptures, meditation and yoga practices, etc. since she was a little girl. In 1994, she was introduced to the knowledge of the Brahma Kumaris. In 1996, she began writing articles. Her first book "Holographic Universe: An Introduction" was published in January 2015. The book "Grow Rich while Walking into the Golden Aged World (with Meditation Commentaries)" was published in October 2016. Around the beginning of 2017, she began writing her third book titled "Expansion of the Universe".

Chapter 1: Introduction

In accordance with the knowledge of the Brahma Kumaris, at the end of each Cycle of Time, people walk into the new, perfect, heavenly world which exists in the Golden Age. The Golden Age is the first Age in the Cycle of Time. The Cycle of Time is about how time flows in a cyclic manner in the following order:

1. Golden Age or Satyuga.

2. Silver Age or Tretayuga.

3. Mid-Confluence Age (Confluence between the Silver and Copper Ages).

4. Copper Age or Dwapuryuga.

5. Iron Age or Kaliyuga.

6. Confluence Age or Sangamyuga (Confluence between Kaliyug and Golden Age).

The Golden Aged world is paradise on earth. Everyone lives a heavenly life as deities because all souls are spiritually powerful. No-one suffers and one can get whatever one wants, including wealth, in the Golden Aged world.

Currently, people are living in the Iron Aged world or Kaliyug. In Kaliyug, souls are in a spiritually weak state and so they suffer. People will find it very difficult to get what they want while they are living in Kaliyug. Those who use the practices in this book can bring themselves out of this bad Kaliyug state, through walking into the Golden Aged world. Even if one was not interested in walking into the Golden Aged world, one can use the practices in this book to get whatever one wants, including money.

While walking into the Golden Aged world (hereafter referred to as "walking in"), one is walking out of the current Kaliyug world and is beginning to live in the Golden Aged world. It begins with living in the Golden Aged subtle dimension. Then, as the Golden Aged world materialises, one lives in the Golden Aged Holographic World and Golden Aged Real World.

According to the knowledge of the Brahma Kumaris (hereafter referred to as the 'BK knowledge'), the rich people in the first half cycle will be helping the royalty who rule the world, and trade will be carried out like a game.

It is the rich people, who walk in, who will be establishing the trading system that will be used in the Golden Aged world. This trading system will be like a game which entertains the people in the first half cycle.

Life is a game which was meant to be enjoyed. If you have more money, you have more play stuff to play around with. Read this book, and use the suggested practices, with this attitude. Then, you will not be caught up with greed, which is a vice. Vices will not allow you to get the best. You will understand why I am saying this, as you read the rest of this book.

Those who walk in will also be helping to establish the Golden Aged governments. So they establish the system where the royalty work along with the rich people for what has to be done in the world.

A lot of rich people will be walking into the Golden Aged world to set up the kingdoms, trade systems etc. You can also be one of these rich people walking in to play a role as a rich person. You can start accumulating your wealth from now and so your role will begin from now.

The people who walk in can use the wealth which they get, via the walking in process, while they are living their lives in the Kaliyug world. When the Golden Aged world materialises, they will use their wealth in the Golden Aged world.

Even during the Mid-Confluence, the rich people played a significant role for getting things done for the second half cycle. These rich people will play a role, in their afterlife, at the end of the cycle, during the walking in process. The souls, of those Mid-Confluence Aged rich people, would have taken a birth which will be involved with the walking in process now. This birth would be their final birth in this Cycle of Time. While walking in, during the present birth, they would also be influenced by their Mid-Confluence Aged past births which would be playing their role in their afterlife. These souls will regain all their wealth, which they had during the Mid-Confluence, because they had done worship to use their wealth in their afterlife. These worship practices included burying the wealth of the person with the corpse. Through using this wealth, now, the soul would be able to establish whatever is needed for the Golden Aged world. They will help to set up the governments, get buildings built, establish the trading system as part of the game of life, etc. Until the Golden Aged world materialises, they can use their wealth in the Kaliyug world. It may be possible that you are also one of those Mid-Confluence Aged souls who will be regaining your wealth now. If you were, you will find that you can easily get wealth through using the practices in this book.

Those who walk in, as the rich people, can also become part of the royal or ruling clan. The scientists will play a significant role with them. In their present life itself, these people can get name, fame, wealth etc. through participating in the development of the new Golden Aged kingdoms.

There will be rich kingdoms in the Golden Aged world because many wealthy people will be working with the rulers to bring the kingdom a lot of wealth. Some of these wealthy people will also be rulers. In fact, the rulers will also be wealthy.

It does not matter if you belong to a kingdom or not because you can just walk in and live as you like in your own place or in your own kingdom. There will be lots of land, outside the huge kingdoms, which you can live in as you like. There will be complete freedom in the new

Golden Aged world. If you have a trade, others will contact you for what you have to offer.

The Brahma Kumaris are involved with training the 900,000 souls who have to be ready for transforming the world into the Golden Aged world (hereafter referred to as 'world transformation'). When they are ready, world transformation will take place. Then, you can walk into the materialised Golden Aged world. Until then, you will be involved with the walking in process.

Through the walking in process, you attain the ability to get whatever you want with just a thought. Since your spiritual power increases, as you use the practices in this book, your ability to get what you want, through just a thought, increases. For this same reason, your visualisations, desires, goals etc. will also easily materialise. If you asked God for something, God will also give it to you. In this book, I have explained about how God, the Kundalini, World Drama, Cosmic Consciousness, Collective Consciousness, QE Light, etc. will be helping you to get what you want, visualise etc.

The Quantum Energies' Light ("QE Light" hereafter) is the spiritual light of quantum energies. Quantum energies have QE Light instead of having a soul. The QE Light initiates what needs to be done for the people in the Corporeal World. The quantum energies provide what is in the Real World (physical world or material world) as initiated by the QE Light. The QE Light serves the people well, in the Golden Age. So, what the Golden Aged people want is materialised in the Real World. Those who walk in can also enjoy this benefit when their spiritual stage is high (as they walk into the Golden Aged world).

In the chapters of this book, there are also explanations about:

1. how the Law of Attraction works to bring you an abundance of wealth and prosperity through resonance of frequencies, aura, QE Light, etc.

2. how one's thoughts etc. are materialised through the pure frequencies that create what exists in the Real World.

3. why we can get what we want when we are surrounded by the frequencies for abundance and through the resonance of these frequencies. All these are possible because human souls have the ability to be co-creators along with the QE Light and quantum energies. In the first half cycle, the people had the ability to act as co-creators while in the conscious state. However, the people in the second half cycle no longer have this ability while they are in the conscious state. Those who are walking in are re-acquiring this ability. So they begin to act as co-creators even while in the conscious state. You will understand why this is so as you keep reading this book.

In this book, I have also explained about how your visualisations, thoughts etc. materialise through the World Drama within the soul and through the 2D Subtle World Drama ("2D SWD" hereafter) in the Holographic Universe. The 2D SWD is like the Holographic Film based on which everything exists in the Holographic Universe. Whatever exists in the Holographic Universe also exists in the Real World because of the quantum energies' wave-particle duality aspect. The QE Light and quantum energies, in the Holographic Universe, materialise what is in the 2D SWD as the World Drama on earth. Everything that is happening on earth is exactly as it is in the 2D SWD. You will have a better understanding of the 2D SWD, as you keep reading this book. You will also learn how the World Drama deep within the soul and the 2D SWD are used to give you what you visualise etc.

All souls in the Corporeal World are connected to each other via the 2D SWD. Thus, if a person needs something or provides something, others in the Corporeal World would be able to know of it and act accordingly. However, it is only the people in the first half cycle who live in a united manner via the 2D SWD, in this way. Thus, they know of what others want; if they are involved with providing what others want, they will contact the others or the others will contact them (since both are connected via the 2D SWD). Through the 2D SWD, they become aware of all the relevant circumstances which will help them to play their role well in the World Drama that is taking place in the Corporeal World.

However, in the Kaliyug world, the spiritual energies of the souls are weak. So people are not aware of what others want and they do not know of who to go to if they need something. Visualisations and meditation are necessary to keep people connected via the 2D SWD. The content in this book explains all this further and helps the reader to get connected to others via the 2D SWD. Through using what has been written in this book, one will be able to participate through the 2D SWD, as one should be participating.

The universe which we live in is like a god. For convenience, I am going to refer to this aspect of the universe as the Universe God. The Universe God includes:

1. the energies of the soul which are entangled with the QE Light,

2. all the QE Light energies in the universe,

3. all the quantum energies in the universe, and

4. all the laws which govern the universe.

The energies of the soul are part of this Universe God because we play a role as co-creators along with the QE Light and quantum energies everyday while we are living in the Corporeal World, though we are not aware that we are. We are not aware of this because the energies of the soul which are used as the Conscious Self are not entangled with the QE Light energies for co-creation. It is the deeper energies of the soul which are entangled with the QE Light energies for co-creation and it is these deeper energies which are playing a role as co-creators with the QE Light and quantum energies. It is not easy to understand the Universe God because of the huge complex system that is involved with providing the Real World which we live in. We might have just understood one aspect of it but not the other aspects. In this book, I am briefly explaining what I have understood so far. More explanations will be given in subsequent books.

It should be noted that I have used the concept 'Quantum God' while referring to all the 'QE Light and quantum energies acting as a god during the creation process'. Actually, the Quantum God has a point as the source of energies and it includes:

1. the point source of the QE Light energies.

2. the point source of the quantum energies.

The Quantum God does not include the role of the energies of the soul during the creation process. The concept 'Universe God' includes the energies of human souls playing a role together with the QE Light and quantum energies for the creation process.

The QE Light links everything in the Corporeal World. Through this, you will be able to get whatever you want, including money, land, success, etc. This has been explained further, in this book.

In this book, I have also explained what you need to know about the chakras, Siddhis (powers), specialties, silence, etc. so that you will understand how and why you are able to get what you want through thoughts, visualisations etc.

The people of the Golden Aged world are deities. These deities don't have to do anything to materialise what they want. Nature, the World Drama, QE Light and quantum energies and everything else serves them well. The deities and the QE Light, together, play the role of the creators in the Golden Age. So what the deities' desire will be materialised. Those who walk into the Golden Aged world also acquire these abilities while walking in and they will have these abilities after having walked into the Golden Aged world. Thus, they will find it easier and easier to have their desires materialised. Most present day people are not consciously playing a role as creators with the QE Light because of the weak energies of the Conscious Self. Thus, their desires are not easily materialised. This will be understood better as you keep reading this book.

World transformation takes place through the Confluence Age, at the

end of the cycle. Thus, it is taking place now. Those who walk in have to
be in the Confluence Age. To come into the Confluence Age, one has to
be introduced to the BK knowledge. God's Sounds of Silence accompany
the BK knowledge. These assist to give you a link to God so that you can
be brought into the Confluence Age and walk into the Golden Aged
world. As a result, in this book (from Chapter 2 to Chapter 10), you are
introduced to the knowledge which is given during the Brahma Kumaris'
7 Days Course. New comers, in the Brahma Kumaris, receive their link to
God when they are given this 7 Days Course. Acceptance of this
knowledge, which is given during the 7 Days Course, will automatically
enable you to get your link to God. Knowing this knowledge, before
reading about the walking in process, will make sure that you have your
link to God so that you can begin your walking in process as you are
reading this book. You need this link to God for the walking in process
because you need God's help to get uplifted into the Higher Universe
where the new Golden Aged world is getting created. In the Higher
Universe, you will be using lokas (worlds/dimensions) while in a state
where you are empowered with magical abilities. While you are in those
lokas, you will easily get what you want. Though those walking in are
using the lokas and dimensions in the Higher Universe, their physical
body will still be in the Lower Universe (where the Kaliyug world exists)
until the Golden Aged world materialises in the Higher Universe. I have
explained all this further, in this book. Knowing about these lokas, their
relevant chakras and auric fields, etc. will help you to understand what
is happening to you, during the walking in process, and why you can get
whatever you want, think, visualise etc.

The Mid-Confluence Aged gods had established the loka systems,
worship systems and had left a lot of knowledge behind which were to
be used during their afterlife (now). These Mid-Confluence Aged gods
are the past births of those walking in as the Sun Dynasty souls. Thus,
those walking in will be greatly benefiting from all that which had been
left behind and they will also be able to easily use the higher
dimensions. More on all these are explained in the later chapters of this
book.

In Chapter 12 and Chapter 13 of this book, I have also introduced the murlis (God's classes in the Brahma Kumaris) which BKs are introduced to, after receiving the 7 Days Course. Contemplating on the knowledge in these murlis will help you to become spiritually powerful. As you become spiritually powerful, your ability (to get what you want) improves. This is so because you are in the process of walking into the Golden Aged world.

To walk in, one must use the BK knowledge. At least, they must use the BK knowledge which I have provided in this book. The contents in this book provide you with all the relevant BK knowledge which you will need to get your link to God.

This book was written as part of God's service for world transformation. Thus, God is keeping an eye to help all those who read this book. Therefore, they get their link to God and begin their journey to walk into the Golden Aged world.

In the Brahma Kumaris, the BK Knowledge is considered as wealth. Constantly contemplating on the BK knowledge will enable one to accumulate their rights to wealth which they will enjoy in the first half cycle. However, those walking in can enjoy their wealth in this birth itself.

Since the practices in this book are for the walking in process, God only plays the role of the Mother for all those who use the practices in this book. This means:

1. you are not expected to follow all the strict Maryadas which the BKs follow. You can live your life, as you wish.

2. You will not be exposed to a lot of God's vibrations directly unless you have a strong link to God through constantly and seriously making spiritual efforts through using the BK knowledge. If you do not make serious spiritual efforts through using the BK knowledge, you will be receiving a lot of God's vibrations indirectly through the Confluence Aged Prana. Thus, you will easily experience and remain in the blissful

stage.

3. God will always be there helping and guiding you like a loving Mother who is not able to take Her Eyes off her child.

All the above will help those walking in to live an easy life with easy effort making so as to enjoy bliss and happiness, and so as to easily get that which is desired.

In the Brahma Kumaris, God initially plays the role of the Mother for those who have just received the BK knowledge. Then, God plays the role of the Father so that they can become spiritually powerful. This means that initially BKs have a good time with easy effort-making. God will help them to have a good stage easily and give them experiences to keep them entertained. He showers them with His vibrations, even though they are not making spiritual efforts seriously. However, with time, God will begin to play the role of the Father to these BKs. Thus, these BKs are expected to make serious spiritual efforts to get their link to God so that they can enjoy the blissful stage and get purified. BKs will also be expected to follow the BK Maryadas strictly. However, God never plays the role of the Father to those who walk into the Golden Aged world. God only plays the role of the loving, giving Mother to all those who walk into the Golden Aged world. Among other things, the myths about the 'Mother and child' reflects God's role as the Mother to His child (those walking into the Golden Aged world). It reflects how God takes good care of those walking in (as a mother would take care of her child). Those myths were a reflection of what happens at the end, during the creation of the Golden Aged world.

The Brahma Kumaris discourage worship because they have to train their members to become powerful souls, since God has given them the duty to make sure that the 900,000 most powerful Confluence Aged souls are ready for transforming the Real World into the Golden Aged Real World. World transformation takes place through self-transformation. Transforming the world through 'transforming the self' is not easy. As God has said in His teachings in the Brahma Kumaris: it is not like going to your auntie's house. Thus, the Brahma Kumaris do not encourage their members to get involved with bhakti/worship. However, those who are walking in do not have the duty to make sure that they are ready for world transformation. Thus, those who are walking in can still get whatever they want, including wealth, through worshipping God.

In the Kaliyug world, people earn money and accumulate wealth because they can use it to have a good time and enjoy happiness. The happiness which is experienced from this is temporary happiness. You can be happy without using your wealth. You will just have to emerge the virtues of happiness which are there deep within the soul. Through emerging the divine energies, you can easily establish a strong link to God. Then, through your link to God, you will be receiving an ocean of happiness and bliss from God, and so you will be enriched with happiness and bliss. This means: you can be happy without being dependent on the use of money. You become a master of the world, a god and a master of all virtues and powers. Thus, you will be able to remain happy all the time.

Further, since you are in the process of walking into the Golden Aged world, you will be able to easily experience happiness through easily remaining in the higher dimensions. God's energies, which are in those higher dimensions, will help you to remain happy.

In the Golden Age, you will experience constant bliss and happiness since you will constantly be in the soul conscious state. You are acquiring this ability now, during the walking in process. So you will find it very easy to enjoy happiness, bliss etc. while walking in and this is worth more than that which money can buy.

Use what I have written in this book to initiate the walking in process. Continue using the practices suggested in this book until you have completely walked into the Golden Aged world. Keep the thought that you are walking into the Golden Aged world, in your mind constantly, and you will be walking into the Golden Age. You will be using various higher lokas in the Holographic Universe since the world is getting uplifted into a dimension which exists beyond the current Corporeal World. All these are explained in this book so that you will understand what is happening to you as you are walking into the Golden Aged world. It will be very easy to experience bliss in the higher dimensions and you will understand why this is so, as you keep reading this book.

Through the practices in this book, you will be enriched with money, property, long life, good health, happiness, bliss, etc. (whether you are walking in or not). Through reading the explanations in this book, you will understand why the practices given in this book will work.

In this book, I have provided meditation guide-lines which you can use to walk into the Golden Aged world and get what you want. The more you use these meditation practices, the greater your abilities to get what you want, with just a thought or a visualisation, and the easier it will be for you to receive the solutions through which you can get what you want.

Though I have provided knowledge and practices in this book, you can choose to do what you want to do. You have the freedom to make your own choices, during the walking in process.

In this book, I have simplified my explanations on the World Drama, Holographic Universe, chakras, auric fields, etc. If you wish to know more on these, read my book 'Holographic Universe: An Introduction'.

Chapter 2: Introduction to the Brahma Kumaris' Seven Days Course

The BK knowledge, which is also referred to as Gyan/Knowledge, is from the murlis which are the direct teachings of God. In the Brahma Kumaris, the new students are introduced to the BK knowledge through an introductory 7 Days Course, before they can listen to the murlis. The 7 Days Course gives the basic knowledge on the following:

1. Soul.

2. Supreme Soul (God).

3. Three Worlds.

4. Cycle of Time and World Drama.

5. World Tree.

6. World Ladder.

7. Law of Karma.

8. Powers and other original qualities of the soul.

9. Benefits of using Brahma Kumaris Raja Yoga, how the Brahma Kumaris was founded through Brahma Baba, etc.

When you are introduced to the BK knowledge, which is given during the 7 Days Course, you get your link to God. Thus, from this chapter until Chapter 10, you are introduced to the BK knowledge which is given during the Brahma Kumaris' 7 Days Course. My explanations on the QE Light and quantum energies, etc. are sometimes also briefly included in some of these chapters, so that the reader will find it easier to connect my explanations in the later chapters to what has been said in these chapters. However, I have tried my best to only give the BK knowledge in these chapters.

The knowledge given in the 7 Days Course is based on what has been said in the murlis. You will not understand what is being said in the murlis unless you have taken the 7 Days Course. Thus, it is only in Chapters 12 and 13, that you are given extracts from murlis (God's teachings in the Brahma Kumaris).

The members of the Brahma Kumaris have to live a strict lifestyle through following the disciplines called the Maryadas. Since those walking in will not be using the BK life-style, I am not going to go into the BK lifestyle and Maryadas, in this book. The BK 7 Days course, in this book, has been made suitable for those walking into the Golden Aged world because they are being geared to walk in. Those walking into the Golden Aged world should be able to live a free lifestyle and they should have their freedom to do anything that they want. However, the Law of Karma is being taught in this book because those walking in are still capable of using the vices. All those who are capable of using the vices are subject to the Law of Karma.

The BK knowledge which is provided in this book is sufficient for you to get your link to God. If you want to hear more on the BK knowledge, go to the nearest BK center. All the BK classes are given for free. Even if you did not do that, it is okay. You can get your link to God and begin the walking in process through using what has been written in this book. The knowledge given in this book is based on the BK knowledge, my research, experiences and analysis.

You will find it very easy to experience your link to God and have other experiences if you take 7 days off and just concentrate on using the knowledge that has been given in this book. When your mind is saturated with the BK knowledge, you will begin experiencing your link to God and you will also have other spiritual experiences because the saturation of knowledge in your mind influences your intellect to become divine, i.e. it becomes the divine intellect.

Brahma Kumaris Raja Yoga, which is used to establish one's link to God, involves the control of the mind and thoughts. The BK method used for meditation is basically as follows:

Step 1: relaxation. Make sure that you are in a relaxed, calm, peaceful state with no stress or tension.

Step 2: concentration. Take your mind away from everything else and keep it on what you have decided to concentrate on. Begin concentrating by focusing your mind on:

- the words in the meditation commentaries.

- the BK knowledge.

- thoughts or visualisations, which you have decided to use, that are based on the BK knowledge.

Step 3: contemplation. This involves deeply thinking about the BK knowledge which you are concentrating on. The contemplation helps you to understand it and experience it.

Step 4: realisation/experience/enlightenment. This happens when you have contemplated on the BK knowledge for a long time.

Chapter 3: Soul (Day 1 of the BK Seven Days Course)

Within each living human body, there is a soul. Though you may feel that you are the body, you are not; you are actually the soul (atma) who is in the body. The soul is like the driver while the body is like the chariot of the soul. The soul uses the body to do everything. You (the soul) use your eyes to see, your mouth to speak and your ears to hear.

The soul exists eternally but the body perishes. Thus, when a person dies, the soul leaves the body. The soul cannot be created nor destroyed. Only the body gets created and decays.

The human body is created by the QE Light and quantum energies. You are not the QE Light and quantum energies either. You are the soul who uses your physical body which is materialised by these energies.

The soul is a point of white living light and it is in the center of the forehead where its seat is situated. Though the seat of the soul is in the space of the brain, the soul is not part of the brain. The brain is like the computer while the soul is like the programmer. The soul is like the driver seated in its seat in the control-room (brain) of the vehicle (body). From there, the brain is used to control the body. The soul uses the brain to think, remember, decide etc. The soul is able to do this while in the brain because the energies of the soul are closely entangled to the energies of the QE Light which provide the brain. These QE Light flow along with the soul when the soul intents to move etc. Thus, it is actually the soul which is moving the body since the movement is done based on the soul's intentions etc. It is also through the body that the soul experiences happiness etc. The soul cannot live without its body.

Since the soul is metaphysical, it cannot be seen with the physical eyes. The soul is neither male nor female.

You (the soul) use the body to think, contemplate, feel, visualise, live, experience pain, etc. You also express yourself through your body. Without the body, you (the soul) will not be able to express yourself.

You can feel love, peace, happiness, bliss etc. because the soul is filled with virtues and powers. The virtues and powers are the original qualities of the soul. Thus, the soul will seek these if it does not experience these. When you identify yourself with the body, you will be limiting your ability to experience the soul's virtues and powers. Brahma Kumaris Raja Yoga helps you to:

1. experience yourself as the soul, and

2. experience the original qualities of the soul.

Using the Brahma Kumaris' practice of seeing yourself and others as souls, will help you to easily experience the soul conscious stage. When you experience the soul conscious stage:

1. you are in a pure high stage.

2. you (the soul) are linked to God and, through this link, you are absorbing God's vibrations into yourself (the soul).

3. the soul gets purified and through this purification process the soul is in the process of being transformed into the divine state.

4. you experience yourself as the soul and not as the body. You will feel that you are the soul using your physical body.

5. you can have various kinds of beautiful subtle experiences.

6. you will be experiencing the natural original qualities of the soul.

7. you will be living a blissful life.

8. you observe everything as a detached observer.

9. you are not body conscious.

While remembering that you are the soul, remember the original qualities of the soul and keep these qualities in an emerged state within your mind. This will help you to become and remain soul conscious. If one was not soul conscious, one is body conscious.

One is body conscious while one is in a state where one can use the vices. The vices include anger, lust, greed, arrogance, ego etc. When one is body conscious:

1. one feels that one is the physical body.

2. one's stage is not good. One is in the ordinary stage which is why one is capable of using the vices.

When you are body conscious, you trap yourself into limited identities, i.e. you identify yourself with the body, profession, sex, race, religion, nationality, family, etc. This limits what you, the soul, can do. As the soul, you use your body to do your duties, take care of the body and family, etc. You have to be aware that you are the soul who is doing this.

When one is body conscious, one looks for happiness outside the soul and one depends on external things for peace and happiness. One even tries to use one's sense organs to experience happiness and the other virtues. What is in the physical world does not give anyone permanent happiness since the situation and feelings keep changing.

In the body conscious state, one might also keep using the vices without realising that it brings one into the habit of using them. When one keeps using the vices, one is taken away from one's happy, peaceful state. Without being aware of this, one may try to use the vices to see if there are opportunities to enjoy happiness and peace. When one does not get something that one wants, one loses one's happiness because one is overcome by the vices. When one gets a little, one becomes greedy and one begins to desire for more; one can lose one's happiness through this.

During the body conscious state, one may even try to be somebody else or one might envy someone else because one thinks that the other has something which can give one happiness etc. Actually, each human soul is unique because its spiritual strength, personality traits, role in the World Drama etc. are all different. Therefore, one should learn to accept one's role in the World Drama. Further, one should learn to experience the happiness which is within the soul without being dependent on external situations.

Human souls can only re-incarnate into human bodies and not into animal bodies. If you had a belief, in past births or in this birth, that human souls can re-incarnate in animal bodies, then, based on that belief, you might have an experience that you were an animal in one of your former lives.

As the soul, you would have entered your body when it was 4 to 5 months old in your mother's womb. When you enter the foetus, it is given life. You begin this new life with a new slate for the memories of your current birth.

The soul has three functions or faculties: mind, intellect (buddhi) and sanskaras (memories or Memory Bank). The sanskaras is where all the memories are stored within the soul. It can also be said that the soul uses the mind, intellect and sanskaras as its servants or ministers. The mind, intellect and sanskaras are used in the following manner:

1. Mind (Conscious Mind):
- The soul creates new thoughts, emotions/feelings, desires, ideas, images or visualisations in the mind.

- Whatever information the person gets through the 5 senses (sees, hears, etc.) comes into the mind for the soul to see it.

- Memories are brought into the mind (from the Memory Bank) for the soul to see, consider or use.

2. Intellect:

- The intellect takes whatever is in the mind and places them in the Memory Bank.

- The intellect emerges memories etc. which are in the sanskaras faculty (Memory Bank) and places them in the mind.

- The soul uses the intellect to understand, make judgements, discriminate, reason, assess, etc.

- The soul subtly communicates with God and others through the intellect (after the thought, desire etc. have been created in the mind), etc.

- The soul uses the intellect to materialise whatever is in the mind since the energies of the intellect are entangled with QE Light energies. Due to the entangled state, the QE Light initiates the materialisation process based on what is in the mind of the soul and the quantum energies materialise it in the Real World.

3. Memory Bank (Sanskaras):

- Stores sanskaras, i.e. memories of present and past births, instincts, habits, tendencies, emotions, tendencies, temperaments, behaviour, personality traits, desires, believes, values, experiences, information that was received by the person, etc.

Whenever you (the soul) re-incarnate, all the former memories of your past births remain in your Memory Bank. However, they will go deeper down in your Memory Bank. So you do not have access to them similar to how you have access to the memories which were created during your current lifetime.

Since the mind, intellect and Memory Bank are all part of the soul, you will feel that you are doing something when the mind, intellect or sanskaras are used. For example, when you have a subtle experience, your intellect flies around to get information for you; but you will feel that you are leaving the corporeal body to get the information. Actually, you are not leaving the corporeal body. If you (the soul) leave the corporeal body, you die. Thus, only some of the energies of your intellect are sent out. It will feel like you are leaving the corporeal body because the energies of the mind, intellect and sanskaras are all part of you (the soul). They are your energies.

Whenever you want to remember something, your intellect will pick it out from your Memory Bank and place it in your mind so that you (the soul) can see. In this way, you remember it. If you no longer want to remember or use the memory or information, your intellect places it back in your Memory Bank. When a memory is emerged into your mind, you will feel that you remembered it because it is your own energies of the soul which had retrieved the information from the Memory Bank.

When you see, hear, speak, smell or touch something, impressions are left on the soul's energies in the mind. As the soul, you perceive what has come into your mind. Your intellect, then, takes these impressions (of whatever is in your mind) and places them in your Memory Bank. These impressions will be stored in the Memory Bank as memories until you need to use them.

When you think of something, the intellect picks up all relevant memories from the Memory Bank and places them in the mind. For example, if you think about a pineapple, all memories of its taste, shape, texture etc., including an image of the pineapple, are placed in your mind by your intellect. If you had a bad experience in respect of the pineapple, that would also be placed in your mind unless you do not want to remember that experience.

You think, imagine and form ideas through using your mind. What you create in your mind and the impressions of everything that you learn, are also taken by your intellect (from your mind) and sent to the Memory Bank. These will also be stored there for future use.

When you do something, a new sanskar is formed. This can begin a habit. As you keep doing it, it reinforces the habit. So the habit becomes a stronger one.

When you feel an emotion, it first comes into your mind. You feel that emotion while that emotion is in your mind. Since impressions are vibrations, they can influence the others and the whole world. Thus, others can become aware of how we feel, what we want, etc.

All the impressions that are in the Memory Bank exist in the form of vibrations. They can project a holographic image of an image, in the mind, when required.

You also use your intellect to make decisions based on observations and facts retained in your Memory Bank or from outside. For example, when you decide to contemplate on all relevant facts in order to make a decision, your intellect picks out all those relevant facts from your Memory Bank and places them in your mind. As all the information and memories are placed in your mind, you use the intellect to decide which relevant facts, from those that are in your mind, should be given more importance in order to make a good decision. As you keep using your intellect to make decisions, to understand knowledge etc., your ability to use your intellect improves.

If you have an intellect that has been trained to get information from outside your Memory Bank, your intellect will also get information from outside when you are trying to make a decision. When your intellect goes outside your corporeal body, to get information, the intellect is like your subtle third eye because it helps you to see what is outside your body. All the information from outside:

1. can come into the mind for the soul to view. If this happens, the soul will remember what it had seen outside the body. However, sometimes, one might not remember it for a while if one had just changed the spiritual stage which one was using. To remember it, one must keep remembering it while one's stage is changing or write it down while your stage is good. This is a little similar to how you have to remember

your dream as soon as you wake up; if not, you might not remember your dream.

2. can go straight into the Memory Bank. If this happens, one will not remember the experience because one did not see it in one's mind. However, sometimes, what was seen can emerge, or the intellect can bring it into the mind, at a later point in time. If this happens, the person will remember it at a later point in time.

3. can remain temporarily in the mind for just a while without the soul seeing it, before it goes into the Memory Bank. This happens if one was losing one's stage as the information was brought into the mind. However, since the information had come into one's mind, one might vaguely remember it. If one tries to remember it properly, the intellect will bring it into the mind again for the soul to see. Then, the person will remember it. You have to be spiritually well developed and in a pure stage for your intellect to do what you say. If not, the vices might give you a vision of something else to confuse you up, when you try to remember what you had seen.

In the second half cycle, the vices will try their best to reign. Thus, the vices will try to:

1. discourage you from having a higher pure stage.

2. make you feel unhappy.

3. confuse you.

They might bring doubts into your mind or try to take you away from the pure blissful stage by pulling your attention to something which will make your stage drop. For example, during one experience, while I was meditating to remain in a powerful stage, the energies of my vices had emerged into my mind (looking just like me in a human form and holding a watermelon etc.) and it was making sentences such as "Look! Watermelon! Very tasty! Do you want one?" I looked at the watermelon which it was holding and I was having the feeling that it would be nice to eat a watermelon. Then, I realised that Maya (the vices) was trying to pull me away from my meditation. So I gave that subtle human form, in my vision, a hard kick and it shattered as it went flying out of the scene/mind/vision. Actually, in this experience, there were many human forms looking like me and they were having all sorts of fruits. The human forms, which were looking just like me, were a reflection that my own energies were bringing the images of 'tempting fruits' into my mind from my Memory Bank. I love to eat fruits and so these images, which were coming into my mind, were tempting me. Since the vices are the energies of the soul, they can play a role along with weak energies of the intellect, if we were in a weak state. This was why the vices (along with the energies of the intellect) were bringing fruits into my mind as I was trying to meditate. Sometimes, due to the weak state of the soul, the memories just emerge into the mind on its own and the intellect is not bringing them into the mind. Since the memories are imprinted on the energies of the soul, it would seem like our energies are bringing the images (fruits etc.) into our mind.

Since the images, in the vision and impressions, are created through the energies of the soul adopting the frequencies of the images, these vibrations lost the information of the images when I gave the images a hard kick. This was portrayed through the shattering of the images in this vision.

Actually, we are the virtuous self. However, since the vices are also the energies of the soul, it is as if there is a bad side within us, tempting us away from the pure state. The bad side tries to divert the person's attention away from trying to meditate. All these kinds of situations have also been portrayed in the myths as battles between the evil forces (vices) and the good forces (virtues).

Some non-BKs would say that we are half good and half bad. This is not a good way of looking at it because it associates us to the bad side as well. We should not associate ourselves to the bad side. The BK knowledge teaches us to see ourselves as the virtuous self. This is how we should see ourselves. When we see ourselves as the virtuous self, we can easily establish our link to God.

You use your mind to initiate your link to God. This is so because you initiate it through your thought, which is created in the mind. Since it is in your mind, your intellect flies to give you the connection. If your desire, intent and faith are strong, it is as if you have given the instruction to the intellect to act upon that desire, intent and faith. Your mind, intellect and sanskaras always act based on your desires, intent and faith.

The intellect also acts based on the strong impressions which are in the Memory Bank. Thus, if we constantly have faith that we are guided by God, these impressions will accumulate within the Memory Bank to become strong. The vibrations of the strong impressions will then influence the intellect to link the soul to God so as to get guidance.

The thoughts are also like instructions to the intellect. So the intellect acts accordingly. As a result, whatever the soul thinks, will happen. If we have the thought that we want to link ourselves to God, the intellect will act accordingly and we will have an experience. When you remember this earlier experience, the intellect will emerge the experience from the Memory Bank; since the experience consists of pure energies, the intellect is influenced to become divine again, thus, it establishes the link to God again. By remembering the earlier experience, it is as if you are instructing your intellect to link you to God again, as it did when you had the previous experience.

When your intellect is in a divine state, the decisions, which you take, will be the best because of the perfect state of the intellect. It is when you lose your divine state, and go into the weak ordinary state, that you will find it very difficult to use the intellect well so as to make the best decision. So, you might need more time in order to make a good decision. You can also become confused and find that you are unable to make a decision.

In the weak ordinary state, sometimes, the intellect unnecessarily brings up information from the Memory Bank and places them in the mind. So you have numerous stuff coming into your mind. Memories can also just pop up from the Memory Bank and come into your mind. Due to the weak state of the energies in the mind, numerous unnecessary thoughts can also get created in your mind.

When you are in the soul conscious state, the divine intellect will not unnecessarily bring irrelevant information into the mind. It will only bring relevant information as per the desires of the soul. Memories also do not pop up into the mind when one is in a powerful stage. During a powerful stage, you will also not unnecessarily create thoughts.

However, to go into a powerful stage, you will first have to make your mind quiet (by not allowing unnecessary thoughts to get created in the mind, etc.) and just contemplate on something that is in the BK knowledge. Through constantly doing this, it is as if you are giving instructions to your mind, intellect and memories to act in this manner and so they will act accordingly. Further, if you keep a check on your thoughts etc. then, out of habit, you will only create relevant thoughts.

The BK knowledge and meditation practices help you to have control over your mind, intellect and Memory Bank; it also helps you to use a divine intellect. The minute your energies touch God's energies, they immediately get energised and transform into the divine state. Thus, when your intellect touches God's vibrations, it transforms into the 'divine intellect'. This divine intellect is the third eye or Confluence Aged third eye.

When you receive the BK knowledge, whether in the BK center or through this book, you will have the ability to link yourself to God. Acquiring this ability to link yourself to God is the 'opening of your Third Eye'. Your Confluence Aged third eye is opened when you first receive the BK knowledge so as to take your Confluence Aged spiritual birth. The opening of the Confluence Aged third eye is for world transformation through self-transformation.

The intellect is used as a 'Third Eye' (divine intellect) when you contemplate on the BK knowledge. It can also be said that both, the 'divine intellect' and the BK knowledge, are the Third Eye because both are used to open the soul's third eye. Among other things, the Third Eye enables you (the soul) to know the past, present and future based on the truth.

Once your Third Eye has been opened, you have to keep using it so that it does not close again. You keep it open through contemplating on the BK knowledge.

When you contemplate on the BK knowledge, it is as if you are instructing your intellect to help you to understand the knowledge. Your intellect thus helps you to understand it through linking you to God. As you keep contemplating on the BK knowledge, the intellect will keep linking you to God.

Though through contemplating on the BK knowledge you will automatically link yourself to God, you will not get linked to God if you do not have the desire to get the link to God. So everything depends on what you want too. If you have decided that you want your link to God, then, you will be able to use the BK knowledge and your intellect to:

1. keep God's Company,

2. understand the Truth, etc.

It is only when you 'accept the BK knowledge with faith that it is true' that your intellect will act upon it to link you to God. When your intellect links you to God:

1. you go into the soul conscious stage and get purified.

2. God gives you visions and spiritual experiences to help you to understand the knowledge and the path which you are taking.

3. God uses you for the creation of the new world.

4. God gives information, guidance, finances and whatever else you need.

God also has the 3 faculties of Mind, Intellect and Sanskaras. When we link ourselves to God, our intellect gets linked to God's Intellect, our mind gets linked to God's Mind and our Memory Bank gets linked to God's Memory Bank. As a result, God is able to purify, strengthen, protect and guide us.

One has to learn the art of going within before they can go upwards to link themselves to God. Many struggle to go within because they have not developed this ability from the time when they were children. However, this does not mean that adults cannot develop this ability. Through constantly trying, you will be able to do it. You will also find that it is easy to go within if you are old, past 60.

When you were a baby, you (the soul) were detached from the body. Then, as your body began to develop, you began to become and more like a mortal. A mortal is one who feels that he is the body and not the soul. As you grow up, it is as if you are overcome by the body and so you go into the mortal state. The body gets more powerful as it grows and develops. Then, when you are around 60 years old, since the body is decaying, it is getting quite weak and so you slowly get detached from it. You slowly also get detached from it because you will have to leave the body when you cannot use it (when it too old due to decay). Thus, as you grow older you will find it easier to meditate. Sometimes, you can remain attached to the body until you die, even though you are very old. Thus, it is good to start your meditation as soon as possible and not wait until you are old.

You are in a detached state when you are in the soul conscious stage and so you watch everything as a detached observer. This means you watch everything as if you are watching a drama. In this detached soul conscious stage, you do not react to whatever you see, hear, etc. For example, if a person was scolding you or praising you, you are not affected in anyway. You would have just observed and remained in the blissful state. It would not have left an impression on the energies of the soul, i.e. it would not have left an influential impression because it is within an impression which consists of pure powerful energies. This non-influential impression is as good as not leaving an impression. Even though a memory of it is there in your Memory Bank, it will not emerge to disturb you because it did not leave a strong impression on weak energies. Only strong impressions on weak energies will easily emerge to disturb you. After having seen something as a detached observer, if you recollect the incidence when your stage is not good, your recollection will leave an influential impression on weak energies. So if you have to recollect the incidence, make sure that you are in the soul conscious stage first. You develop your ability to remain in the soul conscious stage and watch everything as a detached observer as you keep practicing Brahma Kumaris Raja Yoga.

I have provided some meditation guidelines below (based on the BK knowledge) which can be used during meditation or to begin meditation. As you read them, flow along with the words while in a meditative state. You flow along with the words by creating the relevant thoughts and visualisation in your mind. This will help you to go within and easily become soul conscious. When you want to attain the high spiritual stage, think that you are already in that stage and you will be enjoying that stage.

You can use whatever posture you like when doing the meditation practices suggested in this book. You can do it while:

1. sitting with legs crossed (as done during hatha yoga).

2. sitting on a chair (straight or on a reclined chair).

3. in a sleeping posture.

4. doing your daily activities because BK Raja Yoga trains you to remain in a meditative state no matter what you are doing.

Brahma Kumaris Raja Yoga is also done with eyes open because it trains you to remain in a meditative state no matter what you are doing.

Meditation Guidelines 1:

1. Sit relaxed in a comfortable position.

2. Turn your mind away from all the sounds and sights around you.

3. Let go of all limited bodily identifications.

4. Focus your attention on the point of light in the forehead. You are that point of light and you are seated on your seat in the forehead.

5. If you remember anything other than this, push them out of your mind.

6. Gently keep bringing your attention back to seeing yourself as the soul, who is seated on your seat.

NB: As you keep doing this, you train your mind, intellect and sanskars to come back under your control. You also increase your power of concentration and develop the habit of seeing yourself as the soul. This helps you to easily attain the soul conscious stage and enjoy the blissful, peaceful, virtuous state quickly.

Meditation Guidelines 2:

1. Push aside all wasteful thoughts and nurture pure thoughts.

2. Create the thought that you are peaceful. Experience yourself as being peaceful. Enjoy the feeling of being peaceful.

NB: Do this whenever you can, no matter what you are doing. Also try to have fixed times, once or twice a day, when you can actually sit in meditation (in a quiet place) so as to do this. The next time, concentrate on another virtue, e.g. bliss, happiness, love, joy, patience, serenity, purity, etc. All these practices will help you to regain control over yourself, your thoughts and feelings. However, remember to relax and enjoy yourself. Do not push yourself because it is easier when you enjoy it.

Meditation Guidelines 3:

I close my eyes and feel relaxed... I become aware that I am the soul... I am free of the limitations of the physical world... I have the freedom to be just me, the virtuous self... I feel content to just be who I am... I love myself and everyone else on earth... I see each of them as a soul (in the center of their forehead) filled with pure love, peace, co-operation and all the other virtues... I have a good relationship with them and they are very co-operative.

NB: This meditation practice influences others to become peaceful and co-operative. Thus, you can easily achieve what you want. Seeing others as a point of light, in their forehead, also helps you to remember that you are a soul seated in your seat, in your forehead.

Meditation Guidelines 4:

I am the infinitesimal point of living white light energy which exists eternally and I am in my present body now... I take my attention away from the body and go within... As I go within, I experience a huge reserve of love, peace and happiness emerging from deep within me (the soul)... I experience each of my limitless treasures of peace, happiness, love, bliss, and all the other virtues that exist deep within me (the soul)... I am the embodiment of bliss and peace.

Meditation Guidelines 5:

As I see myself as the soul, my awareness of my body fades... I feel light as I go beyond the awareness of my body and become conscious of being the soul seated in the center of the forehead... I am the soul... I am like a star that radiates light... I am living light energies, emanating from a point of light... I am also radiating out as light and vibrations.

NB: You can concentrate on a thought and then go deeper and deeper within until you are not aware of what is happening around you. However, you can also go deep within while remaining aware of what is happening around you. This is what BK Raja Yoga trains one to do, i.e. to remain aware of what is happening around one and to continue doing one's daily activities while in a meditative state. However, for a beginning, you will find it easier to go within by taking your attention away from your surroundings. Then, when you are used to going within, try going within while you are aware of what is happening around you.

Meditation Guidelines 6:

I am the soul seated in the center of my forehead and I am using my body, which is my vehicle/chariot... I use my body to think, decide, visualise and feel... I also move my body from my seat... When I have the thought that I want to move my hand, I will be able to move it because the complex system in my physical body was designed to serve me... Throughout the day, while carrying out my activities, I am aware that I am the soul doing the acts through my body which is made up of the 5 elements. I do all actions while in the soul conscious stage.

NB: If you can keep concentrating on the same thing for a long time, your power of concentration will improve. However, if you keep concentrating on the same thing, you might get tired or bored, and so find it difficult to concentrate. So improve your power of concentration slowly. Do not push yourself too hard with high expectations. You may get fed up. Meditation should be enjoyed. If you enjoy meditation, you will find it easier to meditate. Meditating regularly will make it easier for you to attain a high stage quickly. You will find it easier to meditate regularly if you keep concentrating on new points. There are a lot of new points to concentrate on in the BK knowledge and in this book. Find something different to concentrate on if you are finding it difficult to concentrate. Keep using new ideas too so as to improve your power of concentration during meditation.

Chapter 4: God (Day 2 of the BK Seven Days Course)

In accordance with the BK knowledge, God is the Supreme Soul (Paramatma). God is referred to as the Supreme Soul because He is the Supreme or highest among all souls. However, God does not take births in the Corporeal World like how human souls do.

God is a metaphysical self-luminous point of white incorporeal light (Jyoti Bindu) like how each human soul is a point of light (jyoti bindu). However, there is a difference between the human soul and the Supreme Soul. God is like an ocean whereas the strength of the human soul is like a drop in comparison. God is an Ocean of all Virtues and Powers. He is the Ocean of Peace, Ocean of Bliss, Ocean of Love, Ocean of Knowledge, Ocean of Mercy, Ocean of Purity, etc. He is eternally unchanged and so He remains powerful. When one is having yoga with God, one can feel "Might" in His strength.

God is worshiped in all religions through one form or another. He is referred to by different names in different religions. It does not really matter as to what name you are going to use while referring to Him.

Through the knowledge given in the Brahma Kumaris, God referred to Himself as Shiva since Shiva means "World Benefactor", "Point", "Seed of the Entire Creation" etc. BKs refer to God as Baba (Father) or Shiva Baba or Shiv Baba because He is the Father of all Confluence Aged souls.

There is only one God and He is the Father of all human souls. So everyone can call God "Baba", "Father" etc. Those who walk in should see God as their Mother too so that God takes good care of them similar to how a mother takes good care of her children. For those walking in, "Baba my Mother" is like a mantra that connects them to Baba playing His role as the Mother.

God plays various roles, for example, God acts as our Father, Mother, Teacher, Guide, Purifier, Liberator, Bestower of Salvation, Almighty Authority, etc. God is detached but loving. He dispels sorrow and bestows happiness. His energies can purify all impure human souls by burning away all their sins.

Though God is not visible, His presence can be experienced during meditation/yoga. When we have yoga with God, we can experience the various roles which are used by God. For example, we can experience Him as the Purifier when He purifies us. We can experience God as an Ocean of Love when we experience an ocean of love flowing to us from Him.

God is completely pure and virtuous. There are no vices within Him. So God cannot get angry or unhappy. During meditation, one can only experience His powerful virtues.

God is filled with knowledge of the truth. Thus, He is able to guide well. Through our yoga with God, we are gently guided to attain victory through experiences. When we have an experience, we should keep recollecting it because this recollection will help us to have more experiences.

Yoga means connection or union. BK Raja Yoga gives a direct connection or link to God. When you have this link, you receive God's vibrations which purify you (the soul). Those who practice BK Raja Yoga are Raja Yogis. The word 'Raja' in the word 'Raja Yogi' means that the yogi is a king or master of the self.

Raja Yoga meditation involves three steps:

1. the journey inside or inward journey.

2. the journey upwards.

3. linking oneself to God.

In the previous chapter, you learnt how to go within which is the inward journey. In this chapter you will be provided with meditation practices which put you on the journey upwards so that you get linked to God.

The journey inwards is the first step which is consciously taken to experience oneself as the original pure virtuous self (soul). You become soul conscious through this. You have to forget who you are as a bodily being.

The second step is the journey upwards which leads to the third step of getting linked to God. Through the link, God's energies charge you (the soul) up with spiritual power and so the soul is recharged with inner strength. When we are empowered, we will find it easier to live a happy virtuous life and we are also transformed into the divine state. Thus, when you sit for meditation or while carrying out your daily activities, stay relaxed and do the following meditation practices.

Meditation Practice 1:

Sit comfortably and visualise yourself as the soul, a point of white living light, in the center of your forehead... Then, visualise God as a Point of White Living Light... You are receiving God's energies and they are filling you up with pure divine bliss... Visualise that God's Virtues and Powers are empowering you with all the divine virtues and powers... God's energies are so powerful that they also instantly transform your energies into the divine state when they touch you (the soul). Thus, even your virtues transform into the divine state... Feel the bliss, happiness, joy etc. as they empower you (the soul)... Have the feeling that you are safe now because you are in God's Company.

NB: You can do this to empower yourself with a specific virtue at a time, for example, you can empower yourself with God's Bliss. Then, later empower yourself with the vibrations of happiness that are flowing from God to you. In this way empower yourself with each of God's Virtues.

Meditation Practice 2:

Begin your journey inwards by seeing yourself as the soul filled with virtues and powers (you can use a different virtue for each meditation or you can visualise all the virtues and powers as existing within you). Enjoy the feeling of the virtues... Then, turn your attention to the Supreme Soul... Visualise a subtle, powerful link of love between you and the Supreme Soul... Absorb God's vibrations of love directly from Him (you can also visualise another virtue/power within God and see yourself absorbing that virtue/power from God)...Visualise yourself channeling God's vibrations of love into the world (or towards others)... Now, come back to the awareness of being in your body and in the room where you are in.

Meditation Practice 3:

As soon as you wake up, remind yourself that you are the soul and remember God. Have the view that God is your Father, Mother, Teacher, Wife, Husband, Friend etc.

NB: Have one of these relationships with God for a few days or even longer. This is beneficial because:

1. it will help you to get over relationship problems which you have in your life since your desires for love etc. are being fulfilled by God's pure love, God's Company, etc.

2. through constantly remembering God, your sanskaras/nature changes into a divine one.

3. it will improve your power of concentration. The more you concentrate on God, the BK knowledge and on what has been written in this book, the greater your power of concentration.

The following are examples of what you can do while you are carrying out your daily activities.

Meditation Practice 4:

NB: This can be done while washing clothes.

I am a point of white light having my link to God, my Laundryman, who is cleaning me... He is washing me with His divine loving vibrations... He is washing away all my unhappiness... He is making me clean and pure... and I am able to feel greater happiness and peace as a result of this...

Meditation Practice 5:

NB: This can be done while you are eating food.

I am the soul using my corporeal body to eat. As I eat, God's powerful vibrations are flowing into me (the soul) and then flowing out to the food which I am eating. Thus, the food is getting purified and strengthened as I am eating. Since God's vibrations are also strengthening me at the same time, as I am feeding the corporeal body, God also feeds me with His lovely powerful vibrations of love.

NB: Eating while in remembrance of God will make sure that God's vibrations purify and strengthen the food which you are eating. This will help you to have yoga more easily.

Meditation Practice 6:

NB: This can be done while you are cooking.

I, the soul, am using this corporeal body to cook. Since I have my link to God, God's vibrations are overflowing from me (the soul) to go into the food which I am cooking. So the food is getting filled with pure spiritual energy. As the food gets strengthened by God's powerful vibrations, I (the soul) am also getting strengthened by His powerful vibrations.

NB: Cooking food, while in yoga with God, will purify and strengthen the food. Thus, those who eat this food will be empowered to easily become pure.

Good spiritual experiences are had through having a strong link to God. When you have an experience, keep remembering it. As a result, you will experience it again or experience something better because remembering it helps to bring you into the pure state. During the pure state, you are linked to God and you are also able to lift yourself up into the higher dimensions.

Chapter 5: Three Worlds (Day 2 of the BK Seven Days Course)

In accordance with the BK knowledge, during the Confluence Age, there are three worlds: Soul World, Angelic World and Corporeal World.

A clearer picture of the three worlds can be seen at the author's website at: http://www.gbk-books.com/3-worlds.html.

The physical realm which we live in is referred to as the Corporeal World. There are physical forms in this physical world where we play our roles. The sciences can be applied to understand this realm.

The Incorporeal World called Soul World (Paramdham) is an infinite, metaphysical and timeless dimension where complete silence and peace exists. The Soul World, which is egg shaped and filled with the red light called Brahm, is the Home of God and all human souls. God resides in the Soul World permanently. All human souls reside in the Soul World until they come into the Corporeal World to play their roles. At the end of the cycle, God descends into the Corporeal World, when it is the darkest time, to begin the Confluence Age and create the new Golden Aged world. Then, He takes all human souls back into the Soul World. All human souls are in the peaceful, resting state when they are in the Soul World.

During the Confluence Age, God and all Confluence Aged souls reside in the Angelic World. The Angelic World, which is beyond the Corporeal World and beneath the Soul World, is only used during the Confluence Age. The Angelic World is a world of light where we have pure thoughts. There can be movements here but no sounds are heard in it. Only subtle communications can be done there. One can also only use a subtle body of light in the Angelic World. This world is not visible to physical eyes; it

40

is only perceived through experiences and visions. Confluence Aged souls meditate to remain in this Angelic World. Within the Angelic World itself, there are three different kinds of subtle regions: Brahmapuri, Vishnupuri and Shankerpuri. Brahmapuri is just beyond the Corporeal World. All Confluence Aged souls reside in Brahmapuri. Beyond Brahmapuri is Vishnupuri. Confluence Aged souls have experiences of being the Golden Aged divine self in Vishnupuri. Beyond Vishnupuri is Shankerpuri. Confluence Aged souls are in the most powerful Confluence Aged stage when they are in Shankerpuri. The subtle regions in the Angelic World can only be experienced through experiences during meditation and in visions. I have explained a lot about Brahmapuri, Vishnupuri and Shankerpuri in my book "Holographic Universe: An Introduction" and in my articles which can be read for free on my website (See http://www.gbk-books.com/articles.html for a list of my articles).

During Raja Yoga meditation, one journeys inwards and then one's intellect journeys upwards to the Angelic World and Soul World where God resides. You have to go beyond the awareness of the physical body and Corporeal World, in order to journey upwards to the Angelic World. Through this, one experiences the pure soul conscious stage. During this stage, one feels pure, divine, completely free, peaceful, blissful, rested and comfortable. One feels this way because one is linked to God.

The following are meditation experimentations which you can do at any time during the day:

Meditation Experimentation 1:

1. I, the soul, am resting in my home (the Soul World) which is a world of golden-red light. This world is filled with peace and silence. I am in a dormant state.

2. Then, I leave to take my first birth in the Golden Aged world. I descend into a body which is in a womb that feels like a golden palace. I feel comfortable and experience happiness.

3. Then, I take birth and begin living in the Golden Age. I am in paradise where there is unlimited happiness, wealth etc. It is a golden world and my home is built of gold bricks. Everything is so heavenly.

Meditation Experimentation 2:

1. I close my eyes to go beyond the world of people and objects.

2. I reach God, in the Soul World, with just a thought.

3. I am bathing in God's loving vibrations and I am in a loving state too.

4. I now see myself as being in my body but with my intellect still linked to God who is in the Soul World.

5. I am getting filled with God's love and these vibrations are flowing out from me and making others feel comfortable and loving.

Chapter 6: Cycle of Time, Swastika and World Drama (Day 3 of the BK Seven Days Course)

In accordance with the BK Cycle of Time (hereafter referred to as the 'Cycle'), time flows in a cyclical manner. Each Cycle lasts for 5000 years and it has five Ages or Yugas: Satyuga, Tretayuga, Dwapuryuga, Kaliyuga and Sangamyuga. Each Cycle, which is also known as the World Drama Wheel or Wheel of Time, has an identical World Drama taking place in the Corporeal World. The souls, who come into the Corporeal World from the Soul World, are the actors in this World Drama. Having come into the Corporeal World, souls keep taking births in this World Drama.

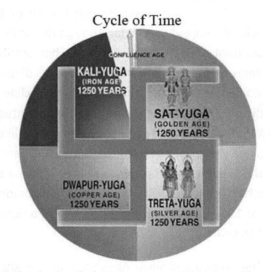

Cycle of Time

A clearer picture of the Cycle of Time can be seen at the author's website at: http://www.gbk-books.com/cycle-of-time.html.

The Brahma Kumaris teach the Cycle of Time through the picture of the World Drama Wheel which has the fylfot (swastika) in the centre. This swastika divides the four ages in the Wheel of Time. In the first part of this Wheel is the Golden Age. In the Golden Aged section of the Wheel, the arm of the swastika is pointing towards the right indicating that there is righteousness.

The BK Cycle begins with Satyug or the Golden Age. This is heaven or paradise on earth because the souls are satopradhan, i.e. the souls are divine, pure and complete with all virtues and powers. The spiritual strength of the souls is 16 celestial degrees. The Golden Age lasts for 1250 years and the average age of a human being is 150 years. People are in perfect health eventhough they live long. They are immortals because they are constantly soul conscious. They know that they are the souls who use the bodies to keep themselves entertained in the Corporeal World. Thus, when it is time to leave their bodies to take a new birth, they willingly leave their bodies. The population at the beginning of the Golden Age is 900,000. These are the children of those who walk into the Golden Aged world.

The Golden Age is followed by the Silver Age (Tretayuga) which is also paradise. The world is still a viceless, pure, divine, happy and perfect world. However, the arm of the swastika, in the Silver Aged section of the Wheel, points down though it is still on the right hand side of the Wheel. This indicates that, though the souls are still righteous, their spiritual strength has decreased. Their spiritual strength is 14 celestial degrees, i.e. they are two degrees less divine than the souls in the Golden Age. Though there is a slight decline in divinity, they are still divine. They are not aware that their spiritual strength is decreasing. Whatever spiritual state they are in feels like their normal perfect state. Since the spiritual strength of the souls here is less than that of those in the Golden Age, the spiritual state of these souls is at the Sato level, which is a lower level than that of Satopradhan. The Silver Age also lasts for 1250 years but the average age of a human being is between 100 to 125 years.

The Golden and Silver Ages are together known as Heaven on earth or Paradise. It is remembered as the Garden of Eden (Jew and Christian), Garden of Allah (Muslim), Vaikuntha (Hindu), Fields of Osiris (Egyptian), etc. There is a total of 2500 years in the first half cycle.

All the souls who take births during the Golden and Silver Ages (or first half cycle) are deity souls. The souls are completely divine, during the first half cycle. There is just one religion, one culture, one dynasty, one language and the people were not worshippers because they had everything. At the end of the Silver Age, they lose their divine state and transform into the weaker ordinary state. Thus, they begin to use the vices.

After the Silver Age, comes the Copper Age (Dwapuryuga) when souls are no longer in the perfect divine state. The third section in the Wheel is this Copper Age. The arm of the swastika turns towards the left indicating that the people have turned to the impure path (where the vices are used and so there is unrighteousness and sorrow). The souls are in the Rajo or Rajopradhan state and Mankind gets divided into various religions, kingdoms etc.

At the beginning of the Copper Age, souls begin to experience sorrow (at the depth of the soul) since, at the depths, the soul is aware that it is losing its perfect world; though, as the Conscious Self, they may not be aware and so they remain happy. Since the Conscious Self is influenced by what is happening at the depths of the soul, the people begin to worship God. Thus, at the beginning of the Copper Age, the Deity Religion of the first half cycle becomes a religion where devotion begins to be done. With time, it becomes known as the Hindu religion. After worship was introduced into the Deity Religion, other religions get created (one after the other). Many cultures, many languages etc. also begin to exist. History begins to get recorded.

The Copper Age lasts for 1250 years. Then, there is the Iron Age (Kaliyug) which is also for 1250 years. Thus, there is a total of 2500 years in the second half cycle.

The fourth section, in the Wheel, is Kaliyuga (Iron Age). The arm of the swastika turns upwards on the left hand side. This indicates that impurity increases in the souls. Therefore, there is a rise in conflicts, sorrow, etc.

In Kaliyug the souls are at the tamo or tamopradhan spiritual state. This means that souls are most impure in Kaliyug. It is the darkest age where people are greatly over-powered by the vices. Therefore, there is intense suffering, irreligiousness, injustice etc. In accordance with the knowledge of the Brahma Kumaris, this is hell on earth.

Then, around the end of Kaliyug, God descends into the Corporeal World so as to establish the fifth age called Confluence Age (Sangam Yuga) which overlaps the ending phase of Kaliyug and the beginning phase of the Golden Age. He enters the body of Lekhraj and names him Brahma. Then, through the mouth of Brahma, God gives knowledge and teaches Brahma Kumaris Raja Yoga. Through using these teachings, the deity souls are purified via their link to God and the world is also transformed into the Golden Aged world. God uses all the Confluence Aged souls who are willing to play a part for this creation process. Through the Confluence Age, which lasts for around 100 years, the new Cycle of Time is brought into existence and God brings about the resurrection of Mankind. All souls will enjoy a heavenly life in their first birth, in the next cycle. Those who use the BK knowledge will take their first birth in the next first half cycle. All others will start taking births in the next second half cycle.

At the end of the Cycle, after all human souls have come down into the Corporeal World, God takes all souls back to the Soul World (which is also referred to as Shantidham or the Land of Peace) where they are in the peaceful (nirvana) state. Those who walk into the Golden Age are taken back to the Soul World, later, after the Golden Aged deities have grown up and are able to continue living there on their own.

All souls are the children of God. This is why God helps all human souls and why, at the end of the cycle, every soul will receive salvation and liberation, regardless of their religion and lifestyle, when God takes them back to the Soul World. However, each soul has its own part to play. Without that part, the World Drama will not be great to be in. This is so even though we can face bad situations in the second half cycle. When BKs see something bad happening, they will have the view that it is happening as per the World Drama and watch it as detached observers in the soul conscious stage.

Brahma Baba is Adam (the first man created through the Confluence

Age) for Paradise (Golden Aged world). When He is born in the new Golden Age, he is born as Krishna. All the deity souls born in the Golden Age are Krishnas. When they get married, the couple becomes Lakshmi and Narayan.

The Corporeal World exists eternally and so Time on earth exists eternally. Since the Cycle of Time keeps repeating, civilisations exist eternally on earth.

In my subsequent books, I am explaining why the BK cycle is only for 5000 years whereas the cosmological cycle, Hindu cycle etc. have figures which go into millions and billions of years.

Below are some meditation commentaries which you can use during your meditation.

Meditation Commentary 1:
I, the soul, am resting in my home (the Soul World) which is a world of golden-red light... I am not aware, though I am in peace and silence... I am in a dormant state, not performing any actions... Then, as per the World Drama, I descend into the Corporeal World to play my part in the World Drama... I descend into a foetus in a womb which feels like a palace... I am in heaven, the Golden Age.

Meditation Commentary 2:
I am a pure soul living in the Golden Aged world... I am full of my original qualities (divine virtues and powers)... I am happily living my live... I do not have the capacity to use the vices... Evil does not exist anywhere... It is heaven on earth and the state of each soul is one of complete bliss... I and the others do not lack anything... Half a cycle passes by with me living in this heavenly world... Then, I take births in the Copper and Iron Ages until I come into the Confluence Age... I am now in the Confluence Age with my Baba (Father/God/Supreme Soul)... I experience bliss as I experience God's love... I, the soul, constantly absorb God's love and shower it into the Corporeal World... I observe everything as a detached observe... I know that it is just a predestined

drama.

Meditation Commentary 3:

I, the soul, am a world benefactor like my Father (the Supreme Soul)... I am linked to God, so extreme peace and bliss flows into me and then, through me, into the world... I spread God's love to every part of the world.... I dance internally with joy during this pure, lovely experience ... I can see God's vibrations making the world pure and divine. The world is transforming into the Golden Aged world... I move around in the world with the awareness that I am the pure soul, constantly showering God's gifts of peace, purity and love to everyone and the whole world... I am constantly linked with God, the Supreme Soul, who is the Ocean of Happiness and Love; so I am constantly showering happiness and love to all souls in the Corporeal World... Through what I am doing, the new Cycle of Time comes into existence.

Meditation Commentary 4:

I, the soul, am in the Confluence Age and I see the contrast between the old world and new world (visualise the old world as being at the end in the Kaliyug section of the Cycle and the new world as being in the beginning of the Golden Aged section of the Cycle). One is impure and the other is pure. I am in a boat that is tied to the old world. I cut the ropes that keep the boat tied to the shores of Kaliyug and I begin my journey to the Golden Aged world... Once I was a deity in the Golden Age... I was a divine being who had lived beautiful lives in the Golden and Silver Ages... Then, I had taken births in the old world and now, I am sailing towards the new Golden Aged world... I enjoy bliss as I am on this journey because I am with God in the boat.

Chapter 7: World Tree (Day 4 of the BK Seven Days Course)

A clearer picture of the World Tree can be seen at the author's website at: http://www.gbk-books.com/world-tree.html.

The World Tree is also called the Kalpa Tree because it reflects the religio-political history of the whole Kalpa. The Kalpa consists of one full Cycle of Time with all 5 ages. The beginning of the Kalpa starts at the beginning of the trunk, i.e. from the beginning of the Golden Age. Since the World Tree depicts the state of religions and civilisations through the Cycle, it is also referred to as the Tree of World Religions, Tree of Religions, Tree of Life or the Genealogical Tree of Mankind.

The Genealogical Tree of Mankind illustrates the growth and developments in the religions of the world. The root of this Tree consists of the members of the Brahma Kumaris since God uses them to create the Deity Religion which exists in the first half cycle. The Confluence Aged souls will then live as deities in the first half cycle and this is the first religion that exists in the Cycle and World Drama. This religion, which exists in the Golden and Silver Ages, is later known as the Adi Sanatan Devi-Devta (meaning 'Original Eternal Deity Religion'). Though it is the Deity Religion, there is no worshipping in the first half cycle because people do not have to ask God for anything. They get everything that they want and need, as per the World Drama. The trunk depicts how there is only one Deity Religion and unity in the Golden and Silver Ages. There is the Sun Dynasty in the Golden Age and the Moon Dynasty in the Silver Age. The deities rule and there is righteousness. No-one is capable of using the vices and so there is perfect order in the whole world. Even Nature is in an ordered and perfect state. At the end of the Silver Age, the Copper Age begins. The people lose their pure divine state and become body-conscious. They begin to get influenced by vices like lust, anger, greed, attachment and ego. So the world becomes an impure, imperfect world. Natural Laws begin to be violated and so Man begins to turn to God and begins to establish religions. Thus, various religions are established in the Copper Age. These religions are the branches from the World Tree and are founded in the following order:

1. Abraham founded Judaism.

2. Buddha founded Buddhism.

3. Jesus Christ founded Christianity.

4. Shankaracharya established the path for recluses and hermits.

5. Prophet Mohammed founded Islam.

These branches also reflect how Mankind split into the different religions. Since each religion has a different set of beliefs, culture, etc., the branches branch out from the trunk. The last twigs of the Tree represent the Kaliyug phases of the religions.

The population is increasing and so the number of people in each religion increases too. Since, as the population is increasing, impurity is also increasing, there is more and more diversity in the religions.

The innermost section of the branches is the Golden Aged section of each religion; and the outermost section of each branch is its Iron Aged section. The twigs and leaves that are growing further away from the Tree represents that Mankind is becoming more and more impure, i.e. they are going further and further away from the original nature of the soul.

As branches grow, they divide into sub-branches. This reflects how, with time, there are divisions within the religions. There are more branches branching out from the outermost section to symbolise that there are more splits within each religious group, at the end of the Cycle. These religions are also passing through different stages of purity, as a result of which there is diversification and disunity. By the end of Kaliyug, many cults, sects and 'isms' also emerge. Religion and philosophy also become more materialistic.

The Tree reaches its maximum growth at the end of the Iron Age. Then, the Tree decays and dies. However, before it dies, a new seed is planted by God for the new Tree. God, the Supreme Soul, is the Seed of this Tree since the next civilisation is begun through what God does through the Confluence Age. The Seed (God) has complete knowledge about this Tree and so He gives it through the mouth of Brahma. Thus, from the

Seed come the roots which provide the foundation for the new Tree to grow. This reflects how the deity souls have to be transformed for the creation of the new Golden Aged world before the Mankind of the next Cycle begins to exist. The new leaves that emerge from the Tree (young plant) represent the deities who take birth in the Golden Aged world. Then, the Tree continues to grow and this represents the growth of civilisation in the new Cycle. As the Tree grows, the trunk develops. The trunk represents the Golden and Silver Ages. In this way, the Cycle and World Drama repeats itself.

There are meditation exercises, below, which you can use during your meditation.

Meditation Commentary 1:
I, the soul, am in the Soul World and I begin my journey to go into the Corporeal World... I take births in the Corporeal World and became part of the trunk in the Golden and Silver Ages where I experience happiness, unity and harmony... After half the cycle, I take births in the second half cycle. The branches grew in the World Tree and I was searching for God... Now, I have found God since I have come into the Confluence Age, and the Seed Himself is explaining everything to me.... I am journeying into the other worlds where I keep God's company... I am in the company of the Master of the Tree, Shiv Baba... I enjoy bliss in His Company.

Meditation Commentary 2:
God, the Seed, is explaining about the World Tree to me... I understand that I was originally from the Deity Religion which existed in the Golden Age... I was part of the trunk of the World Tree... Then, in the Copper Age, I was no longer aware that I was the soul and I forgot that I belonged to the Deity Religion... As many religions were established, I searched for the truth and for God... Now, I am in the Confluence Age among the roots of the World Tree because I have found God and have understood the truth... I feel overjoyed because the new Tree has begun to grow.

Chapter 8: World Ladder (Day 5 of the BK Seven Days Course)

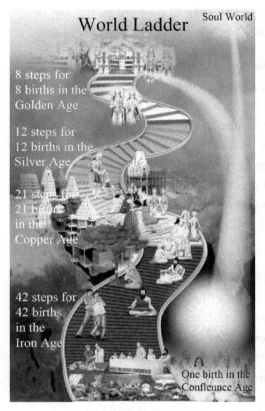

A clearer picture of the World Ladder can be seen at the author's website at: http://www.gbk-books.com/world-ladder.html.

The knowledge given through the Cycle and the Tree can also be explained through the World Ladder. However, the World Ladder or Ladder of 84 births is specifically used to explain the rise and fall of humans. It is used to explain how the deities of the Golden and Silver Ages walk down the ladder, as the spiritual strength of the soul decreases. They are deities in the Golden and Silver Aged section of the Ladder. Then, in the Copper Aged section of the Ladder, it has been reflected that they begin worship, and become devotees, after transforming into the ordinary state. The people lost their divine virtues and righteous state to become impure as they walk down the ladder.

In the World Ladder, each step represents a birth. There are 8 steps in the Golden Aged section of the World Ladder. This represents that Lakshmi and Narayan, the rulers in the Golden Aged world, take 8 births in the Golden Age. During their first birth, Lakshmi and Narayan are on the highest step in the World Ladder. Then, during the next birth, they are on the step below the highest step. This reflects that the soul has lost some spiritual strength and so is walking down the World Ladder. Thus, they will be on the third step during their third birth and they continue walking down during each birth until they are on the eighth step at the end of the Golden Age.

In the Silver Aged section of the World Ladder, there are 12 steps. This represents that Rama and Sita, the rulers in the Silver Aged world, take 12 births in the Silver Age. During each birth, their spiritual strength decreases and so they are on the step below during the next birth. In this manner the souls continue to walk down the World Ladder until they reach the end of the Silver Aged section of the World Ladder. Since the spiritual strength of the souls, in the Silver Age, is lower than that in the Golden Age, the Silver Aged world can be said to be semi-paradise. This is so since the world which souls live in is based on the spiritual strength of the souls.

There are 21 steps in the Copper Aged section of the World Ladder. This represents that souls take 21 births in the Copper Age. Since during each birth their spiritual strength continues to decrease, they continue walking down the World Ladder as they keep taking births. They will be on the last step, at the end of the Copper Aged section of the World Ladder, during their last birth in the Copper Age.

There are 42 steps in the Iron Aged section of the World Ladder. This represents that the soul takes 42 births in Kaliyug. During each of these births, the soul keeps losing spiritual strength and so the person is on the next step below that step, during the next birth. The soul continues walking down each step, in this manner, until the soul is at the end of the World Ladder.

When a soul takes its next birth, the new body which it takes will be based on its lower spiritual strength. So it is as if the 'person' (and not just the soul) has taken a step down the World Ladder.

The deity soul that takes its first birth at the beginning of the Golden Age is on the highest step in the World Ladder. This deity soul will take 83 births to completely use up what exists as its store of pure spiritual energy, as it walks down the World Ladder. Then, during the Confluence Age, in just one spiritual birth, the soul can get recharged. The soul is recharged just before its flame extinguishes, i.e. just before it completely uses up its store of pure spiritual energy.

No matter how many incarnations the soul takes in the Confluence Age, the soul only takes one spiritual birth in the Confluence Age because the soul will be continuing to regain its spiritual strength, during each incarnation, when the soul continues making spiritual efforts after being re-introduced to the knowledge of the Brahma Kumaris. Since only one spiritual birth is taken in the Confluence Age, the deity soul can take a maximum of 84 births in a cycle. Brahma Baba is one of those who take 84 human births during each cycle. The minimum number of births, a human soul can take in a cycle, is one.

The number of births which a soul takes is based on its spiritual strength. For example, if the deity soul has not accumulated a lot of spiritual strength during the Confluence Age, the soul takes its first birth in the later part of the Golden Age or in the Silver Age. This means it leaves the Soul World and comes into a lower section in the World Ladder, i.e. its first birth will be on a lower step and not on the first highest step in the World Ladder.

Through the Confluence Age, the deity souls take a high jump back up to the top of the ladder, as souls walk into the Golden Aged world and as new deity souls take birth again on earth. Souls return to the Soul World after the purification process and then return to play their parts from the top of the World Ladder.

Below is a meditation commentary which you can flow along with, during meditation.

Meditation Commentary:

I, the soul, leave the Soul World to take my first birth in the Corporeal World... I am, now, on the first step of the World Ladder.... I am in the Golden Age where I experience happiness, bliss, purity and all other virtues and powers. I am 16 celestial degrees complete... As I take births in the Golden and Silver Ages, I walk down the World Ladder... After 20 births in the heavenly world, I take a birth in the Copper Age. I keep walking down the World Ladder until I reach the last step which is in the Kaliyug section of the World Ladder... Then, I am in the Confluence Age and I take a high jump up to the top of the World Ladder... I am in the Golden Age again, enjoying a heavenly life.

Chapter 9: Law of Karma (Day 6 of the BK Seven Days Course)

The Sanskrit word Karma means action or deeds. Actions are performed in the Corporeal World, based on which we reap the fruits as per the Law of Karma. The Law of Karma is a Spiritual Law which plays its part during the second half cycle since Mankind is capable of doing good or bad actions. A different set of Spiritual Laws apply in the second half cycle and the fulfilment of one's desires is based on the Law of Karma.

Actually, what we get is only based on what exists in the World Drama. However, we are supposed to be living and so we are subjected to the Law of Karma while living during the second half cycle.

There are **three kinds of karma/actions**:

1. Akarma which is neutral karma,

2. Sukarma which is positive or good karma, and

3. Vikarma which is negative, bad or sinful karma/action.

Whatever God does is Akarma because:

1. God is not subjected to the Law of Karma, and

2. God is not capable of being influenced by the vices.

Even the **actions done in the first half cycle are Akarma** because in the first half cycle:

1. the people are not capable of being influenced by the vices.

2. the souls are enjoying the fruits of their actions which were done during the previous Confluence Age. Thus, they are beyond the cause and effects of karma.

3. the Law of Karma is not in force.

The people in the first half cycle did not know of the Law of Karma because:

1. their actions were Akarma.

2. the Law of Karma only comes into force from the beginning of the Copper Age.

3. people only began to know of the Law of Karma from the Mid-Confluence when people began to do bad karma and they began to realise that they were accumulating bad karmic accounts.

In the second half cycle, the Law of Karma is a force that is bound with the World Drama to allow human souls to reap the fruits of their actions on earth. So if one does something good, one will get something good in return. It follows suit that if one does something bad (Vikarma), one will get something bad in return.

One should constantly check the quality of one's actions and interactions with others to make sure that one is not performing Vikarma because, since every action creates a reaction through the Law of Karma, one will experience the effects of those reactions through happiness or suffering. One experiences the effects, of these reactions, in this life itself or in a subsequent birth.

There is disharmony, suffering, conflict, impurity in the world, etc. when a person's actions are based on the usage of the vices. The fruit received, through the Law of Karma for such actions, is bad. When a person's acts help bring harmony, purity etc. the fruit received, through the Law of Karma, is good.

The Confluence Aged souls and those walking into the Golden Aged world are still capable of using the vices. Thus, they are still bound by the Law of Karma. Making spiritual efforts to become and remain soul conscious, during the Confluence Age, is good karma (Sukarma) because it is a benevolent action. It helps others to remain pure and so they experience happiness and not unhappiness. It also helps to transform the world into the pure Golden Aged world. Getting involved with the creation of the New Golden Aged world is the most charitable act. A multimillion-fold is earned in return for such actions. The returns are received through the World Drama.

Through purifying yourself, via the Confluence Aged spiritual effort making and the walking in process, God's powerful vibrations are sent out from you and you are also involved with the good karma of changing the world into the heavenly divine Golden Aged world. Thus, through the Law of Karma, you will get good fruits for your good karma.

The thoughts which you have can also determine what you get through the Law of Karma. BKs have thoughts based on the BK knowledge. This enables them to earn a multimillion-fold because contemplating on the BK knowledge links the soul to God. As a result, there is purification of the soul and the world is being transformed into the Golden Aged world.

When you get involved with the Confluence Aged spiritual effort making or the walking in process, you earn a spiritual income. This spiritual income is earned through the Law of Karma. During the present birth, this spiritual income is spiritual upliftment because it involves a greater accumulation of spiritual strength within the soul. If you accumulate your spiritual income, you can become spiritually powerful and then, you can enjoy your income in the first half cycle as wealth and status. You will be able to instantly accumulate spiritual strength, via the Law of Karma and World Drama, when you make spiritual efforts. The more you make spiritual efforts, the greater your income.

Those walking in can reap the fruits in this birth itself or/and they can also enjoy the benefits in their births in the first half cycle. Thus, they will be given an opportunity to be exposed to God's vibrations so that, without much spiritual effort-making, they can enjoy the blissful stage. In addition to this, they can also use their spiritual income in this birth itself to enjoy wealth, etc. If they prefer not to enjoy the wealth etc. in this birth itself, they can enjoy it in later births, during the first half cycle

59

or during the Mid-Confluence. Their efforts to walk into the Golden Aged world, and the world service which they do, will accumulate a lot of wealth for them. Thus, they can become rich in this birth itself or they can become rich in subsequent births. They have a choice to decide when they want to enjoy this wealth. If they use the money (which they get) for service, they keep accumulating more spiritual wealth which they can use in their births in the first half cycle. If they use the Confluence Aged knowledge to get involved with transforming the world into the Golden Aged world, as BKs do, it is as if they accumulate wealth and the royal status. Thus, in subsequent births, in the first half cycle and Mid-Confluence, they will be born in a royal family to become a wealthy king or queen.

In the second half cycle, actions which are done through the influence of the vices are bad karma (Vikarma). These actions create bad karmic accounts (sins) which need to be settled through the Law of Karma. Vikarma can be created through every act which you do. For example, using somebody else's water to wash your clothes is a Vikarma which creates a karmic account because, one day, somebody else is going to use your water to wash their clothes. However, it may be possible that you are using someone else's water now because, in the past, you had allowed somebody to use your water. So you are reaping the benefits of that earlier act. Since we are living with others, we create good and bad karmic accounts. These get settled as we continue to live our lives.

Settling of karmic accounts sets you free of your bad karmic accounts and it also purifies you. Karmic accounts can be settled quickly or slowly. If you wish to burn off karmic accounts quickly, establish your link to God, as BKs do. As you get purified, your sins are burnt off. However, the severe karmic accounts might take some time to get burnt off. If it is taking some time to get burnt off, just watch what is happening as a detached observer.

One can also settle one's bad accounts through one's own body (e.g. through diseases etc.) and through suffering (mentally or physically). If you are making spiritual efforts and your diseases have not disappeared, keep making spiritual efforts until they disappear. They will disappear when you have settled the karmic account which is making you suffer through the disease.

Karmic accounts can be settled while you are doing Karma Yoga, as you interact with people, through the body, etc. Karma Yoga involves meditating while performing actions (while working and/or moving around). This means you have to carry out your daily activities etc. while in a meditative state, i.e. while having your link to God. Thus, you get purified while you are carrying out your daily activities. If you do activities for world service, while in yoga with God, you can get spiritually powerful through two ways, i.e. through the service and your link to God. Through doing this kind of Karma Yoga, others and the world get a huge benefit while you are being purified. Karma Yoga includes transforming yourself, through which the world is transformed. This is being done via your link to God. While doing Karma Yoga, if you find yourself in a situation where people are giving you a bad time:

1. remind yourself that you are settling karmic accounts and that you should not react in anyway, i.e. watch it as a detached observer, and

2. keeping sending them God's vibrations to bring them into a pure peaceful state.

World service can be done:

1. through sending God's vibrations into the world while sitting in meditation.

2. through sending God's vibrations into the world while doing actions (Karma Yoga).

3. through doing something that will put God's Confluence Aged service on the world stage, e.g. informing others and/or the world of how God is getting the Golden Aged world created now. Even if your stage is not good, you will earn a huge spiritual income because this service is for world benefit, i.e. it is world service.

All deity souls have to play their part for world transformation to take place. So through playing your part you are helping with this transformation process. This is also world service. Spreading the news so that others can also play their parts is also world service which will help you to earn a spiritual income.

World service is also done through using the practices in this book because it helps God to achieve the goal of creating the Golden Aged world in the materialised form together with all those who will be living there. You earn a spiritual income through doing this via the Law of Karma.

The spiritual income which you get through spiritual effort making, Karma Yoga, world service and the walking in process can be enjoyed in this birth itself. If you have only enjoyed some of it in this birth, the remainder remains with you and you can accumulate them for your births in the first half cycle.

BKs prefer to use their spiritual income during the first half cycle. They have faith in the BK knowledge and so they know that they will be able to use their spiritual income, as wealth and status, in the first half cycle.

Since this book is for those who want to walk into the Golden Aged world, there is guidance, in this chapter, on how the Law of Karma affects them and on what kind of actions are beneficial to them until they completely walk into the materialised Golden Aged world. Those walking in can enjoy the fruits of their actions while walking in, after having walked in and also in their subsequent births in the first half cycle (Golden and Silver Ages).

If those walking in do not get involved with practices to bring them an abundance of wealth, they will acquire money if they need money to do service. If they are only getting the wealth for service, they are not using their spiritual income for these. They can keep their spiritual income if they use this wealth with the view that they are doing so on God's behalf (as His trustees) for getting the service done.

Informing others about the walking in process will give you a great spiritual income because it will bring all the deity souls into the Confluence Age and those walking in will get together to do something or the other for the walking in process and for what needs to exist in the new world. Don't worry about doing things that need to be taken into the new world. Just live your life happily and keep making spiritual efforts. As you do this, you will be guided on what to do and how to use your money for the walking in process (if you are interested in that). What you do with your money is your choice. However, to earn a greater spiritual income, see the money as being God's money. God is your Father and Mother; a Parent will always give money to His children so that they can live their lives. So don't think that you cannot use that money on yourself.

Even if you were not a deity soul, you are a blessed soul if you decide to go on the pure path for world benefit through the practices in this book because you will be helping to maintain the purity of the Lower Universe where the Kaliyug world exists. It was the pure souls who were sustaining the world from the Copper Age onwards. They would have received a lot of benefits through the Law of Karma for this part, e.g. they would have easily enjoyed purity, happiness, wealth and prosperity in subsequent births. However, now, God is purifying the world through His children who are living on earth.

Chapter 10: Powers and other Original Qualities of the Soul (Day 7 of the BK Seven Days Course)

The original qualities of the soul are the virtues and powers. It can be said that love, peace, truth, happiness, purity, power and bliss have all the virtues and powers within them. However, actually, virtues are the specific beneficial qualities such as joy, happiness, peace, bliss, love, etc. Since all good values and qualities can be seen as virtues, even 'power' can be seen as a virtue.

The virtues are used to live righteously. When we use the virtues, we are considered to be good and our actions are also considered to be good. A virtue is experienced as a feeling by the soul.

All virtues can also be used as powers. Powers are the soul's ability to use the virtues, BK knowledge etc. in an efficient and accurate manner for self-transformation and for world transformation. Powers are used to influence others or to have control over the self. Through using the powers, the soul is able to achieve something. For example, when we take God's vibrations of love and send it to someone so as to influence them, we use that virtue (love) as a power. If we are just experiencing love during meditation and while doing activities, 'love' is not really being used as a power. When people are capable of using the vices, we need to use the virtues as powers so as to influence them to become virtuous. But we should not send them our own virtues because our virtues are weak, we should absorb God's virtues and send that to the people around us. When we keep doing this, our own virtues become powerful and divine. When you are battling with the vices to remain virtuous, the virtues are used as a power. So if your virtues are in a more powerful state and you are able to use them as powers, you can easily win that battle to remain in the virtuous state. While in the virtuous state, you experience the virtues as 'virtues' through your feelings. However, when you use the virtues to empower yourself and others, they are used as powers.

The aim of Brahma Kumaris' meditation is to experience each and every virtue and power. Eight significant spiritual powers which the Brahma Kumaris give emphasis to are:

1. Power to Withdraw.

2. Power to Pack-Up.

3. Power to Tolerate.

4. Power to Accommodate/Adjust.

5. Power to Discriminate.

6. Power to Judge.

7. Power to Face.

8. Power to Co-operate.

Through using the above powers, one remains in the virtuous state. So one can easily go beyond into the Angelic World. As you keep meditating, these powers increase within the soul:

1. as God's energies fill the soul up with these powers, and

2. as the soul's energies are strengthened or purified through the purification process.

Though these powers exist naturally within the soul, they are in a weak state in the second half cycle. They can be strengthened through one's link to God. As you keep using the powers they keep increasing. This and meditation, together, will increase your stability. There are also other benefits in applying the powers. For example, it helps to reduce conflicts. So check to see which powers you are lacking in or are weak in, then strengthen those through meditation and during your interactions.

Powers Through Yoga

A clearer picture, portraying the eight significant powers of the soul, can be seen at the author's website at: http://www.gbk-books.com/powers. html.

This picture is used by the Brahma Kumaris, during the 7 days course, while explaining about the powers. So I have also used it in this book.

1. Power to Withdraw:

The Power to Withdraw is your ability to step back and disengage yourself (the soul) from the ordinary world which you are in. The Brahma Kumaris use the picture of the tortoise while explaining about the Power to Withdraw. When the turtle or tortoise senses some kind of danger, or when it wants to rest, it goes within its shell. In the same way, a person should be able to withdraw from any situation and remain protected within their "shell of soul consciousness" or "God consciousness". God keeps you protected like the shell that protects the turtle. You detach yourself from the situation, yet, you remain fully aware of what is happening around it. You do not run away from the situation by detaching yourself from the body so that you are unaware of what is happening around you.

The Power to Withdraw is also used to begin meditation, through taking away your attention from your external environment. It helps you to calm down for meditation. Just like how the tortoise is able to easily pull its head, two arms and two legs inside its shell, you should be able to withdraw all your 5 senses from the external environment. You withdraw your senses to become a point (the soul conscious state). You are aware that you are the soul and not that body. You are aware that you have to use that body and 5 senses well so as to play your part well. You are in a situation where you see, yet, you do not see; you hear, yet, you do not hear. You see and hear; however, you are not influenced or disturbed by what you see or hear. Through developing this ability, you become the master of your senses. If not, you become a slave to your senses and you are not the master, they are. When you withdraw in this way, you observe the situation as a detached observer. It is as if you are looking at the situation as a third party or as an actor who is assessing the situation before playing his part. In this way, you can understand the situation better and even become aware of your own weaknesses.

The Power to Withdraw also includes the need to occasional find time when you can quietly sit so as to meditate. Going within, regularly, helps you to accumulate inner strength and also draw on your stock of inner strength. It helps you to accumulate more energy through your link to God. It helps you to fill yourself up with God's energies so that you have His energies assisting you to remain powerful in all situations. So it is beneficial to withdraw so as to meditate.

2. Power to Pack-Up:

The Power to Pack-Up gives you the ability to bring things to an end and to stop wasteful thinking. The Brahma Kumaris use the picture of the luggage while teaching about the Power to Pack-Up. This is used to teach that there must be a spiritual packing-up. A well-versed traveller would normally travel light. He would only be having a few clothes and necessities in his luggage. The soul is also like a traveller who flies from one body to another, during re-incarnation, and then the soul has to travel back Home to the Soul World at the end of the cycle. You are also like a traveller carrying your luggage around with you while carrying out all your daily activities. Thus, the soul has to learn to remain light. You should not carry all the waste thoughts with you. You should just keep the virtues and powers with you because you will need to use these. You do not have to use waste thought. Waste thoughts make one feel heavy. Thus, carrying waste thoughts is like making the luggage unnecessarily heavy.

When you go within, during meditation, you will find that a lot of waste thoughts come into your mind. Your mind will be constantly chattering, your intellect will be constantly trying to analyse everything (including waste), wasteful memories will also be constantly popping up from the Memory Bank. All these will make you heavy and so you will not be able to meditate. When you learn to pack-up everything with just one thought (that you are a soul linked to God) you have control over your Mind, Intellect and Memory. You will be able to easily pack-up all unwanted paraphernalia from your mind, and throw it off, so that you can travel light with only that which you need.

The Power to Pack-up is your ability to put aside all the wasteful thoughts (which have come into your mind) in one second. This enables you to remain light and free from burdens and worries. A soul who knows how to pack-up, will throw off what is not needed and pack those that are needed. You can also pack-up all the unwanted stuff into a luggage and throw off that luggage; and keep the luggage which has what you need.

When you are in a situation where the vices have emerged because you are getting angry etc., immediately pack all that anger and all other unwanted odds and ends into a bag and throw it off. You can also give it to God. This means, establish your link to God and let all those vices and waste thoughts get burnt away. As they get burnt away, imagine that God is taking them away from you.

Sometimes, you may have left an object in a place, however, you are no longer able to see it there. This may have happened as part of the settling process. It should be noted that everything that exists in the Real World is in a dual state, i.e. the wave-particle state. As a result, it can exist in the wave state or in the particle state. If you had done some wrong in the past and you need to settle it, the World Drama provides for that settling in one way or another. If the thing disappeared to attain the wave state and so you are not able to see and use it, it is part of the settling process. Use your powers to deal with this. i.e. don't let waste thoughts take over. Use your power to pack up and remain light.

3. Power to Tolerate:

The word 'tolerate' has a different meaning from that which is used by non-BKs. Often, when non-BKs say that they are tolerating something, it means that they may be reacting internally but are not reacting in an external manner. For example, they might not like what is happening but they do not do anything to show that they do not like it. Where Confluence Aged souls are concerned, they should not react internally and externally because they should be a detached observer.

BKs teach about the Power to Tolerate through the picture of the boy hitting the tree with the stone so that he can get its fruit. The tree is unaffected by the external events and continues to respond in a positive manner by continuing to give fruits to the boy even though he is throwing stones at it. We have to develop our Power of Tolerance so that we can be like that tree. When you have the Power of Tolerance, you have the ability to remain undisturbed by external and internal situations. You have this ability when you are in the soul conscious stage and are thus watching everything as a detached observer. You watch everything as if it is part of a game or drama. So you are not emotionally involved in that situation. You will keep absorbing God's energies into you through your link and you will reflect those energies to the one who is behaving badly, so as to help transform them into the pure state. You will keep behaving in a virtuous manner and not retaliate. Though people are doing hurtful actions, the soul conscious person is not hurt by it. They understand that the other person is in a weak state and so he is behaving in that bad manner. They understand that it is happening as per the World Drama and so they observe it as a detached observer without getting hurt. When you have the Power to Tolerate, hurtful memories and emotions do not emerge to influence you.

4. Power to Accommodate/Adjust:

The Power to Accommodate or Adjust is symbolically represented by how the rivers meander to accommodate the obstructions by adjusting its path and changing shape, while on its way to the ocean. This power is used to accommodate situations, people, and the views and ways of others through using the soul conscious stage. For example, if you did not get what you want, you would adjust to this and not lose your high stage. The Power to Adjust also refers to one's ability to accept, flow along with and/or expand upon ideas, desires and the work of others. It allows you to accommodate and adjust when someone is crossing the line to come into your territory. One has to adopt and adjust while in the detached state so as to make sure that impressions of what is happening around one are not left in the soul.

One should also be able to accept what one is faced with, like how the ocean accepts all types of rivers to flow into it, irrespective of whether the river brings a benefit or not. This means one must be able to adjust oneself and accommodate all that is happening around one. One is broadminded when using the power to accommodate.

Another scenario in respect of the rivers flowing into the ocean is that the rivers represent the Confluence Aged souls who are linked to God (the Ocean). From this angle, the qualities of the river are given importance to since it is adopting and adjusting to flow between all the rocks and other obstacles while flowing towards the Ocean. This reflects how those who have a powerful soul conscious stage will naturally adopt and adjust without being influenced by what is in the way. We still keep maintaining our link to God (the Ocean) no matter what obstacles come our way. At the same time, since we have a link to God, we are able to adopt and adjust to all the situations which we are put in.

The eight main powers given importance to, by the Brahma Kumaris, involve using more than just one virtue. Thus, when you are using the Power to Adjust and Accommodate, the virtues that develop within you are respect, acceptance, mercy, flexibility, the ability to listen, broadmindedness, openness, etc.

5. Power to Discriminate:

This is explained through using the picture of the jeweller picking out the true gems. The Power to Discriminate is your ability to pick that which is true and not the false. You pick out what is true by using your intellect which is the inner eye or third eye.

An untrained person will not be able to differentiate between a synthetic, fake diamond and a true one. However, an experienced and trained jeweller will know the difference. Similarly, one can use one's power of discrimination well when one uses one's spiritual knowledge, divine intellect and experiences. One's spiritual sight is one's divine intellect. This divine intellect is like an experienced jeweller's eye. Through using this divine intellect, we will understand the Divine Laws which govern the course of human life. For example we will understand how the Law of Karma apply to karma. Through using this divine intellect we will be able to make a proper discrimination between a good action and a bad action.

The Power to Discriminate also helps one to distinguish the truth from that which seems like the truth. One will be able to distinguish between things of temporary value and those of eternal value. This power will help one to recognise the traps of Maya (vices) even when they present themselves as something great.

Through the use of this power, we will know if someone is pretending and we will act accordingly in a soul conscious manner, understanding that it is happening as per the World Drama or like a game. Through remaining in the soul conscious stage, we will be able to choose the right from the wrong within a second.

6. Power to Judge:

The Power to Judge is one's ability to make good decisions after properly assessing the choices, actions etc. The picture of an accurate scale is used to represent this power. The accurate scale represents that an accurate judgement has been made.

One does not use the Power to Judge to judge others. Judging another is bad karma. The original qualities of all souls are the virtues and powers. So the soul is good. However, the soul is in a weak state and so is not playing his part well. When you have a proper understanding of this, you will not judge another. The Power to Judge is only used to judge actions (to see if an action is worth doing) or to know if something is worth contemplating on because you should not waste your time contemplating on wasteful matters. Use the Power to Judge on yourself: to assess your thoughts, words and actions. This helps to make sure that you are on the angelic path. However, don't be too harsh on yourself.

Through using the Power to Judge, you will be able to assess the situation which you are in accurately. Thus, you will know how to conduct yourself. This power is developed further as you keep remaining in the soul conscious stage and have your link to God. When one's spiritual stage is very high, one will be able to make a good decision quickly. If a decision should not be taken, because you have to just watch it as a detached observer, you will be just watching it without making any decision. If you have to flow along with what is happening, then also, you will not make a decision because when your stage is good, your acts are accurate.

7. The Power to Face:

The picture used to explain the Power to Face is also symbolic. People find it hard to face the death of a loved one. They will even run away when they are faced with a tempestuous, storm-like situation. However, if you are in the soul conscious stage, you will be able to face the death of a loved one and even the other terrible situations (which have been represented through the fierce storm etc. in the picture). You should not lose your soul conscious stage, which has been represented by the flame, during such situations. Only then will you be able to easily face the situation. The flames of the powerful soul conscious soul will not get extinguished when confronted by all these. With confidence they face each and every situation, knowing that God is there with them, to protect them in all situations. If you have your link to God, God will be there to protect you and His vibrations will be soothing you to keep you comfortable.

The Power to Face is the ability to face a situation and at the same time carry out an appropriate act without running away from the situation. Through meditation, you develop your ability to face hardship.

When using the Power to Face, you also use courage, forgiveness, confidence, faith, determination, purpose etc. to face any situation or person. Thus, as you use the Power to Face, these virtues and powers are also developing within you. As you keep using them, they keep increasing and you will find it easier and easier to face a bad situation. Thus, when you have to face someone who has been giving you a lot of problems, you will not turn away from the situation. You will be able to deal with it since you have an increased amount of the relevant virtues and powers. Since you remain in the peaceful state, there cannot be any fight between you and the others. So you are helping to transform the situation into a peaceful one. Further, you will be giving God's vibrations to the others. As a result, people will be influenced and they will stop giving you a bad time. Think of God, while facing people who give you a hard time and God will take care of it. When you use the Power to Face, you would be conquering fear, hatred, jealousy, insecurities, doubts on your abilities, etc. (if those were the reasons why you might not have been able to face a situation or person). If you find these existing in your mind, remove them from your mind and establish your link to God. You become powerful through your link to God and so the vices stay away. The vices will also get burnt through being exposed to God's powerful energies. Entertaining these negative qualities will increase them within you. When there are more of them within you, you will find it more difficult to face a situation. Thus, don't entertain them. Remember that the people who are born in the Golden Aged world will have all the virtues and powers. As a person walking in, you should try to develop these. If not, you will find it difficult to uplift yourself into the higher dimensions.

8. Power to Co-operate:

The Power to Co-operate involves your ability to do something together with others. The picture used to explain this shows how if each person just gives a finger in a co-operative manner, together, they will be able to lift a mountain. This reflects how powerful a team can become if they co-operated with each other. The fact that they can co-operate with each other also demonstrates that they have very good characteristic qualities because it is not easy to work together in a team.

When people do things together, often, their weaknesses get revealed. Thus, there can be conflicts, etc. This gives one an opportunity to study one's own weaknesses and to work on it.

During teamwork, one has to give one's time, attention, experience, wisdom etc. to get something done. A person who co-operates will not be competing with the others in the team. However, sometimes, someone may try to take control of the whole project and if others do not follow along, the whole project can fail completion. If they have successfully co-operated in that teamwork, then, they were able to have control over themselves.

Those who are masters of the self will be able to flow along with each other. One will find it easy to co-operate when one is in the soul conscious stage. A person who is in a soul conscious stage does not try to take control of a project. They are just helpers. So others will find it very easy to work with them. When you are in the soul conscious stage, God's vibrations are also vibrating out from you. So others are also helped to remain peaceful and co-operative. God has an ocean of the powers to co-operate; these are received and vibrated out of those who are in the soul conscious stage. As a consequence, all the others in the team are also influenced to become co-operative.

Simply seeing the other's highest qualities of character, instead of seeing their weaknesses is also an act of co-operation because by seeing their highest qualities you are helping it to exist in their mind. They get influenced by it.

When you have good wishes that the others must succeed, feel good etc., these will help them to succeed, feel good etc. Your good wishes are 'co-operation'.

Your positive attitude, when the group is faced with a difficult task, inspires the others to successfully accomplish the tasks. Your positive attitude is also 'co-operation'.

When you appreciate, encourage, accept or acknowledge another or his work, ideas etc., you are co-operating with him. When there is co-operation in a team, there is unity, harmony and prosperity. When there is co-operation, the members of the team share and learn from each other. You share virtues, specialties, ideas, knowledge, etc.

Through meditation, we develop and increase our ability to co-operate. These powers are emerged from within us through meditation and we also get more of these powers from God through our link to Him. God's energies transform our weak energies into powerful ones and so our Power to Co-operate becomes more powerful. This in turn increases our ability to be co-operative.

The greatest charitable task which a person can do is to co-operate for world service, i.e. to help transform it into the Golden Aged world. As the divine world is getting created, God's energies in the environment will make the world a heavenly place to live in. Nature and all the people are influenced. The greatest spiritual income, through the Law of Karma, can be earned through participating for world transformation. Together, without competing with each other, we can lift mountains with just a finger each.

In the above picture, the powers opposite to each other are normally used together in a situation. For example, the Power to Discriminate is opposite the Power to Judge and so these two are normally used together. You discriminate and decide/judge when making decisions. The Power to Accommodate is opposite to the Power to Face because you normally use these together. You have to face the situation while you accommodate and adjust. The Power to Tolerate is opposite to the Power to Co-operate because you use these two together. You tolerate and at the same time, you co-operate. The Power to Pack-Up is opposite the Power to Withdraw because both of these are used together. If you pack up your unwanted waste, you will find it easy to withdraw. Further, when you with withdraw, you will find that you need to constantly use your Power to Pack-Up, i.e. you need to throw off unwanted stuff and keep the good ones in your luggage for use.

Through using the eight powers mentioned above, you will develop your ability to cope with every challenge and live well in every situation. In the present world, where we can use the vices, we need to use powers to a great extent. In the Golden Aged world, since everyone is virtuous, there is not much of a need to use the powers.

As we take births through the Cycle of Time, as the spiritual strength of the soul gets weaker, even the powers get weaker. Thus, by the end of the cycle, we do not efficiently use our powers. The fact that one lacks the ability to use one's powers reflects the weak state of the soul.

To become more powerful, increase the virtues and powers within you. As you keep inculcating virtues, you are also developing your powers. When you (the soul) are filled with powers, you are a Shakti (power). Shakti has been portrayed as a goddess in the Hindu scriptures. This reflects the powerful state of the soul who is filled with powers. As a Shakti, you are unshakeable. So empower yourselves by gaining experiences on each virtue. Contemplate on a virtue at a time. Emerge it from the depths of the soul and enjoy it. When in an emerged state, it is there in your mind and so you can enjoy it. You experience it or feel it. At the same time, establish your link to God and draw the virtue, which you are contemplating on, from God. Then, you can use that virtue as a power. Whatever virtue or power you want, will come from God in abundance because God has an ocean of it. The following are some virtues (values or qualities) which you can inculcate and use as powers: happiness, peace, bliss, love, joy, purity, truth, contentment, faith, harmony, obedience, wisdom, trust, uprightness, zeal, flexibility, unity, decisiveness, courage, steadfastness, generosity, friendliness, sincerity, gratitude, cheerfulness, openness, righteousness, bravery, gratitude, consideration, tranquillity, trustworthiness, gentleness, orderliness, detachment, determination, perceptiveness, mercy, mindfulness, majesty, dignity, appreciation, modesty, independence, prudence, perseverance, initiative, nobility, kindness, freedom, forgiveness, compassion, understanding, benevolence, loyalty, simplicity, humility, enthusiasm, acceptance, strength, serenity, tact, innocence, integrity, reliability, helpfulness, honesty, confidence, respect, purposefulness, truthfulness, caring, responsibility and patience.

You can contemplate on one of the above virtues/powers every day. When contemplating on each virtue/power, make sure that you are using it based on BK Gyan/knowledge. For example, when you contemplate on thankfulness, be thankful that God has found you or be thankful that you have such a heavenly life due to the walking in process. These visualisations will materialise and so God would be helping you and you would be living a heavenly life through the walking in process.

Meditation Guideline:

I, the soul, nurture pure thoughts based on the BK Knowledge... and so I have a strong clear link with God... This gives me the highest experience of bliss...While experiencing this blissful state, I carry out my daily activities... I use the powers in all the situations which I am faced with, while remaining in the detached soul conscious stage.

NB: after having visualised what had been provided in the above meditation guideline, visualise something that is based on what is happening in your life. However, in your visualisation, see yourself participating in the detached soul conscious stage while using all the relevant powers. This helps you to act in the way that you had visualised.

Chapter 11: Silence

There are various aspects to 'silence' such as the:

1. virtues and powers of the soul which are one's power of silence.

2. God's Virtues and Powers which can be received and used as the Power of Silence. When capital letters are used for 'Power' and 'Silence', God's Power of Silence is being referred to.

3. quiet place for meditation (within the Real World).

4. room/space of silence within the soul.

5. silence in the metaphysical dimension (within the Corporeal World), lokas, auric fields, Confluence Auric Field, dimensions within the Holographic Universe and Angelic World.

6. silence in the Soul World.

7. sounds of silence.

The vices and waste thoughts are 'noise' within the soul. When there is no noise of the vices and waste thoughts, and only the virtues and powers are in an emerged state within the soul, then, there is only silence within the soul. Through experiencing silence, you become aware that you are the soul.

All the virtues and powers of the soul are 'silence' because they do not create any noise within you (the soul). These pure virtues and powers have a 'power' since they influence the self, other souls and the environment. This 'power' influences the self to become the Inner Self and to use the energies at the deeper levels within the soul. This 'power' helps one to easily establish one's link to God. When one is in the pure virtuous state, one is enjoying the power of silence.

When you have the link to God, you are filled with God's energies, and so your energies transform into the divine state. Your energies now have the divine power of silence and you experience divine silence within the soul. While you experience this divine silence, you are also filled with God's Power of Silence (God's Divine Virtues and Powers). God's energies have a 'Power' which can do magical miracles and wonders. God's Power of Silence will help you to remain as a detached observer, transforms you into the divine state, keeps you away from noise that can exist in your mind and it also gets the Golden Aged world created. The Power of Silence gives you an enormous inner power. It is like a shield that protects you from the vices, waste thoughts etc. It helps you to experience being the soul and stay connected to God.

As you keep using the virtues, more and more impressions of the virtues are formed. You become more virtuous because your virtues are increased. This means that your power of silence is, likewise, increasing.

Further, through your link to God, the soul's energies are transformed through the purification process. Therefore, as you keep remembering God, the vices are burnt away or transformed into the pure energies and the divine virtues and powers increase within the soul. As your divine virtues and powers increase, your divine power of silence increases and the space of divine silence, within your soul, also increases.

If one keeps using the vices, more and more impressions of the vices are created. These are noise that has a negative effect on the physical body, hence the body can get diseased. This situation can be changed through one's link to God.

By filling oneself with one's power of silence and God's Power of Silence, the soul and body are healed. One's body can also be transformed into the perfect state through being exposed to God' Power of Silence during the walking in process.

It is not possible to remain without a thought. However, you can easily remain silent through holding a specific thought in your mind. This is also silence because you are not allowing all the waste thoughts to create noise within your mind. This is what Brahma Kumaris Raja Yoga teaches. It teaches you to stabilise your mind while you hold one thought, e.g. seeing yourself as a peaceful soul or seeing yourself receiving God's energies, etc. You have control over the thoughts and the thoughts are positive thoughts. They are not waste thoughts. Acquiring the habit to have control over your thoughts, in this way, helps you to use the Power of Silence.

Being filled with the power of silence does not just mean that there is 'silence' within the soul. The pure divine virtues and powers have magical abilities and so it can be said that the power of silence can do magical marvels. However, the power of silence of the human soul is not powerful enough to transform the world into a Golden Aged world. It is only God's Power of Silence which can transform the world into the Golden Aged world and transform you into the Golden Aged self.

People often do meditation in a silent room because it helps them to take their first step inwards where there is silence. Silence is also the place which you, the virtuous self, occupy in your mind and soul. From your silent space within the soul, you can see all the thoughts, emotions etc. that exist in your mind. From that silence, you can look at everything that is happening around you, as a detached observer, when you have your link to God.

Since your original qualities are the virtues and powers, this is the real you (since you are the soul). This aspect of you is silent and it should fill your room of silence within your mind and soul. Since the energies of the soul are metaphysical, your room of silence is in a metaphysical dimension (within the Corporeal World) which is also silent.

As you contemplate on the virtues, your room (within the soul) gets filled with silence. When you contemplate upon peace, your room (including your mind) becomes more and more quiet, until only the relevant thoughts, which you hold, remain.

Om means "I, the soul". Om Shanti means "I, the soul, am peaceful". When one keeps repeating this, one actually goes into the peaceful soul conscious stage. As you keep filling your mind with the thought "Om Shanti", it acts like a mantra to connect you to your own power of silence and to God's Power of Silence. So you (the soul) become an embodiment of peace and silence. You will be in your room of silence (within the soul).

When you are using only the virtues and powers, you will feel very light and you will be able to float up into the higher dimensions. Silence is experienced when you visualise something of your own choice, e.g. when you visualise yourself as being in the higher dimension. During these visualisations, you are not entertaining the vices and waste thoughts, since you are concentrating on your visualisation. Thus, you are in silence. You will naturally move into the higher dimensions when you experience silence because your energies will resonate well with the pure silent energies in the higher dimensions. You will learn more about these higher dimensions as you keep reading this book.

Since you have a link to God, and are using the Confluence Auric Field (the aura of Confluence Aged people) it is as if you have a room of silence which you can constantly use in your Confluence Auric Field. This room is connected to the Angelic World and your room of silence can also exist in the Angelic World (beyond the Corporeal World). So long as you are using the BK knowledge, you are in this room of silence. There is silence in the Angelic World because:

1. there are no vices there since only the pure energies of souls can remain in the Angelic World.

2. God's Power of Silence fills the Angelic World.

3. only your power of silence exists there.

You will understand more on the Confluence Auric Field as you keep reading this book.

It is while experiencing silence that you can begin your journey to the Soul World which is your silent Home. You are in complete silence in the Soul World.

There is silence within you when you are peaceful because there isn't any noise of wasteful thoughts etc. However, silence has a deeper meaning when it refers to the silence experienced when one is in deep meditation. It can be said that those who practice meditation use an aspect of silence which are not used by those who do not meditate. This is so because those who meditate go deeper within the soul, they subtly journey into the silent dimensions in the Holographic Universe, etc. From this viewpoint, it can be said that silence is different from peace because one can be peaceful even though one is not experiencing silence.

There are various aspects to energies. One of these is the 'light' aspect and another is the 'sound' aspect. All energies have a sound aspect to them. The pure energies have a sound of silence. The sounds made by the impure energies are not the sounds of silence.

Though all energies have the sound aspect, not all energies have a 'light' aspect. Only QE Light and the energies of the souls and Supreme Soul have a light aspect.

The human souls and the Supreme Soul use both: their light aspect and their sound aspect. Through the sound aspect we are able to subtly communicate with each other, with God and with the QE Light. The light aspect of the energies of the soul and Supreme Soul reflect wisdom, purity and the spiritual strength of the energies. The 'light' is used as consciousness.

God's Power of Silence consists of the light aspect and the sound aspect. The sound aspect is the Sound of Silence. God's Sound of Silence includes the subtle vibrations that accompany the knowledge which God has given to the Brahma Kumaris.

When you keep saying "Om Shanti" or "I am a peaceful soul" you become that because these words are accompanied by God's vibrations since these words are also part of the 'knowledge' that was given by God in the Brahma Kumaris. The vibrations of the sounds of these words will resonate with God's vibrations to link you to God.

The light aspect of God's Power of Silence purifies and strengthens the energies in the soul and Corporeal World. Thus, it is involved with transformation of the world into the Golden Aged world. The magic which is done, through the light, can be seen in visions. The sound aspect of the Power of Silence has subtle magical abilities which cannot be seen since it does not involve 'light'. The greatest Magician is God because only He can create the Golden Aged world and only He can open the gateway to heaven so that you can walk into the Golden Aged world.

The frequency of the pure energies of the 'OM' (soul) resonates with the frequencies of the pure energies in the universe. The resonance of the waves/frequencies of all pure energies, in the universe, is in a harmonious state.

In the Corporeal World, there are various kinds of pure vibrations that are involved with the creation processes. All of them have a sound of silence aspect. The main one is the souls' sound of silence (OM). It can be said that the sound of silence (OM) is everywhere in the Corporeal World because:

1. the pure QE Light have the same frequencies as the pure energies of the soul (OM).

2. the QE Light are entangled with the energies of the soul (OM) and the quantum energies are the other half of the QE Light. It is like this because the universe exists to serve the soul (OM), i.e. the Supreme Soul and all human souls. As a result, the souls' thoughts, visualisations etc. are fulfilled, while they are living their lives in the Corporeal World. The universe hears the thoughts, desires etc. of the human souls because of the sounds of silence aspect of all energies.

The original qualities of the soul also consist of the sound of silence or 'OM' (since these are part and parcel of the soul). Since they are the energies of the soul, it can be said that the sound of inner silence is 'OM'. The 'OM' sound is also resonating from the soul when the soul is in silence and enjoys the blissful state. It vibrates out along with the light of the soul. However, BKs do not attempt to hear it. Their concentration is on the light of the soul. Instead of trying to listen to the OM sound, they experience the original qualities of the soul, i.e. the virtues and powers. When one experiences the original qualities, the unheard sounds are in harmony. At the same time, one is enjoying the lovely feelings of the virtues. Through becoming virtuous and pure, one will be naturally vibrating the sound of silence. Thus, you are 'heard' and you get what you want. As your energies become purer and more powerful, you get closer to the finest sound of silence that is vibrated from God, human souls and animal souls. Thus, the energies at the depths of the animal and human souls will hear and respond to what you want, though at the conscious state they are not aware of why they are responding to you. The more powerful your energies, the more others will want to respond to you because they will be influenced to become more pure. In the pure state, the souls will be co-operative. The finest sounds of silence are vibrated while you are in the divine state, which is the state you are in when you walk into the Golden Aged world.

Chapter 12: Sakar Murli

In 1936, when Lekhraj was 60 years old, God gave him visions and experiences on the soul, Supreme Soul, world transformation, etc. All these happened over a few months. As a consequence, Lekhraj surrendered himself to God and God used his physical body for the remaining 33 years of his life. After God had entered Lekhraj's body, Lekhraj was renamed as Prajapita Brahma (Father of the People). Lekhraj is lovingly referred to as Brahma Baba.

The sakar murlis were given by God through using Brahma Baba's physical body. The teachings were given slowly, over Brahma Baba's lifetime, so that the BKs can slowly let go of all their older believes without being put in a state of shock (through something completely and radically new). Thus, though there are numerous sakar murlis, God has given the instruction that the BKs should keep reading the sakar murlis of the last 5 years of Brahma Baba's corporeal life. So BKs, normally, only read these since they follow God's instructions to the dot. All those who hear the knowledge, which God has given through Brahma's mouth, become the mouth-born progeny of Brahma, i.e. they become Brahmins. They become Brahma Kumars (men) and Brahma Kumaris (women). This means that they are the pure sons and daughters of Brahma. The Brahma Kumars and Brahma Kumaris also play the role of 'Brahma' with Brahma Baba. This is also why 'Brahma' is part of their name. These souls have actually become God's "sweet children". The gathering of souls and Supreme Soul, in the Confluence Age, is referred to as the Yagya (sacrificial fire) because God purifies the souls who are in the Confluence Aged Subtle Region.

God has given all deity souls a right to get their link to God when they contemplate on the BK knowledge. Thus, by reading it and listening to it, while contemplating on it, one will get one's link to God. As a consequence, the soul gets purified. As one receives the 7 Days Course, which is based on what has been said in the sakar murlis, one gets one's link to God. One can lose this link, if one was not making spiritual efforts, though one remains in the Confluence Age. BKs give a lot of importance to the sakar murlis so as to maintain their link to God through spiritual effort making.

In the Hindu scriptures, it has been portrayed that when Krishna played his flute (murli) all the Gopis went into an intoxicated state. The vibrations from the flute put them in that state of intoxication. Similarly, the teachings (murlis) that were given by God bring the soul into an intoxicated state. Along with these teachings, we receive God's vibrations which are the Sounds of Silence that influence us to enjoy divine silence when we absorb them by accepting the knowledge which comes with them. Through absorbing the knowledge and vibrations, we become intoxicated. This means we go into the blissful state. Thus, the teachings that were given by God through the mouth of Brahma were called 'murlis'. 'Murli' means flute of knowledge through which God's Sounds of Silence are emitted. When one hears or reads the BK murlis with faith that the words are from God, one is able to absorb the vibrations of the Sounds of Silence that accompany the words, and one goes into a blissful stage. These Sounds of Silence are like the music which is from the flute (murli). The Sounds of Silence are not heard in the Real World, they are unheard by the ears but heard by the soul because the soul also consists of the vibrations of silence. The energies of the soul will easily resonate with God's Sounds of Silence which accompany God's words when there is no noise, of vices and waste thoughts, in the mind of the soul when the soul is hearing the murli. The Sounds of Silence of the murli are coming from the Angelic World while the words of the murli are heard in the Real World. Thus, the knowledge, together with the Sounds of Silence that accompany the words of the murli, will bring your consciousness from the Real World to the Angelic World. It will bring you into a state where you are completely angelic. Therefore, you are no longer in a state where your consciousness is partly in the Real World and partly in the Angelic World. Though you are completely angelic, you can still be aware of what is happening in the Real World and you can do all activities while in the angelic state. However, often, one will slowly lose one's angelic stage when one is no longer reading or listening to the murli. One way of making sure that one doesn't lose the angelic stage is to keep remembering what God had said in the murli. When one does this, one is remembering God's knowledge which is accompanied by God's Sounds of Silence. This helps to keep one in the Angelic World. Listening to the murli helps the soul to detach itself from the body and dance in the intoxicated state with the consciousness completely in the Angelic World. When one concentrates on the external sounds made while the murli is read, one begins to hear the internal or silent sounds, i.e. the Sounds of Silence.

The teachings which God gave, from 1936 to 1969, through the mouth of Brahma Baba are referred to as sakar murlis because 'sakar' means corporeal. The word 'sakar' refers to the fact that Brahma Baba's corporeal body was used to give the murli. The sakar murlis are God's messages that were given through Brahma Baba, when he was alive. Each of God's messages is a murli. These murlis are read by the BKs for spiritual effort making purposes. What has been said in these murlis is constantly remembered by BKs so that they can establish and maintain their link to God.

The knowledge which has been given in the murlis is viewed as points of knowledge. One has to contemplate on each point of knowledge so as to understand more on it. Everything has not been revealed about a point of knowledge, in the murlis, because one is encouraged to go beyond to understand it better through one's link to God. One has to develop one's ability to understand knowledge through constantly practicing Brahma Kumaris Raja Yoga.

One will not be able to understand what is being taught in these murlis without proper explanations. One might misunderstand what was being said. Thus, I have only given extracts from sakar murlis, below, which can be understood quite easily.

In the extracts below, from the sakar murlis, the word 'Maya' has been used. Maya (the female demon) was used to represent the vices at thought level. If we are under the influence of Maya, the vices are in an emerged state in the mind but we are not carrying out any actions under the influence of the vices. If actions are taken based on the vices, then the vices are referred to as Ravana or Ravan.

You can contemplate on the points/teachings in the following extracts during your spiritual effort making:

"Om shanti. You sweetest children come here to the spiritual Father in order to be refreshed... So the Father is now explaining to you children. It should enter the intellect of each one of you that you have to give the Father's introduction... The Father's order for you children is: Sweetest children, consider yourself to be a soul... Also benefit yourself; become satopradhan by having remembrance. You have to make a lot of effort. Otherwise, you will have to repent a great deal. Some say: Baba, I forget You again and again. I have many other thoughts. Baba says: They will come. You have to stay in remembrance of the Father and become satopradhan. Souls that have become impure have to become pure by remembering the Supreme Father, the Supreme Soul. The Father gives directions to the children: O obedient children, I instruct you to remember Me so that your sins will be cut away... I am the Purifier. It is by remembering Me that your sins will be absolved... The unlimited Father comes and teaches you true yoga. The Father makes you children the same as Himself. I am incorporeal and I take this body temporarily. "The Lucky Chariot" is definitely that of a human being; a bull would not be called that. It is not a question of a horse or chariot. There is no question of any battle either. You know that you only have to battle with Maya. It is remembered: Those who conquer Maya conquer the whole world. You can explain very well, but you are still learning... Baba is alone, but He is not going to carry out this task without His children who are His helpers... Baba asks: Are you helpers? You reply: Yes Baba... Some remain very happy. Baba feels that you should remain very happy in this knowledge. You should have the happiness that you have now found the Father, Teacher and Guru in One... Shiv Baba alone is the

Ocean of Knowledge, the Purifier and Bestower of Salvation for All. The Father of all is One... You children now know that He is the knowledge-full One, the Liberator and the Guide. So, you have to follow the Father's directions... The Father says: Constantly remember Me alone... Only those who have loving intellects and who remember Me will gain victory. Even if they do have love but don't remember Me, they will claim a low status. The Father gives directions to the children... Remember the Father and you will become pure and a master of the pure world. According to the drama, Baba has to take an old body on loan. He enters this one in his age of retirement. It is only in their age of retirement that people make effort to search for God. In devotion they believe that they will find the path to meet God by chanting and doing tapasya etc. They don't know when they will find Him. They have been performing devotion for birth after birth. No one has found God. They don't understand that Baba will come when the old world has to be made new again. Only the Father is the Creator... The Father says: I come and make you belong to the Lord and Master. You belong to the Lord and Master for 21 births. You don't have any difficulty... The pure world is the new world. The Father explains everything so simply. You also understand that you now belong to the Father, and so you will definitely become the masters of heaven. Shiv Baba is the Master of the Unlimited. It was the Father who came and gave you the inheritance of peace and happiness. In the Golden Age, there was happiness and all the rest of the souls were in the land of peace. You now understand all of these things. Why would Shiv Baba have come? He would surely have come to make the world new and to purify the impure. He carries out an elevated task. Human beings are in total darkness. The Father says: This too is fixed in the drama. The Father sits here and awakens you children. You now know this whole drama of how the new world becomes old. The Father says: Now renounce everything and remember the one Father... You have to explain this. According to the drama, there has to be the kingdom of Maya. The Father says: Sweetest children, this cycle is now coming to an end. You are now receiving God's directions and you have to follow them. You must no longer follow the directions of the five vices. You have been following the directions of Maya for half the cycle and have become tamopradhan. I have now come to make you satopradhan. This is a play about becoming satopradhan and tamopradhan... This is the cycle of the drama and it continues to repeat. The drama is eternal. The Golden Age has passed and it is now the Iron Age. The Father has now come once again. Continue to say, "Baba, Baba" and you will continue to benefit. The Father says: These things are extremely deep and entertaining. It is said: A golden vessel is needed for the milk of a lioness. How will your intellect become golden? The intellect is in the soul. The soul says: My intellect now goes to Baba. I remember Baba a great deal. The intellect goes in other directions while just sitting somewhere. Your intellects continually remember your business etc. Then it is as though your intellects don't listen to you. This takes effort. As death comes closer, you will continue to stay in remembrance. At the time of death, everyone says: Remember God! The Father, Himself, now says: Remember Me! It is now the stage of retirement for all of you. You have to return home and this is why you have to remember Me... Burdens of the sins of many births are on your heads. Shiv Baba says: At this time, all are like Ajamil. The main thing is the pilgrimage of remembrance through which you will become pure...The Father is the Ocean of Love... Be soul conscious and remember the Father... Have yoga with the one Father alone. The Father says to souls: Remember Me and your vicious vision will end. Don't perform any sinful actions through the physical senses. Storms will definitely come into your mind. The destination is very high. Baba says: When you see that your physical senses are deceiving you, become very cautious... It is said: Those who ascend become the masters of heaven. Nothing can happen without you making effort. A lot of effort is required... You children also understand that you are now claiming your unlimited inheritance from the Father. No one can take that kingdom away from us... The first thing is to become pure, for only then will your intellects be able to imbibe anything. The rules here are very strict. Previously, you were told that you had to stay in a bhatthi for seven days and not remember anyone else at all. You couldn't write a letter to anyone either. No matter where you lived, you had to stay in a bhatthi all day long. Now you study in the bhatthi and then go outside...

Your effort is to change from an ordinary human into Narayan. You have to follow the Father's directions at every step, but this too requires courage. It isn't just a matter of speaking about it... When you come to God, Maya does not leave you alone. She will try a great deal to make you fall down... Maya also becomes very strong and will not leave you alone. This too is fixed in the drama... When new ones come, simply tell them to remember the Father. God Shiva speaks. Krishna is not God. He goes around the cycle of 84 births... You were impure. The Father now tells you how you can become pure. A cycle ago too He told you: Constantly remember Me alone! Consider yourself to be a soul... I have come to grant salvation to everyone... In the Golden Age, there were just these deities. ... Everyone is now impure and tamopradhan. I come and enter this one at the end of his many births. He was a complete devotee; he used to worship Narayan. I enter him and make him into Narayan. Now, you too have to make effort. This deity kingdom is being established... You are now becoming the masters of the land of Vishnu by making this effort. The people of Bharat say: Bharat belongs to us! You also understand that you are becoming the masters of the world... Therefore, the Father says: Children, renounce everything else and constantly remember Me alone and your sins will be absolved. It isn't that someone should especially sit in front of you to conduct meditation and give you drishti. The Father says: Remember the Father while walking and moving around. Keep your chart. How long did I stay in remembrance throughout the whole day? For how long did I talk to the Father after waking up in the morning? Did I sit in remembrance of Baba today? Make effort on yourself in this way. You have the knowledge in your intellects... The destination is very high. The Father has come to purify the impure... Achcha.

To the sweetest, beloved, long-lost and now-found children, love, remembrance and good morning from the Mother, the Father, BapDada. The spiritual Father says namaste to the spiritual children."

More extracts from the sakar murlis are given below:

1. Sweet children, you are the spiritual, incognito salvation army. You have to salvage the whole world and take the sinking boats across... The parlokik Father has taken this body on loan and is explaining through it. Only once does the unlimited Father come and teach you to consider yourself to be a soul and to remember the Father so that your boat will go across. Everyone's boat is sinking. To the extent that you make effort, so your boat will accordingly go across. It is said: O Boatman, take my boat across. In fact, each one has to go across by making effort for himself. Once you have learnt how to swim, you swim by yourself. Those are physical aspects. This here is a spiritual aspect. You know that souls are now trapped in a dirty swamp. There is the example of a deer. It went forward thinking that there was water ahead, but there was nothing but a swamp there, and it became trapped in that. Sometimes, even steamers and cars become stuck in mud. They then have to be salvaged. That is the Salvation Army; you are the spiritual army. You know that everyone is completely stuck in Maya's swamp. This is called Maya's swamp. The Father comes and explains how you can you be removed from that. He salvages you. There, one person would need the help of another person. Here, souls are trapped in the swamp. The Father shows you the way to get out of it. You can then also show this path to others. You yourself have to see how to take your boat across the ocean of poison to the ocean of milk and then show others this path. The Golden Age is called the ocean of milk, which means the ocean of happiness. Here, this is the ocean of sorrow. Ravan drowns you in the ocean of sorrow. The Father comes and takes you to the ocean of happiness. You are also called the spiritual salvation army... The Father comes in order to teach you Raja Yoga. There is no other study like this one. The double-crowned kings existed in the Golden Age. There are also the kingdoms of those with single crowns. Even those kingdoms don't exist now; it is the rule of the people by the people. You children are studying in this Godfatherly University for a kingdom... Here, there are many languages. Every king adopts his own language. The Sanskrit language is not the language of kings. Baba doesn't teach Sanskrit; the

Father teaches Raja Yoga for the Golden Age... There is no question of violence. Your study is incognito. You are the spiritual salvation army. No one knows what this spiritual army is. You are the incognito, spiritual salvation army; you salvage the whole world. Everyone's boat is sinking... To the sweetest, beloved, long-lost and now-found children, love, remembrance and good morning from the Mother, the Father, BapDada. The spiritual Father says namaste to the spiritual children.

2. What is your relationship with that Supreme Father, the Supreme Soul? He is the Truth. He gives you true knowledge to change from an ordinary human into Narayan. You children know that the Father is the Truth and that He creates the land of truth. You come here to change from an ordinary human into Narayan... Those who become pure will then go to the pure world. Here, it is a question of Raja Yoga. You will go and rule there. All souls will have to settle their karmic accounts and return home. This is the time of settlement. Your intellects now say that the Golden Age will definitely be established. The Golden Age is called the pure world. All the rest will go to the land of liberation. They then have to repeat their own parts. You too continue to make effort for yourselves to become pure and the masters of the pure world. All of you will consider yourselves to be the masters. Even the subjects are the masters... The Father knows that He gives His children the nectar of knowledge to imbibe, sits them on the pyre of knowledge, awakens them from their deep sleep and takes them to heaven. The Father has explained that souls are residents of the land of peace and the land of happiness. The land of happiness is called the viceless world. The deities are completely viceless. The other is the sweet home! You know that that is the home of you actors and that you come here from that land of peace to play your parts. We souls are not residents of this place. Those actors are residents of that place. They simply come from their various homes, change their dress and play their parts. You understand that your home is the land of peace where you are to return to. When all the actors have come onto the stage, the Father comes and takes everyone back home. This is why He is called the Liberator and the Guide. He is the Remover of Sorrow and the Bestower of Happiness... Those who

study well and have yoga with the Father will claim the inheritance from the Father. Achcha.

3. The Land of Angels is now being established. You are at the Confluence Age. You can look at the Iron Age and also the Golden Age. At the Confluence Age, you see everything as detached observers. When people come to the exhibitions or museums, make them aware of the Confluence Age. On this side is the Iron Age and on the other side is the Golden Age and we are in the middle. The Father is establishing the new world where there are very few human beings... It has been explained to you children which religion comes at what time. In the human world tree, there is first your foundation. The Seed is called the Lord of the Tree. The Father says: I, the Lord of the Tree, reside up above. When the tree reaches a state of complete decay, I come to establish the deity religion. There is a wonderful banyan tree which is standing without any foundation. In this unlimited tree too, the original, eternal, deity religion doesn't exist. All the other religions exist here.

You were resident of the incorporeal world and you came down here to play your parts. You children play all-round parts. Therefore, there is a maximum of 84 births and a minimum of one birth... The Father explains: Each Age is 1250 years. There has to be the account of 84 births. There also has to be the account of the ladder showing how you come down. First, there are the deities as the foundation... The Father has also explained to you the secrets of the tree. No one, except the Father, can teach you this.

4. This knowledge is not in any books that need to be studied. There is the name: Gyan Vigyan Bhavan, but they don't know why that name has been given or what the meaning of it is. There is great praise of gyan vigyan. Gyan means the knowledge of the world cycle that you are now imbibing. Vigyan means the land of silence; you go even beyond the stage of gyan. You rule a kingdom again on the basis of the study of knowledge. You understand that the Father of souls comes and teaches us. Otherwise, the versions of God vanish. God does not come after having studied the scriptures. God has both gyan and vigyan. Whatever

someone is, he would make others similar to himself. This is a very subtle matter. Vigyan is more subtle than gyan. You have to go even beyond gyan. Knowledge is gross; noise is made when teaching it. Vigyan, in which you go beyond sound into silence, is subtle. It is this silence that you have been wandering around for... You have now received the entire knowledge. Achcha.

To the sweetest, beloved, long-lost and now-found children, love, remembrance and good morning from the Mother, the Father, BapDada. The spiritual Father says namaste to the spiritual children.

Chapter 13: Avyakt Murli

In 1969, Brahma Baba left his physical body at the age of 93. Avyakt murlis are God's teachings that were given after Brahma Baba had left his physical body. God uses the physical body of Dadi Gulzar to give these teachings.

'Avyakt' means subtle or non-physical. The avyakt murlis were given by God when Brahma Baba began to play an avyakt (subtle) role from the Angelic World, after he had left his physical body. Both, God and Brahma Baba, enter Dadi Gulzar's body to give these avyakt murlis.

During spiritual effort making, the reader can also contemplate on the points or teachings that have been given through the avyakt murlis since it is also BK knowledge. Contemplating on the BK knowledge will automatically link you to God, because God enables this to happen to all the deity souls when they come into the Confluence Age and begin the Confluence Aged spiritual journey. The following are extracts from an avyakt murli:

"Today, Baba has come to meet the long lost and now found children of the previous cycle, who are dearly loved, loving, co-operative embodiments of power. BapDada always stays with His co-operative children... You have experienced love. There is only you and the Father and no third one in between. To have found the Father is to have found everything... You have changed from being those with a divorced intellect into those whose intellects have love, have you not? So, where there is love for God, how long would it take to become bodiless? To become bodiless out of love is like a game of a second. As soon as you say, "Baba!" you forget your body. The word "Baba" is the bomb of soul consciousness that makes you forget the old world. (The lights went out.) You can now see how the lights play the game of switching off. In the same way, your switch is the switch of awareness. As soon as you put on the switch of the Father, you turn off the switch of awareness of your body and the bodily world. This is a game of just a second. Even to say the word "Baba" with your lips takes time, but how long does it take to bring Him into your awareness? To remain in love means to become bodiless easily... Constantly remain in love with this imperishable Friend and, all your labouring will end out of love. Since you know how to love, why do you still labour? BapDada is sometimes a little amused. When someone has the practice of carrying a burden and you invite him to put it down and sit comfortably, he is not able to do so. He would constantly run to his burden again and again. He would then become breathless and cry out to be freed. Therefore, constantly remain in love with your true Friend and all your labouring will end. Do not step away from your Friend, but continue to move forward as a constant companion. In the same way, constantly continue to sing songs of the virtues you have attained from BapDada. There are so many songs of praise of you and the Father and the melodies of these songs play automatically. The more songs of praise of virtues you sing, the more the melodies of happiness will automatically play. These singers have come here. (Bharat Vyas and company were visiting Madhuban). Your music is a little different. This is the music of happiness. This would never get damaged that you would have to repair it. So, constantly continue to sing such songs. All of you know how to sing these songs, do you not? Constantly continue to sing these songs and you will easily become bodiless. There just remains the method. The right method is a matter of a second. "I am a bodiless soul" is the easiest method of all to use in order to become bodiless. It is easy, is it not? The praise of the Father is that He makes anything difficult easy. In the same way, you children should also make anything difficult easy. You are those who make the difficulties of the world easy, and so how can it be possible for you to experience anything to be difficult yourselves? Therefore, may all of you always be easy yogis. As Confluence Aged Brahmins do not say or even think such words as "labour" or "difficult", never let these words be on your lips or in your thoughts. So the special attention you have to pay this year is to be "Always be an easy yogi". Just as the Father has mercy for you children, so, have mercy for yourselves and also be merciful towards everyone else. The title 'merciful' applies to all of you too, does it not? Do you remember your title? However, sometimes, instead of being merciful, you make a small mistake. Instead of having feelings of mercy, you have feelings of self-importance. You then forget to have mercy. Some of you have self-importance and others have self-doubt. You think, "I don't know whether I will be able to reach that stage or not. Is this the right path or not?" In this way, you have many types of self-doubt and you sometimes also doubt this knowledge. This is why your feelings of mercy change. Do you understand? Do not become disheartened, but remain constantly seated on Baba's heart-throne. So, do you understand what you have to do this year? This is the homework Baba is giving you for this year: Become easy yogis. Be merciful and remain seated on the heart-throne. Every day at amrit vela, the Father, the Bestower of Fortune, will put tilaks of success on the foreheads of such obedient children. There is praise of the tilak because God Himself came and put tilaks on the foreheads of the devotees. So, this year, the Father Himself will go to the service places, the pilgrimage places, of His obedient children to put the tilaks of success on them. The Father goes on a tour of these places every day anyway. If you children are still sleeping at that time, that's your mistake! At the time of Diwali, devotees put ignited lamps everywhere. They also clean everything and invoke Lakshmi. They have cleanliness, light and that invocation. Those people invoke Lakshmi, whereas this is the invocation of the Creator of Lakshmi. Only when you keep your light ignited will the Father come. Many wake up, but they then go back to sleep again. Although they hear the sound, they then go back to sleep in the sleep of carelessness. In the Golden Age, there is nothing but gold. There is double "sona" (sleep and gold). Therefore, become an ignited light now. You do not think that with the sanskar of sleeping now you will receive gold there, do you? It is those who stay awake now who will receive gold there. It is because you forget that this is the time of destruction that you fall asleep in the sleep of carelessness... This is the way to become rulers of the globe. To those who constantly fulfil the responsibility of love, to those who constantly stay with the true Friend, to those who constantly sing songs of praise of the attainments and virtues, to those who become easy yogis by knowing the right method of just a second, to those who are constantly merciful, to those who make difficult things easy, to the children who conquer sleep and become rulers of the world, BapDada's love, remembrance and namaste."

Chapter 14: Structure of the Holographic Universe

In this chapter, I have explained about the dimensions in the Holographic Universe etc. because:

1. those who walk into the Golden Aged world use various kinds of lokas via the chakras and auric fields. They will have their visualisations, intentions and desires materialised through the chakras and lokas; these lokas are used in the auric fields within the dimensions in the Holographic Universe.

2. the QE Light initiate the materialisation of our visualisations, intentions and desires. This QE Light exists in the higher dimensions within the Holographic Universe.

3. everything in the Holographic Universe serves the souls in the Golden Aged World. Thus, they also serve those who walk in.

In this chapter, I am only giving a brief explanation on the Holographic Universe so that one will understand what I am saying in the subsequent chapters on the walking in process - how to get money etc. via the 2D SWD etc. If you wish to know more on the Holographic Universe, please read my book "Holographic Universe: An Introduction".

The dimensions within the Holographic Universe are in different orders in the first and second half cycle. Thus, I have created two diagrams reflecting the differences. These two diagrams can be found at the end of the book as Figure 1 and Figure 2. You can also see a bigger and clearer image of these two diagrams at my website (http://www.gbk-books.com/figure-1.html and http://www.gbk-books.com/figure-2.html). The dimensions in the two diagrams are in descending order with the lightest holographic dimension at the very top, above the Real World, and the densest holographic dimension at the very bottom, below the Real World. The Real World has been placed in the diagrams to reflect:

1. the order of holographic dimensions from the earth.

2. how the holographic dimensions will be situated in visions reflecting the density of the dimensions.

3. to explain what the ancient people had left behind in scriptures, myths etc.

In this book, I have reflected the densities of the dimensions based on:

1. spiritual experiences, where we see the materialised world below us, and

2. how energies and particles become denser for the materialisation process.

In this book, I have not depicted density based on the theories of Quantum Mechanics where scientists say that quantum energies, in the quantum vacuum, are denser than mass. It is only in my next book "The Expansion of the Universe" that I give importance to the theory that energies in the quantum vacuum are denser than mass. In this book, I give importance to the spiritual experiences and to the materialisation process. Based on spiritual experiences, the dimensions can be said to be in the following order:

1. QE Light (the highest). The QE Light energies are lighter than the quantum energies because they have higher frequencies.

2. Quantum World (mid-way).

3. Real World or visible universe (the lowest).

During the Copper and Iron Ages, the dark outer space is on top of the sky of the world stage because the Real World is in a submerged state within the Quantum World (Garbhodaka Ocean). The Real World is in the same space as the Unified Field, and the dark Quantum World is all around the earth and Unified Field. This is so since the earth is in a sunken state within the Quantum World.

The Real World has been placed within the diagrams, which I have created, to reflect that the Real World overlaps the Unified Field (since the energies in the Unified Field provide the Hologram of the Real World and the Real World).

Figure 1 (at the back of the book) gives an illustration of where the dimensions are located, based on density, in the First Half Cycle.

Figure 2 (at the back of the book) gives an illustration of where the dimensions are located, based on density, in the Second Half Cycle.

The illustrations in Figure 1 and Figure 2 will be understood better after reading:

1. Chapter 15: Higher Universe and Lower Universe within the Universe.

2. Chapter 22: White Hole and Black Hole.

3. The chapters which explain about the QE Light source.

During the first half cycle, all the dimensions in the Corporeal World can be said to be part of the Holographic Universe since:

1. all the energies in the Corporeal World are involved with providing the Hologram of the Real World which the people live in.

2. all the energies in the Holographic Universe serve the people who are playing their roles on the World Stage.

During the second half cycle, all the dimensions in the Corporeal World can be said to be part of the Holographic Universe since:

1. one can have subtle experiences anywhere in the Corporeal World, based on one's spiritual strength.

2. all energies in the Corporeal World are involved with providing the

Hologram of the Real World which we live in.

The **Holographic Universe basically consists of** the:

1. Subtle World of Light,

2. Subtle World Drama, and

3. Quantum World.

Among other things, the Subtle World of Light (hereafter referred to as the 'SWL') consists of the spiritual light energies of all the quantum energies, i.e. it consists of the QE Light. These QE Light energies provide QE Light bodies for plants, animals and human bodies. The QE Light also initiates the creation of everything that exists in the Real World, including what is being materialised based on our visualisations, thoughts etc.

The Quantum World, which has been referred to as the Garbhodaka Ocean in the Hindu scriptures, is filled with quantum energies such as Dark Energy, Dark Matter, etc. When present day scientist look into outer space, they see it filled with Dark Energy and Dark Matter because we are in a sunken state within the Quantum World, now.

Actually, there are various kinds of quantum energies and many quantum dimensions within the Quantum World. These quantum energies complete the creation of material forms when the QE Light initiates the creation of something. What is being created exists in the Real World due to the wave-particle duality aspect of the quantum energies. Actually, even the photons etc. from the QE Light become part of the Real World. However, without the quantum energies from the Quantum World, the QE Light and their photons etc. will not be able to complete the manifestation of the 3D SWD and Real World in the Corporeal World. The Quantum World is generally involved with providing the Real World while the QE Light is more involved with:

1. playing a role with the human souls, and

2. initiating the creation process by providing an outline for the manifestation process, e.g. through the QE Light forms.

So in this book, and generally, I state that that the quantum energies from the Quantum World are for the materialisation of the Real World. Currently, it is the Quantum World which is providing the space in which the Real World is materialised.

In the second half cycle, the Real World is in the Quantum World. However, in the First Half Cycle, the Real World will be in the SWL which is above the Quantum World. So there is a difference in the order of dimensions in the first half cycle and second half cycle. In this chapter, I am going to briefly relate how it is in the first half cycle and in the second half cycle.

There are **many dimensions within the SWL**. However, for convenience, I have divided the SWL into two:

1. Depths of the SWL.

2. Border of the SWL.

The **Depths of the SWL** consists of the Ocean of QE Light Energies (referred to as 'QE Light Ocean' hereafter). It can be referred to as the Cosmic Consciousness because it plays a role with:

1. all human souls who are in the Corporeal World, and

2. God.

In the first half cycle, the **Border of the SWL** is divided into two:

1. Upper Part in the Border of the SWL.

2. Lower Part in the Border of the SWL.

In the first half cycle, the Shore of the QE Light Ocean (Shore of the Cosmic Consciousness) is within the Upper Part in the Border of the SWL. Within the Lower Part in the Border of the SWL, there are the:

1. Cosmic Field.

2. 2D SWD.

3. First Field.

4. Second Field.

5. Real World.

The Subtle World Drama (SWD) consists of the 2D SWD, 3D Subtle World Drama (3D SWD) and Nature's 2D World Drama.

When we are living our lives on earth, in the Real World, we are also living our lives in the 3D SWD (in the Holographic Universe). The 3D SWD is the subtle or holographic movie in the Holographic Universe whereas what is happening in the Real World is in the material form. The 3D SWD includes the wave and particle aspects of quantum energies. The 3D SWD actually overlaps the material forms in the Real World. So as we live on earth, we are also living in the 3D SWD (in the Holographic Universe) in the same space though we are not aware of this. The QE Light and quantum forms are all part of the 3D SWD.

Everything that is happening in the World Drama on earth and in the 3D SWD is exactly as it is imprinted in the 2D SWD. The 2D SWD is like the Holographic Film of the Hologram (3D SWD). Since the quantum energies have a wave-particle duality aspect, what is in the Hologram (3D SWD) also exists in the material form in the Real World.

The Unified Field, as referred to by the quantum physicists, consists of the First Field and the Second Field. This is the Ocean of QE Light and Quantum Energies (hereafter also referred to as the 'Quantum Ocean') which has both energies: QE Light and quantum energies. These QE Light and quantum energies are involved with providing the Real World and 3D SWD.

The Unified Field is lighter and higher than the Quantum World because the QE Light is also there in the Unified Field (since both the QE Light and quantum energies are involved with providing the Real World via the Unified Field). Since the Real World overlaps the Unified Field, the Real World is in the same space as the Unified Field. This is one reason why the Real World is higher than the Quantum World, in visions. It should be noted that the visions are seen in the space of the Unified Field which provides the Real World. All these have been reflected in the illustrations in Figure 1 and Figure 2.

The QE Light also produces quantum energies such as photons which only exist in the Unified Field. These quantum energies from the QE Light do not exist in the QE Light Ocean, Shore of the QE Light Ocean and Cosmic Field because they are denser energies which are involved with providing the Real World.

Actually, instead of saying that the photons are produced from the QE Light, it can also be said that there are various levels of ether/light energies. The QE light is in the highest dimensions/levels, in the Corporeal World.

In the Unified Field, the QE Light and quantum energies have quantum wave function. Since they can act as waves or as particles, they are involved with providing the Real World and the 3D SWD (a world of light). The 3D SWD also has a wave form in the Unified Field. All the energies in the Unified Field act like strings.

The 3D SWD, which is the holographic form of what is happening in the World Drama on earth, is in the space of the Unified Field which includes the First Field and Second Field. The energies from the First Field keep coming into the Second Field continuously for the creation process and the energies of the Second Field keep going back into the First Field so as to get re-energised. The holographic form that exists in the space of the Unified Field will also have a material form in the Real World. This system is also used to materialise the visualisations etc. of those walking in, when something is materialised in the new Golden Aged world.

In the first half cycle, below the SWL is the Black Energy Field. Below the Black Energy Field is the Quantum World. The Quantum World consists of the:

1. Border of the Quantum World.

2. Depths of the Quantum World.

In the first half cycle, the Depths of the Quantum World consists of the Ocean of Quantum Energies ('QE Ocean' hereafter). The Border of the Quantum World consists of the Shore of the QE Ocean.

In the second half cycle, the Border of the SWL consists of the Shore of the QE Light Ocean. The Shore of the QE Light Ocean can also be referred to as the Shore of the Cosmic Consciousness. From the QE Light Ocean the QE Light energies flow into this Shore of the QE Light Ocean.

In the second half cycle, below the SWL there is the:

1. Cosmic Field.

2. 2D SWD.

3. First Field.

4. Second Field.

5. Real World.

All these are similar in position to how it is in the first half cycle. However, in the second half cycle, these and the SWL are in a sunken state within the Quantum World. So they are in the Upper Part in the Border of the Quantum World.

In the second half cycle, even the Black Energy Field (which is below the Real World) is in the Upper Part in the Border of the Quantum World.

In the second half cycle, below the Black Energy Field is the Lower Part in the Border of the Quantum World. The Shore of the QE Ocean is in the Lower Part in the Border of the Quantum World. Below this is the Depths of the Quantum World where the QE Ocean exists.

There are differences in the Holographic Universe that exists in the first half cycle and second half cycle because the SWL sank into the Quantum World during the Mid-Confluence. The Quantum World is the Garbhodaka Ocean.

The people of the first half cycle will be living in a universe where the SWL is above the Quantum World. So their subtle environment consists of the pure divine QE Light energies. Thus, the pure divine QE Light energies will also be providing an environment for those who are walking into the Golden Aged world as the SWL gets lifted out of the Quantum World through the Confluence Age. As a result, those walking in can easily enjoy a wonderful blissful feeling unless their stage has dropped and they are living in the Real World of the old universe.

As the Golden Aged world is getting materialised, what is provided through the First Field and Second Field will be different because the energies have transformed into the divine state. So a perfect world and perfect bodies are provided through the First Field and Second Field, as per the 2D SWD. The 2D SWD is just above the First Field.

The higher dimensions, in the Holographic Universe, provide the pure QE Light energies which are sent into the First Field, lokas etc. Though the QE Light provides the photons, generally the quantum energies are sent into the First Field from the dark Quantum World. The Quantum World provides various kinds of quantum energies including dark energy, etc. For simplicity sake, hereafter, when I refer to 'quantum energies' I am often not referring to the photons.

The quantum energies do not exist in the Cosmic Field and higher dimensions. Generally, the quantum energies only exist in the First Field and Second Field. It is the quantum energies which provide the material forms. Thus, all the higher dimensions are like pure spiritual dimensions. The 2D SWD is like a border separating the material world from the spiritual world. Though the QE Light energies are the spiritual energies of the quantum energies, they are not like the spiritual energies of the soul. Further, the QE Light does not live a life similar to how the human soul lives a life. The QE Light only serves God and the human souls so that human souls can live their lives on earth, as per the World Drama.

Due to the wave-particle state of quantum energies, there are numerous universes of different densities constantly coming into existence. This is also why there are various states of existence for the photons, from the virtual photon state to the real photon state, as the real photons are created from the virtual photons.

There are different universes at different densities due to the creation of the Real World from the least dense form to the densest form. Thus, it is as if there are many Real Worlds at different densities (all of which are like different universes of different densities). There are also many 3D SWDs at different densities (all of which are also like different universes of different densities).

As the world is lifted from the Kaliyug Real World to the space which is above the present Corporeal World, many different sets of QE Light and quantum dimensions are capable of providing the visible universe or Real World for us. In my book titled "Holographic Universe: An Introduction", I have referred to each of these sets of QE Light and quantum dimensions as the "Real World Quantum Dimension".

Only one Real World is provided at a specific point in time. Thus, currently, we only have the Kaliyug Real World. However, each of the Real World Quantum Dimension is capable of providing the Real World at a different level, though a different Real World is not materialised until we are about to completely walk into the Golden Aged world. Since so many Real World Quantum Dimensions exist all along the space to the edge of the Corporeal World, those walking in can use the QE Light and quantum dimensions in these other Real World Quantum Dimensions, as they get uplifted into each of them due to the walking in process.

It can be said that the visible universe (Real World) is our universe. From this angle, it can be said that each Real World Quantum Dimension provides a universe. When in these other universes, it will be as if the Corporeal World is structured differently since these universes are not in the same place as our present universe, within the Corporeal World. Despite this, I have created generalized structures of the Corporeal World and Holographic Universe.

In the first half cycle, it is as if the people are living in the holographic 3D SWD though they have a body in the material world which is not like the present Real World. Thus, they can hold an object, if they wish to hold it, and their hand can also pass through the object if they do not wish to feel the object.

The Real World, in the Golden Age, is a less dense Real World. The consciousness of the people can easily shift between the less dense Real World to the densest 3D SWD; however, normally, their consciousness will be in the densest 3D SWD.

In the second half cycle, our consciousness/awareness is not in the holographic 3D SWD. We see ourselves as living in the Real World. We are actually living in both, the 3D SWD and in the Real World. However, it is a matter of where our consciousness/awareness lies. Actually, in the second half cycle, our consciousness is in the 3D SWD, subtle dimensions, metaphysical dimension and in the Real World. These are all within the Corporeal World because the Corporeal World consists of the Holographic Universe and the Real World. Though our consciousness is in more than one dimension, in the second half cycle, one is only aware that one is in the Real World unless one has a subtle experience.

In the first half cycle, one does not see what is in the densest Real World which is what is seen at the end of Kaliyug. The Golden Aged people live in a universe which is in the border between the Real World and 3D SWD. Since their awareness is in the 3D SWD, they easily become aware of what is happening in the subtle and metaphysical dimensions within the Corporeal World.

At the end of the cycle, those walking into the Golden Aged world will have their consciousness slowly leaving the Real World and going more and more into the 3D SWD and other subtle realms. As this happens, they will be entertained by a lot of visions, as I am easily entertained by visions now.

The dimensions of the Holographic Universe are being lifted up so that the Golden Aged Real World can materialise in a higher dimension. The contents of this book help you to hop into that boat which is being lifted up. So you can easily go into the higher dimensions. Through this, you will be walking into the Golden Aged world. Those who are walking into the Golden Aged world will be given wealth, authority and everything else which they need. You become spiritually more powerful as you begin to use the higher dimensions. Thus, the QE Light and quantum energies, the World Drama, God, Nature etc. will all serve you well. The Holographic Universe consists of various kinds of QE Light and quantum energies. All these and everything else in the Holographic Universe will serve you well. This is why the thoughts and visualisations of all those walking in will get materialised.

The Real World is provided through a complicated holographic system, just as the body is provided through a complicated holographic system. What is happening in the Holographic Universe can be viewed from various angles. Thus, one might find it hard to understand everything that exists in the Holographic Universe. Anyway, even if you do not understand, it is alright, just use the practices in this book and take the benefits that can be got through the walking in process.

Chapter 15: Higher Universe and Lower Universe within the Universe

Actually, there is only one universe which I am going to refer to as the 'Universe'. In the Universe, there is the Quantum World and the SWL. When in the perfect state, the Quantum World exists at the bottom of the Universe, in the Lower Universe, and the SWL exists in the upper portion of the Universe, in the Higher Universe.

In the first half cycle, since the Universe is in the perfect state, the SWL is above the Quantum World and the earth is in the SWL above the Quantum World. The SWL and earth are in the Higher Universe. In the second half cycle, since the Universe is in the imperfect state, the Earth is in the sunken state within the Quantum World. It is in the Lower Universe. The earth drowned into the Quantum World during the Mid-Confluence. Thus, in the Hindu myths, the earth was portrayed as having drowned into the Garbhodaka Ocean. The Garbhodaka Ocean is the Quantum World, at the bottom of which lies the QE Ocean.

At the end of the cycle, when God transforms the world into the Golden Aged world, the Real World (including the Earth) gets lifted out of the Quantum World and it goes into the higher section of the Universe. It gets lifted into the Higher Universe. The Real World (including the earth) exists in the Higher Universe during the first half cycle; it exists in the Lower Universe during the second half cycle.

The Universe can be divided into two: Higher Universe and Lower Universe. It is also as if there are two universes within the Universe because:

1. the people do not experience what is in the Quantum World (which has the black holes) during the first half cycle. They can only see the White Hole (which is in the Higher Universe) and not the Black Hole, at the center of the Milky Way Galaxy. So it is as if they are in a different universe, within the Universe.

2. the people in the second half cycle are not able to see the White Hole. They are not able to see any white holes in the universe because the white holes are above the Quantum World, in the Higher Universe. Since the earth is in a sunken state within the Quantum World, people are not able to see or go beyond the Quantum World. Thus, it is as if the people, in the second half cycle, are in a lower universe within the Universe.

These two universes within the Universe were also reflected through the Hindu scriptures via the lokas, talas etc. In the Higher Universe, a different set of QE Light and quantum dimensions (Real World Quantum Dimension) provides the Real World. In the Lower Universe, a different set of QE Light and quantum dimensions (Real World Quantum Dimension) provides the Real World. It is only during the Mid-Confluence and during the walking in process (at the end of the cycle) that people can live in either the Higher Universe or in the Lower Universe depending on the spiritual state of the soul. During the first half cycle, the people are only in the Higher Universe, whereas during the second half cycle people are only in the Lower Universe.

Those walking into the Golden Aged world are going from the Lower Universe into the Higher Universe. They will use dimensions and lokas in the Higher Universe and Lower Universe. While in the Lower Universe, they would not be able to see any white holes, but they will be able to see white holes when they are in the Higher Universe.

There is a White Hole in the Higher Universe which keeps everything within the Universe. Thus, the Universe consists of one universe which has two divisions. There aren't really two universes within the Universe. It is just a matter of which section of the universe you are in.

During the Mid-Confluence, as the QE Light Ocean was dropping into the Quantum World, the SWL dropped into the Quantum World. Though the QE Light Ocean and SWL dropped into the Lower Universe, the white holes and the source of the QE Light remained beyond the Quantum World, in the Higher Universe. All the QE Light energies are actually from a point source (QE Light source) which exists in the Higher Universe. The source of the QE Light consists of pure energies.

At the end of the cycle, through the Confluence Age, the QE Light Ocean and SWL get lifted out of the Quantum World. As this happens, they get uplifted into the Higher Universe.

During the second half cycle, though the QE Light source remained in the Higher Universe, it continued to play a significant role through the QE Light Ocean which exists in the Lower Universe because, in the Holographic Universe, QE Light energies flow from this QE Light Ocean into the various dimensions.

The QE Light Ocean began sinking at the end of the Silver Age and it has continued to sink until the end of the cycle. Through the Confluence Age and the walking in process, it gets uplifted to a higher point (in the Golden Age) as the SWL gets lifted out of the Quantum World.

There is a barrier between the Higher Universe and the Lower Universe. Thus, when souls have come into the Lower Universe, from the Higher Universe (as had happened during the Mid-Confluence), souls cannot go back into the Higher Universe again until God uplifts Mankind through the Confluence Age.

Figure 1 and Figure 2 (at the back of the book) give illustrations of where the Higher Universe and Lower Universe are located, in the Holographic Universe, during the first and second half cycle. During the walking in process, it is as if the Higher Universe also exists on the other side of the higher dimensions which are in the Lower Universe. Thus, in Figure 2, it can be said that the Higher Universe also exists on the other side of the Unified Field, SWD, Cosmic Field and SWL. Actually, all the energies are in the same space. However, since one can either be in the Higher Universe or in the Lower Universe, it is as if the dimensions of the Higher Universe are on the other higher side.

Currently, the Higher Universe only has QE Light dimensions; there are no quantum energies in any of the dimensions, in the Higher Universe.

When the Golden Aged world gets materialised, the Golden Aged Real World will also be in the Higher Universe because the quantum energies which are in the Unified Field will begin to exist in the Higher Universe. Just as the Black Hole is visible in the Kaliyug Real World, the White Hole would be visible in the Golden Aged Real World in the Higher Universe. However, for the time being the Real World does not exist in the Higher Universe, the Real World only exists in the Lower Universe.

Currently, only the QE Light dimensions exist in the First Field and Second Field, in the Higher Universe. It will be like this until it is time to materialise the Golden Aged Real World and Golden Aged physical bodies in the Higher Universe.

Currently, since there are pure QE Light energies in the Higher Universe, they will serve those walking in well since the energies of these souls will be surrounded by the pure QE Light energies. Since the pure QE Light energies are close to those walking in, they will initiate the materialisation process for what those walking in want. Since the QE Light in the Higher Universe and Lower Universe are all connected, those walking in can easily get what they want even though they are getting it in the Lower Universe.

Since the Golden Aged world has not materialised, it is as if the 2D SWD lies between the Higher Universe and the Lower Universe, for those walking in. It is as if the 2D SWD is between the Lower Universe and Higher Universe because their physical bodies are in the Lower Universe.

The Higher Universe is the Universe which is being used by those walking in and the Lower Universe is where their physical bodies exist in. Thus, even though they are living in the Higher Universe (since their consciousness is there) they use whatever they get in the old Real World until the Golden Aged world materialises.

Chapter 16: Light and Darkness

The SWL consists of QE Light which is white light energies. Thus, it is lighted up. The Quantum World consists of black quantum energies, so it is dark. When one has experiences in a dimension in the SWL, one is in a lighted up environment. When one has experiences in a dimension within the Quantum World, one is in a dark environment. When you go within during meditation (the inward journey) you will find that you have two options:

1. a dark room or dimension, and

2. a lighted up room/dimension.

Both of these rooms are quiet and there is silence in both. The dark room takes you into the Quantum World, in the Lower Universe. Through taking the path to the lighted up dimension, you go into the SWL (either in the Lower Universe or in the Higher Universe) or you go into the Angelic World. After going within, if you are in the dark room, look up and you will see the lighted up dimension and:

1. if you are a deity soul in the Confluence Age, you will be seeing the light from the Higher Universe or God's light from the Confluence Aged Subtle Region.

2. if you are not a deity soul or not in the Confluence Age, you will be seeing the light from the SWL or from other higher dimensions where there is QE Light. These higher dimensions are actually submerged within the Quantum World, i.e. in the Lower Universe.

Even if you go into a dimension in the SWL, which is within the Lower Universe, you are still in the Quantum World because the SWL is in a sunken state within the Quantum World during the second half cycle. In the Lower Universe, the dark dimension which you go into is a safe dimension for the energies of the soul to be in, even though it is in the Quantum World. The energies of the soul will not be exposed to the powerful quantum energies, in this dark dimension.

During the second half cycle, you will find that there is a small spot within the mind which easily brings you into the dark dimension. If you have taken this spot to go within, don't go any further into the dark dimension. After having gone within, look up and journey upwards to go into the lighted up dimensions. If you were walking in, then, the journey to the lighted up dimension will bring you into the Higher Universe or Confluence Aged Subtle Region. The lighted up dimension, in the Higher Universe and Confluence Aged Subtle Region, includes the Light of God.

As you begin your journey inwards, you easily go into the darker room through the dark spot because you use the physical body to begin the spiritual effort making and the physical body is in the Lower Universe. Since the Lower Universe is in the Quantum World, you have gone into the dark room. The dark spot is connected to the body. This dark spot, which can be experienced by the soul, will be removed with time as the soul completely transforms into the divine state because the soul will be completely lifted out of the Lower Universe. For so long as it can be experienced by the soul, you can use it to easily go within. However, as said earlier, look up and you will see the light. See yourself as being within that lighted up dimension and you will be within the lighted up dimension with just a thought. Everything happens through just a thought because you are in a state where thoughts materialise, since you have already gone within. Thus, the darker dimension will disappear and you will be surrounded by light. You will have a better understanding on the dark spot when you read about the gross mind in Chapter 19 (Lower Self, Higher Self, Deeper Self, Deity Self and god self).

The Lower Universe also has the vibrations of the sound of silence (OM) everywhere because the pure QE Light are entangled with the pure energies of the soul (OM) and the pure quantum energies are entangled with the pure QE Light energies. However, in the Quantum World, the sound of silence is in darkness. There are no vibrations of light there. There are only the vibrations of the sounds of silence.

During the Mid-Confluence, when souls began dropping into the Quantum World, a Real World was materialising in the Lower Universe for them. The human souls could go into the Real World of the Lower Universe, with just a thought. Thus, the dark Quantum World was like a thought. The Real World in the Lower Universe would exist for them if they just had a thought that it should exist for them. Thus, through the thought they journeyed into the world which was in the Lower Universe.

The dark dimension in the Quantum World is also like a thought because the energies there resonate so well with the sound aspect of the soul (OM) via the QE Light. It is as if the sound of silence of the pure thoughts exists in the Quantum World for the thought to be materialised.

Now, the word 'OM' should not remind you of the sound of silence, it should remind you of the light of the soul and the light of the Supreme Soul. Then, with the thought 'OM' you go into the lighted up dimension and not into the darker dimension.

Beginners might find it easy to go into the quiet darker dimension first. So you can learn to go within there first. Then, find your way up. Later, when you have learnt the art of easily going within, learn to go straight into the lighted up dimension. All that this requires is just a thought and the thought can bring you there provided you are not entertaining the vices at that time.

Most of the time, you will not know if you are going into the darker or lighted up dimension. If you are feeling good, you are in the lighted up dimension. You can go into any dimension with just a thought. Have the faith that contemplating on the BK knowledge will take you into the lighted up dimension in the Higher Universe (if you wish to walk in) or into the Confluence Aged Subtle Region if you are not interested in walking in.

Chapter 17: My Experiences with the Impure QE Light

Between 1996 and 2001, my lokik sister had given me some herbs and she had told me to consume them. Since she was a doctor, I took it that she was giving me good advice and I grew them for consumption.

In 2014, I noticed that one of the herbs was no longer there in my garden. I had some old seeds of the herb and I decided to grow some of them in my nursery (on soil). Since they were quite old, they did not germinate. So I decided to sprout some of them in my trays (without any soil). I was always successful in sprouting my seeds in this way. But these seeds were so old that they did not sprout for a long time. I was washing them regularly to make sure that fungus did not grow on them as I was sprouting them. Since they were not sprouting, I began to get worried. I had a lot of attachment for that sister, who had given this herb to me, because she was always trying to take care of me. That sister had already left her body and so I did not want to lose the herbs which she had given me. So I was having a lot of transferred attachment to the herb, thinking that I should not lose it like how I had lost her. So I decided that I was going to tell those seeds to sprout when I was washing them. It should be taken note that I was instructing them and it was not done through visualisations within my mind.

Anyway, since I had taken the decision to instruct those seeds to germinate, every time when I was washing the seeds, I subtly told the seeds to sprout. I think it was my 'attachment' which was making me do this. In accordance with the BK knowledge, attachment is a vice.

With time, I began to realise that there was an evil force hanging around me. It was waiting for me to tell it what to do. I could feel its presence in the air around me and also in objects such as the bathroom door. I began wondering if it was a ghost and so I looked closely at it and realised that it was not a ghost. I realised that it was everywhere in the environment because it was the impure QE Light energies which act like evil gods who serve the vices. I realised that they were not doing anything evil and that they were just waiting to serve me. I could not understand why they were hanging around me. Their impure and evil nature had frightened me. However, since I was a spiritual effort maker, I kept getting over that fear through spiritual effort making.

When I made spiritual efforts to become powerful again through using the BK knowledge, they would disappear. I had also noticed that when my spiritual stage was very powerful, the QE Light energies acted like pure divine gods who were waiting to serve me.

Through experiences one can feel the differences in the pure and impure QE Light. Further, QE Light consists of white energies which look golden in visions if they are in their pure state. In the impure state they will look greyish white.

Anyway, going back to my experience, every time I noticed the presence of the evil QE Light, I made spiritual efforts to absorb God's energies so that it can receive God's energies from me. It did not like the fact that I was making spiritual efforts. It did not want me to make spiritual efforts. But when it received God's energies through me, it would transform into the pure state and everything would be alright. Once, when I saw it, I started making spiritual efforts and I could feel its desire to push me down the staircase. It wanted to cause harm to me since I was beginning my spiritual effort-making. I looked to see if it could do that and realised that it could not. It could only have such desires/thoughts but it could not do anything based on its own desires/thoughts because it was destined to serve the humans. This means that it will help to materialise the desires of human beings but it cannot fulfil its own desires.

Anyway, going back to my experience, one day, as I was about to wash my plants, I was in a detached state as I was about to tell the seeds to sprout. In that detached state, I saw living evil worms in the place where the seeds were supposed to be. I quickly tried to bring myself out of that detached state so that I could see if worms actually existed there. When my consciousness was back in the Real World, I only saw the seeds and there were no worms. I went beyond to see what I could subtly see there, while in the detached state, and again I saw evil worms in the place where the seeds were. I was shocked. I realised that I was doing something wrong. As trained by the Brahma Kumaris, I had automatically begun to absorb God's vibrations so that I could purify the energies of the seeds. The evil energies did not like what I was doing but I managed to purify them. The next time when I was going to wash the plants, I went into the detached state again to see what state the seeds were in. Their QE Light and quantum energies were in the evil impure state again. I was surprised that it had gone back to that state. I started making spiritual efforts so that they would get purified. They started telling me fiercely that I should not make spiritual efforts. But I did it and they became pure again. The next time when I was washing the seeds, while in the detached state, I noticed that they were in the evil state again. They were looking at me in a very evil way as if they hated me because I was going to give them God's pure energies. They were fiercely trying their best to expose me to their evil impure energies so that I would find it very difficult to link myself to God. I was in a very fierce battle until I finally got my link to God. Then, God saw the battle which I was having and He was watching what I was doing. I finally managed to become victorious in sending them God's energies. I felt so exhausted after that. It was as if I had won in the fierce battle against the evil forces, similar to how Hercules won the battle against the fiercest monsters and finally reached the heavenly realms after having become completely victorious over the evil forces. I knew that I had become victorious, like Hercules. God was also congratulating me over the victory and that was a good blissful experience. Later, I threw away the seeds, having realised that it was my attachment which had brought about this whole situation where evil QE Light forces were waiting to serve me. When I was giving the seeds the instruction to sprout and grow, they must have been getting the command from my energies which consisted of 'attachment'. Since the seeds were exposed to my vices, they became impure. Since the impure QE Light energies in the seeds are connected to the impure QE Light everywhere in the environment, I could feel the presence of the impure QE Light around me (soon after I began instructing the seeds to germinate and grow). The QE Light energies in the seeds must have looked like worms because energies behave like strings. Anyway, I have not faced such a situation since then, because I was always more careful after that.

The QE Light acts as evil energies when they serve the vices because the QE Light transforms into the impure state when they are exposed to the vices. In the evil state, they wait to serve us just as the pure QE Light wait to serve the pure souls.

Recently, from around the beginning of 2016, I had sometimes wondered if the impure consciousness in the QE Light were actually my own vices which play a role with the impure QE Light for getting black magic done. This is something that I would not want to look closely into because I prefer to remain in the pure state.

In accordance with the BK knowledge, the vices are the devils, not us. Since the original qualities of the soul are the virtues and powers, we should not classify ourselves into the category of the devil unless we have taken on the form of the vices to act as Ravana (the demon). We should not succumb to the vices and see ourselves as the vices. If we do not take actions while under the influence of the vices, the vices are just 'Maya' and not 'Ravana'. Despite all this, it has to be noted that the vices consist of the energies of the soul.

According to BK knowledge, the more spiritually powerful we become, the greater the vices will try to prevent us from succeeding in becoming pure. So, sometimes, I wondered if my own vices, which were in an entangled state with the impure QE Light, were trying to prevent me from becoming spiritually powerful. Since the energies of the soul are entangled with the QE Light energies, it would be very difficult to distinguish as to whether we are dealing with only the QE Light energies or with a combination of both energies (the energies of the soul and the QE Light energies). The QE Light vibrates at the same frequencies as the energies of the soul. For this reason too, it will be very difficult to distinguish between one and the other. However, from experiences, I know that there is a difference between the two because the QE Light is waiting to serve me while my own vices are not waiting to serve me in a like manner. The vices are just trying to confuse us and keep us on the impure path. To get the impure QE Light and quantum energies to serve us, we will have to:

1. use the vices.

2. use a belief system which has an Evil Collective Consciousness.

3. become one with the Evil Collective Consciousness of the Underworld which is an entanglement of the vices of all those who are trying to do black magic through the impure QE Light and quantum energies.

Maybe, the fact that the QE Light forms, in my experiences, were trying to prevent me from going into the higher pure spiritual stage was a reflection that my vices were in an entangled state with them, influencing them to act in that way, and so they were flowing along with my vices. However, there was a need for the soul (me) to succumb and become part of the Evil Collective Consciousness so as to complete what needs to be done for doing black magic. Since the QE Light never got this co-operation from me (the soul), black magic was not committed.

Sometimes, people can be in such a desperate situation that they may become part of the Cosmic Consciousness to take control of the situation and do magic, instead of trying to get something through worship. The desire to be in control may be so subtle that they may not realise that they are being influenced by it. It is better to get what one wants through worship since worship is a pure path, instead of taking control of the QE Light and bringing them onto the evil path with you.

What is black magic in the Kaliyug world is white magic for those walking in (while they are on the walking in process and not when they are under the influence of the vices). The difference is whether we are dealing with is the impure QE Light or the pure QE Light. In the Golden

Age, the pure souls are served well by the pure QE Light. Further, in the Golden Aged world, all souls are part of a pure Collective Consciousness. In the second half cycle, one has to leave the pure Collective Consciousness which one is in and join an Evil Collective Consciousness in order to do black magic. Both, black magic and white magic involve the QE Light and a Collective Consciousness.

Anyway, in this book, I am going to just state that one should not try to get the impure QE Light to serve one. More on how the vices may be used through the Evil Collective Consciousness of the Underworld will be discussed in a later book.

Chapter 18: QE Light Mind and Ether

The QE Light energies, of all the QE Light dimensions in the Holographic Universe, serve the souls who are living in the Golden Aged world. Therefore, as people walk into the Golden Aged world, they acquire the ability to get whatever they want. As a consequence, the people who are walking into the Golden Aged world will have to be very careful about what they are thinking and desiring because the QE Light will begin the process which will fulfil their thoughts and desires. This is begun in the QE Light Mind. The QE Light Mind is within the brain.

The brain has quantum forms which are just like the physical brain, except that these are quantum in nature. This is so because of the wave-particle duality of everything that exists in the Real World. There is also a QE Light brain which overlaps the physical brain. The QE Light brain has a QE Light Mind aspect to it. The mind of the soul is in an entangled state with the QE Light energies in the QE Light Mind. So what is in the mind of the soul also exists in the QE Light Mind. All visualisations that are done by the soul, in the mind of the soul, also exist in the QE Light Mind as holographic scenes.

The QE Light Mind is the living aspect of the QE Light brain which acts like how a computer does. When what we want is in our mind, it is in the QE Light Mind. Thus, the QE Light becomes aware of what we want and acts accordingly, like a computerised Mind.

When you create a thought that you want to move your body, this thought also exists in the QE Light Mind. The QE Light Mind is connected to a complex subtle system in the QE Light body, via the QE Light brain. The complex subtle QE Light system provides the complex system in the physical body via the quantum energies. Your body is designed to serve you. Thus, through the QE Light Mind, QE Light brain and subtle QE Light system, your hand is moved as you wish to move it.

This QE Light Mind is like the Mind of the Cosmic Consciousness because whatever is in the QE Light Mind will also be there in the Mind of the Cosmic Consciousness if the person was having a high spiritual stage. If the person was not in a pure stage, the QE Light Mind would not be having that high frequencies and so it would not really be resonating well with the pure QE Light energies of the QE Light Ocean and Quantum Ocean. The Cosmic Consciousness consists of all QE Light energies in the Corporeal World. However, since the QE Light source and QE Light Ocean play the most significant role, it can be said that the Cosmic Consciousness represents the QE Light Source and the QE Light Ocean. Actually, the QE Light is only the 'Cosmic Consciousness' because they play a role together with the energies of the human souls in the Corporeal World and with God.

Anyway, since what is in our mind is in the Mind of the Cosmic Consciousness, all QE Light energies in the Corporeal World become aware of what is in the soul's mind. All QE Light and quantum energies in the Corporeal World are in an entangled state because the QE Light is the spiritual aspect of the quantum energies. Through this everything in the Corporeal World are connected. Thus, the desires, thoughts etc. which are in the mind of the people in the first half cycle are fulfilled by the QE Light and quantum energies. This is so because energies of the soul are divine in the first half cycle. In the second half cycle, the energies of the soul are in the weak ordinary state. Thus, the pure QE Light reverts to God before fulfilling the desires of a person unless it is there in the 2D SWD that the person's desires should be fulfilled. In the second half cycle, God sees what is in our mind:

1. since it is in the Mind of the Cosmic Consciousness via the QE Light Mind.

2. if it is in the World Drama within God for God to fulfil it.

Whatever is in the QE Light Mind is sent to God via Ether. In the Corporeal World, the QE Light and quantum energies are 'Ether'. However, Ether also includes the Mid-Element (element between the Soul World and Corporeal World) and the Brahm element (element in the Soul World). The quantum energies, QE Light, Mid-Elements and Brahm element can all be classified as Ether because they are energies which are not the energies of the soul or the Supreme Soul. All the other energies in the Corporeal World are only products of the QE Light and quantum energies. Thus, all these other energies do not fall into the category of 'Ether".

It can be said that there are many different levels of Ether energies. Alternatively, different names can be used for these different energies. In the BK murlis, God has referred to the red light energies in the Soul World as the Brahm element. So I prefer to use this name while referring to the red light in the Soul World. I prefer to refer to the energies between the Soul World and Corporeal World as 'Mid-Element' so that the reader can understand which light energy I am talking about. Since the Mid-Element and Brahm element are also light energies, like the QE Light energies, what is in the Mind of the Cosmic Consciousness easily gets transmitted to reach God who is in the Soul World.

During the second half cycle, when one does worship or visualisations to get something, the QE Light begins the process to send the request to God. From the QE Light which is within the Corporeal World, it gets sent to God via other Ether light energies which are outside the Corporeal World.

Since whatever is in the QE Light Mind is sent to God, the Mind of the Cosmic Consciousness (or QE Light Mind) is like the Mind of God in the Corporeal World. Since the energies of our thoughts are entangled with the QE Light energies in the QE Light Mind, our thoughts are passed into the Cosmic Consciousness. Then, the QE Light energies of the Cosmic Consciousness send the soul's thoughts, visualisations etc. to God.

When you visualise, your visualisation is near the World Drama in the soul and this helps you to get what you want. In addition, the visualisation is also there in the QE Light Mind. Thus, the QE Light energies also become aware of what is in your mind through the sounds of silence (provided you were in a pure state and so your sounds of silence are able to resonate well with the pure QE Light energies). If you have vices in an emerged state then this will influence the QE Light energies which are there to serve you and they become impure.

The QE Light uses the sounds of silence to understand the thoughts and communications of the human souls and Supreme Soul. Thus, it can play its part well for initiating the processes for materialising the instruction etc. of God and the human souls.

Chapter 19: Lower Self, Higher Self, Deeper Self, Deity Self and god self

All the energies of the soul are one's own energies. However, not all the energies in the soul are used as the Conscious Self. There are lots of energies deeper within which are quietly playing their own roles, while we live our lives, though we are not aware of it. In order to understand how one can materialise what is being thought, visualised etc., one needs to know what is quietly happening deeper within the soul. For convenience, I am only going to divide the soul into the following divisions or levels:

1. Lower Self (when one uses the energies at the surface of the soul). During the second half cycle, this is normally the Conscious Self.

2. Higher Self or Inner Self or Subconscious Self (when one uses the energies just below the surface of the soul, i.e. at the first deeper level within the soul).

3. Deeper Self or Inner Self or Subconscious Self (when one uses the energies just below the first deeper level within the soul, i.e. at the second deeper level within the soul). The Deity Self (the soul conscious self during the first half cycle) is in this level after having sunk at the end of the Silver Age.

4. Deepest level (World Drama and 'god self' at the core/center of the soul). The god self is also the Subconscious Self deep with the soul. One can only become aware of what is in this section of the soul when one is in the unconscious state. Within this level there is the World Drama.

Whenever I use a capital G for 'God', in my books or articles, I am referring to the Supreme Soul. If I am using a small 'g' for the word god, then I am referring to one of the following:

1. the deities in the first half cycle.

2. the gods who lived during the Mid-Confluence.

3. the Confluence Aged souls.

4. the depths of the human soul which is like a god in itself, i.e. the god self (as mentioned above).

5. the QE Light energies.

6. the quantum energies.

7. the QE Light bodies which are provided by the QE Light for plants, human bodies, worship, etc.

The Lower Self and Higher Self are used during the second half cycle. The Lower Self (at the surface level) is used when one is not on the religious or spiritual path, while the Higher Self (at the first deeper level) is used while one is on the religious or spiritual path. Thus, during the second half cycle, one is normally only using the Lower Self as the Conscious Self. The Lower Self lives a life with the awareness that he is the body. When one is the Lower Self, one uses the energies at the surface of the soul.

During the second half cycle, the surface of the soul easily transforms into the vices because the energies of the soul are in the ordinary weaker state. If the Conscious Self is using the energies at the surface of the soul, the person would feel that he is the body and not the soul due to the weaker state of the energies which one is using at the surface.

Through meditation or through living a religious life, one becomes the Higher Self. When one is the Higher Self, one uses the energies which are at the first deeper level within the soul. These energies from the first deeper level emerge to the surface to play the role of the Conscious Self. When one keeps using the Higher Self as the Conscious Self, it will be as if the first deeper level occupies a greater space (from the first deeper level to the surface of the soul). One will be living one's life as a spiritually developed self.

The Higher Self, at the subconscious level, is beneath the surface of the soul but not that deep within the soul. The deeper the energies of the soul, the less dense the energies become. Thus, in experiences, when one is using the energies which are deeper within the soul, one would feel that one is higher up; the self would be like a higher self and not the lower self.

According to the knowledge of the Brahma Kumaris, the soul is a point of living white light. Despite this, one can experience space within the soul when one goes within. As a result, in experiences, one can feel as if one is:

1. spiritually higher up (when one's consciousness/awareness is deeper within the soul), or

2. the Lower Self (when one's consciousness/awareness is at the surface of the soul).

Among other things, the second deeper level within the soul has the Deity Self who is only used during the first half cycle. The Deity Self consists of divine energies. When the deity souls lost their divine state, at the end of the Silver Age, this Deity Self sank to exist at the second deeper level. The Deity Self is something additional that exists within the deity souls. During the Confluence Age, God empowers the deity souls to use the energies from the Deity Self. They are empowered through God's Power of Silence which accompany the BK knowledge and through God's energies which are in their Confluence Auric Field (aura). As a consequence, the Confluence Aged souls can easily emerge the divine energies from the Deity Self with just a thought, during their spiritual effort making. This helps them to have a stronger link to God. The stronger their link, the more spiritually powerful the souls become and so the closer they are to using their Angelic Body in the Confluence Aged Subtle Region to the fullest.

When the Confluence Aged souls take their births in the first half cycle, it would be the Deity Self which would be at the surface of the soul.

Since all the energies of the soul would be in the divine state, the whole soul is the Deity Self (including the god self at the core of the soul).

During the second half cycle, we are blocked from using the energies of the Deity Self which is in a sunken state (in the second deeper level within the soul). We are blocked because we are in the ordinary state. It is only during the Confluence Age, that we would be able to emerge the divine energies from the Deity Self that lies deep within the soul. One becomes the soul conscious self by emerging those energies from deeper down. Since God's vibrations energise the soul, the energies from the second deeper level automatically emerge to influence the soul even if we did not intentionally emerge them. This is because the Deity Self is in the process of being lifted up to play its role again. Thus, those walking in will have the benefit of using the Deity Self as it gets lifted through the walking in process.

One cannot constantly use the Deity Self during the walking in process because one is not constantly soul conscious. The energies of the Deity Self cannot remain in an emerged state, if one's stage was not good. Thus, those walking in will have to keep emerging energies from the Deity Self so as to establish one's link to God.

When one's Golden Aged physical body gets created, only then can one constantly use the Deity Self for living one's life. The energies of the Deity Self emerge to the top and it begins to live as the Conscious Self.

If you are interested in walking in, maintain the view that you are walking into the Golden Aged world and visualise yourself as the Deity Self living this life. This will help you to walk in and have a higher stage where you will be the Deity Self.

When the souls use the energies from the Deity Self, the energies of the soul are in the Higher Universe. We cannot emerge the energies from the Deity Self while we are in the Lower Universe because of our ordinary state.

The soul has three ministers: mind, intellect and Memory Bank. These also function at the different levels within the soul. Some of the energies of the mind and intellect function at the surface level while the rest function at deeper levels within the soul.

The mind of the Lower Self exists around the surface of the soul and its Memory Bank is just beneath that. The intellect plays its role between this Memory Bank and the mind at the surface of the soul.

The soul does things through the body, via the entangled state with the body. This entangled state provides the soul with a gross mind via the QE Light Mind. This gross mind includes the aspect of mind and brain where the QE Light and quantum energies connect the soul to what has been provided in the Real World. Since the Real World is in the Quantum World, during the second half cycle, the soul is also connected to the dark dimension in the Quantum World through the gross mind. A dark spot exists in the mind of the soul since the gross mind connects the mind of the soul to the Quantum World via the QE Light Mind. During the second half cycle, since the energies of the soul are weak, the gross mind is 'one' with the physical body. This is one reason why the Conscious Self, in the second half cycle, feels that he is the body.

The Higher Self and Deeper Self use different energies of the soul which are deeper within the soul. So the person is able to have different kinds of subtle experiences. For example, when one's Conscious Self is the Higher Self, one can experience oneself as being one with the QE Light of the physical body.

The Higher Self is closely connected to the QE Light Mind, QE Light bodies, the auric fields and lokas which are provided by the QE Light energies and QE Light dimensions. Through the QE Light Mind, the person is also closely connected to the QE Light energies which supply the body. Through all these connections, the Higher Self can easily get connected to the QE Light and quantum energies in the universe. The energies of the soul are also closely entangled with the QE Light energies for living the life on earth. Thus, in the second half cycle, the Higher Self can feel like he is the QE Light energies. Since the QE Light is closely entangled with the quantum energies, one can even feel as if one was the quantum energies which are providing the body. Since all QE Light and quantum energies are one with all other QE Light and quantum energies in the whole Corporeal World, one can feel like one is 'one' with the universe and as if there is no difference between you and the universe. All these can be experienced as the Higher Self.

Further, in the body conscious state, the QE Light in the body is playing a greater role like the master, and we are like the slave because we are no longer co-creators while we are the Conscious Self. Since the QE Light is playing the more superior role as the creator, we feel that the QE Light and quantum energies are god. In experiences, it can feel as if we are the QE Light and quantum energies because:

1. we should be playing the role of the main co-creators.

2. the QE Light and quantum energies serve us, i.e. they fulfil our thoughts, desires and visualisations.

3. the QE Light and quantum energies create based on what is in the 2D SWD, and what is in the 2D SWD is also based on what exists in the World Drama deep within the soul.

4. we are in an entangled state with the QE Light energies, and the quantum energies are in an entangled state with the QE Light.

Since the QE Light is playing the more superior role as the creator, we could feel that we have to become 'one' with the QE Light and quantum energies. This is because we are supposed to be co-creators. Since we should be playing the more superior role, we could feel like we are the QE Light and quantum energies which are playing the more superior role in the second half cycle. This experience is due to the influence of Maya (the vices) which is trying to become and remain as the 'master'. In the soul conscious state, the soul plays the role of the master and the QE Light is the slave which serves us.

Deeper within the soul is the Deeper Self. Normally, it is only the Deeper Self who realises that he is a soul and that he is not the body, QE Light or quantum energies (which provide the body). However, during the second half cycle, souls normally do not go deeper than the Higher Self level because they are not powerful enough to go within. The Deity Self is in the level where the Deeper Self exists, thus, Confluence Aged souls and those walking in would be able to easily accept that they are the souls.

Normally, we do not use the god self while living, i.e. we do not use the god self as the Conscious Self. However, we can use the Higher Self, Deeper Self or the Deity Self as the Conscious Self. These Inner Selves (Higher Self, Deeper Self and the Deity Self) can also be used to guide us based on our desires etc. The god self only guides us based on what exists in the Detailed World Drama.

Normally, one does not become the god self (whose energies are at the core of the soul) because the soul is in a weak state and so Maya (the vices and also the illusory aspect of the quantum forces) pulls one into the Real World and keeps one there (to give one the experience that one is the body). However, during the Mid-Confluence, since the souls were spiritually powerful, they were able to get close to the energies of the god self which are at the core of the soul. The more powerful souls could even experience being the god self in experiences. This was also a reason why I refer to them as the Mid-Confluence Aged gods. I also refer to them as the Mid-Confluence Aged gods because they were gods in the first half cycle and they were still like gods after having walked out.

Since the energies of the god self plays a role with the QE Light, in the concept of the Universe God, the Mid-Confluence Aged gods (who were using the energies of the god self as the Conscious Self) could understand what was happening within the universe. Their experiences and explanations had been passed down. With time, these were put into writing. Thus, in the Hindu texts etc., we can find a lot of descriptions and explanations on the Universe God who has been referred to as God, Brahma, Vishnu or Shiva.

During the Mid-Confluence, since the Quantum God materialised what the Mid-Confluence Aged gods wanted, the sound of OM (soul) could be heard in the universe (within the Quantum God), during experiences. Actually, since the energies of the god self (of all human souls) play a role with the QE Light for the creation process in the concept of the Universe God, it is as if the sound of 'OM' is everywhere in the universe.

There is a World Drama that exists deep within the soul, at the core of the soul. Everything that exists in this World Drama is what the soul is doing in the World Drama on earth. This World Drama has two types of World Dramas within it: the Outlined World Drama and the Detailed World Drama. It is as if the Outlined World Drama is just above the Detailed World Drama.

While living a life, the energies of the god self at the deepest level (at the core/center of the soul) influence the person through the brain and at the same time the causal energies of the soul place what is about to happen into the Outlined World Drama (from the Detailed World Drama).

Scientists have found that 3 to 5 seconds before we look at something that will arouse our emotions, our bodies are already being prepared for the arousal. This also reflects that what is happening is only as per the World Drama, and so what is in the Detailed World Drama is able to begin the arousal in the body so that the soul can properly feel the emotion through the body when the person is aroused.

Normally, the soul (while using the deeper levels) can only become aware of what exists in the Outlined World Drama and not of what exists in the Detailed World Drama. The Outlined World Drama only has an outline of what the souls' life will be like. Actually, there isn't much of an outline here. It will only look as if one has a path to walk on and there are details of what has already happened in one's life.

Normally, people are not aware of their future because one can only see what exists in the Outlined World Drama during meditation. However, since the Detailed World Drama exists within the energies of the soul, one might vaguely know about something that would happen in the future. Normally, what exists at the Detailed World Drama is only known when the person dies, i.e. as the soul gets detached from the physical body to take another birth.

During the Mid-Confluence, the spiritual strength of the souls was still quite high since they were still soul conscious. Since they were using energies from the second deeper level within the soul, they were close to the World Drama within the soul. Since they were still pure and powerful, they were easily getting information from the Detailed World Drama. They could easily merge into the Outlined World Drama, 2D SWD or into the Detailed World Drama, to get information on what exists in the future etc.

Since the Mid-Confluence Aged gods were able to know what is in the Detailed World Drama, as the god self, and since the Confluence Aged memories were emerging to influence them (because the Confluence Age is connected to the Mid-Confluence), the Mid-Confluence Aged gods knew of the Confluence Aged subtle regions which exist at the end of the cycle. Thus, they had reflected what happens via the Confluence Aged Subtle Region through the myths, loka system and other knowledge which they provided to the people.

The Mid-Confluence Aged gods who were originally using the soul conscious Deity Self had begun to use the god self through their meditation practices. They had also used their meditation practices to facilitate themselves during their afterlife at the end of the cycle. Thus, people who walk in can easily get wealth. The meditation practices which those ancient people had used were modified for religious practices.

Normally, past lives are all in the Detailed World Drama that is at the deepest level. Therefore, one does not know of one's past lives.

However, when one is a child (in the womb or just born), one is not completely connected to the body as yet. So one lives as the Subconscious Self and could still be strongly connected to one's past life which has gone back into the Detailed World Drama (as a life that has just been lived). A child could easily remember its past life even though it has been given a clean slate to begin a new life. This clean slate includes a Memory Bank (with none of the past memories in it) and the Outlined World Drama of the present life emerging above the Detailed World Drama so that the soul can live that new life. However, in the second half cycle, if the soul is attached to anything that existed in its previous life, it can still remember it and the life until the person forms new attachments in the present life. The soul still identifies itself with the previous life because the soul has not identified itself with the new body as yet.

However, since the Mid-Confluence is connected to the Confluence Age, the memories of those who play a role in the afterlife are in an emerged state. As one continues to read this book, one will understand how memories remain in an emerged state in one's Ancient Past Birth Auric Field which exists high up beyond the aura of the person. See Chapter 41 (Mid-Confluence Aged Vaikuntha) for more on the Ancient Past Birth Auric Field.

For many of those walking in, what was done in one's past lives will be significant because the worship done by those past lives will be helping the soul to become wealthy now, in their present birth. Those ancient practices will also help one to easily become the god self, in this birth.

In this book, I have explained a lot about the World Drama so that the reader will understand what is happening as our visualisations, desires and intentions are materialised through the World Drama in the soul and 2D SWD.

Please note that as you are spiritually developing, you will have to be very careful of what you are thinking. Thoughts such as "I am getting old, so I will begin to get body pain" etc. will make it happen. Even checking to see if you have body pain etc. is like a thought/visualisation informing that you do or can have body pain. This is so because you are now thinking as the Subconscious Self and not as the Lower Self.

Chapter 20: Chakras (Including the Specialities and Siddhis which they provide)

The physical bodies and everything else in the Real World are provided through vortices which are energy centers. The vortices in the physical body are referred to as chakras. These chakras are located in the Holographic Body of the person. The physical body overlaps the Holographic Body and it is also provided through the Holographic Body. So it can be said that the chakras are in the physical body.

Actually, there are numerous chakras in the physical body. However, there are seven main chakras along the spine which perform various functions such as:

1. creation and sustenance of the physical body.

2. enabling the soul to use Siddhis (powers), specialities etc.

3. allowing one to live one's life in the Corporeal World.

4. enabling spiritual effort making.

5. providing what needs to be given to the person as per the World Drama.

In this chapter, importance is only being given to these seven most important chakras which are situated along the subtle central channel called Sushumna/Avadhuti (hereafter referred to as the 'subtle central channel') that exists along the spine. In descending order, these chakras are:

1. Seventh Chakra: Sahasrara Chakra or Crown Chakra. This chakra is at the top of the head.

2. Sixth Chakra: Ajna Chakra or Third Eye Chakra. This chakra is in the

forehead.

3. Fifth Chakra: Vishuddhi Chakra or Throat Chakra. This chakra is in the region of the throat. It is situated at the neck, near the spine.

4. Fourth Chakra: Anahata Chakra or Heart Chakra. This chakra is around the heart.

5. Third Chakra: Manipura Chakra or Navel Chakra. This chakra is positioned around the Navel.

6. Second Chakra: Svadhishthana Chakra or Sacral Chakra which is situated at the lower belly.

7. First Chakra: Muladhara Chakra or Root Chakra. This chakra is located at the bottom of the spine.

The chakras are used for different purposes. Four significant ways through which the seven chakras are used, which will be relevant for those walking in, are as follows:

1. The chakras are used for the creation of the new perfect bodies which will be utilised in the new materialised Golden Aged world.

2. The 5 higher chakras (along with chakras which exist higher than these) are used for living a pure life.

3. Each chakra, if it is functioning properly, provides different specialities and Siddhis which the person can employ while living his life. The Siddhis are psychic powers/abilities. These specialities and Siddhis develop as the chakras are activated and while the Kundalini rises.

4. Different kinds of subtle experiences are experienced through the different chakras. Thus, one can have experiences in various kinds of QE Light and/or quantum dimensions, depending on which dimension the chakra is providing an outlet/gateway to. This will be discussed further in subsequent chapters.

QE Light and quantum energies flow in and out of the body through these seven chakras for creating and sustaining the physical body. Even the Golden Aged bodies are created and sustained through these chakras.

The chakras and vortices join the First Field and the Second Field, in the Unified Field (Quantum Ocean or Ocean of QE Light and Quantum Energies), for providing the physical body and everything else that exists in the Real World. Energies flow into the First Field from the QE Light Ocean and QE Ocean. Then, from the First Field, these energies flow into the Second Field. The QE Light and quantum energies in the Second Field are in a dual state (wave-particle state) in order to provide the Real World and physical bodies. The Unified Field (First Field and Second Field) is in the Border of the Quantum World during the second half cycle. During the first half cycle, the Unified Field is in the Border of the SWL, above the Quantum World. During the walking in process, a new Unified Field slowly gets created in the Higher Universe for the creation of the new Golden Aged bodies and Real World. At first, during the walking in process, only new QE Light dimensions get created in the Higher Universe where the Unified Field will exist. These QE Light dimensions get uplifted into the space of Brahmapuri, when the new Golden Aged body has to be materialised in the Higher Universe. Then, even the quantum dimensions begin to exist in the Unified Field, in the Higher Universe. After that, when no-one remains in the Lower Universe, the Unified Field will no longer exist in the Lower Universe. The Unified Field is completely lifted into the Higher Universe.

The chakras consist of black hole like vortices and white hole like vortices. The vortices that bear a resemblance to black holes are in the Lower Universe and the white hole like vortices are in the Higher Universe. Thus, some parts of all the chakras are also in the Higher Universe since the vortices that resemble white holes are in the Higher Universe. When one is walking into the Golden Aged world, and so one is in the Higher Universe, one is on the side of the chakras in the Higher Universe. This is also where the new Golden Aged QE Light bodies are getting created for those who are walking in. These Golden Aged QE Light bodies are being created through the seven chakras, in the Higher Universe, for the materialisation of a new perfect Golden Aged body. The new body materialises as the Golden Aged world materialises. Currently, the QE Light bodies, in the Lower Universe, provide a physical body in the Lower Universe.

In addition to providing the bodies, the chakras are also used while living one's life. Normally, the first three lower chakras are used when a person is not on the spiritual path. When one begins to make spiritual efforts, one begins to avail oneself of the Third Chakra for this purpose. From there one begins to draw on the Heart Chakra for beginning to live the spiritual life. Then, one begins to use the higher chakras which are above the Heart Chakra for living the spiritual life. This is one way in which the chakras are made use of.

The chakras are also used during spiritual effort making through the following ways:

1. randomly for spiritual experiences. The chakra which gets activated depends on the experience which one has to have, as per the World Drama.

2. as the Kundalini rises. The chakras get activated from the bottom to the top, as a person makes spiritual efforts to walk into the Golden Aged world. Having ascended, the Kundalini remains in the Seventh Chakra. In the second half cycle, the Kundalini will descend again (after having ascended) because the Kundalini will have to be in the Root Chakra because of the conditions which are in the second half cycle. However, there can be exceptions to this general rule if the soul has just come down from the Soul World.

One will be able to understand how the chakras are used during spiritual experiences as one reads the subsequent chapters on the auric fields, Kundalini and lokas. Though there is more to the chakras, hereafter, in this chapter, I am only going to discuss some of the functions of the chakras and how some of the 'specialities and Siddhis' are developed as one's chakras are used or activated.

Through spiritual effort making, the chakras are activated temporarily or permanently. When they are activated, one acquires specialities and Siddhis depending on which chakras are activated or used.

Specialities are like gifts which the person can use in his/her life; for example, the gift to understand and explain the BK knowledge, experience God's love, have control over the 5 senses etc.

Siddhis are psychic powers/abilities. One can acquire all or some of these abilities as one becomes powerful spiritually. However, one should not intentionally try to acquire and use any of these Siddhis because it can involve instructing and having control over the QE Light and quantum energies. If one was influenced by the vices while trying to use the Siddhis, one might become involved with black magic. So do not intentionally try to walk on water or try to materialise money magically. Allow the money to come through the World Drama.

Often, as the chakras are getting activated (whether temporarily or permanently) a person may experience Siddhis such as: healing abilities, levitation abilities, ability to have control over the 5 elements, ability to remain disease free, astral travelling abilities, change one's form, participate in visions and dreams, attain whatever one wants, become invisible, experience being the body of light, walk on fire, walk on water, breathe fire, "manifestation of one's thoughts, visualisations and words", improved psychic awareness, ability to know the past, present and future, etc. The lower three chakras are used for psychic clairvoyance. The highest three are used for spiritual clairvoyance.

Each chakra can provide different kinds of Siddhis and specialities, as per the World Drama. For example, when the **Root Chakra** is activated, one can acquire the following:

1. ability to materialise one's thoughts.

2. ability to easily achieve success in one's undertakings.

3. ability to remember memories of past lives.

4. ability to become tremendously clever.

5. ability to remain free of diseases, etc.

It should be noted that a properly functioning Root Chakra will assist one to attract wealth and material possessions, and it also makes one hard-working and energetic so that the person can do something to get the money.

The **Second Chakra** is used:

1. for experiencing positive emotions which helps one to attract money, materialise what one needs etc.

2. as an astral dimension when one is not making spiritual efforts.

3. for having dreams. Through the Second Chakra, one's emotions are expressed. Thus, one's emotions are also expressed in dreams.

Through the **Third Chakra** your stomach area will function well and so you will have no digestion problems etc. In addition, the Third Chakra is used for:

1. using one's thoughts and mental capabilities while living. Thoughts can have a causal effect when one goes onto the religious or spiritual path.

2. experiencing sovereignty.

3. experiencing power/energy to get something done while doing it without much effort.

4. providing one with the ability to move around from subtle dimension to subtle dimension.

5. easily conquering diseases and achieving longevity.

6. easily materialising gold. One can also know where one can find gold and other hidden treasures.

7. easily manifesting what one wants.

8. communicating with animals and plants.

9. easily going beyond.

10. experiencing a flying sensation.

11. walking on water, etc.

The **Heart Chakra or Fourth Chakra** helps one to express and experience love. If one wants to go onto the spiritual or religious path, one begins to use the higher chakras through using the Heart Chakra. Love has a causal effect and so one becomes a causal self through using the Heart Chakra. The Fourth Chakra helps one to subtly communicate with others in the subtle dimensions through love. Further, through the Heart Chakra:

1. one can easily acquire the Siddhis (powers).

2. one can use love to attract more money for world service.

3. one can subtly see and subtly communicate.

4. one's heart will function well.

5. one can acquire the ability to walk in the air, etc.

The **Throat Chakra**:

1. helps the throat area to function well.

2. helps one to have the ability to get and materialise whatever one wants including wealth, fame, success, comforts, etc.

3. provides magical abilities.

4. helps to bring about lucidity in dreams. It helps to give a connection between the conscious state and the dreaming state.

5. helps one to easily go within.

6. connects the heart and the brain.

7. begins the journey towards self-realisation.

8. connects the Conscious Self to the Inner Self.

9. allows one to perceive oneself as the soul.

10. helps the person to live a spiritual path.

11. projects one's consciousness externally during subtle experiences.

12. helps one to subtly express oneself in the subtle dimensions.

13. enhances one's psychic perception.

14. helps a person to achieve what the person was destined to do so.

15. gives one creative abilities.

16. helps one to have great control over the mind.

17. opens the door for knowledge, wisdom, etc. and provides the ability to explain knowledge very well. It gives a beneficial influence on one's voice and speech. The words uttered by these people will be influential, effective and, will have wisdom and beauty. Their words can become a reality. People will love to listen to them and read what they write. They will become good writers, teachers, actors, singers, politicians, etc. It should be noted that the chakras also get activated as per the World Drama so as to allow a person to use certain specialities or Siddhis, even though the person is not involved with spiritual effort making. This is why singers, etc. can enjoy the specialities that are provided through

this chakra.

The **Sixth Chakra or Ajna Chakra or Third Eye Chakra**:

1. allows all the Siddhis, received through using all the other chakras, to be enjoyed.

2. gives the ability to get whatever one desires. The Ajna Chakra, along with other chakras, also help to manifest what you visualise.

3. makes one intuitive.

4. gives greater abilities to subtly communicate and see. Thus, it helps one to have visions during experiences.

5. gives one an increased ability to know the past, present and future.

6. makes one knowledgeful. One will be able to get further knowledge, which one is seeking, and have a better ability to understand that knowledge. Thus, one will be able to explain this knowledge well through using the Throat Chakra.

7. helps one to have yoga with something or the other. In the Confluence Age, the souls can have yoga with God for world transformation through self-transformation.

8. is used by Confluence Aged souls to establish their link to God and become soul conscious.

9. gives an increased ability to remain in the enlightened state.

The **Seventh Chakra or Crown Chakra** enables one to:

1. have the ability to use all the Siddhis.

2. attract money while on the spiritual/religious/pure path.

3. have the ability to instantly know what others are feeling, thinking etc.

4. become a master of the senses.

5. be free of diseases.

6. proceed into the higher dimensions.

7. experience the truth.

8. experience bliss.

9. remain in the enlightened state.

10. be a master of the QE Light & quantum energies, master of the world/universe etc. As a result, one is assisted to instantly get what one wants.

11. experience liberation. In the second half cycle, people experience liberation when they are 'one' with the Cosmic Consciousness. They will not feel that they are enclosed within their bodies and they get God's assistance easily via the Cosmic Consciousness. They are liberated from their vices because they are experiencing a pure stage and using the higher dimensions. Those walking in and the Confluence Aged souls experience liberation through their link to God. They are liberated from the vices through the purification process. At the end of the cycle, all souls leave the body to go back to the Soul World with God after having left the body through the Crown Chakra. So they receive liberation through the Seventh Chakra.

From the Throat Chakra to the Seventh Chakra: the higher the chakra one uses, the greater one's ability to understand knowledge, the past, present and future. One's magical abilities also increase. Thus, one's thoughts, visualisations, desires and intentions get manifested more easily as one uses the higher chakras. As one activates the higher chakras, one's knowledge of the self and the universe deepens. Psychic perception also improves as one begins drawing on the higher three chakras. However, each of the three higher chakras is also used for specific abilities.

Though the BKs also do use the Seventh Chakra for various purposes, it is the Sixth Chakra which plays the most significant role for them, in the body, as if it is the highest chakra among all the seven chakras in the body. However, the Seventh Chakra is also significantly used to bring them into the Confluence Aged Subtle Region which is beyond the Corporeal World.

It should also be noted that the Confluence Aged souls receive God's energies through all the chakras, even though the Ajna Chakra plays the most significant role for receiving and reflecting God's energies into the world. During visualisations, if one sees oneself as receiving God's energies through the forehead, one would be using the Ajna Chakra to receive God's energies, more than the other chakras. If one sees oneself as receiving God's energies through the top of the head, the Crown chakra would be used, more than the other chakras, to receive God's energies.

Each of the lower 5 chakras is associated to one of the natural elements as follows: earth (Root Chakra), water (Second Chakra), fire (Third Chakra), air/wind (Heart Chakra) and ether/space/akasha (Throat Chakra). Thus, through the Root Chakra, one can easily control the earth element. Through the Second Chakra, one can easily control the water element and so on. Through the usage of these 5 elements via the 5 chakras, one can materialise whatever one wants and do magic. The higher chakras flow along with these chakras to get the magic done. However, one should not try to do magic because one may be influenced by the vices and thus, one may end up doing black magic.

As those walking in use the higher chakras and as all their chakras get activated, they will be acquiring the Siddhis. However, BKs are not involved with developing the Siddhis, though they do use the specialities provided by the chakras. For example through using the Ajna Chakra and the Throat Chakra, they understand and explain the BK knowledge. They use the Heart Chakra to experience God's love because love is experienced through the Heart Chakra.

Those walking in can have spiritual experiences through all the chakras. At the same time, when using a specific chakra, they can also experience the specialities and Siddhis provided by the chakra.

As those who walk in and others keep doing meditation, their chakras are activated. Each chakra helps the soul to utilise specific specialties or Siddhis. Thus, when a soul wants to employ a specific specialty, the relevant chakras play a more significant role for the soul. In addition, all the other chakras are also being used (though not to the extent which the chakra that gives the specialty is used).

Each of the seven chakras in the body has numerous vortices. Each of these vortices is used to provide something for the person. Thus, when we talk of activating the chakras, what we are talking about is the activation of specific vortices for an ability, speciality, etc.

In the first half cycle, the higher chakras are always open because the people in the first half cycle live a pure and divine life. Thus, they are like yogis. However, they are not like the yogis of the second half cycle because they do not make attempts to live a pure life. They naturally live a pure life. This means they do not have to make spiritual efforts to develop the ability which makes their thoughts powerful. Naturally, the thoughts of the people in the first half cycle are powerful. Since the souls are in the powerful state, the chakras are functioning perfectly. This is the state that is being attained by those who walk into the Golden Aged world.

When we are involved with spiritual effort making, the energies from deeper within the soul are put to use. Some of these energies also move into the Heart Chakra and from there, they get expressed through the higher chakras. This happens because they are pure and finer energies. In the second half cycle, as the energies from deeper within the soul move into the Heart Chakra during spiritual effort making, the Higher Self becomes the Conscious Self. As they keep activating the higher chakras, they are using energies from deeper and deeper within the soul. The energies from the god self are used when one avails oneself of the Seventh Chakra.

Where the Confluence Aged souls and those who walking in are concerned, they begin using the Third Chakra when they are first introduced to the BK knowledge. Then, they begin to wield the higher chakras as they keep making spiritual efforts.

At the beginning of the Confluence Age, the Angelic Bodies are created through the vortices that had opened, at the edge of the Corporeal World, as God was coming into the Corporeal World. QE Light energies flowed through these vortices to fill the space where the Angelic Bodies were to exist in the Confluence Aged Subtle Region via the chakras that exist at the feet of the Angelic Bodies. When one receives the BK knowledge, some of the energies of the soul go through the chakras in the Angelic Body so as to remain in the Angelic Body, i.e. they adopt the Angelic Body as their own. When one is a weak spiritual effort maker, one uses the lower chakras in the Angelic Body. When one is a more powerful spiritual effort maker, one begins to use the higher chakras in the Angelic Body. The lower chakras in the Angelic Body are used when one is in Brahmapuri; the higher chakras in the Angelic Body are used when one goes into Shankerpuri and Vishnupuri. The chakras which provide the Angelic Body, in the Confluence Aged Subtle Region, are also the chakras of the person after the person begins to use his Angelic Body. Thus, the Confluence Aged souls have higher chakras in the Confluence Aged Subtle Region where the Angelic Body exists.

Chapter 21: Auric Fields

In this chapter, I am going to begin by explaining the situation as it exists in the Lower Universe because one needs to know this so as to understand what is happening through the walking in process.

Each person has an aura which is an invisible field of energies that surrounds the physical body of the person. QE Light energies flow through the chakras to provide the QE Light bodies from which the aura vibrates out. Each QE Light body provides one auric field in the aura. The seven main chakras of each person provide the seven QE Light bodies from which the seven auric fields vibrate out. Thus, it can be said that the seven chakras provide the seven auric fields. These auric fields are the aura of the person, in the Holographic Universe.

It can be said that the QE Light bodies are the Holographic Body and that the auric fields are an extension of this Holographic Body. Thus, the Holographic Body overlaps the physical body, exactly. However, the QE Light Bodies and their auric fields can collectively also be referred to as the Holographic Body. In fact, even the aura can be said to be the Holographic Body.

The Holographic Body, which overlaps the physical body, is used in the 3D SWD and the physical body is used in the World Drama on earth. The QE Light bodies and their auric fields connect one to everything in the Holographic Universe while one lives one's life on earth. The consciousness of the person is also expressed through aura.

The first auric field (Etheric Field) is provided by the First Chakra. This Etheric Field stretches from within the border of the Real World to go into the Second Field which is in the Holographic Universe. It is more accurate to say that the Etheric Field is in the Second Field. I have created a diagram (see Figure 3 at the back of this book or at my website http://www.gbk-books.com/figure-3.html) illustrating where the Etheric Field is situation in the Lower Universe and Holographic

Universe. However, Figure 3 will only be completely understood after reading all the remaining chapters in this book.

The QE Light body which provides the Etheric Field:

1. is part and parcel of the Etheric Field.

2. initiates the creation of other QE Light and quantum bodies which exist in the wave or particle state.

Among the abovementioned QE Light and quantum bodies, there are also quantum bodies which are created through the quantum energies from the Quantum World. All these QE Light and quantum bodies are also part and parcel of the Etheric Field. Since these QE Light and quantum bodies materialise the physical body, it can be said that the:

1. physical body exists since the Etheric Field exists.

2. the Etheric Field is the double of the physical body.

It should be noted that, normally, one can easily see the Etheric Field but not its QE Light body.

When one lives a non-spiritual life, one is using the 4 auric fields which are closest to the physical body. When one lives a spiritual life one uses the higher auric fields.

One can use the Etheric Field during subtle experiences, even though one is not on the spiritual path. However, normally, it is the second auric field which is used during subtle experiences when one is not on the spiritual path. It also through the Second Chakra and its auric field that one has dreams, if one was not on the spiritual path. The second auric field (or Astral Plane) is provided, in the Second Field, through the Second Chakra (see Figure 3 at the back of this book). The Astral Plane exists beyond the Etheric Field. Through the Astral Plane, one can:

1. communicate with ghosts.

2. communicate with people who have just died and have not taken another birth.

3. subtly observe and/or communicate with others, who have come into the Astral Plane.

4. observe your dreams.

5. carry out astral travelling during Lucid Dreams.

6. have visions of angelic beings, etc.

If one was not on the spiritual path, one's emotions are also expressed in the second auric field while one's thoughts and mental activities go into the third auric field (Mental Plane).

The Third Chakra provides the Mental Plane in the Second Field (see Figure 3 at the back of this book). The Mental Plane is a causal plane because thoughts are used for initiating the materialisation process.

One begins one's spiritual effort making through the Mental Plane (and Third Chakra) for living a spiritual life. Through using the Mental Plane properly, one can begin to use the higher chakras. From the Third Chakra and Mental Plane, one begins to engage the 4th auric field (through the Heart Chakra) for the spiritual or religious life. After this, one begins to use the higher auric fields (via the higher chakras) which are beyond the 4th auric field and Fourth Chakra. It takes time for one to develop spiritually. Thus, it takes time to use the higher chakras and higher auric fields. However, one does not have to wait until one activates the higher chakras so as to have a heavenly experience. Since one has already begun living a spiritual or religious life, one can begin to live a heavenly life through the Third Chakra and its auric field. This is because:

1. the third auric field is in the higher region of the Second Field where pure energies are constantly coming from the First Field.

2. one is connected to the spiritual life through the Heart Chakra which

is above the Third Chakra.

In the Mental Plane itself, one can have visions of God, the gods, etc. Often, these influence one to take the spiritual path.

One engages the Heart Chakra and its auric field when one experiences love (whether for a person or for God). When the love is for God or the spiritual life, one begins to use the higher chakras and their auric fields; and one becomes angelic when one uses the Heart Chakra and its auric field. The Heart Chakra provides the 4th auric field which is in the border between the First Field and Second Field (see Figure 3 at the back of this book). From the Heart Chakra, one begins to involve the higher chakras and higher dimensions which are in the First Field. The 5th auric field, 6th auric field and 7th auric field are in the First Field (see Figure 3 at the back of this book). One experiences oneself as a subtle being, in the higher auric fields, via the Throat Chakra and the other higher chakras.

When one has subtle experiences through using the three lower chakras, the light body which one uses would be denser because it is in the Second Field. The subtle body is lighter (less dense) when one uses the 4th to 7th auric fields because they are provided by QE Light energies in the First Field.

The seven chakras and their auric fields are in the Unified Field. This Unified Field, along with the auric fields, is the sphere of influence of, and for, the person and his body. When the energies of the soul leave through the Seventh Chakra, they leave via the 7th auric field to go into dimensions which are beyond the Unified Field. Through this, the Seventh Chakra and its 7th auric field get connected to what is outside the Unified Field.

In the second half cycle, there are 5 more relevant auric fields beyond the 7th auric field which are used during the spiritual/religious life. Thus, there are 12 chakras, in the Holographic Body, which are providing the 12 auric fields in the Holographic Universe. The 8th, 9th,

10th, 11th and 12th chakras provide the 8th, 9th, 10th, 11th and 12th auric fields, respectively. The 8th to 12th chakras are all above the physical body. However, they are in the Holographic Body because the Holographic Body includes all the auric fields. Above the 12th auric field is another crucial 13th chakra which allows the energies of the soul to get connected to the energies from the QE Light Ocean. Those who use the BK knowledge also use this higher 13th chakra and its auric field. This is explained further in the later chapters of this book.

The 8th, 9th and 10th auric fields are in the Cosmic Field (see Figure 3 at the back of this book). The 11th and 12th auric fields are in the Shore of the QE Light Ocean which is in the Border of the SWL (see Figure 3 at the back of this book). It can also be said that the 10th auric field is between the Cosmic Field and the Border of the SWL (see Figure 3 at the back of this book) since the Cosmic Field is connected to the SWL around the edge of the SWL. This connection allows QE Light energies to flow into the 2D SWD via the Cosmic Field. When souls use the higher auric fields, in the second half cycle, they can be exposed to the finer QE Light energies in these higher dimensions within the Holographic Universe.

All the specialties and Siddhis of the chakras are also enjoyed while one uses the auric fields that are provided by the chakras. Thus, the ether or space element of the Throat Chakra allows the expansion of the auric fields for experiences. One's auric field can expand into the higher dimensions because, when one wishes to go into the higher QE Light dimensions, one's energies (of the soul) will flow outwards and upwards. The auric fields, which contain the energies of the soul, will have to expand so as to allow the flow of the energies of the soul.

The soul is a point, the QE Light Ocean is from a point source and the QE Ocean is also from a point source. So there is no space involved. However, from the point, there is expansion. Thus, there is space in the Real World in which the energies of the soul roam around in via their auric fields. The QE Light and quantum energies provide dimensions in the Holographic Universe, and the auric fields extent into these dimensions. Thus, the soul is able to experience the various dimensions that exist in the Holographic Universe.

Some chakras have specialised functions. This allows the soul to use a speciality. However, numerous chakras can also be involved for that speciality, whether they are within the main chakra or outside it. Similarly, even though there are the seven main auric fields, other dimensions etc. may be within a main auric field or they may be connected to it so that the soul can use the specialities of that auric field. For convenience, I have ignored all the other numerous chakras and auric fields and have combined them all with the main chakras and auric fields which they play a role with. This has made it easier for me to give explanations on the functions of the main chakras and their auric fields.

Just as one shifts from the non-spiritual life to the spiritual life through using different chakras, a shift also takes place during the Confluence Age and during the Mid-Confluence because different universes begin to come into play.

Where those walking in are concerned, since the Golden Aged Real World has not materialised, the physical body with its Etheric Field remains in the Lower Universe. Even Confluence Aged souls have their physical body and Etheric Field in the Lower Universe.

In experiences, I saw that the Etheric Field, which provides my physical body in the Real World, is in the lower, darker dimension (Lower Universe). I noticed that when I was in my first auric field, it was as if I was caged within a small space which extended a little beyond my physical body. This was because:

1. I am generally using the Higher Universe and not the Lower Universe, therefore I am not able to move around in the subtle Lower Universe.

2. The Etheric Field does not extend very far from the physical body.

Confluence Aged souls, including those walking in, begin their spiritual life through the Third Chakra and third auric field. This Third Chakra and its auric field are used to initiate the process through which one is able to use one's Angelic Body (when one first receives the BK knowledge). Thereafter, one uses the Angelic Body and so one has the Confluence Auric Field as one's aura. Through this one is lifted into the Higher Universe, from where one goes into the Angelic World. Through all this, one begins to live a spiritual life in the Confluence Age and not in the Kaliyug world.

When Confluence Aged souls begin to use the Confluence Auric Field (aura of the Angelic Body), all their other auric fields become part of the Confluence Auric Field. So the Confluence Auric Field becomes their aura.

The Confluence Auric Field of each Confluence Aged person acts like a chakra to absorb God's energies and the energies of the environment from the Subtle Region. Thus, it can be said that the Subtle Region also exists within the Confluence Auric Field. This Confluence Auric Field is connected to the body in the Real World, through the first auric field.

When one is first given the Angelic Body, one's spiritual strength is still very low. One has to make spiritual efforts to become powerful. As one makes spiritual efforts, one's higher chakras get activated and so one begins to use the higher auric fields in the Confluence Auric Field. Though one begins using the higher chakras, they do not function so well, initially. One has to keep making spiritual efforts to keep them in an active state. As one's spiritual strength keeps increasing, these chakras slowly begin to function better and better. Thus, it is easier for one to go beyond into the Confluence Aged Subtle Region. As a result, initially, when BKs are learning to go beyond through the third auric field, they will be struggling to establish their link to God. Once BKs are constantly using the Seventh Chakra, they would be able to easily go beyond into the Confluence Aged Subtle Region which is beyond the Corporeal World via their Confluence Auric Field.

Though BKs have their third auric field and higher auric fields in the Higher Universe, these auric fields, which are provided by the chakras, are just getting filled with God's vibrations to give the BKs a more powerful spiritual stage and environment. BKs are not using dimensions in the Higher Universe nor are they developing the Siddhis (though they can develop the specialities that are used via the chakras).

Those walking in will also be developing auric fields for Confluence Aged spiritual effort making, similarly to how the BKs do, as explained above. In addition to this, something more is happening to those who walk in.

During the second half cycle, all the chakras are also involved with providing a properly functioning physical body in the Real World, while they provide all the auric fields in the Lower Universe. During the walking in process, QE Light bodies and auric fields are developing in the Higher Universe for the creation of the new perfect bodies.

The Golden Aged physical body is created through the Golden Aged QE Light bodies and auric fields. The Golden Aged auric fields are provided by the Golden Aged QE Light body. Within this QE Light body, there are numerous QE Light bodies, each providing an auric field. These Golden Aged QE Light bodies and their auric fields begin to be provided for you as you begin to make spiritual efforts through using what has been written in this book or as you use the BK knowledge. The creation of the perfect bodies begin with the Seventh Chakra creating a 'Golden Aged QE Light body and auric field' in the Higher Universe. When that has been established, then, through the Sixth Chakra, its Golden Aged QE Light body and auric field are created in the Higher Universe. After this gets established, the 5th Golden Aged QE Light body and its auric field are created through the Fifth Chakra. Then, the 4th Golden Aged QE Light body and its auric field are created through the Fourth Chakra. When this is completely created, the 3rd Golden Aged QE Light body and its auric field are created through the Third Chakra. Then, the 2nd Golden Aged QE Light body and its auric field are created through the Second Chakra. Finally, the 1st Golden Aged QE Light body and its auric field are created through the First Chakra. When the first QE Light body and its auric field are completely created, the physical body is transformed into the perfect state and it is brought into the Higher Universe.

The Golden Aged QE Light bodies and auric fields are created on the side where the white holes and the white hole like vortices (of the chakras) exist, in the Higher Universe. Since the white holes are in a lighter dimension and it is further away from the Kaliyug world, the auric fields which are created in the Higher Universe are higher up. Since the vortices that bear a resemblance to white holes are connected to the physical body, via the chakras, it is as if the auric fields of the person stretch from the Lower Universe into the Higher Universe. Thus, those walking in, and the Confluence Aged souls, will have gigantic auras since their aura goes beyond the present Corporeal World.

There are two ways of creating the golden aged auric fields in the Higher Universe: through the gathering of the Confluence Aged souls and through one's own spiritual effort making. The physical bodies will materialise in the Higher Universe when the 900,000 Confluence Aged souls are ready for world transformation. Thus, all the QE Light bodies and auric fields have not completely developed as yet. As a consequence, they do not have the capability to materialise the physical body in the Higher Universe.

When one has walked into the Golden Aged Real World, one will have a physical body and a Holographic Body in the Higher Universe. The old physical body transforms into the perfect state, when the first auric field is in the Higher Universe and not in the Lower Universe.

Sometimes, due to the settling process, one's chakras might not function well. Thus, the energies in the auric fields which are in the old world become impure since they are not being energised through a constant flow of energies from the First Field. However, this does not affect the Golden Aged auric fields which are developing in the Higher Universe because different vortices in the chakras will be constantly nourishing them as they develop. Further, God's energies will also be helping to keep your auric fields pure, in the Higher Universe.

One should not intentionally focus one's mind on opening any chakra so as to use specific auric fields, specialities or Siddhis. The chakras open naturally as we progress along this spiritual path for the walking in process and so we will be naturally using the relevant auric fields etc. One should allow all these to happen naturally, as we make spiritual efforts.

All the relevant chakras also get opened for experiences and the relevant auric fields will also exist for the experiences. These chakras and auric fields are all connected to the QE Light Mind. So the soul will be able to become aware of the visions which the soul sees in the auric fields. The QE Light Mind is part of the holographic brain. The holographic brain is the quantum aspect of the physical brain. So what comes to the holographic is coming into the physical brain. As a result, various parts of the brain will get activated accordingly for the experience. Since the brain is connected to the body, the body is also used accordingly. All these enhance the experiences etc. which the soul has, and the person will also be able to see and experience the visions, though using the body.

An auric field is like a dimension of its own in the Holographic Universe. The position of the auric fields in the Lower Universe and Higher Universe (during the walking in process) can be seen in:

1. Figure 3: Dimensions in the Lower Universe (based on Density).

2. Figure 4: Dimensions during the Creation of the Golden Aged World.

Both the above illustrations can be found at the end of this book. These illustrations can be understood better as one keeps reading this book.

Chapter 22: White Hole and Black Hole

In this chapter, I have explained my experience in the white hole
dimension because it gives a rough idea of how those walking in will not
be able to easily move between the Lower Universe and Higher
Universe. One's stage must be very bad or one should have let go of
God so as to have one's consciousness in the Lower Universe. The
explanations on the white holes, in this chapter, will also help the
readers to have a better understanding of what is happening in the
Higher Universe as they walk in.

Since 1996, I had seen visions where a White Hole was providing the
entrance to the Angelic World. In January 2016, I decided to understand
a bit more on the white holes through subtle experiences. I decided to
see if I could see any white holes in the universe of the Real World
where the body was in. So during meditation, I was trying to roam
around in outer space. I was finding it very difficult to move out from
the body and the Etheric Field. It was as if I was caged within the body
and Etheric Field. I could not understand why I was not able to go out of
the body because I was able to do that before I was introduced to the
Brahma Kumaris. Anyway, I kept on trying until, during an experience,
my subconscious self was able to move around outside the body. After
searching around, my subconscious self subtly informed that white
holes were not to be found anywhere. During this experience, I was in
darkness and this was not how it usually is during my experiences.
Further, I could not believe that there was no white hole because,
during experiences, I had sometimes gone through one when I entered
the Angelic World. I began wondering why I was being given this
information. I realised that the energies of my sub-conscious self, which
gave me this information, had looked weak. They were energies of my
intellect which had gone to look because I had given the instruction to
look around. Since these energies had looked weak, I couldn't accept
what it had just told me. So I subtly looked around into the universe and
I could not see the white holes. When I subtly looked, I was also using

my intellect to look. However, this was a situation where I was doing it and not a situation where 'I had instructed my intellect to do it and so it brought back information to give me based on my instruction'. Anyway, almost immediately (after I had subtly looked) God gave me a vision. This vision showed that there was an upper white dimension (Higher Universe) and a lower black dimension (Lower Universe). The vision showed that there was a barrier between the Higher Universe and Lower Universe. Nothing can enter the Higher Universe from the Lower Universe. I began to understand that I must have been in a bad spiritual stage, during the experience, and this may have been why I could not see any white holes. Maybe, I was in a body-conscious state since I was wondering too much about it. Maybe God had allowed me to subtly move around in the Lower Universe because I had to be given experiences which I could use for further explanations. Anyway, after that, I began to seriously contemplate on the BK knowledge until my spiritual stage was high. Then, I had an experience in the dimension of the white holes. I had this experience while I was in the Higher Universe. We go into the Higher Universe as we are on our way to the Confluence Aged Subtle Region.

The dimension of the white holes was so hazy because there were white energies spinning and white smoke-like energies bursting out everywhere. So I could not see clearly. However, I could see that there were many white holes, some large and some small, because there were white energies spinning in a cyclic manner in many places. I also saw the huge White Hole which provided the entrance to the Confluence Aged Subtle Region. It was at the very top, near the edge of the Corporeal World. From the dimension of the white hole, I had to look up to see the entrance to the Angelic World. There were also a lot of white energies spinning around the White Hole which was the entrance to the Confluence Aged Subtle Region.

When I began to have the experience in the white hole dimension, I began to feel the power of the powerful energies which existed there. Thus, I clung very closely to God and God must have also come very close to me. I knew that God will make sure that nothing bad happens to me. Anyway, since God was so close to me, my body had begun to shake. Since my body was shaking, I let go of God a little and my body stopped shaking. However, I knew that God was still there since I could feel His vibrations, I could not see Him because the place was so hazy. I could only see Brahma Baba vaguely and I could only experience a little of God's vibrations. So I made spiritual efforts to get closer to God again and I saw the angelic body of Brahma Baba getting clearer; and God came very close to me again. Subsequently, my body started trembling again. My attention turned towards my body and I noticed that there was a prickly sensation all over my physical body. I wanted to see what was causing it. I had to look down to look at it since the dark Lower Universe was below. Imperceptibly, I could see the body way below but I could not see what was in it. It was as if I was blocked from seeing it clearly and I also could not go there to see it clearly, since the physical body was in the black Lower Universe. Then, God assisted me so that I could see what was happening in my body. I was no longer in the dimension of the white hole. I was in the body and I could see that there were short bursts of white smoke-like energies everywhere in the body. They were constantly bursting out everywhere similarly to how bubbles keep bubbling out when water is boiling. However, these short bursts did not look like bubbles; they looked like smoke that was being released into the environment as short bursts. They were not being released simultaneously; they were irregularly released throughout the body. The white holes of the body were in the dimension of the white hole, but they were emitting white energies into the body. This was why I was able to feel the prickly sensation all over my body. However, I could not see the white energies spinning around any white hole in the body, like how I saw them in the dimension of the white holes. I only saw the smoke-like bursts everywhere. I knew that the white holes were in the Higher Universe and that the smoke-like white energies were being released into the Lower Universe.

It may be possible that my body was shaking due to one of these reasons:

1. the energies of the White Hole that sustain the universe were too powerful and my body was not able to tolerate it.

2. I was being exposed to the powerful energies of God since He was too close to me. God may have purposely exposed me to more of His energies so that my body shook. Through this, my attention was turned towards what was happening in my body.

The way my body was quivering reminded me of another experience which I had had when I went to the BK center for amrit vela and to listen to the murli. This had happened sometime between 1996 and 2001. I wanted a short cut to become spiritually powerful quickly. I wanted to be exposed to a lot of God's vibrations, like how we are exposed to His vibrations during Judgement Day. I wanted this because I wanted to get purified quickly. Through the purification process, we become spiritually powerful. During the Confluence Age, God has provided a protective shield to the BKs so that they are not exposed to a lot of His energies as souls are during Judgement Day. If God was not protecting them, they would experience pain when exposed to a lot of His vibrations because His vibrations have a purifying effect and this purification is only done on Judgement Day, when souls have left their bodies and are taken back to the Soul World.

During the Confluence Age, as souls become more powerful, they get exposed to more of God's energies through Shankerpuri. If not, they are in Brahmapuri where there are less of God's vibrations. Even those in Shankerpuri are given a protective shield to make sure that they are experiencing bliss and not pain.

Since I wanted to be exposed to a lot of God's energies, God lifted the protective shield (a little) so as to allow me to get exposed to more of His energies. As I was being purified, it felt good because God was still giving me protection. However, my physical body could not take the powerful vibrations of God since it was getting exposed to God's vibrations through me (the soul); the physical body was not getting a good protective shield since God was protecting the soul. As a result, my body started shaking violently, since it was in the imperfect state; it was not able to tolerate God's powerful energies. Since the body was not able to take it, I understood that I should not attempt that again. Judgement Day should only be experienced after the soul has left the body, not while the soul was in the body.

My body was shaking in a similar manner during the experience in the white hole dimension. This was why I formed the opinion that my body was trembling due to being too close to God; as a result of which, I let go a little and my body's tremors stopped. However, the energies of the white holes were so powerful that it was scary. Therefore, I started making spiritual efforts to maintain a good link to God in order to make sure that He was protecting me.

Anyway, since the energies in the dimension of the white hole felt very powerful and since the body was shaking so violently, I decided that it was not a good idea to attempt that again. So I never tried to go into the dimension of the white hole again.

After the experience, I was being given a better understanding of the Universe without having to go into the dimension of the white holes. From the understanding which I was being given, I knew that apart from all the huge black holes and white holes all over the Universe, there are also tiny ones which are close to us.

In our body there are numerous chakras. These chakras are vortices. Within each chakra there are more than one vortex, some of these are black-hole-like vortices and others are white-hole-like vortices. However, we cannot see the white-hole-like vortices from the Lower Universe. We can only see the black-hole like vortices in the Lower Universe. And vice versa, while in the Higher Universe, we cannot see the black-hole-like vortices; we will only be able to see the white-hole-like vortices. This is because there is a division between the Lower

Universe and the Higher Universe. This was also why, when I was trying to see the cause of the prickly sensation all over my body, I could not see it; it was something that was happening in the Lower Universe and my consciousness (awareness) was in the Higher Universe. God had to assist me by putting my consciousness (awareness) back in my body so that I could see what was happening there. I must have been given a vision of what was happening in the body, which was why I was able to see it all in an enlarged form.

Present day scientists put forward the theory that eruptions of matter and light energies occur from white holes. Maybe the white smoke-like quick eruptions/bursts, in my experience, were these. Maybe, they were QE Light energies and the denser particles that get created from the QE Light's energies as the QE Light comes into the dimensions which are closer to the Real World.

In the second half cycle, pure QE Light energies and quantum energies flow into the Second Field and body, via the First Field; all these are within the Border of the Quantum World. Since the Quantum World is in the Lower Universe, the Real World (including earth and our bodies) is in the Lower Universe.

Even in the first half cycle, the pure QE Light and quantum energies flow into the Second Field and body, via the First Field, however, all of these are in the Border of the SWL. Since the SWL is lifted out of the Quantum World and into the Higher Universe, through the Confluence Age, even the Unified Field is lifted into the Higher Universe. Thus, the Real World, including earth, would be in the Higher Universe during the first half cycle.

When the 'walking into the Golden Aged world' process begins, pure divine QE Light bodies get created in the Higher Universe via the white hole like vortices of the chakras which exist in the Higher Universe. The chakras in the physical body are actually connected to the white hole like vortices of the chakras, in the Higher Universe, though the people of the second half cycle are not able to see the white hole like vortices of the chakras.

The chakras in the bodies are not powerful like the huge Black Hole and White Hole at the center of the Milky Way Galaxy. The black hole like vortices and white hole like vortices, within the chakras, are also not that powerful. I am using the words black hole like and white hole like because of the similarity in appearance to the black holes and white holes.

Though people, in the Lower Universe, are not able to see what exists on the other side, in the Higher Universe, the white holes which are there play a part from there for what exists even in the Lower Universe. In some experiences, I knew that there is a White Hole on the other side of the Black Hole which exists in the center of the Milky Way Galaxy. Its forces contribute to empower the Milky Way Galaxy and the universe. Its gravitational pull makes sure that cosmic bodies do not fly out of the visible universe (Real World), in the Lower Universe. However, as the Real World sinks further and further into the Quantum World (from the Copper Age to the Iron Age), the gravitational pull from this White Hole gets weaker and weaker because we are getting further away from this White Hole. Thus, scientists have noted that the visible universe is expanding.

Other factors and forces are also contributing to the expansion of the visible universe. For example, as the SWL is sinking into the Quantum World, an abundance of QE Light energies are coming closer to, and into, the Unified Field and Real World. This is also contributing to the expansion of the visible universe. Since the Unified Field provides the Real World, it can be said that even the Unified Field is part and parcel of the visible universe. The sinking of the QE Light energies, into the Unified Field and Real World, is bringing about an expansion to the visible universe since more space is needed to contain the increasing energies in the visible universe. The expansion is also taking place because, as the QE Light energies from the higher dimensions are moving into the dark space of the Quantum World, the Dark Energies of the Quantum World are allowing those energies to occupy the space in the Quantum World. Thus, the Dark Energies of the Quantum World are spreading out so as to give the descending energies space to move in. Further, since the pull of the White Hole decreases, other forces are able to push the galaxies further away and so the expansion of the universe is taking place. The visible universe is like our universe since we can see it.

There are great benefits in the 'QE Light sinking into the Unified Field' because, during the Confluence Age, it will help to bring more of God's energies into the universe; as a result of which, the world will easily transform into the divine state. In the Sumerian myths, the 'QE Light coming closer to earth which is within the Real World' has been reflected through Nibiru coming close to earth. 'Nibiru coming closer to earth' was also reflecting God's coming, at the end of the cycle, because that is when the QE Light energies and God are closest to the earth. Nibiru has also been used to portray the Soul World because that is the place of residence of God and all human souls. All souls are actually aliens in the Corporeal World.

In the second half cycle, it is the Black Hole in the center of the Milky Way Galaxy which plays a significant role in the Lower Universe. In the first half cycle, on the other hand, it is the White Hole which will be playing a similar significant role. Though the huge White Hole has a gravitational pull which keeps cosmic bodies within the visible universe, the cosmic objects cannot get pulled into the White Hole in a similar manner to how they can get pulled into a black hole. This provides the perfect state in the sky/cosmos that exists in the perfect world of the first half cycle. People, of the first half cycle, would be able to use the powerful energies around the White Hole because the instruments that are left there, to absorb the powerful energies from the White Hole, would not be pulled into the White Hole. I am not sure if people were doing this in the Golden Age, but people were doing something like that at the end of the Silver Age when the divine world was being lost. When they were no longer able to go into the Higher Universe, they had used the powerful forces around the black hole and later, mankind on earth stopped doing that.

In the second half cycle, the Black Hole in outer space is a dangerous zone because everything that is too close to it will get pulled into it. Thus, current day scientists are not able to use the powerful energies which are around the Black Hole. They will be taking a lot of risks if they attempt to use it. The fact that the Black Hole area is a dangerous zone reflects what kind of world people are provided with in the second half cycle.

There is no gravity in the auric fields. Thus, when one looks at what exists in the Holographic Universe, from within the auric fields, one is in safe grounds. However, if one becomes the Holographic Body and has experiences of what is in the Holographic Universe, one can experience the strength of the gravitational forces. This was why I could feel the forces of the white holes and the black hole, sometimes, in some experiences, though not in all my experiences since some of the experiences may have been experienced from within the auric field. In the experiences where I could not feel the gravitational forces, God may also have been protecting me during the experiences or He may have just given a vision of what exists there. Thus, I was not able to experience the strength of the forces. Even if we experience the gravitational forces, we (the energies of the soul) cannot get pulled into the black hole because:

1. the gravitational forces only have a pull on what is in the Real World which are considered 'material' in nature.

2. the energies of the soul are spiritual and not material.

We are only able to see the Black Hole at the center of the Milky Way Galaxy because the Black Hole is in the Lower Universe, i.e. it is in the Quantum World. We can see it because the Real World is in a sunken state within the Quantum World. In the Lower Universe, the source of the quantum energies (hereafter referred to as the 'QE source') can be felt through the black holes.

At the end of the Silver Age, when the QE Light Ocean dropped into the Quantum World, the whole SWL dropped into the Quantum World. However, the source of the QE Light and the white hole dimension had remained above the Quantum World, in the Higher Universe.

The white holes can be said to be part of the SWL. However, the white holes are not in a sunken state within the Quantum World, like how the rest of the SWL is. The white holes are everywhere but they are not within the Quantum World and they are not within the Lower Universe. However, they are within the Corporeal World. The white holes can only be seen while one is in a dimension that is in the Higher Universe. In the Higher Universe, the QE Light source can be felt through the white holes.

The sources of the QE Light and quantum energies are like Vishnu because they create and sustain the universe. Among other things, Vishnu represents:

1. the QE Light source lying on the QE Light Ocean,

2. the QE source lying on the QE Ocean, and

3. QE Light and quantum energies lying on the Unified Field or Quantum Ocean.

The universe, which we live in, is created and sustained through the energies from all the above three Vishnu. This universe is materialised through stages. Denser universes are created progressively until the Real World is materialised. In each stage, there is a universe which looks like our universe. It is as if all these universes are emerging out of Vishnu for the creation of the universe which we live in. Even the new universe of the first half cycle gets created through Vishnu (lying on the QE Light Ocean, QE Ocean and Quantum Ocean); though it is created through a different Real World Quantum Dimension. Actually, in the BK knowledge, the word 'Vishnu' does not reflect the QE Light and quantum energies. In the BK knowledge, Vishnu refers to the combined spiritual state of the energies of the married royal couple (a male and a female acting as one spiritual strength) in the Golden Age. However, in the Hindu scriptures, Vishnu was also used to represent the QE Light and quantum energies. Thus, I am also using the word 'Vishnu' to represent the QE Light and quantum energies.

Those who were born in the Copper Age could no longer see the White Hole in the sky because they were in the Lower Universe and they could no longer go into the Higher Universe as the Mid-Confluence Aged gods could. Even the bodies of the Copper Aged people were on the black hole side of the chakras. Thus, people in the second half cycle have experiences of going through a black tunnel. Sometimes, they leave the tunnel and remain in a black dimension because they remain in the dimensions of the Quantum World instead of going into the SWL dimensions.

When the Confluence Age begins, a white hole provides the entrance to the Confluence Aged Subtle Region. In my experience in the dimension of the white holes, this White Hole which is the entrance to the Angelic World was more powerful than any of the other white holes in the dimension. This may be because the QE Light energies (which provide the entrance to the Angelic World through the White Hole) are powerfully energised since it is so near the Angelic World. God's energies via the BKs are coming into the Corporeal World, through that White Hole. For this reason too, that White Hole is powerful. It may also be possible that I could experience its powerful state more than the powerful state of all the other white holes there because I was closer to this White Hole than all the other white holes.

In the Hindu scriptures, Siva and Kailash have been used to represent various things, including the powerful forces of the QE Light and quantum energies. Thus, the abode of Sadasiva was also used to represent the powerful dimension within which exist the white holes.

Since the energies of the white holes and black holes are powerful energies, the ancient people had also associated these to the Hindu god Siva and his abode or to Vishnu and his abode. The ancient people had sometimes even portrayed Siva and Vishnu in a similar manner because both of these gods were used to represent the powerful forces of the QE Light and quantum energies.

A powerful vortex is high and so the vortex of the White Hole (which provides the entrance to the Angelic World) has also been portrayed as Mount Kailash in the Hindu scriptures and myths. The top of Mount Kailash represents the pure powerful elevated energies of the Confluence Aged Subtle Region. One reason why it was portrayed that the residence of God Shiva is on top of Mount Kailash is that, during the Confluence Age, the residence of God is on top of the White Hole which provides the entrance to the Angelic World. From the Corporeal World, one would be able to see God on the other side of that White Hole. Around the north of India, Mount Kailash is on the other side of the Himalayan Mountains. This was also used to symbolically represent that God is on the other side of the white hole dimension. The Himalayan Mountains represents the white hole dimension.

Normally, in all my previous experiences, when I saw the White Hole which was the entrance to the Confluence Aged Subtle Region, I never saw white energies spinning around that White Hole. I only saw God's energies on the other side of the White Hole. This may have been because God and the QE Light give us a safe dimension for our energies to fly in, as we fly from the Corporeal World to go into the Confluence Aged Subtle Region. We can safely use this dimension without being exposed to the powerful QE Light energies from the QE Light source.

Those who are walking into the Golden Age would have additional QE light bodies which allow them to use dimensions that are on the same side as the white holes. One needs one's link to God to go into the Higher Universe to use these bodies and dimensions. This was why I was able to go into the dimension of the white hole, after establishing my link to God.

Though the black holes are within the Lower Universe and the white holes are within the Higher Universe, the white holes are not confined to just one area in the Corporeal World and neither are the black holes just confined to one area in the Corporeal World. Actually, the white hole dimension can be said to exist everywhere because there are numerous white holes all over the universe which are linking various dimensions, just as there are numerous black holes all over the universe linking various dimensions. Vortices spin in and out of the QE Light Ocean, QE Ocean and Quantum Ocean (everywhere in the universe) for the creation of black holes, white holes, dimensions etc. There is also no specific space for all the dimensions. They are everywhere in the same space. One can only distinguish dimensions based on their density and based on how close a role they play for the creation of the Real World. I was probably shown a vision of the Higher Universe being on top and the Lower Universe being at the bottom because the vision was reflecting the density of the energies.

Space only exists in the Real World. From the subtle, holographic or quantum point of view, this space is an illusion. It does not exist. Thus, there are no barriers for the energies of the soul to travel from one dimension to another. However, there seems to be a barrier between the Higher Universe and the Lower Universe.

In my white hole experience, when I looked down, it was as if my physical body was very far below in a dark space. When I tried to go there, it was as if it was below me, however, I could not go there. I could not see any walls separating my dimension and that one; yet, it had seemed as if there was a transparent wall which did not allow me to go into the dimension where my body was.

Chapter 23: Manifestation through the World Drama

In the present day world, people keep visualising what they want, in order to get it. In the first half cycle, people's thoughts, desires etc. will surely get materialised. All these happen through the Outlined World Drama within the soul which is entangled with the 2D SWD.

The World Drama deep within the soul is an impression on the energies of the soul. Thus, it can be said that the energies of the soul have been used to create the scenes in the World Drama within the soul. Visualisations are also impressions that are left on the energies of the soul. Thus, it can be said that the energies of the soul are used to create the scenes in the visualisations. Since there are similarities, what is visualised can easily become part of the Outlined World Drama within the soul.

When a soul takes a birth, an outline of the World Drama (in respect of that birth) emerges from the Detailed World Drama and exists as the Outlined World Drama at a higher level within the soul. The Outlined World Drama, within the soul, does not have all the details which are there in the Detailed World Drama. A lot gets recorded in the Outlined World Drama, as we play our roles on earth. When we visualise something, it can also get inserted into the Outlined World Drama as that which is happening. So our desires and thoughts can be materialised through the visualisations and 2D SWD.

Just as a World Drama exists deep within the soul, a Subtle World Drama exists within the Holographic Universe. Inter alia, this Subtle World Drama consists of the 2D SWD and 3D SWD. The Outlined World Drama within the soul is entangled with the 2D SWD. Therefore, the scenes in the World Drama within the soul are there in the 2D SWD. What is in the 2D SWD is materialised to become the 3D SWD. The 3D SWD is materialised as the World Drama on earth.

If what we visualise becomes a scene of our Outlined World Drama, it also becomes part of the 2D SWD since the Outlined World Drama is entangled to the 2D SWD. As a result, the QE Light and quantum energies materialise it since they materialise whatever exists in the 2D SWD. Thus, our desires are fulfilled through the visualisations.

What is in the Detailed World Drama are powerful scenes since they are impressions on the energies which are in the god self or deepest level within the soul. To become similar to these, powerful scenes (of the visualisations) have to be created for the visualisations to be materialised.

Visualisations are created in the mind of the soul. For convenience, I am going to divide the mind, within the soul, as follows:

1. Inner Mind (which is the Subconscious Mind of the Subconscious Self).

2. Outer Mind (the mind which is normally used by the people in the second half cycle).

The Outer Mind is at the surface of the soul. The Inner Mind extends to roughly where the Outlined World Drama exists within the soul.

When we visualise while in meditation we, normally, use the Inner Mind to create the visualisations. If we are visualising while we are not in a meditative state, we use the Outer Mind while visualising. The Outer Mind is not near the Outlined World Drama. Thus, one's visualisations are also not deep enough to be within the range of the Outlined World Drama. As a result, one's visualisations, which are created through using one's Outer Mind, do not get materialised. Further, the energies of the soul in the Outer Mind are weak because they are at the surface of the soul. Thus, powerful impressions cannot be created on it. However, if one keeps visualising a scene with faith, a lot of impressions get accumulated within the Memory Bank. The Memory Bank is situated where the Inner Mind is situated. Thus, it is as if what is accumulating in the Memory Bank is accumulating in the Inner Mind. Since there are a lot of impressions of the visualisations in the Memory Bank, it becomes a strong impression in the Memory Bank. Every time one thinks about it with faith that it is true, the visualisation strengthens the impression that exists within the Memory Bank and Inner Mind. Since it is strong, it becomes part of the Outlined World Drama within the soul. These strong impressions look similar to the powerful impressions of the scenes, in the Outlined World Drama, which are from the Detailed World Drama. As a result, it is materialised as the World Drama on earth via the 2D SWD. If the visualisations are not strong or powerful, they are only in the Memory Bank and not in the Inner Mind, Outlined World Drama or 2D SWD; and so they do not get materialised.

If you are not using pure powerful energies to create the visualisations, you are not creating powerful visualisations that look like the powerful scenes in the Outlined World Drama. If you are not capable of creating powerful visualisations, you should create strong visualisations through repetitive visualisations.

During the second half cycle, when the soul uses the Subconscious Self to visualise, the soul normally uses the Inner Mind and pure, powerful energies to do these. How close the visualisations are to the Outlined World Drama depends on which level, within the soul, is used to create the visualisations. If the visualisations are created by using the energies of the god self, the visualisations become part of the Outlined World Drama; and they will definitely get materialised. This is so because:

1. the energies used to create the visualisations are as powerful as those in the Detailed World Drama and Outlined World Drama.

2. the Inner Mind is used for the visualisation and the visualisation exists where the Outlined World Drama is situated.

If the visualisations are created by the Deeper Self, the visualisations are so close to the Outlined World Drama, and they are so powerful, that they easily become part of the Outlined World Drama. If the visualisations were created by the Higher Self, they are further away from the Outlined World Drama. However, if powerful and/or strong impressions were created, they become part of the Outlined World Drama.

It should be noted that the soul is just a point of light. Since there is no space within the soul, all the visualisations are created in the same space where the Outlined World Drama exists; however, the visualisation will only become part of the Outlined World Drama and 2D SWD if it is a powerful and/or strong impression.

In the first half cycle, people would not do visualisations to get what they want and they would not have desires; but if they did have desires, they would easily succeed in getting what they want. Since their thoughts and desires are created through the soul's divine powerful energies, the pure divine powerful QE Light would automatically begin the process to fulfil those thoughts and desires. It would be as if the QE Light and the divine energies of the soul are, together, playing the role of the 'creator' in the perfect divine manner. The World Drama would also be such that the desires of the people are definitely fulfilled. Thus, the changes that take place in the Outlined World Drama would be to fulfil the desires of the person. However, people would only have desires as per the World Drama. Everything would actually be happening as per the World Drama though the people would not be aware of this. They would enjoy living, while thinking that they are getting what they want. If the reader is reading this book, it is due to it being there in the World Drama. If it is there in the World Drama, they will succeed in materialising what they want. If a person keeps trying and trying until he succeeds in getting what he visualises, then, this person was meant to be successful in manifesting his visualisations. If a person is able to use the practices in this book to easily and quickly get what he wants, then, that is also happening as per the World Drama.

In the second half cycle, the human souls are normally not in the pure powerful state, unless they are new souls who have just come down from the Soul World. The souls who have been long in the Corporeal World will find it hard to get their visualisations materialised because:

1. the souls are in a weaker state due to more impurities existing in the souls.

2. the ordinary energies of the souls are not so efficient nor powerful.

So strong visualisations have to be created before one's desires are fulfilled. Those walking in will begin to use more powerful energies since they are being transformed into the divine state. Thus, their desires will be easily fulfilled through the resonance of frequencies. This will be explained further in Chapters 27, 28 and 29. Until those walking in become more powerful, they will have to use visualisations, while in meditation, so as to get what they want.

When in a non-Confluence Aged meditative state, one is using the energies from deeper within and so, one is closer to the Outlined World Drama within the soul. One's Conscious Self would be using the energies which are deeper within. Thus, one's thoughts, desires and visualisations would be created through using powerful energies and they easily influence the energies in the Outlined World Drama.

When doing visualisations, one can have the desire to be involved with:

1. only the pure energies and/or God, or

2. the impure energies.

Impressions of the visualisations on the pure energies of the soul are deeper within, while the impressions on impure energies are around the surface of the soul. The pure impressions which are deeper within the soul become part of the 2D SWD, via the Outlined World Drama. The impure impressions are entertained by the impure QE Light energies which are in the Second Field.

While QE Light energies flow from the QE Light Ocean to the Second Field, they bring the information that is in the 2D SWD with them so as to materialise the Real World via the 3D SWD. Thus, it can also be said that the 2D SWD exists everywhere in the Unified Field (including in the

Second Field) and not just in the space of the 2D SWD because the QE
Light and quantum energies have to have the information which exists
in the 2D SWD for the manifestation of the Real World. When the
impure QE Light energies (which are entangled with the impure
energies of the soul) fulfil one's visualisations, its energies camouflage
the information (impressions) from the 2D SWD, which are in the
Second Field, with the visualisations of the soul.

When the pure QE Light in the Second Field, which have information of
what exists in the 2D SWD, are exposed to the impure energies (impure
energies of the soul and the impure QE Light which are entangled with
the energies of the soul), they transform into the impure state too.
Though in the impure state, they still have information of what exists in
the 2D SWD since they came into the Second Field as the pure QE Light,
with information from the 2D SWD, for the sustenance and creation of
what exists in the Real World. However, due to their impure state, they
co-operate with the impure QE Light energies which play a role together
with the impure energies of the soul. Thus, the impure impressions of
one's visualisations camouflage the information of the 2D SWD which
these impure QE Light energies have (even though these impressions of
the visualisations are not within the 2D SWD proper). This means that
the impressions of the visualisations have not gone into the 2D SWD;
yet the impure QE Light energies in the Second Field are making it look
like the impure impressions of the visualisation are also from the 2D
SWD and so the visualisation has to be materialised. The weaker QE
Light and quantum energies will materialise it. Due to their weak state,
they will just flow along with that which is false. Even the soul's impure
energies can camouflage the information from the 2D SWD, in the
Second Field. All this involves black magic.

To make sure that one's impressions are imprinted in the pure QE Light
energies in the 2D SWD, it is better to keep God in one's mind while
doing the visualisations or one should use a worship system. When God
is also in one's mind or if one uses a worship system, it is as if we are
letting it be known that the fulfilment of the visualisation should be like

how it is done through worship. Thus, the impure energies cannot get involved with black magic and the visualisation will be fulfilled through the pure QE Light sending the message to God; as a result of which, God assists to get the visualisation fulfilled via the 2D SWD. These pure QE Light assist to send the message to God even if one does the worship or visualisation based on greed or one of the other vices.

When God gives instructions through Ether, to get the visualisation materialised, these powerful vibrations influence the energies of the pure QE Light to vibrate in a similar manner and so the relevant powerful impressions are left in the 2D SWD; as a result of which, the QE Light and quantum energies materialise it. Actually, God also helps as per the World Drama. So it will also be there in the Detailed World Drama that the visualisation will be materialised. However, based on the information in the Detailed World Drama, the impression is only left on the 2D SWD and Outlined World Drama, when God gives a Helping Hand.

During your visualisations, if you were in a spiritually high stage while worshiping God, what you visualise will be there in the 2D SWD, via the Outlined World Drama, due to your powerful stage. In addition, due to the worship which you had done, the message is sent to God, so God also helps you. All these make sure that you get what you visualise.

If God was not in one's mind while the visualisation was being done, the impure QE Light might end up serving one because, without realising it, one might be instructing the impure QE Light energies to fulfil one's desires. Sometimes, out of desperation and without realising it, one might try to take the situation into one's own hands. In a later book, I will explain why it is better to walk on the pure path instead of getting involved with black magic.

Those who wish to walk into the Golden Aged world should not try to do black magic. Since they are capable of using the vices, they should always use God and allow Him to create the magic. While having your link to God, you can visualise what you want or subtly inform God of what you want. If your link was strong, God will hear it and so He will fulfil your desires via your link to God. Your link to God is like your telephone wire through which God hears what you want. God hears what you want through the sound of silence aspect of the soul. Thus, you don't have to say it out loudly. You can subtly communicate your desire. BKs are not supposed to ask for anything unless they need it for service. However, those walking in can ask for whatever they want.

The 2D SWD and the World Drama deep within the soul also consists of the pure sounds of silence aspect in addition to the scenes which are created through light. In the pure state, the sound of silence and the light aspects of the soul are used to create the scenes, during the visualisations. The sound of silence, of the soul, is used to create sounds of silence for the scenes in the visualisations; and the light of the soul is used to create the picture-like scenes. These energies resonate well with the pure light energies and sounds of silence in the World Drama within the soul and in the 2D SWD. For this reason too, one's visualisations easily materialise.

The vibrations of the soul (OM) are:

1. entangled to the 2D SWD. Thus, all souls are connected through the 2D SWD.

2. vibrating out from the soul into the universe. Thus all souls, in the Corporeal World, are connected to each other, through their sound of silence, in the Holographic Universe.

Since all the QE Light and quantum energies in the Corporeal World are in an entangled state, everything in the Corporeal World (including human souls) are connected like a network via the 2D SWD and also through the sound of silence (hereafter referred to as 'silence'). Since all souls are connected through the 2D SWD and silence, they respond to the thoughts and visualisations of others, without being aware that they are responding to the thoughts and visualisations of others. As far as they are concerned, they were looking out for an opportunity (based on their own needs and desires) and it so happens that they found someone through one way or another. Actually, they were brought together via the connections in the 2D SWD and through silence. As a result, while the QE Light and quantum energies materialise what is wanted, others in the world are also touched to respond to the 'call'. All these, collectively, help people to get what they want.

In the Holographic Universe, all people are connected via their QE Light Mind. The pure energies of the QE Light Mind and the QE Light of the Corporeal World vibrate at the same frequencies. Through this, what is in the mind of the soul is also conveyed to the QE Light in the Corporeal World, including to that which have the imprints of the 2D SWD. Through the QE Light, the minds of other souls can also get information of what is in the mind of others. In addition to this, loved ones are also connected via the energies of the soul, i.e. through love. All these help one to get what one wants and it is all happening as per the World Drama.

During the second half cycle, God also helps to connect you and others because people are not able to get information and help, through the subtle connections, due to the souls' weak state. God gives the connections as per the World Drama and so, others contact you or you contact them.

In the first half cycle, due to the powerful subtle connections which people have, the human souls in the Corporeal World (who are participating in the World Drama) will be influenced to give what others want. Thus, the kings will give the subjects what they want and the subjects will serve the kings as desired by the kings. All these also happen as per the World Drama.

In the Golden Age (since you are in the pure state) your desires and thoughts have a pure sound of silence aspect. This resonates well with the pure sounds of silence of the 2D SWD and World Drama deep within the soul. It is as if your desires and thoughts become 'one' with the resonance of the sounds of silence in:

1. the World Drama within the soul,

2. the 2D SWD, and

3. all the QE Light and quantum energies in the Holographic Universe.

As a result, all the above serve you well and so, your desires and thoughts materialise. Therefore, as you walk in, you will slowly acquire the ability to materialise each thought. While in the pure state, your thoughts will naturally begin to get fulfilled even though you are not forming visualisations so as to get your desires fulfilled. If one has the ability to materialise one's thoughts instantly, one should be careful of the thoughts etc. which one has and one should make sure that one remains in a pure state as much as possible.

When you are in the impure state, your energies cannot resonate with the pure energies in the Outlined World Drama and 2D SWD. So the energies of the Lower Self cannot go near the Outlined World Drama and into the 2D SWD. Thus, what is in your mind is not materialised. Others also do not hear your silent call for the same reason.

In the Holographic Universe, people are also connected via their chakras, QE Light bodies and auric fields. One's thoughts etc. are not just in one's mind; they are also in one's auric fields. If one was not spiritually powerful, one's thoughts etc. would be in the third auric field. If one was spiritually more powerful, one's thoughts etc. would be in the higher auric fields. If these are in the higher auric fields, they are closer to the 2D SWD. From here, these thoughts, desires etc. easily influence what is in the 2D SWD. Thus, one can easily get what one wishes for, even if one was not doing visualisations to get it. One will understand all these better after reading Chapter 27 (Vibrational Frequencies), Chapter 28 (Law of Attraction) and Chapter 29 (Frequencies for Abundance).

During the walking in process, one begins to use higher dimensions because one's world is getting uplifted into the Higher Universe. These higher dimensions are also closer to the QE Light energies in the 2D

SWD, SWL environment, QE Light Ocean and QE Light source; thus, one's thoughts etc. easily influence these QE Light energies and so, one acquires the ability to get what one wants (without visualisations).

If those walking in have not been lifted into the higher dimensions as yet, they can meditate to go into those higher dimensions which are close to the 2D SWD, QE Light Ocean and QE Light source. In these higher dimensions, their visualisations easily get materialised since the visualisations are close to the 2D SWD, QE Light Ocean and QE Light source. This is another way, through which one's visualisations are manifested.

BKs fly straight up into the Angelic World via the Higher Universe. They do not linger around in the dimensions, in the Higher Universe, where the Golden Aged world is beginning to be materialised. However, those who walk in do linger around in these dimensions in the Holographic Universe, in addition to using the Confluence Aged Subtle Region. Further, those walking in are also having Golden Aged QE Light bodies being created, in the Higher Universe, to give them a Golden Aged body to walk in with. For this reason too, those who walk in are close to the 2D SWD and QE Light which are in the Holographic Universe. As a result, their visualisations etc. easily materialise. If you have decided to walk in, you surely will walk in and you will be able to use these higher dimensions in the Higher Universe of the Holographic Universe.

In the first half cycle, if you were supposed to have a desire and so you had it, the World Drama will make sure that your desire is fulfilled so that you experience happiness through every possible way. However, this is not how it is, in the second half cycle, due to the settling process.

Those walking in are acquiring the ability to get whatever they want. However, since they are still settling and they are still subjected to the Law of Karma, they can still face situations where they do not get what they want and need. Despite this, they will not be settling as badly as the BKs because the aim of BKs is to become completely pure. Those walking in might only be settling to a lesser degree, if they do not have the aim to become completely purified, as BKs do, and they only wish to walk in. However, through this, those walking in will not become very powerful. If you have only chosen the path to walk in, it is also happening as per the World Drama and so you might as well enjoy it.

Be that as it may, it should be noted that the purification process will help to reduce a lot of the bad karma of your past births. Thus, with time, your settling process will get reduced and you will find it easier to get what you want.

You can also use the spiritual income which you get, for helping with world transformation, to reduce the effects of the settling processes (if you wish to do this). Then, you will easily attain what you want. However, when you use your spiritual income to enjoy life now, you will not become so powerful spiritually. This in turn will affect the rate at which you acquire the ability to get what you want.

BKs prefer to enjoy their spiritual income through receiving benefits in their subsequent births in the first half cycle. They are not interested in enjoying it in this birth itself, though they can.

Through the thought that you want to use it now, those who are walking in can use it now. If you have decided to use the spiritual income now, it is also happening as per the World Drama because there is a need for that to happen. So enjoy living the drama.

Sometimes, you will be given money, status, name and fame etc. for service. If you enjoy these while doing the service instead of doing the service in a detached manner as an instrument of God, you are also using your spiritual income.

Everything that happens is based on what exists in the Detailed World Drama within the soul. If it is there in the Detailed World Drama, you will obtain what you want through your visualisations because:

1. it is there in the Detailed World Drama for it to materialise and so strong impressions are left in the Outlined World Drama from the

Detailed World Drama, and

2. your visualisations strengthen what has been brought into the Outlined World Drama, from the Detailed World Drama, and so it will surely be materialised.

If your wants are not fulfilled or if you are not capable of creating a strong impression of the visualisation, that is also happening as per the World Drama. Your attempts and failures will be like a settling process for a wrong which you had done in the past or in past lives. However, this does not mean that you will never get them. Keep on doing until you succeed.

When doing an activity or visualisation, consider that you are doing it for mankind. Consider that what you are doing is your contribution towards what needs to exist in the World Drama. Have good intentions for doing it because your good intentions will help you to receive more via the Law of Karma.

If you want to become rich, prosperous etc., information can also come to you from the World Drama (since that information is in the World Drama) and using this information can help to bring what you desire. Based on what exists in the World Drama, you might be given guidance on what you have to do or who to meet in order to get money etc. If you have to start a business, you will get whatever you need in order to succeed in that business. You will have a choice on whether you want to do it or not. You will not be forced to do anything.

Sometimes, you have to do something in the Real World to give an outlet for money to come in. Though people can give money to you, as a gift, it would be good to create an outlet through which money can come in, e.g. through starting a business venture, etc. These activities can be taken into the Golden Aged world as part of the game of life. Even if it is not taken into the Golden Aged world, the income from the business can be used to do service for bringing in the Golden Aged world. If you were only interested in getting cash the easy way, just keep visualising that you are receiving money and a way will be created in the World Drama for you to easily get the money.

In the Kaliyug world, riches are being used in an attempt to enjoy happiness; though money only brings temporary happiness and it does not always bring that happiness. In the Golden Aged world, people are naturally happy, whether they have money or not. Thus, they are like wealthy beings. The Golden Aged people and those walking into the Golden Aged world are like royalty because of the pure, perfect divine state which the souls are in. In addition to all these, the Golden Aged people and those walking into the Golden Aged world can enjoy having an abundance of money because the Holographic Universe will flow along to provide them with whatever they want, as per the World Drama.

In the Golden Age, everything in the Holographic Universe serves the souls who are living in the Corporeal World. Thus, as people walk into the Golden Aged world, everything in the Holographic Universe will begin to serve them. Therefore, as people walk into the Golden Aged world, they can get what they want, including money. They can acquire what they want because those living in the Golden Age play the role of the 'divine creators' along with the QE Light and quantum energies. All this happens as per the World Drama.

As you walk in, you become a master of the universe because everything in the universe will exist as per your thought. However, there are certain things which cannot be changed. In the pure state, you will understand that the universe and World Drama were meant to be in the state which they are in and you will just accept it.

No matter what happens, just remember: whatever is happening is only a drama. We are given this body to play a role in this drama so that we can enjoy happiness. So detach yourself from the body and experience happiness, no matter what is happening to you and around you. Watch what is happening in the World Drama, as a happy detached observer. Only then will you be doing what you have come into the Corporeal

World for, i.e. experience happiness. See life as a Life Drama, Game, Dream or with an optimistic view and keep saying "Wah Baba Wah" (Hey Baba/Father/God! This is great!) while seeing the variety play. Adopt and adjust beautifully to whatever is taking place as a detached observer. It is a variety play and variety plays are supposed to be entertaining. So stay entertained and just watch the World Drama unfold itself while continuing to enjoy bliss through your link to God.

Below are some meditation guidelines which you can use until you have walked into the Golden Aged world.

First Meditation Guideline:

1. See yourself as the soul seated in your seat, in the center of the forehead. See God, the Supreme Soul, as a Point of Light vibrating out pure powerful light onto you. See yourself going into a deep meditative state.

2. While keeping God before you, visualise your aims or desires. If you have more than one desire, visualise one at a time, spending at least 5 minutes on each visualisation.

3. Visualise that God is fulfilling your desires in the World Drama on earth.

Second Meditation Guideline:

1. With faith that you are walking into the Golden Aged world, visualise yourself as the soul who is being helped by God during the walking in process.

2. Visualise that God is giving you whatever you want. See yourself enjoying what you get in the World Drama on earth. Rejoice! Be happy that you have been given this wonderful life where you are healthy, wealthy and wise.

Chapter 24: QE Light and Quantum Energies serve the Souls

Since the QE Light and quantum energies play a significant role for enabling those who walk in to get what they want, a better understanding of these will help one to understand what is happening through the walking in process. It will also help one to understand how one's desires, thoughts, visualisations etc. are manifested in the Corporeal World through the QE Light and quantum energies.

The QE Light plays a significant role in the Corporeal World. They provide lokas, dimensions in the Holographic Universe, chakras, subtle bodies, environment in visions, initiate the creation of the Golden Aged body, initiate the process for bringing the person's desires etc. to God, initiate everything that materialises in the World Drama (as per the 2D SWD), etc. At the end of the cycle, via the QE Light, connections are also given between the Lower Universe and Higher Universe so as to materialise the Golden Aged Real World in the Higher Universe.

The QE Light provides two different kinds of worlds in the first half cycle and the second half cycle based on:

1. the purity of the energies, and

2. what exists in the 2D SWD and Nature's 2D World Drama.

Nature's 2D World Drama has the Laws of Nature which provides for how Nature works in the world which is being provided for Mankind. In the second half cycle, the laws which are applicable make sure that the people are given a hell-like world, especially for when the vices are used to a great extent. A different set of laws are in operation when the perfect divine world is being provided and this set of laws makes sure that Nature serves Mankind in the first half cycle. The QE Light flows along with the relevant laws based on what kind of world is provided; so it serves Mankind perfectly during the first half cycle. Thus, they will serve those who walk in too, since the Golden Aged world is getting created through the Confluence Age. As a result, the thoughts of those walking in have creative abilities.

There are 5 elements in the Corporeal World: earth, water, fire, air and ether. In the Corporeal World, the QE Light and quantum energies are 'Ether'. These 5 elements are used to materialise everything that exists in the World Drama which we are participating in on earth. The materialisation begins with the QE Light initiating it based on:

1. what exists in the 2D SWD and Nature's 2D World Drama.

2. initiations from God.

3. initiations from human souls.

For example, in the second half cycle, when one does bhakti/worship to get what one wants, the QE Light begins the process for sending one's message across to God. Then, when God has taken the step to give you what you want, through sending the relevant frequencies, the QE Light (which resonates in accordance with the frequencies that had been sent by God) will act like God in the Corporeal World; nevertheless, the QE Light is not God. It is only serving God and the human souls. Since the QE Light has the frequencies for giving you what you have asked for, the quantum energies manifest it for you in the Corporeal World. You will have a better understanding on all this when you read Chapter 27 (Vibrational Frequencies).

Since the quantum energies materialise based on what has been initiated by the QE Light energies, they work together symbiotically in a computerised manner in order to:

1. serve the human souls and God, and

2. materialise what exists in the 2D SWD.

All QE Light and quantum energies are naturally entangled with each other. Thus, they play a role together, in the Holographic Universe, for creating what exists in the Real World. Since the energies of the souls are entwined with the QE Light energies, it is as if the energies of the soul are likewise entangled with the quantum energies. Thus, it is as if both (the QE Light and the quantum energies) serve the human souls, and it is as if the energies of the soul are also creating the world since the energies of the soul are entangled with the QE Light. However, the true picture is that the energies of the soul are not creating the world; it is the QE Light and quantum energies which are creating the world. The QE Light and quantum energies are serving Mankind and so they are creating the world. Your mouth salivates when you think of eating something sour because the QE Light and quantum energies are serving you. From this angle, it is as if we start the creation process, while the QE Light and quantum energies complete the process because they serve us.

Since the QE Light and quantum energies serve Mankind, things can disappear based on our desires too. For example, if we did not like to see something, it will not exist as far as we are concerned. But others would be seeing it. Subsequently, when we want to see it, it will appear and we will be able to see it. This has happened to me, and I would wonder how something can just disappear from sight and then just reappear. With time, I began to understand that it is because the QE Light and quantum energies are serving us based on our desires. Things can also disappear as per the World Drama, if someone needs to settle for a wrong. When the settling process is over, the thing (which was searched for) will reappear. Things can disappear and reappear at any time because the Real World is being manifested at every point in time.

Everything that exists in the Real World is created through the Holographic Universe. It can be said that the creation process is taking place at every point in time because the QE Light and quantum energies have to materialise what exists in the 2D SWD, at every point in time too. If they did not do this, the Real World will not exist. The fact that the World Drama is constantly taking place in the Real World reflects that the creation processes is taking place at every point in time. Thus, changes keep taking place at every point in time.

The First Field is always situated between the 2D SWD and the Second Field. Since the QE Light and quantum energies, in the First Field, are next to the 2D SWD, these QE Light and quantum energies are influenced by what exists in the 2D SWD. Through this influence, they begin the process to materialise what has to exist in the 3D SWD (which is within the Second Field) and World Drama on earth. Through this, they are serving Mankind at every point in time.

When one takes the path to walk into the Golden Aged world, this is reflected in the 2D SWD and this influences the QE Light energies to provide, in the Higher Universe, all that is needed for the walking in process. Thus, divine QE Light dimensions of the First Field and Second Field begin to exist in the Higher Universe. Divine 'QE Light and quantum dimensions' only begin to exist in the First Field and Second Field, within the Higher Universe, when it is time to materialise the perfect bodies for those walking in. All these are done as per the World Drama, at every point in time, because the QE Light and quantum energies serve the souls.

Since the QE Light and quantum energies serve the souls, they also materialise their thoughts, visualisations etc. When they do this, it is actually happening as per the World Drama. So the QE Light is actually serving as per the World Drama.

In the Golden Age, the World Drama will be such that the people will get what they want. Even where the people walking into the Golden Aged world are concerned, the World Drama will allow them to get what they want. Since the QE Light serves Mankind as per the World Drama, the QE Light initiates what these people desire and the quantum energies materialise it in the Real World.

We are in the QE Light dimensions during the walking in process and in the first half cycle. Since the QE Light is close to us, it serves us well. It should be noted that the impressions of the World Drama, or 2D SWD, are on the QE Light energies. Thus, we are close to these QE Light impressions when we are in a QE Light dimension in the Higher Universe or SWL. Hence, our thoughts and visualisations easily materialise.

In the second half cycle, since the souls are in an impure state, they are in lower dimensions and not in the SWL. They are far away from the pure and powerful QE Light energies which are in the higher dimensions of the SWL. As a result, these pure QE Light do not serve the souls well and so the quantum energies do not materialise the desires of the human souls. The QE Light does not become aware of what a person wants, in the second half cycle, because it is as if there is a barrier between the Conscious Self (whose energies are at the surface of the soul) and the QE Light. This barrier exists because:

1. the energies of the Conscious Self (from the surface of the soul) are in a different lower dimension and not in the higher QE Light dimensions of the SWL. The different dimensions are like different worlds.

2. the QE Light from the higher dimensions are playing the 'leading role' with the energies of the god self. They are not assuming a subservient role with the energies of the Conscious Self (whose energies are at the surface of the soul).

In the second half cycle, the energies of the Conscious Self are playing the 'leading role' in the lower dimensions. The god self does not engage in a leading role because it does everything as per the World Drama. However, through meditation, we can use the energies of the god self to play a leading role. When we do this, the QE Light begins to assume a subservient role with the Conscious Self since the Conscious Self is using pure, powerful energies.

It is only through meditation that one can lift one's consciousness into the dimensions where the QE Light exists. Thus, generally, one can easily get what one wants through meditation.

In the first half cycle, the QE Light and quantum energies are sustained to remain in the pure divine state by the pure divine energies that are flowing out from the divine human souls. So the QE Light and quantum energies serve the human souls well.

During the Confluence Age, the QE Light and quantum energies are energised by God's energies which are sent into the world by the Confluence Aged souls. Thus, the QE Light and quantum energies are transforming into the pure, divine state. So they begin to serve the Confluence Aged souls well. They serve the BKs well by providing the perfect world for them to take their next birth in. Further, during the Confluence Age, God gives whatever is needed for service. Whatever is being given by God will also be manifested in the Real World via the QE Light and quantum energies since they serve God and those who do the Confluence Aged service.

During the walking in process, God gives you whatever you want. So the QE Light and quantum energies flow along to manifest what God is giving you. They are serving those who are walking in, when they do this. Further, since the QE Light and quantum energies serve the souls well in the Golden Age, you are developing your ability to be served in this way too (since you are in the process of walking into the Golden Aged world). Hence, the QE light and quantum energies serve you better and better with time.

If one was in the pure state when one creates a visualisation, the visualisation is there in the:

1. 2D SWD (via the Outlined World Drama and higher auric fields).

2. QE Light Mind.

Since the visualisation is there in the 2D SWD, the QE Light and quantum energies serve to materialise it. Thus, people's desires can be fulfilled through visualisations. Even one's desires, thoughts etc. can be fulfilled via the 2D SWD. This will be explained further in Chapter 27 (Vibrational Frequencies), Chapter 28 (Law of Attraction) and Chapter 29 (Frequencies for Abundance).

When the visualisation is created in the mind, it also exists in the QE Light Mind. Thus, it comes to the attention of the QE Light energies in the Corporeal World through the QE Light in the QE Light Mind, body and aura. Then, the QE Light and quantum energies encode, decode and recode information so as to materialise what we visualise. They also create everything else that needs to exist for you, in the Real World, through encoding, decoding and recoding information.

The quantum energies are like the other half of the QE Light energies. Thus, what is in the QE Light Mind is materialised through both of them acting conjointly together. This happens based on the Natural Laws which the QE Light and quantum energies flow along with. Thus, the quantum energies are bound to materialise what is initiated by the QE Light energies. Based on the Natural Laws, the QE Light and quantum energies act like the gods (lower gods) who serve us (the souls who are the higher gods).

Together with the QE Light and quantum energies, we can play the role of the creator so that whatever we want gets created. Nevertheless, we have to be careful since we are still capable of using the vices. One should not try to materialise something through instructing the QE Light. If one decides to instruct the QE Light, one should make sure that one is in the pure state, when one instructs the QE Light. If the vices are in an emerged state, it is the impure QE Light which will be waiting to serve one. Instructing the impure QE Light is bad as it takes one away from the pure path.

The pure QE Light naturally serves the pure souls. If you and the QE Light were simultaneously in the pure state, they will act according to your thoughts, desires, etc. You don't have to instruct them to do anything. Only in the impure state do they wait for your instructions. So there is no need to instruct the QE Light to do anything.

As one's power of concentration etc. increases, one can easily do black magic with the assistance of the impure QE Light energies. The impure QE Light initiates what one wants and the impure quantum energies provide what one wants. However, it is better to turn to God for fulfilment of desires. This can be done through worship or through one's link to God during the walking in process. One has to be careful while involved with materialising in the Lower Universe because one can be resonating with impure energies in the universe if one was not involved with worship to God or is not having one's link to God.

The BKs are not allowed to get involved with materialising things magically. God gives them whatever they need. BKs are only trained to absorb God's light and send it into the world for global transformation through self-transformation. The BKs are taught on how to use the virtues and powers, and they are involved with the purification process. All their visualisations involve God and His knowledge; they keep filling themselves with His vibrations. They do not do visualisations to become rich etc. Be that as it may, those walking in can do visualisations to become wealthy. Just visualise and these visualisations will be in the QE Light Mind. Based on what is there, the QE Light will initiate actions, provided your visualisation has a powerful impression because what is there also needs to be in the 2D SWD. Then only will your desires be fulfilled. If at the same time, one has one's link to God or one is doing worship, one can also get God's help to get what one wants.

The people in the first half cycle are naturally virtuous all the time and so they are not involved with black magic when the pure divine QE Light serves them. The people in the first half cycle are gods; it is the pure QE Light which serve the gods and not the impure QE Light.

Though those walking in are becoming pure, they are still capable of using the vices. Thus, those walking in should make sure that they remember God while doing their visualisations for fulfilment of their desires. If not, they might end up walking on the dark, impure path since the dark and impure energies would be waiting to serve them.

Since the souls consist of 'light' energies, the QE Light is able to be influenced to initiate the materialisation of what the souls have visualised etc. For the same reason, even other human souls are able to participate in order to help others to get what they want. The QE Light, quantum energies and others are all able to participate in this way because everything in the Corporeal World is connected through the QE Light and 2D SWD. Since the QE Light serves human souls, it gives a connection to everything through various ways, including through the 2D SWD.

Through the 2D SWD, all the pure energies in the universe act in a collective manner through the sounds of silence. All these energies subtly communicate with each other via the sound of silence aspect and so they are able to act as 'one'. They act as 'one', through the QE Light, for the sake of Mankind.

Everything that exists in the Holographic Universe consists of energies which are constantly vibrating. It is through these energies that everything is connected. The most important among all the energies that are vibrating in the universe are that of the soul's and therefore the most significant sound of silence in the universe is that of 'OM'. This is so because the universe exists to serve the human souls. In the universe, the pure QE Light energies are the energies which are involved with initiating the creation processes. Since they serve the soul through their entangled state, 'OM' is the most significant in the Corporeal World. It is as if the 'OM' is everywhere in the Corporeal World because:

1. the QE Light and the energies of the soul act as one; the quantum energies are just the other half of the QE Light.

2. all energies in the universe, including all the energies of all the human souls, act as 'one' in the universe for Mankind.

3. the universe exists to serve the soul (OM), i.e. it serves all human souls who are in the Corporeal World. Furthermore, the universe exists for the human souls to come from the Soul World and play their roles in the universe.

4. God, the Supreme Soul, who is also a soul (OM) plays the most significant role in the universe at the end of the cycle for transforming

the world into the Golden Aged world. It is when the universe is filled with God's energies that the new creation takes place. The creation takes place through God's Sound of Silence. The QE Light and quantum energies in the whole universe will flow along with God's Sound of Silence and serve God as they are being divinised.

5. during the second half cycle, the QE Light plays a role as God's representative in the Corporeal World because it sends the souls messages to God and does what God wants to do for the human souls on earth. Connecting oneself to the QE Light is like connecting oneself to God. Thus, since the QE Light and their quantum energies fill the whole universe, it is as if God (OM) is everywhere in the universe.

In the first half cycle, since the OM (soul) is in a pure, powerful and divine state, it plays the most significant role in the universe; thus, the people in the Corporeal World are served very well. Together with the QE Light, the human soul is capable of creating and having its desires fulfilled because the frequency of the soul's sound of silence is everywhere in the universe since the energies in the universe are vibrating in resonance with the energies of the soul. The souls will never have an impure desire because of their pure state. However, since the souls who are walking in can have an impure desire, it is always better to use God in every possible way.

In the body conscious state, when the soul is using the vices, the sounds of the energies of the soul are in disharmony and they do not resonate well with the pure energies. Thus, the pure QE Light will not be serving the individual.

In my book titled "Holographic Universe: An Introduction", I have explained how the QE Light and quantum energies materialise the world which we live in. Thus, I have only briefly discussed it here.

Chapter 25: Kundalini

The Kundalini consists of powerful QE Light energies from the QE Light source. It can be said that all the QE Light energies in the Holographic Body are part of the Kundalini of the person. However, it can also be said that these other QE Light energies are playing a secondary role with the Kundalini or that they are a product of the Kundalini, and that the 'Kundalini' actually only consists of the powerful QE Light energies which accompany a soul from birth to birth. This Kundalini, which accompanies a soul from birth to birth, has also been referred to as the Inner Kundalini while the other QE Light energies in the body have been referred to as the secondary Kundalini. When I use the word 'Kundalini', I am referring to the Inner Kundalini.

Some of the powerful QE Light from the QE Light source becomes entangled with the soul, to play a role as the Kundalini, as soon as the soul comes into the Corporeal World from the Soul World. It is these same energies which continue to play a role with the soul during each subsequent birth.

In the Kaliyug world, when the soul enters a body, the Kundalini also enters the body along with the soul. Then, while the soul remains in the brain area to play its role from there, the Kundalini descends down the subtle central channel until it reaches the Root Chakra. In the body, some of the energies of the Inner Intellect (buddhi) from the god self are entangled with the Kundalini. The Kundalini is also entangled with the Detailed World Drama and Outlined World Drama. Through the Outlined World Drama, the Kundalini is also entangled with the 2D SWD.

During the first half cycle, the Kundalini was in the Crown Chakra. It began to drop during the Mid-Confluence. So it went into the Ajna Chakra, during the beginning phase of the Mid-Confluence, and it generally was in the Heart Chakra at the beginning of the Copper Age. Then, it dropped further and so it is at the Root Chakra in Kaliyug.

When the Kundalini was in the Heart Chakra, during the end-phase of the Mid-Confluence, the people would have dropped into the Lower Universe because the switch from the spiritual to the physical takes place through the Heart Chakra. The minute that switch takes place, they drop into the Lower Universe.

During Kaliyug, since the Kundalini is in the Root Chakra, it is as if the consciousness of the soul is also at the Root Chakra. This is so because the energies of the soul, at the core of the soul, are entangled with the Kundalini. Actually, the energies of the soul which are entangled with the Kundalini can only be used as the Self (instead of being the Conscious Self) while one is 'unconscious', e.g. during deep sleep and after death. It can be said that these energies act as the consciousness:

1. in the 'unconscious' aspect (of the lower Conscious Self) when one is awake.

2. though one (as the lower Conscious Self) is not aware that it is doing something on its own.

So one does not feel that one's consciousness is in the Root Chakra. In this book, when I am stating that one's consciousness is in the Root Chakra, I am only talking about the state of the energies, at the core of the soul, which are entangled with the Kundalini. I am not talking about the energies of the soul which are used to live one's life as the lower Conscious Self. I am also not referring to all the energies of the soul (collectively). I am just referring to those energies of the god self which are entangled with the Kundalini. Not all the energies of the god self are entangled with the Kundalini, only some are. There are two kinds of consciousness, existing at two different levels within the soul:

1. the consciousness of the energies that exist at the core of the soul. These energies are doing something in the core of the soul, even though we are not aware of it. For example, some of the energies at the core are constantly bringing scenes from the Detailed World Drama into the Outlined World Drama, yet we are not aware of it. Since these energies

are doing something, it is as if they are in the conscious state, even though we are not aware of what is happening there. They can also be referred to as consciousness because they are energies of the soul which can be used as one's higher Conscious Self.

2. the lower Conscious Self who is aware that he is living the life, i.e. when one is awake and in the conscious state. This consciousness can also be referred to as 'awareness' because we are aware of what is happening in the World Drama on earth.

While living, it is as if there will always be two kinds of consciousness involved with the living process. Only one of these is 'experiencing' while living. Actually, one can experience being the Lower Self, Higher Self, deity self, Confluence Aged Spiritual Effort Maker, Angelic Self or god self, when one acts as the Conscious Self. However, normally, we never experience ourselves as the god self and we are not aware of what the god self is doing while we are living our lives.

In the second half cycle, since the deeper consciousness and Kundalini are in the Root Chakra, one is living in the present dense Real World and one would be trapped within the body. Thus, the lower Conscious Self would feel that he is the body.

The feeling that one is the body is through the usage of the first auric field for living, even though one is not aware that one is influenced by the subtle experience resulting from the usage of the first auric field and Root Chakra. The auric field which one uses also reflects where one's consciousness is. Since the deeper consciousness and Kundalini are in the Root Chakra, one's consciousness is actually in the first auric field. Since the first auric field is the double of the physical body, we feel that we are the physical body, when we use the first auric field for living. Since the first auric field is very close to the body, we feel that we are trapped in the body.

The First Chakra and its auric field help you to live your life in the World Drama that is taking place in the 3D SWD and on earth. We experience living on earth through the first auric field because its QE Light body provides us with the physical body to live our lives on earth.

The first auric field cannot be separated from the physical body because the QE Light and quantum energies, which provide the physical body, exist in the dual form (wave-particle form) and the first auric field is part of the dual form. The body can be in the real form or in the quantum form. This is why bodies can suddenly disappear and suddenly appear.

The place of residence (in a chakra) of the deeper consciousness is based on which dimension the consciousness/awareness of the Conscious Self is in. Thus, if the deeper consciousness is in the Root Chakra, it means that the consciousness/awareness of the person is in the lower dense Real World. As a result, the god self will be conducting itself accordingly. The god self does not choose to conduct itself as it likes. There are specific Spiritual Laws which it naturally flows along with, based on which chakra the deeper consciousness is in. The 'place of residence of the deeper consciousness' can be said to be part of the system that enables the god self to conduct itself in such a way that is suitable to where the consciousness/awareness of the person is in.

Since the Kundalini was in the Heart Chakra at the beginning of the Copper Age (which overlapped the end-phase of the Mid-Confluence) the deeper consciousness of the soul was also at the Heart Chakra. The people began to live in the denser Real World, even though their consciousness/awareness was still able to remain in the subtle dimensions, i.e. in the higher auric fields. Though the Mid-Confluence Aged gods were no longer living in the denser 3D SWD, they could still reside in the denser 3D SWD, instead of in the Real World, through their spiritual effort making.

During the first half cycle, when the consciousness and Kundalini of the people were in the Crown Chakra, the people were aware that they were souls and they were also living in the denser 3D SWD. The people used the higher four chakras for living their lives. They did not use the lower three chakras for living their lives, though all the chakras were involved with the creation and functioning of their body. Though they lived in the 3D SWD, they were capable of using a physical body in a less dense Real World because of the wave-particle duality state of the quantum energies. Even though they were capable of having a body in the Real World, they were not really living in the Real World. The soul was seated in its seat in the center of the forehead, and the Kundalini was at the Crown Chakra, during the Golden and Silver Ages. So they were living a subtle-like life in the Corporeal World. Since the soul was constantly seated on its seat and the deeper consciousness was in the Seventh Chakra, while the people were living their lives, their life was like a subtle experience which continued throughout their life. Since their Kundalini and deeper consciousness were at the Seventh Chakra, their consciousness was not trapped within the body. They were constantly soul conscious and so they were having the feeling that they were the souls who were using the body. The souls were in bodies which were in the subtle quantum state, even though the bodies were capable of being in either the real state or subtle quantum state due to the wave-particle duality aspect. It is only mortals who have their consciousness trapped in the body because the Kundalini and their deeper consciousness are at the Root Chakra. The people of the first half cycle were immortals since they were not trapped within the physical body as the Kaliyug souls are. Since they were immortals, at the end of the life, they will know that it is time to take another birth and play a different role somewhere else. Since they were in their perfect state, they will be happily eager to play their next role just like how present day people are eagerly waiting to travel to other countries to spend some time there. Even those who walk in will be in a similar immortal state, after having walked in. However, when it is time to leave the body, they will know that it is time to go back to the Soul World.

During the second half cycle, the sunken state of the Kundalini reflects the sunken state of the SWL, earth and Mankind. The SWL began to sink as the Kundalini began to sink from the Crown Chakra to the lower chakras. Since the Kundalini is from the QE Light source, it is closely connected to the QE Light Ocean which is also getting its energies from the QE Light source. Both, the Kundalini and QE Light Ocean, sank because they actively play a role for Mankind in the Corporeal World.

The Kundalini plays various kinds of roles with the soul and in the body. For example, the Kundalini:

1. ascends along the subtle central channel during the walking in process and descends during the Mid-Confluence.

2. ascends and descends, along the subtle central channel, during one's spiritual experiences.

As per the World Drama, the Kundalini will not be in the awakened state during the second half cycle. Thus, the Kundalini was portrayed as the sleeping serpent which blocks the entrance to the Sushumna which is the subtle central channel. This opening, at the entrance of the Sushumna, has been referred to as Brahma-Dvara (Door of Brahma). This door will only be opened when the role of Brahma begins to be used again at the end of the cycle. By the end of the Confluence Age, the Door of Brahma will be permanently re-opened.

During the walking in process, as one keeps making spiritual efforts, one's Kundalini will be moving up into the higher chakras, while it moves up along the subtle central channel. This happens because one's Kundalini is entangled with the energies of the intellect at the core of the soul and with the World Drama.

Since the Kundalini will be naturally rising again as souls walk into the Golden Aged world, the ancient people had created the myth that the Kundalini (as Shakti) rises up to meet Shiva (the Supreme Soul or God). This reflects the time during the Confluence Age when the Kundalini rises because the world is being transformed into the Golden Aged world. It has to rise because the people who walk in will have their consciousness at the Crown Chakra. After playing their roles in the Golden Age, they will leave the bodies and go to the Soul World where God resides. Those walking in will temporarily reside in the Golden Aged world before going back to the Soul World. The 'rising of Shakti' also represents the 'journey to reside in the Confluence Aged Subtle Region and then back to the Soul World'. It represents how it is as if the Confluence Aged souls are on their way back to the Soul World as they are gaining spiritual strength. It is as if they are on their way back because the higher their spiritual strength the closer they will be to God:

1. when He takes them back to the Soul World (at the end).

2. when they are in the Soul World.

During the second half cycle, when a person is on the spiritual/religious path, the person's Kundalini gets awakened temporarily. Normally, in the second half cycle, it is only partially awakened (to a greater or to a lesser extent). It is only in the first half cycle that it is completely and permanently in the awakened state while the person is living his/her life in the Corporeal World.

In the second half cycle, since the Kundalini is entangled with the Outlined World Drama and Detailed World Drama, the Kundalini will know when the person has to be given an experience and so it activates the Second Chakra (if the person was not on the spiritual path) so as to enable the person to have the experience. The Kundalini can be partially awakened even if the person was not on the spiritual path. When it is awakened, it rises. While it rises, it activates the chakras and so human souls can use their chakras efficiently. As a result, the person can also use the specialities and Siddhis. This is why some souls (who have just come down from the Soul World or who are enjoying the fruits of their good actions through the Law of Karma) can do magic from the time they are young, but many have lost their ability to do magic because:

1. they are in the weak, impure state.

2. they are settling karmic accounts.

3. the Kundalini is not activating the chakras to allow them to function

well, as per the World Drama.

Those walking in will be able to use all the Siddhis and specialities that are provided through the relevant activated chakras:

1. when the Kundalini is rising due to the walking in process, and

2. when the Kundalini rises to activate specific chakras during experiences.

During the Confluence Age, the place of residence of the consciousness (awareness) of the soul is in the Confluence Aged Subtle Region since God has uplifted our consciousness through the Angelic Body. Those walking in also have their consciousness (awareness) in the Confluence Aged Subtle Region. In addition, during the walking in process, the place of residence of the consciousness (at the depths of the soul) is rising through the rising of the Kundalini. As the Kundalini rises, it is as if one's consciousness rises from the First Chakra to go into the Second Chakra and then, it keeps rising until it reaches the Seventh Chakra. When it is time to walk into the materialised Golden Aged world, the Kundalini constantly remains at the Seventh Chakra.

The chakra which you use is a reflection of where your consciousness is because the Kundalini is entangled with some of the energies of the soul which exist at the core of the soul. The place of residence will affect how well the Conscious Self is served by the energies of the god self, etc.

As the Kundalini rises from the bottom to the top, for those walking in, each chakra along its passage gets activated. The activation of the chakras begins with the activation of the Root Chakra.

In the Kaliyug world, even though one's consciousness is situated in the Root Chakra, the Root Chakra might not be activated and functioning completely well. When the Root Chakra begins to function well, whatever one thinks will happen.

In the Higher Universe, the new QE Light bodies get created from the 7th auric field downwards. Thus, the transformation of the body begins from the 7th auric field. At the same time, the Kundalini also rises. The Kundalini resonates with God's Sounds of Silence, so it rises and flows along with God for the recreation of the Golden Aged world. As the Kundalini is rising to the Crown Chakra, there will be an upliftment of the place of residence of the Kundalini and consciousness of the soul.

When the Kundalini began dropping, during the Mid-Confluence, the Mid-Confluence Aged people began practices to raise their Kundalini. They were spiritually powerful souls who still had healthy bodies. They had also not accumulated much sinful karma which they have to settle. Thus, they could safely raise their Kundalini. However, in Kaliyug, the spiritual state of the souls is impure and the bodies are unhealthy and imperfect. Thus, it is not safe to raise the Kundalini through meditation practices where you instruct the Kundalini to rise or you visualise that the Kundalini is rising. It is not advisable to get involved with these practices because the Kundalini is entangled with the World Drama within the soul and so, if one has to suffer as per the World Drama (for one's bad karmic accounts), one can also suffer through the rising of the Kundalini. Those who have taken more than one birth, in the Corporeal World, should be more careful while raising the Kundalini since it can badly affect the physical body due to the settling process.

Since the Kundalini is closely connected to the settling process through the Buddhi (intellect), World Drama (in the soul and 2D SWD) and the Law of Karma, it is as if it keeps a record of the karmic accounts that need to be settled by the soul. As a result, it can take actions based on them and so, the body can be affected badly due to the settling process.

The Kundalini is from the QE Light source. All the QE Light energies, which play a role in the Holographic Body for providing what is in the physical body, are also from the QE Light source. Thus, everything in the physical body can be said to be a product of the Kundalini. The QE Light energies provide the body for the soul based on what exists in the 2D SWD, World Drama within the soul and based on the Law of Karma.

Even the Kundalini is guided by these. Further, there is a connection between the QE Light energies in the Holographic Body and the Kundalini. Thus, a healthy body is provided for souls who have just come down from the Soul World and their bodies will also not be badly affected by the Kundalini energies. The Kundalini would also be helping them to live a heavenly life. Hence, souls who have just come down from the Soul World can safely raise their Kundalini. They can also safely raise it because they would not have accumulated much sinful karma. However, deity souls have accumulated a lot of bad karmic accounts from the time of the Copper Age. Therefore, even though God is taking care of you during the walking in process, you still have to settle all your wrongs. So don't make attempts to raise the Kundalini through practices that were intended to raise it. That can be dangerous for you. It should rise on its own. The Kundalini is naturally rising on its own without harming the body because:

1. you are walking in as per the World Drama.

2. there are Confluence Aged souls who have become very powerful spiritually and so the walking in process has begun.

3. God's energies are there protecting you during the walking in process.

If you give the Kundalini a command to rise, it will rise irrespective of whether it harms you or not. But when it rises naturally, it will only rise to bring you a lot of benefits. For example, since you are involved with the walking in process, the Kundalini will help transform your body when the Golden Aged world is being materialised.

When something has to happen as per the World Drama, even the Kundalini flows along with what has to happen; thus, even the Kundalini assists to allow a requisite materialisation if that has to happen. For example, if the person has to be given a perfect body to walk in, the Kundalini and chakras will begin to function in such a way that the person is given a perfect body. The Kundalini will safely rise up, as per the World Drama, to do this.

As we keep walking into the Golden Aged world, the Kundalini rises from the bottom of the spine to the top of the head; at the same time, we keep ascending into the higher heavenly dimensions. It can also be said that as you keep using the higher dimensions, your Kundalini rises naturally and your chakras get activated.

Instead of trying to raise the Kundalini, start using the higher dimensions, during the walking in process. As you lift yourself into the higher dimensions, the Kundalini will naturally rise by itself because you are involved with the walking in process. It is better to let it happen naturally instead of trying to force it to rise when your karmic accounts have not been properly taken care of.

Your old karmic accounts will get reduced, during the walking in process, as you are purified through your link to God and through the settling process. Even if you have not settled all your old karmic accounts or have not got them burnt off through the purification process, they can be kept at bay since you are walking into the Golden Aged world. During Judgement Day, if you have not completely purified yourself through your link to God or through the settling process, the spiritual income which you receive, for participating in the walking in process, will be used to off-set your karmic accounts so that you can walk into the materialised Golden Aged world. Since God takes care of the karmic accounts, the Kundalini of those walking in will rise, safely on its own, without consideration of the settling process.

Even as you participate now for the walking in process, there is a multimillion fold return, through the Law of Karma, for the good karma of participating in the walking in process. However, if you use all this spiritual income for enjoying wealth etc. now or for off-setting your karmic accounts before completing the walking in process (i.e. before Judgement Day), you are not going to become a very powerful soul. Then, you might only take your first birth in the Silver Age and not in the Golden Age.

In the second half cycle, the state which the chakras are in is also based on the settling of karmic accounts. Thus, we might not get what we want through visualisations etc. However, this is being changed during the walking in process via the rising Kundalini. The Kundalini will have to activate the chakras when you use the higher dimensions because the Kundalini is also serving God and the deity souls for the walking in process. Further, as your Kundalini activates your chakras naturally, during the walking in process, you are being given the ability to do magic and to easily use the higher dimensions.

As you go into the higher dimensions, you will begin to use the higher chakras more frequently. Then, the environment which the energies of the soul have, when they vibrate out, will often be in the higher auric fields depending on which chakras have opened and which dimension you are in. When the energies of the soul are in the higher dimensions via the higher auric fields, they are exposed to the sounds of silence of the pure QE Light in those higher dimensions. Since these pure QE Light energies serve the soul and God, magic can be performed. However, one should not intentionally try to perform any magic. If you noticed that you had done something magical, just observe and keep quiet. Don't try to use it again or develop it further.

Though all of one's chakras may be activated during a subtle experience, it does not mean that one's Kundalini has risen permanently. During experiences, the Kundalini temporarily moves up and down the subtle central channel so as to enable the person to have an experience. When the Kundalini goes up, it is actually taking the consciousness of the person into the higher dimensions.

During spiritual effort making, if the Kundalini rises and resides in a specific chakra, it will be as if the person resides in the loka, provided by that chakra, while living his/her life. Then, when one loses one's stage and begins to live in the dense Real World, the Kundalini drops back into the Root Chakra. This is another way through which the Kundalini is utilised.

Actually, the chakras can be used and activated without any specific order. A chakra can suddenly function well so that the soul can use it for an experience or if something needs to happen to the soul as per the World Drama. A chakra can become activated temporarily or permanently during a life depending on how it is supposed to be in the World Drama. The Kundalini rises and activates a chakra as per the World Drama. However, for the walking in process, the chakras get activated from the root upwards as the Kundalini rises. This situation is different from that where a chakra is being activated randomly for what needs to happen in the World Drama.

The Kundalini is entangled with the energies of the chakras and subtle systems in the QE Light bodies. Thus, chakras function well as the Kundalini rises. However, the Kundalini and chakras will only function based on what is to happen in the World Drama.

When the Kundalini has activated the relevant chakras in the body, the soul will be able to understand knowledge, experience bliss etc. Thus, the awakening of the Kundalini has been associated with bliss, liberation etc. The soul understands knowledge, experiences bliss, etc. through using the body. Thus, the Kundalini is actually helping the soul to use the body efficiently.

When the Kundalini unites with the energies of the soul at the Sahasrara Chakra, the soul is able to experience the blissful state of the soul to a tremendous extent. It is the body that allows the soul to experience the virtues, including bliss, that are within the soul. The raised Kundalini helps the soul to experience the bliss that is within the soul, via the body. The greater the bliss that is within the soul, the greater the bliss one could experience during an experience.

The people, in the first half cycle, can constantly experience bliss and the pure divine happiness that is within the soul because the Kundalini is always in the Seventh Chakra. They are also experiencing these through the usage of the body.

Chapter 26: Cosmic Consciousness and World-Wide Collective Consciousness

The Cosmic Consciousness consists of the QE Light energies playing a role with the energies of the soul and Supreme Soul. Though I refer to the QE Light as Cosmic Consciousness, it is not really 'consciousness'. It is only souls who have consciousness because we can use consciousness to 'live' while using our bodies. The QE Light is a spiritual force which can give life to plants and living bodies; however, it is not really 'living' a life as we do.

When we want to interact with the QE Light body in a plant, it can interact with us similarly to how humans interact with us, so it can seem like it has consciousness. This is possible because it serves us. Though the QE Light is only the Cosmic Consciousness from the viewpoint that they play a role with the consciousness of human souls and with God, the QE Light can be referred to as the Cosmic Consciousness since:

1. it does seem to be conscious (to a certain extent).

2. it is the spiritual aspect of the quantum energies.

3. its 'light' plays a crucial aspect for, and as, 'consciousness' with the energies of the souls.

Actually, it is the energies of the soul which is consciousness; however, without the QE Light, the soul cannot experience its own consciousness. For example, the Kundalini, which consists of very powerful QE Light energies from the QE Light source, plays a very significant role as 'consciousness' with the energies of the soul.

The QE Light energies which accompany a soul, as the Kundalini, also play a role like it was part of the consciousness of the human being. Thus, it is as if it is part of the human soul in the Corporeal World. The powerful QE Light energies from the source which accompany each human soul, from the time the soul comes into the Corporeal World to play its part, is the Kundalini during every incarnation of that soul. Even for the reason that these energies have to play a role with the soul, it is as if the soul includes these QE Light energies which are from the QE Light source. However, in reality, they are not part of the soul. They are just closely entangled with the energies of the soul. Since they play such a significant role with the soul, the Mid-Confluence Aged gods had given importance to them as if they were the most crucial energies for the human beings which were getting detached from the Cosmic Consciousness (QE Light source) to play a role as human beings. There is truth in this because without the part of the QE Light energies, there cannot be human beings. However, we are not the QE Light; we are the souls who have come from the Soul World to enjoy living on earth. We enjoy living, the QE Light and Kundalini do not.

It can be said that the Kundalini is not really 'consciousness' because it does not live the life. It is the soul which is living the life. However, since the QE Light energies, along with the Kundalini of all human beings, closely play a role with the consciousness of all human souls who are in the Corporeal World, it is as if these are part and parcel of consciousness in the Corporeal World.

It cannot be said that the human souls or their energies are the Cosmic Consciousness because our energies do not provide the universe. The word 'cosmic' relates to the universe. It is the QE Light and quantum energies which provide the universe. The QE Light is the spiritual aspect of the universe and the quantum energies are the material aspect of the universe. Thus, it is more appropriate to refer to the QE Light as the Cosmic Consciousness.

All human souls, who are in the Corporeal World, play a role together as the World-Wide Collective Consciousness. The QE Light and Kundalini connects all souls in this World-Wide Collective Consciousness. The World-Wide Collective Consciousness can also be said to be part of the Cosmic Consciousness because:

1. all human souls are also playing a role with the QE Light as the Cosmic Consciousness.

2. the QE Light connects all souls based on the 2D SWD, what they desire, think, visualise, etc.

As the lower Conscious Self, we are not aware that we are part of the World-Wide Collective Consciousness but as the god self, we are aware. The god self does what the soul needs to do, as part of the World-Wide Collective Consciousness in the Corporeal World, irrespective of what the lower Conscious Self wants and desires.

It can be said that it is through the Inner Mind that we are connected to the Cosmic Consciousness and World-Wide Collective Consciousness. The Inner Mind can be used by any of the Inner Selves. However, it is the god self which plays the most significant role, through the Inner Mind, as part of the Cosmic Consciousness and World-Wide Collective Consciousness.

We get what we want through the Cosmic Consciousness and World-Wide Collective Consciousness. Since the lower Conscious Self is not connected to the Cosmic Consciousness and World-Wide Collective Consciousness, the Conscious Self can instruct a deeper Inner Self to act as the co-creator to get something created through constant visualisations, thoughts etc. When the Inner Self fulfils the desires of the Conscious Self, it does so through the Cosmic Consciousness and World-Wide Collective Consciousness, i.e. the QE Light of the Cosmic Consciousness will flow along to act as co-creators with us and others will also be touched to assist via the World-Wide Collective Consciousness.

When one's spiritual stage is good, one can act as the co-creator to create something with just a single thought because thoughts can initiate the creation process. Creation is, actually, initiated by the QE Light of the Cosmic Consciousness based on our thoughts; and, others can also be touched to act as co-creators via the World-Wide Collective

Consciousness.

The people, in the first half cycle, are in their perfect state and so they will only have relevant positive, accurate thoughts; whereas the people, in the second half cycle, can have negative thoughts. If all the thoughts of the people in the second half cycle were to materialise, life on earth might be in the worst kind of hell. Thus, it is for the benefit of Mankind that people in the second half cycle, generally, will not have their thoughts materialised. If they want to have their thoughts materialised, they will have to get involved with pure spiritual living. During spiritual living, since one tries to remain in the pure state, one does not form unnecessary negative thoughts. Thus, the world will not be affected badly; the world would only benefit through their purity. So it is good that the Spiritual Laws in the World Drama are such that weak impure souls cannot play a role as co-creators while they are living as the lower Conscious Self, though their god-self would be involved with playing the role of the co-creator through the Cosmic Consciousness and World-Wide Collective Consciousness.

It is as if we have to become part of the Cosmic Consciousness in order to act as co-creators in a conscious way. Though we become part of the Cosmic Consciousness, we are not the Cosmic Consciousness, we are the souls.

For the sustenance of what is being provided in the World Drama, QE Light energies are flowing from the higher dimensions into our auric fields and then, finally, they flow out of our chakras in the feet to go into the earth. At the same time, QE Light energies which provide the earth are also flowing, from the Unified Field, into our chakras in the feet and then, they flow upwards to go out of the Crown Chakra at the top of the head so as to go into the higher dimensions. One reason why these energies, from above and below us, are flowing through us for the creation process is that the human souls are co-creators in the Corporeal World. The QE Light that flows down into the lower dimensions from the higher dimensions brings information from the 2D SWD. When they bring information from the 2D SWD, they are also making all relevant connections, through the Cosmic Consciousness and World-Wide Collective Consciousness, so as to provide as per what exists in the 2D SWD.

We are also connected to the 2D SWD, Cosmic Consciousness and the World-Wide Collective Consciousness through the Seventh Chakra. The energies which flow through the 4th, 5th and 6th chakras also use these connections as the soul uses the specialities and Siddhis that can be provided by these chakras.

It should also be noted that the rising of the Kundalini helps to bring the energies of the soul into the higher dimensions, so we get connected to the 2D SWD. While we are there, we can influence the QE Light energies, which are there, to flow down into the 3D SWD and Real World so as to manifest what we desire. At the same time, since the World-Wide Collective Consciousness exists through the 2D SWD, we can also influence all other souls to get their co-operation. Through the Cosmic Consciousness and World-Wide Collective Consciousness, we can also be influenced by what the QE Light is doing based on the 2D SWD.

Actually, we can influence and be influenced by energies from the Cosmic Consciousness and World-Wide Collective Consciousness, through all the chakras and aura. All the seven chakras help to reflect the various aspects of our consciousness into the aura and world. This means that they are also connecting the person to the Cosmic Consciousness and World-Wide Collective Consciousness. Thus, others subtly become aware of what we want, though as the lower Conscious Self, they are not aware.

The energies, which flow through the chakras at the feet and then flow out through the Crown Chakra, help to connect the person to the universe, especially to the Cosmic Consciousness. We also become one with the QE Light or Cosmic Consciousness through our energies which flow out via the Crown Chakra. Through all these we can easily get our desires fulfilled.

We live in a complex Holographic Universe, where all energies are connected and symbiotically influencing each other. So we cannot really say that only one factor is contributing to materialise what we desire etc. The human souls are connected to everything else in the universe via the World-Wide Collective Consciousness and Cosmic Consciousness because everything in the Holographic Universe has to aid us in getting what we want.

After you are purified, on Judgement Day, you leave your Kundalini in the Corporeal World as you fly back to the Soul World with God. As you leave your Kundalini behind, you leave the Cosmic Consciousness and World-Wide Collective Consciousness behind. You no longer play a role with the Cosmic Consciousness, nor do you play a role in the World-Wide Collective Consciousness while you are in the Soul World.

When you leave the Corporeal World, your Kundalini joins back to the QE Light source and remains as 'one' with the QE Light source until you return to the Corporeal World, in the next cycle, to play your roles again. When your Kundalini joins you, as you come into the Corporeal World to play your role, you engage with the Cosmic Consciousness and become part of the World-Wide Collective Consciousness again.

Chapter 27: Vibrational Frequencies

The Corporeal World is filled with energies which are vibrating at different frequencies. The rate at which energy vibrates is called the frequency.

In the original pure state, the QE Light and the energies of the soul naturally vibrate at the same frequency. Thus, the QE Light and the energies of the soul are vibrating in resonance with each other. As a consequence of this and due to the fact that they are entangled with each other:

1. the QE Light and the energies of the soul can influence each other to become pure or impure.

2. the QE Light of the 2D SWD and Cosmic Consciousness can influence the energies of the souls to vibrate in a similar manner while they provide the souls' environment etc.

3. the energies in the Outlined World Drama resonate with the frequencies of the visualisation that become part of the Outlined World Drama, and so strengthen the visualisation. Then, the visualisation becomes part of the 2D SWD for the materialisation process.

4. the vibrations of the QE Light in the chakras, QE Light Mind, QE Light Body, aura, 2D SWD etc. are in resonance with the vibrations of the soul. Therefore, they adopt the relevant frequencies so as to fulfil the soul's desires; and thereby, one gets what one wants.

5. what is in the mind of the soul can influence what is happening in the QE Light brain. For example, the QE Light in the QE Light brain, which provides the neurons of the human brain cells, catches the frequency in the energies of the soul. Through this, it interacts with the soul and fulfils the desires of the soul, so the person can use his body efficiently.

When a visualisation becomes part of the Outlined World Drama, even the energies in the Outlined World Drama vibrate with the same frequencies and this strengthens the visualisation. Thus, the visualisation will surely materialise.

The closer the visualisation is to the Outlined World Drama, the greater it will influence the vibrations in the Outlined World Drama to resonate with the same frequencies which are in the visualisation. The more it influences the vibrations in the Outlined World Drama, the stronger the frequencies in the Outlined World Drama. The stronger these frequencies are, the greater the influence on the QE Light energies in the body, aura, 2D SWD and universe. Hence, the greater the chances of the visualisation being materialised.

When the pure state is used while visualising, the visualisation is there in the 2D SWD through:

1. the Outlined World Drama.

2. the 7th auric field and other higher auric fields.

It should be noted that the energies of the soul are always within the auric fields and the 7th auric field is the nearest to the 2D SWD in the Unified Field. Since the Outlined World Drama and 2D SWD are entangled around the border where the First Field and the 2D SWD overlap, it can be said that the Outlined World Drama is in the higher space of the 7th auric field. If one was using the energies of the god self to visualise what one wants:

1. the visualisation is in the Inner Mind where the Outlined World Drama exists, so it is in the higher space of the 7th auric field since the Outlined World Drama is entangled with the 2D SWD in this space.

2. the visualisation is brought into the 7th auric field through the Seventh Chakra. This is similar to how thoughts are brought into the 3rd auric field if one was not on the spiritual path or if one was just beginning the spiritual path.

Through both of the above, the visualisation is brought into the 7th auric field. In the 7th auric field, these visualisations are in or near the space of the 2D SWD, so they strongly influence the energies in the 2D SWD. As a result, the QE Light in the 2D SWD adopts the frequencies in the visualisations and resonates with the frequencies in the visualisations too. The visualisations will influence the energies in the 2D SWD because the visualisations were created by pure powerful energies of the soul. Thus, it is very easy to get what one wants.

When one's stage is not that high:

1. one might be the Deeper Self and one's visualisations might be somewhere in the 6th auric field or in the lower space within the 7th auric field.

2. one might be the Higher Self and one's visualisations might be somewhere in the 4th, 5th or 6th auric fields, depending on one's spiritual stage.

In the above situations, though the visualisations are brought into the higher auric fields, they are not in the higher space of the 7th auric field, and consequently they will not influence the energies in the 2D SWD unless the visualisation was a strong or powerful one. A strong visualisation is created through numerous visualisations that have left a strong impression in the Inner Mind. A powerful visualisation is created by pure powerful energies of the soul.

If the visualisations are created by the Lower Self, the 2nd auric field and 3rd auric field would be used to reflect these in the aura, depending on what one is visualising. Since these visualisations are far away from the 2D SWD, it would be very difficult for these to influence the vibrations in the 2D SWD unless they consisted of very strong vibrational frequencies, i.e. they were very strong visualisation.

The thoughts, which have been visualised, become scenes around the Outlined World Drama, i.e. they become part of the Outlined World Drama if they were powerful and/or strong visualisations. The thoughts, desires, intentions, faith and beliefs of the person influence the Outlined World Drama, 2D SWD and all QE Light energies through the resonance of all their pure energies. Due to the resonance of the pure QE Light with the pure energies of the soul, the pure QE Light will create the frequencies that will materialise what the person desires etc.

The thoughts, desires, visualisations etc. (in the Mind and Inner Mind) will also exist in the QE Light Mind. If we were in the pure stage, there will be powerful vibrational frequencies of these in the QE Light Mind and this helps to bring what is in the mind of the soul to the Mind of the Cosmic Consciousness. So all QE Light energies in the Holographic Universe become aware of what we want and they flow along accordingly.

The energies of the soul are connected to everything that exists in the universe, through various ways. Thus, when you visualise that you are getting money, a way will be created for you to get the money (through the 2D SWD) if your desires are resonating with the pure QE Light energies which are entangled with the pure energies of the soul. If you are in the pure state, your desires will be fulfilled as per the World Drama because the Spiritual Laws and Laws of Nature are such.

In the first half cycle, people do not use visualisations to fulfil their desires. Since they are in the pure state, the QE Light energies are in resonance with the pure energies of these souls and it is as if they become aware of the souls' desires. This in turn influences the energies in the 2D SWD since they are also resonating with the pure frequencies in the Outlined World Drama and the pure frequencies of the soul. As a consequence, the relevant frequencies are created in the 2D SWD and the person's desires are fulfilled.

The vices have different vibrational frequencies from the pure energies of the soul. Since the frequencies are not the same as the frequencies of the pure energies, these impure energies cannot resonate with the pure energies. As a result, if one was in an impure state, one cannot get what one wants. Further, when the QE Light and quantum energies are exposed to the vibrational frequencies of the vices, they begin to resonate at the same frequencies as the vices.

The higher chakras are involved with spiritual living and assisting in the manifestation process. The frequencies from these influence the frequencies of the soul and all other energies so as to help the soul to live a spiritual life etc.

The lower chakras are the ones that are greatly involved with the materialisation process. They complete the materialisation process, though all the seven chakras are involved with materialising the different parts of the body. Thus, the frequencies that are emitted from these will be greatly involved with the materialisation processes.

It is the low frequencies of the quantum energies, from the Quantum World, which play the most significant role for the materialisation of the body, etc. So they play the most crucial part for the materialisation process. This is also a reason why I keep saying that the quantum energies are involved with the materialisation process.

During the Confluence Age, when the energies of the soul are touched by God's energies, they are influenced to resonate at the same frequencies as God's pure powerful divine frequencies, while they become energised. Thus, we become divine like God and so, God and the Confluence Aged souls are in the "Like Father like son" state. However, even though we become like God (Bapsaman or 'like Father'), we do not become 'a powerful Ocean' like God. Only our energies would be of the same quality as God's, i.e. pure, divine and in its perfect state. Vibrations have to be powerful so as to resonate at the same frequencies as God's. Since God's energies energise our energies, we are able to resonate with the frequencies of God. Thus, if we concentrate on the BK knowledge, we will get God's assistance to go beyond, since our frequencies will fall into step with the divine frequencies of God's energies. The powerful divine frequencies, which we begin to resonate with, cannot be measured because the energies of the soul cannot be measured. The frequencies of God, the soul and the

QE light cannot be measured since they are spiritual in nature. One can only measure frequencies in the Real World.

Since all the vibrations in the Corporeal World influence each other, the 2D SWD and what exists in the Outlined World Drama can be changed based on the changes in the frequencies that surrounds them. For the same reason, those walking in (who are not powerful spiritual effort makers) can be influenced to become divine through coming into contact with God's powerful divine frequencies which have been emitted through other Confluence Aged souls.

Everything (including the chakras, bodily organs etc.) is vibrating at different frequencies, therefore, our thoughts consist of all their different frequencies when we think of them. Since the energies of the soul have a causal quality, the different vibrational frequencies of everything that exists in the universe can be created within a thought or visualisation. This means, in our visualisation, the object which we visualise will be having the frequency which it has in the Real World. Thus, what we visualise will consist of vibrations that are vibrating at numerous different frequencies. Since the energies used for the visualisation etc. have a light and a sound of silence aspect, the visualisations have a subtle movie-like nature.

Whatever has been visualised in our mind is in the QE Light Mind (as vibrational frequencies and as pictures or scenes). If it is also there in the 2D SWD, via the Outlined World Drama, the frequency of the object which is in our visualisation will also be there in the QE Light energies (in the scene/picture form and also in the vibrational frequency form) for manifestation purposes. Since the QE Light initiates the materialisation process, the object which has that frequency will be materialised. So what you visualise gets created.

In the second half cycle, when a person does bhakti/worship to ask God for something, the QE Light initiates the process to get the message sent across to God. God gets these messages as frequencies. Then, God takes the step to give you what you want, through sending the relevant frequencies. These get sent through the Mid-Elements, which exist between the Soul World and the Corporeal World. When these frequencies reach the QE Light, which is in the Corporeal World, the QE Light resonates to have the same frequencies as the messages which have been sent by God. Thus, the QE Light acts like God in the Corporeal World but it is not God. It is just serving God in the Corporeal World by creating what needs to be created.

The Holographic Universe is the womb of creation where different kinds of energies are involved with the creation processes through getting tuned to different frequencies. When the QE Light and quantum energies get tuned to the different frequencies for creation purposes, information is encoded, decoded or recoded in the QE Light and quantum energies so as to create what exists in the Real World.

'OM' is the mother tone because the energies of the souls can contain the frequencies of everything that exists in the universe. The frequency of OM is the sound of creation because the QE Light energies act based on the sounds of silence of the energies of the human souls.

The vibrational frequencies of the quantum energies are also based on the thoughts of the soul because they vibrate based on what is being provided by the QE Light; and the QE Light provides based on the vibration frequencies of the souls' thoughts. Thus, in the Corporeal World, it is as if the vibrational frequency of the souls exists all over the universe. This is also so because, in the pure original state, the QE Light is vibrating at the same frequency as the energies of the soul and the quantum energies are only the non-light aspect of the QE Light.

The quantum energies cannot be seen as being separate from the QE Light, just as the body and soul cannot be separated from each other while a person is alive. Since the quantum energies, in the Quantum World, are the other half of the QE Light, and the QE Light flows along with the frequencies of the soul, it is as if both (the QE Light and quantum energies) are flowing along with the frequencies of the soul. Hence, it is as if the frequency of the sound of OM is also there in the

Quantum World.

Since the QE Light is closely entangled with the energies of the soul, it can be said that the frequency of the sound of OM is also there in the Quantum World, in the second half cycle, because the QE Light energies are coming into the space of the visible universe which is in a sunken state within the Quantum World; as a result of which there is an expansion of the visible universe. The sound of OM is also there in the Quantum World because the energies of the souls are using dimensions in the Quantum World, during the second half cycle.

During the Confluence Age, when the BKs send God's energies into the Corporeal World, God's energies are also sent to the QE Light since the QE Light is part of the Corporeal World. As the QE Light energies sink into the visible universe, due to the sinking of the old world, God's vibrational frequencies go deeper down into the visible universe, i.e. they go deeper down into the Quantum World, in order to reach the QE Light that is sinking. As a consequence, all energies in the universe (including those in the Quantum World) easily begin to resonate with God's frequencies, and so the world will transform into the perfect state. It should be noted that when the QE Light transforms, even the quantum energies will transform. Thus, when God's energies transform the QE Light into the divine state, it is as if even the quantum energies are being transformed into the divine state. When the QE Light and quantum energies have transformed, even what is provided in the Real World will be in the pure perfect state.

Since the QE Light and quantum energies exist to provide the stage for the human souls, in the Corporeal World, people should be able to get whatever they want. However, in the second half cycle, people find it difficult to have their desires fulfilled because of the weak state of the human souls and due to numerous bad karmic accounts.

If you were settling karmic accounts, your thoughts and visualisation would not resonate so well with what is in the 2D SWD and World Drama deep within the soul because these will be in resonance with the frequencies of the karmic accounts. As a consequence, you will find it difficult to get what you want.

Chapter 28: Law of Attraction

You attract what you think, visualise, feel, believe, etc. through the Law of Attraction. If your thoughts are positive, you attract positive responses, e.g. if you feel that you have an abundance of wealth, you will attract that and so you will have an abundance of wealth. If your thoughts are negative, for example, if you think that you are poor, you will attract this and so you will be poor.

The Law of Attraction is about how frequencies attract similar frequencies. When we are happy, others around us are influenced to be happy through our vibrations. When we are unhappy, everyone around us is also influenced to become unhappy through our vibrations. All this happens because the frequencies of people will begin to resonate in a similar way. Further, all happy people are attracted to keep each other's company because they are vibrating at similar frequencies; likewise, unhappy people are attracted to keep each other's company for the same reason. Even those with similar believes are attracted to each other because their beliefs are vibrating at similar frequencies. People are influenced in all these ways via the frequencies which are in their aura. Similarly, when you fill your aura with the thoughts and visualisations that you are wealthy, you are filling your aura with the frequencies of wealth; so this:

1. brings about the creation of wealth in your life. It influences the energies of the QE Light etc. to resonate in a similar way to that of the frequencies of wealth and so wealth begins to exist in your life.

2. attracts wealth into your life. It attracts the frequencies of wealth which exists elsewhere to come into your life.

During Kaliyug, the human souls are in the weak ordinary state and so they are capable of using the vices. They are in the impure state when they use the vices. The impure state will only attract the Kaliyug life-style. Thus, in the Kaliyug world, the Law of Attraction does not bring you an abundance of wealth and prosperity; it only brings you an abundance of poverty and misery. What you get through the Law of Attraction is based on whether you are in the pure state or impure state.

At the end of the Silver Age, our frequencies were lowered when we transformed from the divine state to the ordinary state. Even the frequencies of the QE Light were lowered because they also transformed into the ordinary state. However, the QE Light energies remain pure and powerful unless they get exposed to our vices. With time, those human beings who used the vices began to use even lower frequencies than those of the pure QE Light in the QE Light source and QE Light Ocean. The QE Light source and the QE Light Ocean remained pure, identical to how the core of the soul remained pure. Thus, the pure QE Light frequencies could only remain in resonance with the energies from the core of the soul.

Filling the surface of the soul (which is used as the Conscious Self) with negative thoughts and the vices such as anger, unhappiness, fear, greed, etc. will lower the frequencies at the surface of the soul. The QE Light energies, which are exposed to these, will adopt the lower frequencies. While vibrating at these lower frequencies, they only attract poverty and everything else which makes the world a miserable Kaliyug world because:

1. as per the laws in Natures' 2D World Drama, they have to provide the environment based on the state of the human beings.

2. impure QE Light energies resonate with the vices and flow along to fulfil what the vices want. The vices want to reign and so the impure QE light flows along with this and provides a Kaliyug environment so that the vices can reign. Vices reign when people suffer etc.

In the Kaliyug world, the Spiritual Laws and Laws of Nature will be such that everything in the Holographic Universe allows the vices to reign. This is so because everything in the universe flows along with what the souls want; thus, so long as the human souls allow the vices to reign and/or want the vices to reign, everything in the Holographic Universe will be geared to allow the vices to reign.

Based on the Spiritual Laws and Laws of Nature, when one is in the impure state due to using the vices, one only attracts that which is provided in the Kaliyug world, i.e. misery, poverty, the fallen and degraded state, etc. In this weak and impure state, you only get an abundance of wealth and prosperity if it is there in the World Drama. The World Drama will only provide for an abundance of wealth and prosperity:

1. if you had done some good karma in the past.

2. if you are a new soul who has just come from the Soul World.

3. if you are walking into the Golden Aged world.

The World Drama would also be such that, in the Kaliyug world, you only receive that which allows the vices to reign. Hindus, sometimes, say that it is the bad people who easily get money and that the good people do not. Bad people misuse the money and so, the money is used to help the vices to reign. Actually, it is not always like this because good people will receive wealth and prosperity if they had done something good in their past or past lives. In fact, even souls who have just come down from the Soul World are pure and good natured, and they will be enjoying wealth and prosperity.

In the Kaliyug world, the QE Light does not serve you well for attracting an abundance of wealth and prosperity. It provides based on:

1. what should exist as your reality in the Kaliyug world, i.e. poverty etc.

2. your perception of your environment. Thus, what you see as your reality is what you get. What you see and experience around you often overrides what you are visualising etc. because deep within, due to your weak state, you only belief in what you perceive and not in the Law of

Attraction.

The state of the QE Light energies which are exposed to the Conscious Self will reflect what the soul will be provided with through the World Drama. This is so due to the Spiritual Laws, the Laws of Nature and the Law of Karma. When you are in an impure state, you influence the environment and everyone else badly; so what you get will be bad due to the effects of the Law of Karma.

We can attract at the Lower Self level and at a deeper Subconscious Self level. The surface of the soul consists of lower frequencies; the energies of the souls which are deeper within consist of higher frequencies. What we attract as the Lower Self will be bad because:

1. we use the vices or are capable of using the vices, and are not in the pure, powerful state.

2. we are aware of what is around us and, due to this awareness, we only attract that which we are surrounded by.

In accordance with the knowledge of the Brahma Kumaris, the vices are the devil. This will also explain why we attract a hell-like world, when we use the vices. The weak energies of the soul allow the vices to confuse the soul and bring the soul into a miserable state so that the vices can reign. Thus, the frequencies during the weak state, when we use the vices or are capable of using the vices, will only attract failure, misery, poverty and the like. If money comes into one's life, the vices will try to deceive and bring the soul onto the impure path, so that they (the vices) can reign. So one misuses the money and also loses one's happiness, though one has received wealth.

Actually, it is the soul which should reign and the soul's original qualities are the virtues and powers. This means it is the virtues which should reign and not the vices. When the virtues or soul reigns, only a heavenly environment and an abundance of wealth and prosperity are attracted through the Law of Attraction. This is why Mankind enjoys an abundance of wealth and prosperity in the heavenly Golden Aged world.

In the second half cycle, you are in the pure state if you are using one of the deeper Subconscious Selves as the Conscious Self. In the pure state, even if it was the Kaliyug world, you can attract an abundance of wealth and prosperity.

If one was on the spiritual path, one can attract what one wants during the stage when one is the Higher Self. It is easy to use the Higher Self in order to use the Law of Attraction to attract what one wants but it is not that easy to use the god self to get what one wants. This is because, normally, what we attract at the god self level, will be that which exists in the World Drama within the soul.

From the Detailed World Drama, what has to happen goes into the Outlined World Drama. From there it goes into the 2D SWD. From the 2D SWD, what has to be provided for us, are attracted. Further, since the energies of the god self are also entangled with the Kundalini, what needs to be done through the chakras will get done. So frequencies for attraction are sent into the aura to attract that which has to be provided for us. Though what is provided, through the god self, will normally be as per the World Drama, there can be complete success in using the Law of Attraction if one learns to use the energies of the god self to attract abundance.

When the Mid-Confluence Aged people were dropping out of the Higher Universe, they were losing their ability to remain as co-creators while they were in the conscious state. Only their god self continued to remain as a co-creator with the QE Light and quantum energies. This meant that the pure QE Light and quantum energies were no longer staying tuned to the frequencies of their Conscious Self for co-creation. This was because the frequencies which they were using for visualising objects, while thinking, were no longer the same powerfully pure frequencies that were used by the QE Light energies for materialising the objects that existed in the Real World. So the people had turned to meditation so as to stay tuned to the pure, powerful frequencies in the

Cosmic Consciousness. Current day people will also have to maintain a pure and powerful positive stage, during visualisations, in order to get what they want.

By remaining virtuous and maintaining positive thoughts, one uses the higher frequencies. So even the QE Light energies, around the energies of the soul, vibrate with these higher frequencies; as a consequence of this, one can get tuned to the higher frequencies (of the QE Light in the higher dimensions) which are used to initiate what exists in the Real World. As a result, an abundance of wealth etc. can be attracted through visualisations etc. The greater the loveful and virtuous state one is in, the easier it is to stay tuned to the higher frequencies of the QE Light in the higher dimensions and the greater one's ability to attract that which enables one to live a heavenly life. This is why it is the Golden Aged people who would be able to attract what they want, most easily.

Love, which flows into the aura, also helps to attract through the Law of Attraction because love attracts. So remaining loveful will help to bring success to the frequencies which are in your aura. The love which I am referring to is pure love. Powerful, pure love can exist in one's aura through absorbing God's Love into oneself because:

1. one's own energies (in the aura and soul) transform into powerful energies through being exposed to God's energies, and

2. God's loveful energies can remain in the soul and aura, during the Confluence Age.

The virtuous and powers are one's power of silence. Magic can be done through this power of silence. The pure, divine virtues and powers, of the Confluence Aged souls and those walking in, have greater magical abilities because they have been energised by God's energies. However, along with the virtuous state, you must have a desire or visualisation to get something.

In the first half cycle, people do not normally have desires. They just live, and they get whatever they want and need through the Law of Attraction since the energies of the soul are powerful, pure and divine. However, if they had a desire, they will get what they want because they are filled with pure and divine virtues and powers. Those walking in will be able to attract an abundance of wealth and prosperity since:

1. they have to remain pure and virtuous for the walking in process.

2. the Golden Aged stage will attract the Golden Aged state, i.e. an abundance of wealth, prosperity etc.

Those walking in are developing greater abilities to attract an abundance of wealth and prosperity because the energies of the soul are transforming into divine energies which have even higher frequencies than the ordinary energies of the soul. Those who walk in will have pure desires which get materialised for world benefit, through the Law of Attraction. However, those who walk in can also have other kinds of desires since they are still capable of being influenced by the vices. Ultimately, even if they got something which was not based on pure desires, what they get will be beneficially taken into the new Golden Aged world with them.

Two crucial factors which influence what we get through the Law of Attraction are 'emotions' and 'thoughts'. In the Kaliyug World, during the impure state, the emotions and thoughts attract misery, poverty and a hell-like world. In the pure state, they attract an abundance of wealth and prosperity.

Since emotions attract, the following will help you to attract an abundance of wealth and prosperity through the Law of Attraction:

1. remaining virtuous while visualising, thinking etc.

2. having positive feelings that you do have an abundance of what you want.

3. being grateful for all that which you have been given.

4. having faith that you are getting an abundance of what you want.

Feeling happy that you are living in the Golden World, where there is abundance and prosperity, will also attract this to you. Thus, you will be living in a heavenly place and enjoying an abundance of heavenly blessings. You would be more successful in your visualisations if you experience the joy of walking in, or of living in the Golden Aged world, before doing your visualisations to attract what you want through the Law of Attraction.

The most powerful instrument which you have is your Power of Thought. As is your thought, so is the result. Your thoughts reflect the state of your consciousness. Powerful thoughts are created when one is in a powerful stage.

It is with just a thought that those walking in go into the Higher Universe. It is also with just a thought that the Mid-Confluence Aged gods had come into the dense Real World which existed in the Lower Universe. Since the materialisation process begins with just a thought, it can be said that the universe is created through a thought. Materialisation also begins with a thought where the Law of Attraction is concerned.

Even beliefs, intentions and faith influence what we get through the Law of Attraction. If you believe that what you see around you is how it will be, that is what you get. If you believe that you have an abundance of wealth etc., you get that.

'Intention' can be said to be a thought which gives clarity to another thought. Thus, visualising or having thoughts with strong intentions help to materialise the visualisation or thoughts, i.e. it helps with manifestation through the Law of Attraction. For example if you have the intention to succeed in your visualisation, you will.

Our world is changed based on our beliefs, faith and intentions. Thus, have faith that you are walking in and that you are having an abundance of whatever you want due to the walking in process.

When energies flow into the aura, through the Root Chakra and other chakras, they also flow along with our beliefs, faith, intentions, desires, thoughts etc. which are in the aura. Thus, it is easier to attract wealth when our thoughts are positive, even though our chakras are activated to give us wealth.

The Sixth Chakra (Ajna chakra) emits frequencies, based on our beliefs, and these affect:

1. the frequencies emitted from the other chakras, and also

2. all the other QE Light and quantum energies in the aura, body and universe.

Thus, through the Ajna Chakra, the frequencies in the aura are influenced to attract abundance. When we keep having positive thoughts of abundance, we are actually giving this message to the QE Light in the Holographic Universe.

We also get guidance through the Ajna Chakra on what to do etc. so as to make our visualisations etc. materialise. Though we get this guidance and act on it, we may not be aware that we are doing something based on this guidance. One may think that one was just doing something.

Souls who have just come down from the Soul World, those who are in the pure state and those walking in will find it easy to get money through just visualising that they have a lot of money because pure energies are used to create the frequencies of money and these energies are able to resonate well with the pure QE Light energies.

As people walk into the Golden Aged world, they begin to use purer frequencies. Thus, their ability to get what they think, desire, visualise etc. improves. Further, as their chakras get activated, the Siddhis that are attained through the walking in process will also help with the manifestation of one's thoughts, etc. For example, when their Root Chakra begins to function well, some of the frequencies that are emitted from the Root Chakra will help them to get an abundance of whatever they want.

When doing the visualisation, if you only want money or gold, there is no need to visualise on how you are to get it. With faith, just visualise that you have the money or gold, and you will be having it through the Law of Attraction because:

1. human souls can act as co-creators in the Corporeal World (along with the QE Light and quantum energies) based on Spiritual Laws and the Laws of Nature.

2. the Kundalini will activate the Root Chakra and other relevant chakras to fulfil our desires since they were destined to fulfil our desires. This is also why when a person visualises that the Kundalini is rising, it will rise so as to fulfil the desires of the person.

3. the World Drama was meant to fulfil the desires of human souls.

You will get what you want through the World Drama because:

1. the Outlined World Drama is entangled and entwined with the 2D SWD, and

2. the Seventh Chakra and 7th auric field bring the energies of the soul near and into the 2D SWD.

Thus, when you constantly fill yourselves with the vibrational frequencies of money (through thoughts, visualisations etc.) your frequencies attract an abundance of money via the 2D SWD.

When frequencies involved with the Law of Attraction, in the aura etc., are pure frequencies that are in resonance with the pure QE Light frequencies, they attract the manifestation process. However, those walking in can be in the impure state where their energies cannot resonate with the pure energies in the Outlined World Drama, 2D SWD and QE Light. Hence, their thoughts, desires etc. cannot be fulfilled.

The fact that you can act as a co-creator by remaining happy and virtuous is a reflection that life was meant to be lived happily, in a virtuous manner. This is also a reason why the virtuous people of the first half cycle easily attract and get what they want.

You can create your reality through seeing yourself as walking into the Golden Aged world. As you keep doing this, your life will change to accommodate this and your life will also get filled with an abundance of wealth and prosperity if that is what you want.

God will also give wealth and help one to get what one wants, especially if they were:

1. walking into the Golden Aged world.

2. involved with world service.

3. involved with worship etc.

Whatever God gives is also attracted, via the Law of Attraction, through the frequencies. More on this is explained in the next chapter.

Chapter 29: Frequencies for Abundance

It should be noted that when I refer to the 'frequencies for abundance', I am referring to all the frequencies of money, wealth and other stuff which make you rich or through which your desires are fulfilled (whether for a better job, home, name, fame, etc.). Through the Law of Attraction, the frequencies for abundance attract:

1. what is provided for the person through the chakras.

2. via the Seventh Chakra, 7th auric field and 2D SWD

3. via the Outlined World Drama and 2D SWD.

4. what God has provided through the QE Light (Cosmic Consciousness).

5. what the person wants, desires etc. (i.e. our thoughts and emotions attract).

When we need to be provided an abundance of wealth, as per the World Drama, the frequencies for abundance are emitted from the chakras so that wealth is attracted into our lives. What is in the Detailed World Drama will also emerge into the Outlined World Drama, and the frequencies there which were meant to provide an abundance of wealth are the frequencies for abundance which will attract via the 2D SWD etc. When God gives us an abundance of wealth, we are provided it through the frequencies for abundance which will attract an abundance of wealth into our lives. When we keep thinking, visualising etc. that we have an abundance of wealth, prosperity etc., these accumulate within the soul. If they are strong and/or powerful visualisations etc., they attract as the frequencies for abundance. Thus, if we visualise that we have money, our visualisation will have the frequencies of money in it. If we keep visualising that we have money, there will be a lot of these 'frequencies of money' created and stored in the Memory Bank within the soul. Since there are a lot, they begin to attract as the frequencies for abundance and so money comes into our lives.

One's thoughts and emotions are also reflected in the auric fields and they are also influencing everything in the universe from there, especially if they are in the 7th auric field. The frequencies for abundance are not just emitted into one auric field. They are emitted:

1. into the auric fields where the thoughts and emotions exist,

2. into the first auric field from the Root Chakra, and

3. into the 7th auric field from the Seventh Chakra.

Even the frequencies emitted into the 4th auric field, via the Heart Chakra, attracts through the Law of Attraction because love attracts.

It should be noted that if you were not on the spiritual path, your thoughts are projected into the third auric field and your emotions are in the second auric field. If you were on the spiritual path, your thoughts and emotions are in the higher auric fields. Further, everything that is within the soul is also there in the various auric fields within the aura, and the chakras can also fill the whole aura with these frequencies for abundance. Since the aura surrounds the human body, it will be as if we are surrounded by the frequencies for abundance. We can get what we want through the resonance of these frequencies with the QE Light frequencies in the universe.

Since one's thoughts, desires, etc. also exist in one's auric fields, one's frequencies for abundance can easily influence what exists in the 2D SWD when one is spiritually more powerful, and so is using the higher auric fields. Since the higher auric fields are closer to the 2D SWD, the thoughts, desires etc. in the higher auric fields will easily influence what is in the 2D SWD, and so, one can easily get what one wants even if one was not doing visualisations etc. to get it.

The people in the first half cycle are also close to the QE Light energies since they are living in the SWL and are using auric fields which are close to the 2D SWD. Hence, they can easily get what they want. They get what they want because their thoughts are created by pure powerful energies which have great abilities to attract as the frequencies for abundance.

The energies of the Golden Aged souls have a pure sound of silence aspect which resonates as 'one' with the pure sounds of silence of the 2D SWD and all other QE Light energies. Thus, it is as if one's desires and thoughts become 'one' with these too. As a result, one's desires, thoughts etc. are fulfilled through these resonating frequencies. They are also fulfilled because the Divine Laws make sure that the people enjoy happiness in every possible way. Those walking in are walking into this perfect scenario. Thus, their thoughts begin to have greater abilities to act as the frequencies for abundance.

Those walking in use higher dimensions which are closer to the 2D SWD, QE Light Ocean and QE Light source because the Golden Aged world is getting uplifted into the Higher Universe, and they are also in the QE Light dimensions. Thus, their thoughts, etc. will easily influence the frequencies in the QE Light, everywhere in the universe, to resonate in a similar way. They can easily get what they want since they are in resonance with these pure QE Light energies.

Those walking in can get what they want, even if they are not doing any visualisations, because they are beginning to use the higher auric fields. Since the frequencies of their thoughts are powerful, in the higher auric fields, these can act as the frequencies for abundance; thus, they easily influence the frequencies of the QE Light to resonate in a similar manner.

If those walking in have not been lifted into the higher dimensions as yet, they can meditate to go into those higher dimensions. When one does visualisations while using these higher dimensions and auric fields, one can easily get what one wants for the same reason, through the Law of Attraction, since what is in the mind is also there in the higher auric fields as powerful frequencies for abundance that can easily attract.

When the frequencies in the aura etc. begin to vibrate at the same frequencies which they are exposed to, they will amplify the effects of the frequencies which they have been exposed to. Thus, if the frequencies of the energies of the soul are those that attract an abundance of wealth, the aura will begin to act like a powerful magnet that attracts an abundance of wealth. The human aura acts like a magnet based on the frequencies that are within the aura. Since it is our thoughts, visualisations etc. which affect the frequencies in the aura, etc. by bringing them into resonance to a particular set of frequencies, it is as if the energies of the soul can act as a powerful magnet. When the soul, aura and all other relevant energies of the person are resonating at frequencies for an abundance of wealth and prosperity, it will seem as if the person (including the aura which surrounds him) is like a powerful magnet that attracts wealth and prosperity.

Just as we can attract others to us and influence them to feel the virtue which we feel through the frequencies in our aura, we can attract something which we want through filling our aura with the frequencies for abundance. These frequencies, which we have in our aura, will influence the QE Light energies to vibrate at that same frequency and so the quantum energies will provide what we want.

The synchronisation of frequencies is facilitated by the Law of Attraction, so that they resonate as the frequencies for abundance. The energies in the QE Light Mind adopt the frequencies of the thoughts etc. in the mind of the soul, i.e. there is synchronisation of frequencies. Thus, the energies in the QE Light Mind begins to resonate as the frequencies for abundance since the frequencies of the thoughts etc. were frequencies for abundance. Then, the frequencies in the QE Light Body adopt and synchronise with the frequencies that are in the QE Light Mind. These frequencies in the mind of the soul, QE Light Mind and QE Light body also influence the vibrations in the aura and the vibrations that are being emitted from the chakras. So there is a further synchronisation of frequencies. All these make it easy for one's thoughts etc. to get materialised since all these energies begin to resonate as the frequencies for abundance. They provide the environment to attract the manifestation of one's desires. When the most accurate frequencies are emitted from the soul, they influence the attraction of wealth into one's life since all the energies in the universe get tuned in for the manifestation of what we want.

The energies from the universe are continuously flowing:

1. through your feet to go out from the top of your head and also

2. through the head to go out through the feet.

Through these flows of energies, the QE Light energies of the Holographic Universe are constantly becoming aware of what is in you and your aura, via the frequencies for abundance, and they also begin to resonate at the same frequencies.

When we think or feel something, these also exist as frequencies in the aura (at the same time as the person thinks or feels it in the mind) because the person is living in the Holographic Universe in unity with all other frequencies that exist in the Corporeal World. Through these frequencies in the aura, we are connected or entangled with the environment via the QE Light. However, we are only connected to the universe if the frequencies in our aura consist of powerful frequencies. So it is only the frequencies for abundance, in our aura, which can be materialised in our environment.

All we have to do is to create the thoughts while in a spiritually high stage and the universe will do the rest. We don't even have to bother about the details of how we are going to get the wealth because that can be dealt with by what is in the Holographic Universe.

All mental activities have an electromagnetic aspect to them, via the QE Light and quantum energies. Even the energies of the aura are electromagnetic. Thus, all these energies can function together and they can also resonate with each other's frequencies. They tune in to each other's frequencies very well to carry out the functions which they have to perform so that the soul can live as he pleases. However, the soul is only able to enjoy these benefits if its energies were powerful energies and so the thought, etc. act as 'frequencies for abundance'.

The QE Light energies can also influence the soul since even the energies of the soul resonate with the QE Light energies. For example, when the Root Chakra and other relevant chakras are activated for providing an abundance of wealth to the person, the frequencies that are released through them are the frequencies which attract money etc. These frequencies for abundance influence the frequencies of the soul and so, together, the QE Light and the energies of the soul play the role of the creators to attract money into one's life, etc. Even the activation of the Crown Chakra can help to bring in money through this way. The Crown Chakra can be used to attract abundance through the QE Light Mind, 2D SWD and aura.

When the Crown Chakra is activated, specialities and abilities are received by a person depending on what the person wants and also based on all the circumstances of the case. So if one wishes to live an enlightened life, the Crown Chakra will be used to assist the person on the spiritual path. However, one can also get wealth through the Crown Chakra via the frequencies for abundance that are emitted from the Crown Chakra. This is also why some gurus and ancient sages had easily received and amassed wealth.

The Crown Chakra has numerous vortices within it. Different vortices are used for different abilities and specialities. Specific vortices are activated based on what is needed by the person. Since there are numerous vortices in the Crown Chakra, the people who use the Crown Chakra can be satisfied through so many different ways.

The people in the first half cycle will also be able to get whatever they want, including affluence and gold, because their consciousness will be in the Crown chakra. Their powerful frequencies will act as the frequencies for abundance to influence the QE Light in the 2D SWD etc. since their consciousness is in the Crown Chakra.

In truth, all the chakras in the body, which are in an activated state, will help to fulfil the desires of the person through one way or another, including attracting wealth. When one is doing the visualisation so that one can use the money for service, the higher chakras might be used to bring the riches to the person. However, in the second half cycle, since people are living in the dense Kaliyug Real World, the Root Chakra plays a significant role for attracting money. So when the Root Chakra gets activated, one will find that one can easily get a fortune. In the second half cycle, if a person needs to be given an abundance of wealth, as per the World Drama, the person's Root Chakra would be naturally activated, as per the World Drama. The activation of the Root Chakra also helps one to be prosperous.

The desires of the soul are fulfilled through the Root Chakra, via the resonance of frequencies. The QE Light that comes through the Root Chakra to provide abundance will begin to resonate with the energies of the soul. So, together, they play the role of the creator. Everything happens as per the World Drama and so the chakras only get activated as per the World Drama. However, where those walking in are concerned, the Root Chakra will surely be getting activated as per the World Drama.

One must not associate the Root Chakra to the Lower Universe and to a non-spiritual life. Everyone needs to use the Root Chakra. The Root Chakra assists the soul to use some of the virtues, etc. while living the life (whether the person is on the spiritual path or not). The Root Chakra is also needed for living the life in the Real World and 3D SWD. In addition to all these, through the Root Chakra, frequencies are emitted for abundance of wealth and material possessions. These frequencies will easily influence the other frequencies in the aura to resonate at frequencies that attract abundance and at the same they help to materialise the frequencies for abundance.

When the frequencies for abundance are produced through chakras to fill our aura, wealth, etc. are attracted to us because everything in the Corporeal World acts in a united manner to provide based on the frequencies that surrounds a person. We live in a world of vibrations, and everything happens based on the frequencies which these vibrations have. We, as vibrations, can influence the vibrations and frequencies:

1. that are emitted through the chakras.

2. that exist in the aura.

Thus, we can surround ourselves with the frequencies for abundance so that we easily amass wealth etc. The Law of Attraction satisfies the thoughts etc. and so we can attract.

Since what is in our mind and memory bank is also there in the aura, the aura consists of a variety of frequencies that can attract materialisation if they were frequencies for abundance. These frequencies which you have in your aura and mind can also attract frequencies (of objects etc.) to come to you from elsewhere. For example, when you visualise that you have an abundance of wealth, others in the Corporeal World catch the subtle vibration and resonate accordingly. Thus, they will do something which will make sure that you have it. This is because we are all supposed to be living our lives in a co-operative manner in the World Drama, so souls will be subtly influenced to fulfil the desires, needs etc. of others. One way through which all human souls are connected is also through the frequencies for an abundance of what is desired, visualised, needed, etc. Thus, if someone wants monetary gain and another is willing to give money in return for something (or for some reason) the vibrations of money etc. is in both of their minds or/and Inner Minds. As a result, they get connected to each other via the 2D SWD, Cosmic Consciousness, World-Wide Collective Consciousness and/or aura through having the same frequencies that will begin to resonate with each other. The QE Light energies help to connect all the souls together, in this way, since they provide the environment for all souls. So one's desires get fulfilled by others.

Though all human souls participate in the World-Wide Collective

Consciousness, there are also other levels of Collective Consciousness involving different groups. For example, all people of a specific religion will be participating in the Collective Consciousness of that religion. Similarly, all those who are body-conscious will easily connect with each other since their frequencies are similar. It will be as if they have a Collective Consciousness of their own. All those who are pure will also find it easier to connect with each other since they are using similar frequencies. It is also as if they have a Collective Consciousness of their own unless they are pure due to being on a specific religious/spiritual path.

Those on the spiritual path are usually grouped into the Collective Consciousness of their religion. If there are others in their spiritual/religious group who are involved with attracting an abundance of wealth etc., their auras will merge with each other to assist each other to bring abundance into all their lives. There will be frequencies for abundance in their merged auras which will assist all of them to receive abundance. Their QE Light Minds, etc. will also be used to attract abundance through the Collective Consciousness which they are participating in (including through the Cosmic Consciousness and World-Wide Collective Consciousness).

All those who belong to a Collective Consciousness, which is involved with getting an abundance of financial assets etc., can get the benefits of the frequencies of abundance which will exist in the merged auras of all those in the Collective Consciousness. If the members of the Collective Consciousness are also involved with assisting each other to become wealthy etc., they will also be helping each other via their merged auras. Thus, if a person has the frequencies for abundance, the pure frequencies of others will be influenced to resonate with the pure frequencies of the soul who has the frequencies for abundance; hence they will be influenced to provide the help required by the other for getting abundance.

Those who are on the non-spiritual path will find it very easy to attract similar natured people through the lower chakras because non-spiritual people are using these lower chakras to live a non-spiritual life. This means that they are assisting each other to bring misery, poverty and failure into each other's life.

Spiritual people can easily attract an abundance of wealth, prosperity etc. through the higher chakras and it is easy for others to have the frequencies for abundance when they are blessed by these pure souls. When a pure soul blesses that you should have an abundance of wealth and prosperity, the pure soul's pure frequencies influence your vibrations to resonate in a similar way and so you become pure too. In addition, since the pure frequencies of the pure soul initiates the creation of the pure frequencies for abundance and transfers these frequencies to you (via the blessing) you can attract an abundance of wealth, prosperity etc. These frequencies are transferred to you when your frequencies adopt the frequencies for abundance through resonance with the 'pure frequencies for abundance of the pure soul'.

Even the help from God comes in a similar manner. However, during the second half cycle, God assists through the QE Light energies because souls are only exposed to the QE Light energies and not to God's energies directly. Thus, the frequencies for abundance are sent from God to you via Ether. Then, since the QE Light energies are resonating with those same frequencies, your energies also begin to resonate with those same frequencies. Thus, together, you and the QE Light bring about the manifestation of wealth etc. into your life. However, it is God who had initiated this. Sometimes, the frequencies sent from God only influence the QE Light to initiate the creation process and your frequencies may not be involved with the process for creation. We are living in a variety play and so we can receive help in a variety of ways. In the Confluence Age, God's energies can influence our energies to resonate in a similar manner to His vibrations, which are providing the frequencies for abundance, since we are exposed to God's energies directly. Thus, we attract what has to be given to us.

It is the energies which come from the higher dimensions, i.e. from the QE Light source, QE Light Ocean etc. which will help to manifest what we want. These energies are pure energies and so they vibrate at very high frequencies while initiating the process for manifesting stuff in the 3D SWD and Real World. Our energies have to be able to vibrate at those higher frequencies so as to resonate with them to as to bring about the manifestation of what we want. Our energies can only vibrate at those higher frequencies when we are in the pure virtuous state. When our energies vibrate at those frequencies, then the QE Light energies which are involved with the manifestation process will also be vibrating at those frequencies; thus, they easily manifest what we want. The energies of the soul and QE Light energies influence each other, as the Cosmic Consciousness, during the manifestation process.

The QE Light in the Cosmic Consciousness will definitely initiate the process for providing us with abundance if we have an abundance of specific frequencies, e.g. the frequency of wealth. An abundance of these frequencies of wealth are the frequencies of abundance. When you are surrounded by these frequencies of abundance which were meant to give you wealth, you will get wealth.

Those who are walking in will also have the frequencies for abundance in their aura through God's help. In addition, as per the World Drama, if it is requisite that they be given wealth, the relevant frequencies for abundance are produced by the chakras (via the influence of the Kundalini) and these frequencies go into the aura to act like a magnet that attracts.

The frequencies of our emotions etc. influence our purity and spiritual state. For example, when we are happy, we are in a purer and higher spiritual state. This helps the frequencies for abundance to exist in our aura etc. Since the purity and spiritual state is improved, what is in the mind can easily influence the frequencies in the Outlined World Drama to resonate in a similar manner. This in turn will influence what is provided through the 2D SWD. However, what is in the Detailed World Drama will also influence the frequencies in the Outlined World Drama, energies of the soul, QE Light etc. Thus, what we get will also be based on what exists in the Detailed World Drama. However, normally, if we are involved with the practices for an abundance of wealth etc., it is because we will succeed, one day, in getting what we want.

Since the QE Light energies influence our frequencies, when they surround us with the frequencies for abundance, the energies of the soul are influenced to have the same frequencies. Even if the energies of the soul are not influenced to have the frequencies for abundance, it is okay because we are provided with abundance when we are surrounded by the frequencies for abundance. However, normally, the energies influence each other. Thus, the energies of the soul will also be influenced to have the frequencies for abundance. If we did have the frequencies for abundance, the possibilities of receiving are greater or we will receive more because human souls are meant to act as co-creators with the QE Light and quantum energies. If the energies of the soul did not have the frequencies for abundance, but we are surrounded by the frequencies for abundance as per the World Drama, then, what we receive may not be that much.

Chapter 30: Resistances and Blocks

In the second half cycle, when you do meditation to get abundance, sometimes, you will feel as if there is a resistance which prevents you from being blessed with what you want. At other times, just as circumstances are such that you are about to succeed in getting what you want, the circumstances suddenly change and you do not achieve it. It is as if something blocks it from fulfilment. If the Law of Attraction is not bringing you an abundance of wealth and prosperity, it is because you are not a soul who has just come down from the Soul World. Thus, due to one or more of the following reasons, you are not able to get what you want:

1. Chakras/vortices are not activated for abundance.

2. It is a test paper since you are on the spiritual path.

3. You have taken previous births in which you may have done actions which you have to settle for, i.e. you have bad karmic accounts to settle for.

4. You are in a weak state where you can entertain the vices or you are using the vices.

5. Your current thoughts and beliefs may be negative.

6. All your negative thoughts, which had developed from the time you are young, may come into the way to prevent it from happening.

7. Your awareness of what exists around you is like a resistance to what you want because you belief that what you see is what can exist. You have formed the view that this is the reality.

8. There are no frequencies for abundance in your aura etc. If the frequencies are not strong or/and powerful, it is not an influential factor.

9. It is not there in the Detailed World Drama for it to happen and so the god self does not provide for it to be materialised via the Outlined World Drama which is entangled with the 2D SWD.

10. The QE Light, Kundalini and quantum energies are resisting by not doing anything to get it materialised because it is not there in the 2D SWD.

11. Others resist from giving you a helping hand, through Cosmic Consciousness and World-Wide Collective Consciousness, because it is not there in the World Drama.

If you were trying very hard to get something through visualisations etc. and you were not getting much, it reflects that there is something blocking your abilities to act as a co-creator. For example, your Root Chakra might be blocked or not functioning properly. As a result of which you will find it very difficult to achieve your goals and manifest what you want whether it is a better financial position, better job or something else. When the chakras (especially the vortices for abundance which are in the Root Chakra) are activated, the Siddhis that are attained will also help with the manifestation of one's desires, etc. So you will find it very easy to get what you want. You will not have the feeling that there is a 'resistance' when you are visualising.

You might also receive a test paper if you are on the spiritual path. So you might be blocked from want fulfilment. Test papers give you an opportunity to remove all your negative thoughts through the power of yoga and to make sure that you are in a pure state. So if you have not already been blessed with what you wanted through prayer, visualisations, etc., do not let that create negative thoughts within you. You have to pass the test paper through continuing to have faith while maintaining your happiness.

If the resistance or block is due to your karmic accounts which are preventing you from getting what you visualise, you will be able to get what you want when the karmic accounts are removed. Those walking in can have their karmic accounts:

1. burnt off through the purification process.

2. removed through the settling process.

3. kept at bay since they are walking into the Golden Aged world. During Judgement Day, if they have not completely purified themselves via their link to God or through the settling process, the spiritual income which they receive, for getting involved with the walking in process, will be used to off-set their karmic accounts before they walk into the materialised Golden Aged world. BKs, who are walking in, can have their karmic accounts burnt off, during Judgement Day, before walking into the Golden Aged world. They, including their bodies, will be given a lot of protection during this process. Without any efforts on their own, they will be brought beyond, for the settling process, before being sent back to walk into the Golden Aged world.

If those walking in wish this, the spiritual income which they get, for helping with world transformation, can also be used to reduce the effects of the settling processes or to off-set their karmic accounts so that they can easily get what they want. However, it should be noted that one loses the opportunity to become spiritually powerful through using one's spiritual income. Further, one can become very powerful through the purification process and so this would be the best way to remove karmic accounts.

By July 2016, I was quite successful in bringing an abundance of wealth into my life. Then on the 18th of July 2016 (since I was so used to absorbing God's energies from above) I had subtly stretched out above me so as to grab what was above me and bring it to me. I was editing this book while I was doing that, so I did not really look at what I was grabbing to bring down towards me. I had actually grabbed the energies for the settling process and was bringing that towards me from the 2D SWD. It was as those energies, which looked like dark patches of energies, were pouring down into the area above and near my head that I began to realise that something bad was coming down to badly influence what I get.

When I stretched out above, it was as if I had stretched out my subtle hand to bring what was there to me. The subtle hand actually represented my own energies of the soul. These energies were touched by the frequencies of the settling process which existed in the 2D SWD; so those frequencies had influenced the resonance of energies in the aura. It was obvious that they had changed my luck from good to bad. After a while, the dark patch disappeared. However, it must have already done what it was supposed to do and this may have been why everything began to go wrong after that and I began to have financial losses. From the time when I saw the dark patch dropping, I began filling my aura with the frequencies for abundance, again, through my thoughts, faith, intentions etc. By the next day, the situation was slowly changing and my luck was improving.

Then, on the 20th of July 2016, without realising what I was doing, I had pulled a little of the settling process from above into my aura again. I began to wonder if my god self was doing it as per the World Drama or if I was doing it as the Confluence Aged Spiritual Effort-Maker Self because I have a deep desire to become completely pure so that I can be ready for world transformation.

Despite the abovementioned experiences of mine, have faith that when you surround yourself with a pure positive aura that is filled with the frequencies for abundance, the settling process will not affect you even though it is there in the 2D SWD. What has to be settled is there in the 2D SWD because it involves what has happened between many people. That settling process will not affect you for so long as your aura is pure and filled with the frequencies for abundance.

When doing visualisations for attracting abundance, if one was using the weak energies of the soul, the energies can seem so incompetent, like lazy energies which are incapable of doing it in a competent manner. It might also give wrong information to confuse you, if it was serving the vices. For example, if you were visualising to get something done, it might tell you that it has already been done and that there is nothing more to do, when in reality, it has not been done. If powerful energies inform this, it might mean that whatever needed to be done 'for getting it done' has already been done and so one has to just wait for it to happen. It might not happen immediately because of the settling process. But when weak energies tell you this, it may not be the truth. There may be a possibility that you are getting messages like this because nothing more can be done as per the World Drama. However, don't give up because when the settling process is over, you can get it. So if you want something, have faith that you do have it or that you are currently receiving it and keep making efforts to remain in the pure, powerful state.

You may also be experiencing a resistance because you are doing the visualisation based on the influence of the vices or you are using the vices while doing the visualisation etc. Normally, it is the pure energies which are involved with providing what exists in the World Drama which we are participating in. If you are using the impure energies, while visualising, your energies will not be able to get near these pure QE Light energies. Hence, you may feel that you are blocked or prevented from getting what you want.

When you use the vices, the QE Light which is close to the energies of the soul becomes impure and so through resonance, the message of what the soul wants cannot be sent to the QE Light in the higher dimensions which initiate the creation process. Even for this reason, you may feel a resistance.

Further, there are QE Light energies which are coming from the higher dimensions, and going through the 2D SWD, before coming into the Unified Field so as to materialise what has to exist in the Real World. Through black magic, the information which they have can be camouflaged to give you what you want. If you are not involved with black magic, you will be blocked from getting what you want through this way. On the other hand, it is not advisable to get involved with black magic because what is given through it would only help the vices to reign. You would also be accumulating more sinful actions which need to be settled.

Your thoughts attract. So what you think is what you will be surrounded by, whether you want that or not. Thus, do not think about what you do not want. Just think about what you want. This way you do not attract that which you do not want and only attract that which you want. If you think that you do not want an apple, you will be getting an apple because in your thought you have the frequencies of the apple. For the same reasons, do not wish that you were not in a specific situation and do not be unhappy about anything.

Stay happy and take life easy. Learn to be happy no matter what you are faced with. Be grateful for all that which you have been given. Have the feeling that you are getting all that which you want and appreciate all the stuff that has been brought to you, even if the amount was only small. As you keep doing this, your feelings of appreciation and gratefulness will slowly build up and so, you will be receiving more.

In May 2016, when I was visualising that I have an abundance of money, I was finding a lot of coins all over the place in my house. This may have happened as a result of my visualisations because other incidences (which were bringing in money) were also happening around that time. One should not dislike the situation where one was only receiving coins. There should be pure love for everything, including money (whether it is a small amount or a huge amount). Pure love is love without any attachment involved. If one was in a detached, soul conscious stage through using the BK knowledge, one would be experiencing pure love for everything. The problem is, often, people on the spiritual path are of the view that spiritual people and/or good people should not have love for money. This attitude is wrong because it is as if you do not have pure love for the QE Light and quantum energies which provide the money.

Pay more attention to how you think, speak, feel etc. because there may be some negativity in them. The following negative thoughts and feelings are like subtle instructions to keep money away from you:

1. the view that money is bad or that money is the root of all evils.

2. feeling guilty that you want money.

3. the view that you do not need more than what is needed to survive.

4. the view that you 'do not have enough money'.

5. fears that if you had a lot of money, others might try to take it away from you through one way or another.

Make sure that you are not judging yourself or anything else based on your beliefs or on other beliefs that have been developed by Mankind from time to time. Sometimes, you will be having very subtle views and beliefs about something, and you will be given based on these, even if it was not what you wanted. Since your world is provided based on your beliefs, you have to keep a check on your beliefs.

Though you may be thinking positive now and so you have the view that you are rich, in the past, this may not have been your view. Your old beliefs and views may have been that you were limited in nature and that you could not change the situation which you were in. The problem may be that you cannot let go of all these previous limiting beliefs or they may consist of very strong impressions which are in your Memory Bank. These limiting old beliefs would also be there in your aura since a copy of what is in the Memory Bank is also there in your aura. From the aura and soul, the frequencies of these beliefs will influence all other relevant frequencies, even though you are not aware that this is happening and even though you are not aware that you are still being influenced by these old beliefs.

The negative thoughts and beliefs which you had formed in the past can be removed through the purification process and the walking in process. In addition, constantly keep positive thoughts now because it will increase the volume of positive thoughts in the Memory Bank and aura.

This, then, makes the earlier negative thoughts insignificant if they have not been removed through the purification process.

Do not lose hope and keep maintaining the positive view that you are wealthy etc. Change yourself and everything changes. This means concentrate on remaining happy and being a detached observer through using the BK knowledge. Do not try to change what is in the World Drama, just watch it as a detached observer; but concentrate on changing your thoughts and beliefs. The World Drama is mighty; we cannot change it but we can change ourselves and as we change, the World Drama changes. See what kind of situation you are in, after a few years of practicing this.

Do not scrutinise and look to see if you are getting anything thorough the Law of Attraction. Just believe that you are getting it and remain a detached observer.

Keep remembering that you are walking in. As you walk in, you are acquiring the ability to get what you want. Stop looking at the situation which you are in and concentrate on what you are achieving through using the practices to walk in. Learn to watch everything as a detached observer. Through all this, you can adopt the pure frequencies of what you are seeking in your life and they will materialise in your life. As you keep making spiritual efforts, with time, your beliefs will change and that will also help you to get what you want. As your beliefs change, your environment and the situation which you are in will slowly change. Just have faith that you are getting an abundance of money/gold while you remain a spiritual effort maker, and the money/gold will come on its own or it will find a way to reach you.

Sometimes, the problem is that there are no frequencies for abundance in your aura etc. As a result, nothing in the universe will come forward to help you with your wish fulfilment. So you experience a resistance from all those energies which are resisting helping you.

Your aura, which is your energy field that has been provided by the QE

Light, also has your thoughts, emotions, visualisations etc. as frequencies. These frequencies are connected to everything in the universe through the 2D SWD and QE Light. When these frequencies are strong or/and powerful, they will influence positively to bring you what you want. Visualisations, thoughts, emotions, beliefs, intentions, faith etc. can all help to provide stronger frequencies for abundance in your aura. If your emotions and thoughts are not strong, then, your thoughts and emotions will not attract. Only what has been provided through the World Drama will attract via the 2D SWD.

Further, QE Light energies are constantly flowing in and out of our bodies through our chakras, aura and subtle bodily systems. Thus, all QE Light and quantum energies can become aware of what we are thinking and feeling, provided our thoughts etc. consist of frequencies for abundance.

If you face a resistance during meditation or are blocked from getting what you want, keep doing visualisations because, ultimately, these can help to materialise what you want through:

1. the Outlined World Drama and 2D SWD which are both entangled.

2. the QE Light Mind and Cosmic Consciousness.

3. the Kundalini and chakras.

4. the visualisation going into the aura.

So keep visualising until you get what you want. As you do that, don't keep wondering if you are doing something wrong during your visualisations. This brings you into a weak negative state and so you will not get what you want. The Law of Attraction will not work in your favour. The doubts would also prevent you from getting what you want. Your doubt is like an instruction to the QE Light to the effect, "It will not happen"; and so the QE Light flows along with that.

Despite all that which has been said so far, do not get too carried away with wanting to do visualisations. One should spend most of one's time making efforts to become spiritually powerful while walking into the Golden Aged world. This in turn will bring you into a state where you can get what you want.

If life is very bad and you are not achieving and acquiring, do not worry because you may be a deity soul and so life is very bad for you now as a result of all the wrongs which you had done in all your past births. The Confluence Aged spiritual effort making and/or the walking in process will help to bring you out of this.

Belonging to a belief system which involves bringing abundance into the lives of the believers will help you to have abundance if you belong to that belief system, since the desires of those in the belief system are easily brought to God via the faith in the belief system and through the rituals etc. used in the belief system. The rituals etc. are effective because of the faith of many believers. Thus, the resistances and blocks which you face can be removed. Since the whole world is connected, good vibrations from others in the belief system would also assist to get rid of the resistances and blocks so that you can easily get an abundance of what you want.

The gathering of those who believe in what I have written in this book will also belong to a belief system. Though worship is not done, the strong beliefs held by the gathering will make it a belief system. This will assist to remove any resistance or block which one faces and will also help one to get what one wants. One gets God's help because God helps all those who are in a belief system. However, those using the practices in this book will get greater help from God because:

1. it involves the walking in process.

2. it involves the creation of the Golden Aged world which God has come to establish.

3. those walking in have a link to God.

So enjoy yourself through using the practices in this book, as you see the resistances and blocks being removed and while you walk into the Golden Aged world.

Chapter 31: Loka (World/Dimension)

In this chapter, I am going to explain about the lokas which exist in the Lower Universe. A detailed explanation on what happens in the Higher Universe will only be given in later chapters.

Loka is a Sanskrit word which means world, abode etc. The word 'loka' has also been used to refer to dimensions within the Corporeal World. Though these lokas are like different worlds for us, they are not really 'different worlds' similar to the three worlds (Soul World, Angelic World and Corporeal World) in the BK knowledge. Though we can use two or more lokas (dimensions in the Corporeal World) at any time, we cannot go into the Angelic World or the Soul World without God's help. Further, it is only God who can exist in all these three different worlds (Soul World, Angelic World and Corporeal World) at the same time because He is so mighty and powerful. We do not have that ability.

Based on Vedic cosmology, it can be said that the universe consists of fourteen lokas, in descending order, as follows:

1. Satyaloka/Brahmaloka.

2. Tapaloka/Tapoloka.

3. Janaloka.

4. Maharloka.

5. Svarloka/Swargaloka.

6. Bhuvarloka.

7. Bhuloka.

8. Atala.

9. Vitala.

10. Sutala.

11. Talatala.

12. Mahatala.

13. Rasatala.

14. Patala.

The higher seven lokas are the heavenly lokas and the lower seven lokas are the lokas of the underworld/hell. The higher lokas are higher frequency lokas. The lower lokas are lower frequency lokas. So our frequencies become higher as we go into the higher frequency lokas and it gets reduced as we go into the lower frequency lokas. Another way of reiterating this is that when we have the same frequencies as the energies which provide a loka, we are in that loka. So if we utilise the higher frequencies, we are in the higher lokas and if we use the lower frequencies, we are in the lower lokas.

When one becomes pure one avails oneself of higher frequencies; when one is in the impure state one uses lower frequencies. When one begins to use very low frequencies, one begins to use one of the Talas as one's loka. Generally, if one is using the frequencies of one of the Talas, one cannot easily get what one wants. When we employ a higher loka, we use a higher frequency and so our ability to get what we want correspondingly increases.

One uses the lower seven lokas or Talas (Atala, Vitala, Sutala, Talatala, Mahatala, Rasatala and Patala) through using the lower chakras which are below the spine. These lokas are used in the Black Energy Field and Shore of the Ocean of Quantum Energies (Shore of QE Ocean). Thus, during experiences in these lokas, normally, people experience themselves to be in black subtle dimensions; usually, these experiences are in the Black Energy Field.

It should be noted that the Talas have also been used to represent the places underground where some of the Mid-Confluence Aged people began to dwell in. These places were portrayed as the Talas because there was no light underground and the conditions there were not beneficial for living. Further, these ancient people were considered as gods and sages in the higher lokas when they were doing beneficial actions; and they were considered as living in one of the Talas when they were involved with actions that were not spiritual or beneficial. It was later considered that the actions, which they had done underground, did not bring about world benefit. So their underground residences were associated to the Talas for this reason too.

There are also other hell dimensions below, and around, the bottom of the lowest Tala. The experiences in these other hell dimensions are also either in the Black Energy Field or in the Shore of the QE Ocean; normally, they would be in the Shore of the QE Ocean.

In the first half cycle, the Black Energy Field is above the Quantum World (Garbhodaka Ocean), i.e. at the edge of the Quantum World. It is only during the second half cycle that it is in the sunken state within the Garbhodaka Ocean. The Garbhodaka Ocean can be said to be the Quantum World or the Ocean of Quantum Energies (QE Ocean) since both are dark. The Garbhodaka Ocean or QE Ocean is at the bottom of the universe which we are living in (whether we are living in the Higher Universe or in the Lower Universe).

The Unified Field is for providing the Real World. The higher QE Light dimensions (above the Unified Field and 2D SWD) and the lower quantum dimensions (below the Real World) are not involved with providing the Real World, though they are involved with providing pure QE Light or quantum energies which are sent into the Unified Field that provide the Real World. These higher and lower dimensions are also involved with providing a subtle loka environment for experiences.

In the Holographic Universe, the higher lokas are in the higher dimensions, and the lower lokas are in the lower quantum dimensions. One can be in one of these lokas based on the belief system which one uses and based on one's spiritual stage. So there can be so many subtle lokas (worlds) within these dimensions.

The higher and lower lokas, which were provided for by the ancient people, reflected how, in the second half cycle, you can have good or bad experiences in these different lokas. They reflected how you would be using the lower lokas if you were in an impure stage or did sinful actions, and how you would be availing yourself of a higher loka if you were in a pure stage and did good actions. When you are in an impure stage, the higher chakras do not function well. If you were trying to have subtle experiences while in an impure stage, you would be using the lower chakras during these experiences and you would be in the lower dimensions.

Each loka is like a different planet or world which is separated from the other lokas because each dimension and auric field is different from the others. Just as one moves from one auric field to another or from one dimension to another, one also has to move from one loka to another. It is like this due to the different densities of the lokas.

In this book, I am only going to give a more detailed explanation on the usage of the higher lokas because one needs to use these for getting an abundance of wealth etc.

Actually, as one employs the higher lokas, one is also going deeper and deeper within the soul. Thus, one is getting closer to the god self which is deep within the soul. So one is the causal self while on the spiritual path through using the higher chakras, higher auric fields and higher lokas; and one is the Lower Self while on the non-spiritual path, through using the lower chakras, lower auric fields and lower lokas.

While living one's life on earth, the energies of the soul are constantly going into the auric fields, even though one may not be having an experience in the auric fields. These energies of the soul also act as one's consciousness in the aura. Thus, though one is using the Real World (through the physical body) which everyone else uses, one's consciousness can be in a higher loka that is in a higher auric field. A loka is also the dimension/world in which one's consciousness is in, within the aura. The lokas are the dimensions which are used, in the auric fields and Holographic Universe, during experiences and while living in the Corporeal World. Since one's consciousness is in the loka, one can have an experience in the loka. The loka itself can be experienced within the aura because that is where one's consciousness goes into, to experience 'living' in this world. During experiences, lokas are usually experienced within one's own auric field or within merged auras of people who have the same beliefs. Actually, an experience can be had through:

1. your aura becoming your Holographic Body and so you are in the QE Light dimension or you are in the QE Light and quantum dimension. The QE Light dimension or QE Light and quantum dimension becomes your loka. This loka is not within your aura.

2. your auric field becoming your world, dimension or loka.

3. you having the experience in dimensions within the auric field. These dimensions in the auric fields become your loka. A loka will get created within one's auric field based on all the circumstances.

If one uses one's aura as one's Holographic Body (astral body), the QE Light and Quantum dimensions become one's loka. During such an experience, one can experience the forces of gravity, etc. in the Holographic Universe. However, normally, this is not how we have experiences because we are supposed to be using a mild environment while living and having experiences. Thus, normally, our experiences are in the auric fields.

One should not try to use the aura as one's Holographic Body because when the QE Light and quantum dimensions become one's loka, one will be exposed to their powerful energies, spins of the vortices, etc. This will not be comfortable. In fact, it is quite frightening and one will wonder if one is safe in that dimension. You are the soul and your energies are supposed to be exposed to milder QE light energies which are meant to serve you. These milder QE Light energies exist in your auric fields. So use the auric fields as your loka or, even better still, use dimensions within the auric fields. Normally, people utilise dimensions within the auric fields during their experiences. In the auric fields, one can have a loka which is specifically designed to fulfil one's desires. Though, normally, we do not experience the whole aura as our Holographic Body, the fact that:

1. **our auric fields are in the dimensions of the Holographic Universe** reflects that we are in the dimensions of the Holographic Universe.

2. **our aura is in the Holographic Universe** reflects that we are in the Holographic Universe.

The above reflect that the Holographic Universe and the dimensions in the Holographic Universe can be considered as our loka. As one uses the higher auric fields, it is as if one is going higher and higher up in the Holographic Universe.

Since the auric fields connect the person to everything in the Holographic Universe and the lokas are used within these auric fields, one gets connected to everything in the universe as one uses the lokas. When one avails oneself of the higher lokas, one is closer to the 2D SWD and to the source of the QE Light Ocean. Thus, one can easily get what one wants since one will be easily served by God, the QE Light and quantum energies, the Subtle World Drama, Nature etc.

The QE Light energies from the dimensions of the Holographic Universe provide the environment in the auric fields. These energies, which are in an auric field, provide:

1. the environment of a loka in the auric field.

2. the subtle bodies which are to be used in the loka or auric field.

Each auric field provides a different kind of loka and different kinds of

QE Light bodies. Thus, there are differences in the experiences which one has in the different auric fields. Different kinds of lokas can be provided within a specific auric field, depending on what the person is experiencing.

The auric fields encircle the physical body. Each auric field, which is further away from the body, is a higher auric field that allows an experience in a higher dimension. Since each higher dimension and auric field is provided by less dense energies, each higher loka is also created through less dense QE Light energies. This means that more heavenly experiences can be had in the higher lokas. Through one's spiritual effort making, one begins to employ higher lokas in the Holographic World. God also assists to give an experience, during one's spiritual effort making, so that one can easily avail oneself of a higher loka.

The lokas, which are used during experiences, do not exist permanently. They exist in one's auric field when one has an experience in it. However, when one uses a specific loka, it will be within a specific space within the Holographic Universe.

The seven lokas (Satyaloka/Brahmaloka, Tapaloka, Janaloka, Maharloka, Svarloka, Bhuvarloka, and Bhuloka) are provided by the seven main chakras which exist along the spine. These seven lokas are used within the seven auric fields which are provided by the seven main chakras. Since there are more chakras above the Seventh Chakra, in the Holographic Body, and these provide even higher auric fields, there are also lokas which are above these seven lokas, e.g. Vaikuntha-loka. The auric fields, of the seven main chakras, can be said to be situated in specific areas in the Real World and Holographic Universe because the Real World overlaps the First Field and Second Field. Thus, even the lokas can be said to be situated in specific areas in the Real World and Holographic Universe.

Whatever is provided in outer space is part of the world stage where we live. The sun, moon, stars, planets, Milky Way Galaxy etc. are all part of the world stage since they provide the sky for the world stage. What is in the sky region is in the higher dimensions within the Unified Field since the dimensions there provide these. In fact, the whole Real World, i.e. the world stage, is provided by the dimensions in the Unified Field. Since the seven lokas are in the Unified Field, they can be given regions based on where the sun, Milky Way Galaxy etc. are situated, as has been done in the Hindu texts. For convenience and to keep the explanations brief and simple, when considering the position of the lokas in the Real World, I am only going to use what has been provided for by the ancient people in the Hindu scriptures and I am going to consider how it is positioned in the sky, as the ancient people had done.

The universe which we live in can be measured from two angles: spiritual and scientific. So the explanations should contain both: science and spiritual knowledge.

The spiritual aspect is that we are provided with a world stage based on our spiritual strength. So the world/loka we have in the second half cycle is not the same as the world/loka in the first half cycle.

When you look at it from the spiritual point of view, our world stage is all that which exists up to the sky, including what we see in the space of the sky. Since we play our roles on the world stage, we should also consider this spiritual aspect. So measurements should also be made from the earth up to what exists in the sky. How it exists in outer space is scientific and not spiritual knowledge. When considering it from the spiritual point of view, the position of the sun, moon, Dhruva (pole star), Milky Way Galaxy, etc. is based on where it is located in the sky and not based on where it is located in outer space. Actually, in visions and experiences, this is how we should be seeing it because we are living our lives on the world stage. We should not be seeing it like how it actually is in outer space because the energies there are very powerful and not suitable for an environment similar to how we have a suitable environment within the world stage.

The ancient scientists were spiritual people and they were not like most present day scientists who only give importance to the sciences and not to the spiritual aspects. The world stage is provided based on the Laws of Nature and based on the Spiritual Laws. Since it is provided based on the Laws of Nature, Science and Maths can be used to measure what is provided in the Real World. Different sets of Laws of Nature are used to provide the world in the first half cycle and in the second half cycle because the world is also provided based on the Spiritual Laws. One cannot ignore the Spiritual Laws and just consider the scientific aspects. Thus, the ancient people had included both the spiritual and the scientific aspects, into what they had left behind in the scriptures. Therefore, sometimes, you will find scientific information in the scriptures and at other times what is said does not make any sense because present day people are not looking at the world from the spiritual aspects. The ancient people had also left behind some knowledge of the Sciences in the scriptures because they knew that what they had left behind would be easily accepted, at the end, if the Sciences were also included into it, since the world that exists at the end is Kaliyug and people will be more influenced by the Sciences than by the spiritual.

When you experience the spiritual aspects of the world/loka, you do not see the world/loka as round; you will see it as flat. This is why, even though you are walking around a round earth, you will never experience its round aspect. You will only be aware that the earth is round if you were looking it from outer space. While you are on earth, everything around you can also make it look like it is flat. This is because everything around you is involved with providing a flat world stage for you. This is happening based on the Spiritual Laws, since the QE Light and quantum energies also provide the world/loka for us based on the Spiritual Laws. Since the Sciences and Maths can be used to explain what is provided by the QE Light and quantum energies, when they provide the Real World for us, the Sciences and Maths can be used to explain why the world/loka which we live in is flat and not round. Actually, the world/loka is flat but the earth is round.

When you experience the spiritual aspects, you do not see the world as round, you see it as flat. However, the earth is round from the scientific point of view, though the world/loka can also be seen as flat from the scientific point of view. The earth is different from the loka/world. The earth (Bhuloka) is used to provide the world stage where we live our lives. Those who have a highly spiritual nature will prefer the view that the world/earth/Bhuloka is flat and they will find it very difficult to accept the sciences which point that the earth is round. Actually, one must consider both, the spiritual and the scientific points of view of the world/loka and earth, just as the ancient people had done. If one just looks at it from the scientific point of view or from the spiritual point of view, one is not having a complete vision of what exists as our world/loka and how it is provided through the earth.

The flat earth theory which the ancient people developed also helps one to not get limited by limited space. Thus, you open yourself up to unlimited subtle dimensions which you can use as lokas.

Since this book is not to explain whether the earth is flat or round, I am not going deeply into this. I have just briefly discussed it here because I am trying to explain about the lokas, the earth and Bhuloka. All these explanations will lead to the explanation that:

1. one should use the higher lokas if one wants to easily get what one wants.

2. one will use higher lokas as one walks in and so one can easily get what one wants.

Since one's aura can expand into the space in the sky and one's higher auric fields are provided by energies from the higher dimensions, it is as if the higher lokas are higher up in the sky. Even in experiences, it can seem like the higher lokas are way up in the sky, when seen from the earth, because we experience the less dense dimensions as being higher up. Earth is the densest dimension because it consists of particles and it is provided by the densest energies; and the higher lokas are in the higher dimensions within the Holographic Universe. For all the above reasons, it can be said that:

1. The Second Field stretches up to the pole star (Dhruva) in the sky.

2. The First Field stretches from the pole star and goes beyond the Milky Way Galaxy, which is visible in the sky, up to the end of the visible universe, i.e. until the end of the Real World and Unified Field.

The Real World is the visible universe and it can be seen as our 'universe'. Since the Unified Field provides the Real World, it can also be seen as being part and parcel of our universe. All the seven higher lokas are within this universe since they are within the Real World and Unified Field. Thus, one's experiences will be in the relevant loka that is situated somewhere within the space of this universe.

It should be noted that there are more lokas, such as Vaikuntha, which are above the visible universe. Actually, we can say that all the dimensions which are above the Unified Field are also part of our universe since we can use them. From this angle, our universe includes more than the Real World. Actually, the Corporeal World is the universe. This universe (Corporeal World) consists of the visible universe (Real World) and invisible universe (Holographic Universe). Vaikuntha is in the invisible universe. Vaikuntha is explained in the later chapters of this book.

Bhuloka is from the earth to all the space in the sky which is illuminated by the rays of the sun and moon, i.e. it consists of the terrestrial sphere. It is in the lowest section of the Second Field. Bhuvarloka stretches from this terrestrial sphere to the sun in the sky. It is the atmospheric sphere and it in is the middle section of the Second Field. The five other lokas are situated, above Bhuvarloka, in the sky, i.e. in the higher parts of the Unified Field.

Actually, it can be said that the surface of the earth, where we live, is Bhuloka, i.e. the space which we use in the world stage can be said to be Bhuloka. Since we are seeing Bhuloka as part of the world stage,

Bhuloka is flat. This means that we are living on a flat Bhuloka since the world stage is flat. This is the spiritual point of view. One can also say that the earth itself is Bhuloka (if one wants to look at it from the scientific point of view). From this angle Bhuloka is the earth which provides the world for us to live in. If Bhuloka is used to represent the earth where people live, then Bhuloka is round. For these reasons, the earth with its world stage (as Bhumandala, Bhuloka or Bhumi) has been represented as flat and round in the Hindu scriptures.

If one looks at it from the spiritual point of view and considers the surface of the earth to be Bhuloka, then above that is the atmospheric sphere which is Bhuvarloka. However, it can also be said that Bhuloka is from the earth to the sky because Bhuloka and Bhuvarloka overlap when they are used together; people in the second half cycle, generally, these them in this way.

One uses Bhuloka through the First Chakra. The Muladhara Chakra or Root Chakra is the doorway to Bhuloka; thus, it is the lowest loka. Bhuloka is the realm which we live in and it consists of what exists in the sphere of the earth, i.e. its mountains, rivers, oceans, sky and everything around the surface of the earth. Bhuloka has space, time and gravity. Through Bhuloka, one can feel the earth's vibrational energies.

Bhuloka consists of the lower part of the Real World (visible universe). However, it can be said that parts of the invisible universe (holographic universe) are also included into it because Bhuloka can be seen as being either one of the following:

1. only the physical realm, i.e. only that which can be perceived by our 5 senses.

2. the physical forms and also the quantum aspects which overlap and provide the physical forms.

Since the quantum aspects provide the material world, they can be said to be part of Bhuloka. From the perspective that Bhuloka includes the quantum aspects, Bhuloka encompasses:

1. the Etheric Field (first auric field) since it provides the physical body.

2. lokas used in the first auric field, during experiences.

3. the QE Light body which provides the Etheric Field.

4. all of the body's particle forms and wave/energy forms of various densities which are provided by the QE Light and quantum energies.

All the above forms exist in Bhuloka though we cannot perceive them with our five senses. Some of these exist as part of the Real World while others exist as part of the 3D SWD in the Unified Field.

In the Unified Field, the QE Light and quantum energies have quantum wave function, so they act as waves and particles to provide the Real World and the 3D SWD. Since the QE Light and quantum energies exist as waves and particles, the Unified Field overlaps the Real World. Thus, the Unified Field overlaps Bhuloka since Bhuloka is the lower part of the Real World.

Normally, when living one's life, one is experiencing oneself as the physical body. This is the real form aspect of Bhuloka and one's consciousness can be said to be in a lower dimension because one's consciousness is not in a dimension within the Unified Field. During experiences, one could also experience one's body as consisting of the QE Light and quantum energies. One could experience this as being the true state of the body because the quantum aspects are also part of Bhuloka. While living in Bhuloka, we can experience Bhuloka in its real or quantum forms. When we experience the quantum aspect of it, we can be said to be in a higher dimension.

One has to use the body to make spiritual efforts. Thus, it is from Bhuloka that spiritual effort making begins so that one can easily use the higher lokas via the higher chakras. Since the Etheric Body is the double of the physical body, one is also using that and its QE Light body during spiritual effort making.

One can actually have experiences in the Etheric Field. For example, one can communicate with plants, water, air and clouds (consisting of air and water) through one's Etheric Field. Experiences through the First Chakra, its auric field and Bhuloka are around the surface of the Earth because that is where the physical body and Etheric Field are.

Bhuvarloka is provided by the Second Chakra in the second auric field. Thus, the Second Chakra is the doorway to Bhuvarloka which is the astral dimension. Since Bhuvarloka is higher than Bhuloka, the experiences in Bhuvarloka would be higher up; they can even be experienced near the sun.

If one looks at it from the angle that the first half cycle is the day and the second half cycle is the night, then:

1. the sun at its highest level, up in the sky, represents the first half cycle.

2. the sun at the lower level in the sky represents the Mid-Confluence and Confluence Age.

The Mid-Confluence is the time when the sun is going to set. The Confluence Age is the time when the sun is rising. During both of these times (around the time of dusk and dawn) one can see the sun lower down in the sky as if the sun is in the border between the earth (Bhuloka) and sky/atmosphere (Bhuvarloka). The sun is in a low position, in some places, during winter too. Thus, the ancient people had also associated this time to what happens jointly via the Mid-Confluence and Confluence Age.

When the sun is between the earth and sky/atmosphere, the sun is between Bhuloka and Bhuvarloka. However, sometimes, the sun is higher up in the sky. Since the sun is in various places in the sky during the different times of the year and day, the measurements can vary when measurements are done from the earth to where the sun is located in the sky. The ancient people normally measured the distance to the sun based on where the sun is in our sky since it forms part of our world stage. If the sun is:

1. in the border between Bhuloka and Bhuvarloka, it is just beyond the terrestrial sphere.

2. higher up in the sky, it is just beyond the atmospheric sphere.

For convenience, in this book, I am only going to use the situation where the sun is higher up in the sky so that I can say that Bhuvarloka is between Bhuloka and the Sun. This means that the sun is at the very top of the atmospheric sphere. I am not using the instance when the sun is between the earth (Bhuloka) and sky (Bhuvarloka).

There are differing views in respect of the space which Bhuvarloka occupies, such as the following:

1. The space where the Solar System exists is within Bhuvarloka.

2. The space where the Solar System exists is part of Swargaloka and not part of Bhuvarloka.

3. Bhuvarloka is above Bhuloka. They do not occupy the same space.

4. Bhuloka and Bhuvarloka occupy the same space.

Whether the Solar System is part of Bhuvarloka depends on which 'classification of lokas' one is using. The place where the lokas are situated can differ because:

1. the lokas were dropping into the Real World, during the Mid-Confluence. Swargaloka was originally in the Higher Universe. Then, as their lokas were dropping, they began using Swargaloka and then Bhuvarloka within the higher space of the Lower Universe. Thus, the space of the Solar System would have been within Bhuvarloka.

2. during the second half cycle, from the Copper Age, since the lokas continued to drop in the Real World and Unified Field, Swargaloka and Bhuvarloka occupy a lower space in the Lower Universe. Thus, the space

where the Solar System exists is part of Swargaloka and not part of Bhuvarloka. It should be noted that Bhuvarloka can still include the space where the Solar System exists when one's second auric field expands higher up.

3. during the walking in process, since the lokas are getting uplifted into the higher dimensions, Swargaloka would be higher up, in the Higher Universe.

Though, normally, Bhuvarloka represents the space above Bhuloka, sometimes, both of them have been portrayed as using the space. Bhuloka and Bhuvarloka can be experienced in the same space from the surface of the earth to the sky because, though the Etheric Field is normally not stretched as the aura gets stretched and it is not used for experiences, it can be stretched and used in the space where Bhuvarloka is used. It should be noted that it is Bhuvarloka which normally gets stretched and used for having experiences, as the aura gets stretched, if one was not on the spiritual path. However, both, Bhuloka and Bhuvarloka, are used together while living one's live.

The aura is used for experiences and for living as the Conscious Self in the Real World. While we live our lives, though we are not aware of it, our aura can stretch right up to the sky to stay connected to someone. For example, if our loved one is on an aircraft in the sky, our aura will be in a stretched state so that we can stay connected to our loved one who is so far away from us. The aura is stretched in Bhuloka and in Bhuvarloka, if we are not on the spiritual or religious path, because:

1. we are living our lives in Bhuloka. So auric fields stretch to enable us to live as a community, in Bhuloka.

2. love is experienced through Bhuvarloka. Actually, love can be experienced through the second and fourth auric fields when we are not on the spiritual or religious path.

Since the Mid-Confluence Aged gods had advanced aircrafts and they were spiritually connected to each other, they became aware of how they were staying connected while they were in the sky region. This was also why the ancient people had associated the lokas to the space in the Real World.

One subtly connects with those who have the same thoughts, ideas and beliefs, via the 3rd auric field, if one was not on the spiritual or religious path. All feelings, desires and emotions that are attached to these thoughts, ideas and beliefs are experienced in the second auric field. Thus, there are also connections among the people, with the same thoughts, ideas and beliefs, through Bhuvarloka. For this reason too, the same space is used:

1. for living in Bhuloka, and

2. for staying connected, through Bhuvarloka, while living.

Though we cannot see our aura, we are connected to the group which we belong to and to our loved ones, via the aura, while living our lives on earth. All people are connected in this way. Those who are on the spiritual/religious path are connected through the higher 5 chakras, auric fields and lokas, while those who are not on the spiritual path are connected through the lower three chakras, auric fields and lokas.

When the aura is being stretched to connect to others, the second auric field or Bhuvarloka is also being stretched, as the aura stretches, since feelings are expressed through the second auric field. Though Bhuvarloka is used, people are usually not aware of what is happening through Bhuvarloka; they are only aware of what is happening in Bhuloka. In fact, since the aura is stretching in the space of Bhuloka, it can be said to be stretching in Bhuloka.

One can have experiences while one's aura expands to stay connected. When one is not on the spiritual path, one normally has experiences in the lower auric fields, especially in the second auric field, i.e. in Bhuvarloka. When one's stage is good, one uses the higher chakras, higher auric fields, higher lokas and higher dimensions in the Holographic Universe.

The Etheric Field is not normally used for experiences. It is anchored to and entangled with the physical body since it is involved with providing the physical body. Thus, it just remains close to the body. However, one can have experiences in the Etheric Field and the Etheric Field can also be stretched if one has trained it to be used in these ways. Even if it is used in these ways, it cannot get stretched very far. The aura can get stretched further when Bhuvarloka is used. Bhuvarloka can also be used to subtly travel around in.

Since Bhuvarloka has astral dimensions which are closest to the physical world, all those who have just died are in Bhuvarloka (especially if they were not on the spiritual path and they had not left the body while in a pure state). They can be roaming around anywhere, from around the surface of earth to near where the sun is, until they take their next birth. If one is in an impure state when one dies and one does not want to leave something which one has an attachment to, one can roam around in Bhuvarloka as a ghost after death.

When Bhuloka is seen as just representing the physical world (without any holographic aspects), Bhuvarloka can be seen as representing the holographic aspects. Thus, ghosts can be said to be roaming around in Bhuvarloka.

The ghosts are using energies from the Etheric Field and/or QE Light body which provides the Etheric Field; so they are actually roaming around in the space of Bhuloka where we live (at the surface of the earth). Since the Etheric Field is the double of the physical body, it is as if they are in Bhuloka. However, they are ghosts due to the attachment which they have for what exists in the life that they had just lived. Attachment is experienced in Bhuvarloka. So the ghosts are in Bhuvarloka. These ghosts are in Bhuvarloka which is near the surface of the earth.

Those who play a role in the afterlife would be in the sky region, in Bhuvarloka or in the higher lokas, depending on whether they were in the pure state when they left the body, whether the soul was still spiritually powerful at the time of death, how pure a life-style they had lived, etc. Though they remain in these higher lokas, the soul will continue taking births in Bhuloka. If the afterlife was for what was to be received and done at the end of the cycle, then, when the soul has taken its final birth at the end of the cycle (now), the soul would receive the benefits and be influenced to achieve the aims of the afterlife. The ancient people had made sure that they receive wealth, at the end of the cycle, so that they can do world service. So wealth will also be received during their final birth. The benefits are received through the Ancient Past Birth Auric Field. See Chapter 41 (Mid-Confluence Aged Vaikuntha) for more on the Ancient Past Birth Auric Field.

In the Hindu myths, Bhuvarloka has been portrayed as the abode of semi-demigods (lesser demigods) who are half beast and half god. This reflects that those who used Bhuvarloka:

1. were those who had lesser status and spiritual strength during the Mid-Confluence and early Copper Age.

2. were capable of using the vices during their life-time.

3. were capable of using subtle abilities similar to how animals use subtle perception.

The ancient semi-demigods were less divine because their spiritual strength was lower. At the end of the cycle, their spiritual strength would not be contributing much towards world transformation, i.e. they would not be part of the 900,000 most powerful souls, based on whose spiritual strength the world will transform into the Golden Aged world. Thus, during the Mid-Confluence and early Copper Age, their social status was normally lower. They were serving the demigods who were serving the gods. The demigods generally used Swargaloka, while the gods used even higher lokas such as the Mid-Confluence Aged Vaikuntha. Even where the afterlife is concerned, the semi-demigods will not play a leading role for world benefit. They will be more concerned about receiving benefits which they can enjoy.

During the Mid-Confluence, these semi-demigods were capable of doing magic since they were still very pure. Thus, with time, some of these semi-demigods became wealthy and got what they wanted. Some were able to make spiritual efforts to use higher lokas. When they used higher lokas, they were given higher status on earth. This was also happening because they had the intent for this. When people are in their pure state, they easily get what they want.

The semi-demigods who used Bhuvarloka could be influenced by the vices and thus, sometimes, during those ancient days, they had acted in an uncivilised manner (like an animal). The fact that they were portrayed as being half animal also reflects that they were capable of using subtle abilities, even though they were not on the spiritual path, identical to how animals use subtle perception to live, travel and act as a flock, etc. Normally, in the second half cycle, it is as if people no longer use subtle abilities, though animals continued to constantly use subtle perception after they had dropped into the Lower Universe. When humans have subtle abilities, they are using Bhuvarloka, if they are not on the spiritual/religious path. Those who are born with abilities to do magic use Bhuvarloka, naturally, to do magic.

Each auric field can provide different kinds of lokas, at a higher or lower level, depending on all the circumstances. Thus, there are differences on where Bhuvarloka is situated in the second auric field. It should be noted that the second auric field itself can be used as Bhuvarloka; though often, lokas are created in the second auric field and one has experiences in these lokas which are also Bhuvarloka.

Though the 6 higher lokas are basically within the Unified Field, they can be given a corresponding place within the Real World because the Unified Field overlaps the Real World. The higher lokas are in the higher part of the Real World and Unified Field.

Hence, the ancient people had also given measurements based on the position of the pole star (Dhruva) and the Milky Way Galaxy (as it was visible in the sky as a vaguely lighted up region). In the sky, Dhruva (pole star) was lower down in the sky and the Milky Way was higher up in the sky. Other galaxies existed further away from the Milky Way Galaxy.

As a consequence, the ancient people had placed Svarloka, or Swargaloka, above Bhuvarloka and this Swargaloka occupies the space from the sun to the pole star (Dhruva). So if one was experiencing being in Swargaloka, one's loka can be situated anywhere between the sun and Dhruva. The Third Chakra or Navel Chakra is the doorway to Swargaloka; and Swargaloka is experienced in the third auric field which is within the upper section of the Second Field.

Maharloka was placed above Swargaloka and above Dhruva (pole star) as it is seen in the sky. The Fourth Chakra provides Maharloka in the fourth auric field. The Fourth Chakra or Heart Chakra is the doorway to Maharloka which is used in the borders between the First Field and Second Field.

Janaloka is above Maharloka and it includes all that space which was considered as the Milky Way Galaxy that was be seen in the sky. This is provided through the Fifth Chakra (Throat Chakra or Vishuddha Chakra) within the lowest division of the First Field. The Throat Chakra is the doorway to Janaloka which is in the 5th auric field.

Tapoloka is above Janaloka and it is in the space which is outside the Milky Way Galaxy, in the space where other galaxies are situated, i.e. above what was seen as the Milky Way Galaxy in the sky. It is in the middle section of the First Field. Since an auric field itself can be a loka, it can be said that Tapoloka is within the 6th auric field or that it is the 6th auric field. This loka is provided through the Sixth Chakra (Third Eye Chakra or Ajna Chakra) which is the doorway to Tapoloka.

Satyaloka, which is also called Brahmaloka, is used in the highest division of the First Field. The Seventh Chakra is the doorway to Satyaloka/Brahmaloka which is within the seventh auric field. It is situated in the space from above Tapoloka up to the top edge of the Unified Field. From earth, it is as if one has to go past the Milky Way

Galaxy in the sky and other galaxies to use this loka which occupies a huge space beneath the edge of the visible universe that is within the Unified Field. Since the Unified Field provides the universe for us, it can be seen as being part of our universe too.

What is in the space of Maharloka, Janaloka, Tapoloka and Satyaloka/Brahmaloka are all part of the sky of our world stage. Experiences would be different if they were experienced in outer space.

In outer space, the Unified Field and Real World are both in the environment of the Quantum World. It is as if these two dimensions exist together there as outer space. Since outer space is half material (since it has cosmic bodies belonging to the Real World) and half holographic (since it consists of dark energies etc. which are in the Quantum World):

1. one sees the cosmic bodies in a dark environment.

2. one's experiences in outer space can involve experiencing all the spins, electromagnetic forces etc. that exist in outer space.

Though the seven lokas (provided by the seven chakras) could be experienced in specific areas within the Holographic Universe and Real World, one's loka would be provided in the same space where one lives one's life, though one's environment would be different if one was surrounded by less dense energies.

During the second half cycle, people are not permanently using any of the higher 6 lokas like how they are permanently using Bhuloka. While living on earth, they might be using one of the higher lokas, apart from Bhuloka, depending on their spiritual state, experiences, etc.

Sometimes, in experiences, it is as if one is living a life with others in the higher lokas. This is just a vision, in which one is participating and not just observing. This is different from the walking in process.

The aura surrounds the body and, in the present day world, it does not extend far from the physical body. When one is not on the spiritual path, the aura can be up to about one foot, or less, all around the body. When one is on the spiritual path, the aura can be about three feet away from the body (nearer or further away from the body, depending on one's spiritual strength and spiritual stage). Some of the auric fields can be larger for some and some people may not even have certain auric fields.

The spiritually more powerful souls will have higher auras. Thus, ancient people would have had higher auras. This was also why, in the Hindu scriptures, the lokas were portrayed as being so high up in the sky. Though the present day people's aura is not that tall:

1. the auric fields can be stretched for experiences and living.

2. the higher auric fields are in the higher dimensions and they are also getting their energies from the higher dimensions. So they have experiences in higher dimensions, though the dimensions which they use would not be as high as those of the ancient people.

Since the auric fields can be stretched, the lokas can be experienced anywhere in the stretched auric field. Thus, experiences in the lokas can be near the body (in the lower environment which we live in) or higher up in the universe (in the higher space of the dimension which the auric field is in). If you are using a higher auric field, your experience is experienced higher up, even though you experience it around you. Your loka is in a higher dimension, even though it is only in the lower space of that higher dimension. It should be noted that all the dimensions are also overlapping in the same space and so their energies are everywhere in the space which we use for living. However, some dimensions have a bigger space and so their space extends beyond the other dimensions which have denser energies. All the higher dimensions actually surround the body just as all the auric fields surround the body. However, in addition, if they have less dense energies, they would also occupy a higher space than the dimension which has denser energies. The lokas extend from the chakras right up to a higher space in the

Holographic Universe and Real World. One is in a loka during an experience and one can have experiences near the chakras or higher up.

Normally, when you have an experience, it will be as if your experience is just around the body because your auric fields are not far from the physical body and it can seem like those higher dimensions are also around you. It is only occasionally that you will feel like you are so high up.

Though all the dimensions surround the body, we do not use all of them. The dimension that we use is based on which chakra is providing the environment for us. In the second half cycle, the Root Chakra provides the environment for us since the Kundalini is at the Root Chakra. When the Kundalini rises, higher chakras provide the environment for us.

Since the Unified Field provides the 3D SWD and Real World, all the seven lokas are provided within the 3D SWD and Real World. Thus, our experiences are within the 3D SWD and Real World, and we are also living within the 3D SWD and Real World.

In the second half cycle, since the lower chakras are used, the 3D SWD is in the Second Field. If the higher chakras are also used, then the 3D SWD would include parts of the First Field (depending on which higher chakras are used). Thus, the loka which one uses would be higher up.

One begins to use higher chakras, auric fields and lokas as one's spiritual strength increases. However, this does not mean that one no longer uses the lower chakras. All the chakras are used in various ways for various purposes. However, one does not use the higher chakras for living unless one lives a spiritual life. Thus, this aspect of the chakras does not function until one begins to live a spiritual or religious life by making spiritual efforts.

It is easier to get what one wants through using the higher lokas because the frequencies that are used there are higher. Each higher auric field has a higher frequency and so lokas of the higher auric fields will also have similarly higher frequencies. When one is in these higher lokas, one's energies would also have higher frequencies. Just having gone into the higher lokas is not sufficient to get wealth and prosperity. One must have the relevant thoughts, desires, beliefs, intentions, visualisations and emotions for getting an abundance of wealth and prosperity.

The lower three auric fields, their chakras and lokas have dense energies which have low frequencies; while the three higher auric fields (5th, 6th and 7th auric fields), their chakras and lokas have lighter energies with higher frequencies. The Heart Chakra connects these energies of different densities and frequencies. Without using the Heart Chakra, one will not be able to engage the higher chakras so as to easily get what one wants. Nonetheless, if one was not on the spiritual path, one could use the higher regions in Bhuvarloka and Swargaloka to easily get what one wants because the vibrations there have higher frequencies.

The seven lokas, which are provided by the seven chakras within the auric fields in the Unified Field (Second Field and First Field), are all considered as heavenly lokas. One reason, why this is so, is that it would be easy to get what one wants even if one was using the lower chakras which provide the lower lokas. For example, even if one's Root Chakra is activated, and one is only using Bhuloka, one can get what one wants. However, the Root Chakra normally only gets activated if one was meditating while doing visualisations for receiving wealth, unless it gets activated as per the World Drama. As you keep meditating for many days or years, you would begin to use the higher chakras and their lokas. Then, it would be easier to get what you want through your thoughts, visualisations etc.

Though the same chakras are used to provide many different kinds of lokas, different lokas are used by different groups and people. One uses a loka, in the Lower Universe or Higher Universe, depending on whether one is in the Mid-Confluence, Confluence Age, first half cycle or second half cycle.

All those who are in the Lower Universe will experience all the seven main lokas in the Lower Universe. Those who are walking in will have all the five higher lokas in the Higher Universe. Their Bhuloka will be in the Lower Universe until their perfect bodies materialise in the Higher Universe. In the first half cycle, the earth (Bhuloka) will be like a lotus flower which is provided by the quantum energies that are below. This lotus flower (earth/Bhuloka) will be in the dimension of light and not within the waters (quantum waters of the Garbhodaka Ocean or Quantum World).

Once you become a Confluence Aged soul, you would no longer be using Bhuvarloka because it is only those in the Lower Universe, who are not on the spiritual path, who use it. It will be as if Bhuvarloka does not exist for the Confluence Aged souls (including for those walking in).

The lokas (of the Hindu scriptures) were originally created to reflect the worlds which the Mid-Confluence Aged people used, as their world was dropping from the Higher Universe to the Lower Universe. However, with time they were also adopted to reflect:

1. the dimensions which the ancient people employed, during their afterlife, for their return at the end of the cycle.

2. the stages and dimensions which one uses in the Lower Universe for living and experiences.

3. the dimensions which one could use in the Lower Universe through worship practices.

In this chapter, I have only briefly talked about Swargaloka, Maharloka, Janaloka, Tapoloka and Satyaloka/Brahmaloka. More will be discussed in the subsequent chapters of this book. Vaikuntha-loka will also be discussed in later chapters.

In this book, I am trying my best to keep the explanations on the lokas as brief as possible because I am only trying to give the understanding that:

1. one becomes more powerful through using the higher dimensions/lokas and so one can get what one wants.

2. there are great benefits in using the higher lokas during the walking in process.

3. the Siddhis can be enjoyed while using the higher lokas/dimensions.

4. the Sun Dynasty souls will be able to use all the ancient lokas again; as a result of which, they get the benefits of the worship that was done for wealth and prosperity during those ancient days.

Chapter 32: Swargaloka and Indraloka

There are **various kinds of Swargaloka**, such as:

1. all the dimensions or worlds which are heavenly.

2. the heavenly worlds/dimensions which are used by the people in the first half cycle.

3. the heavenly worlds/dimensions which are used by those walking into the Golden Aged world.

4. the third auric field.

5. the lokas which are provided within the Third Chakra or third auric field.

Indraloka is where Indra resides and this refers to:

1. the residence of god Indra during the Mid-Confluence, and

2. the residence of God Indra (Supreme Soul or God) in the Confluence Aged Subtle Region, during the Confluence Age. The Supreme Soul plays the role of Indra for all Confluence Aged souls (including those who are walking in).

Actually, Indraloka only refers to the residence of God in the Confluence Aged Subtle Region since God only plays a role as Indra for the 330 million deity souls during the Confluence Age. God enables these 330 million deity souls to live in the heavenly world, which exists in the first half cycle, through the walking in process and through the purification process (as a result of which they take their subsequent births in the first half cycle). At the end of the Silver Age, these 330 million deity souls walked out of the Silver Age to become the demigods who lived in the Mid-Confluence Aged Swargaloka. The Mid-Confluence Aged gods had connected themselves to the Confluence Aged Indraloka since they will return to play their roles, in their afterlife, in Indraloka (Confluence

Aged Subtle Region) via the Confluence Auric Field when Swargaloka (the heavenly world that exists in the Golden Aged world) is in the process of getting created. Then, the deity souls will be walking into the Swargaloka of the Golden Age or they will take their next birth there. For all the above reasons, the ancient people connected Swargaloka to Indraloka.

The Mid-Confluence Aged demigods were also portrayed as living in Swargaloka because they were in the heavenly world of the first half cycle which was dropping into the lower dimensions. God (Supreme Soul) was not in Indraloka during the Mid-Confluence. Only His representative for world rule on earth was in the Mid-Confluence Aged Indraloka. However, during the Confluence Age, God Himself is in the Confluence Aged Subtle Region and all the 330 million deity souls will surely come into the Confluence Aged Subtle Region via their third auric field.

Since the Mid-Confluence Aged gods connected themselves to the Confluence Age (when God plays the role of Indra), they had also played a role as Indra, the representative of God, during those ancient days. Since they gave importance to their connection to the Confluence Age and to what happens through the Confluence Age, it has been presented in the Hindu myths:

1. that Swargaloka/Indraloka is the subtle home of the devas/demigods, and

2. that Indra resides in Swargaloka/Indraloka with the 330 million devas/demigods.

The ancient people had also portrayed the Mid-Confluence Aged gods' Swargaloka as being used through the Third Chakra because at the end of the cycle, when the deity souls are introduced to the BK knowledge, they begin using the third auric field as Indraloka. This connection was made since those ancient people were connecting themselves to the next Confluence Age.

In the Srimad Bhagavatam Canto 5, Chapter 19, Verse 28 (SB 5.19.28):

1. the demigods were of the view that they were living in the heavenly lokas because of their spiritual and religious efforts,

2. the demigods expressed their desire to be born in Bharata-varsa (India) as human beings so that they can remember God since God comes to Bharata-varsa to make the people there fortunate.

The above reflected how the ancient Mid-Confluence Aged people, whose world was dropping, had desired to be born as Confluence Aged souls in India (at the end of the cycle) because this is where God descends and establishes the Confluence Age. They valued what would happen through the next Confluence Age because they had just lost their divine world. The Mid-Confluence Aged gods were living in heavenly lokas because of their spiritual and religious efforts which were made during:

1. the Mid-Confluence itself.

2. the previous Confluence Age. The fruits received are enjoyed during the first half cycle and during the life in the Mid-Confluence.

The verses in the Srimad Bhagavatam had also reflected the Mid-Confluence Aged and early Copper Aged history. However, I am not discussing that here.

The Mid-Confluence Aged people had also begun to give a lot of importance to using the thoughts so as to get what they want. Since the Kundalini had dropped to the Heart Chakra by the end of the Mid-Confluence, they would be using the third auric field to express their thoughts, if they were not using the chakras above the Heart Chakra through spiritual effort making. They had used Swargaloka a lot, through the third auric field, to get what they wanted. Through religious practices, they could get even better stuff, including the ability to become Indra and have world rule, because just a little bit of religious/spiritual efforts greatly improved their spiritual stage and ability to get what they wanted. Whatever auric field they used would have been a Swargaloka since they are spiritually still quite powerful.

By the end of the Mid-Confluence, the gods could easily use Swargaloka/Indraloka (the third auric field) to live their lives. If they were less pure, they would be in the lower lokas. With spiritual effort making, they could also use the higher lokas. So Brahma who was a demigod in Swargaloka/Indraloka was also portrayed as residing in Brahmaloka, and Vishnu who was also a demigod in Swargaloka/Brahmaloka was portrayed as residing in Vaikuntha-loka too. Brahma and Vishnu were not involved with world rule and so they could easily remain in the higher lokas unless they had to come into the denser Bhuloka so as to get something done for Mankind in the Lower Universe. Indra and all the 330 million gods were not really living in Swargaloka/Indraloka all the time, during the Mid-Confluence, though those deity souls would be in the Confluence Aged Indraloka all the time, at the end of the cycle, just as the world is about to get transformed into the Golden Aged world.

Swargaloka is provided, in the third auric field, by the Third Chakra. The Swargaloka of those who are in the Lower Universe, is in the Lower Universe. The Swargaloka of those walking in is in the Higher Universe or in the Confluence Aged Subtle Region. The Indraloka of BKs is in the Confluence Aged Subtle Region.

Since all the auric fields, of a Confluence Aged person, become part of the Confluence Auric Field, it is as if all these auric fields become part of Indraloka which stretches from the third auric field to go into the Angelic World which is beyond the Corporeal World. Even though there are numerous auric fields within the Confluence Auric Field, they can all be seen as one auric field, i.e. the Confluence Auric Field. Everyone who is using the Confluence Auric Field is in Indraloka and, since the Confluence Auric Field stretches from the physical body to the Confluence Aged Subtle Region, their consciousness/awareness can be anywhere in this huge space of Indraloka which is also in their Confluence Auric Field. It should be noted that the Confluence Auric

Field is the aura of the Angelic Body. Since the Angelic Body is in the Confluence Aged Subtle Region, which is beyond the physical world, it can be said that their Indraloka is actually in the Confluence Aged Subtle Region which is beyond the present Corporeal World.

Actually, the Confluence Aged Subtle Region is Indraloka because God (Indra) resides there with the Confluence Aged souls. However, since one also uses the environment of the Confluence Aged Subtle Region in one's Confluence Auric Field, Indraloka is also in one's Confluence Auric Field.

At the beginning of the Confluence Age, God had created the Angelic Bodies for all the deity souls, in the Confluence Aged Subtle Region (Indraloka). Thus, Indraloka can be used as soon as one receives the BK knowledge. After receiving the BK knowledge, if one believed in the BK knowledge but was not making much spiritual efforts, one would still be in Indraloka. This is so because:

1. some of the energies of the Confluence Aged souls are anchored within the Angelic Body which is beyond the Corporeal World.

2. the Third Chakra and auric field can also be used to remain in Indraloka.

During the second half cycle, if one was not living a spiritual life, one's thoughts are in the third auric field. Thus, the third auric field has been referred to as the Mental Plane. The Mental Plane is also a causal plane because one's powerful thoughts can help one to get what one wants. The fact that the heavenly Swargaloka exists in the Mental Plane also reflects how one can have a good life through using one's thoughts efficiently.

The Mental Plane is divided into two divisions: the lower one is used for normal living and the higher division is used to begin one's spiritual life. Through availing oneself of the higher division, one begins to use the Heart Chakra for spiritual purposes. Then, after this, one can begin to employ the higher chakras, which are above the Heart Chakra, for spiritual living. Through this way, one acquires the ability to live a spiritual life through spiritual effort making.

Brahma Kumaris Raja Yoga teaches one to use the thought so as to establish the link to God and go beyond. This thought is also in the 3rd auric field because all thoughts exist in the third auric field (apart from existing within the mind of the soul) if a person was just beginning the spiritual life. Thus, when a person is introduced to the BK knowledge, the person will be in Indraloka via his/her thought. As a result, new BKs can easily go into Indraloka with just a thought. Those who have been making spiritual efforts for a long time will be utilising the higher auric fields to express their thoughts. Through using the higher auric fields, they will also be in Indraloka with just a thought since the Confluence Auric Field stretches from the third auric field to the Angelic Body in the Angelic World.

At the beginning of the Confluence Age, when God began using Brahma Baba, God's powerful energies brought Brahma Baba's Indraloka, from the Lower Universe, into the Higher Universe. This also had to happen because Brahma Baba began to engage his Angelic Body through acceptance with just a thought and so his third auric field merged into Brahma Baba's Confluence Auric Field through his thought. All BKs also use Brahma Baba's Confluence Auric Field so as to go into the Confluence Aged Subtle Region. Thus, the minute one is given the BK knowledge, one's third auric field is uplifted into the Higher Universe via:

1. God's assistance,

2. one's thought,

3. Brahma Baba's Confluence Auric Field, and

4. one's own Confluence Auric Field which connects one's physical body to one's Angelic Body in the Confluence Aged Subtle Region.

When BKs are not making spiritual efforts, they are still engaging their

Confluence Auric Field and so they still use Indraloka in their Confluence Auric Field even though their intellect is not linking them to God at that point of time. When one has a link to God, one would be in the space of Indraloka which is beyond the present Corporeal World.

Since BKs use the physical body for spiritual effort making and since the Confluence Auric Field connects the physical body in the Lower Universe to the Angelic Body in the Confluence Aged Subtle Region which is beyond the present Corporeal World, it can be said that Indraloka connects what exists in the Lower Universe to what exists beyond the Corporeal World. It is as if Indraloka occupies a huge space from the end of the Lower Universe right up to beyond the Corporeal World.

The ancient people were becoming aware of what had happened during the previous Confluence Age. Since Indraloka begins from the third auric field and extends into the Confluence Aged subtle regions which are beyond the Corporeal World:

1. Brahma was portrayed as being in Swargaloka/Indraloka and Brahmaloka, and

2. Vishnu was portrayed as residing in Swargaloka/Brahmaloka and in Vaikuntha-loka.

All Confluence Aged souls are taken into the Higher Universe through Indraloka. However, BKs do not use the dimensions or lokas in the Higher Universe. Only those walking in will be using the dimensions and lokas in the Higher Universe.

The thoughts of more powerful Confluence Aged souls do not go into the Confluence Auric Field through the third auric field; their thoughts go into the Confluence Auric Field through the higher auric fields. If they have a link to God and have gone beyond the Corporeal World, their thoughts are in the space of the Confluence Auric Field which is beyond the Corporeal World. While flying to the Angelic World, BKs do not use dimensions within the Higher Universe; they use a passageway which goes into the Higher Universe before providing the exit into the

Confluence Aged Subtle Region.

Though it is as if the Higher Universe is on top of the Lower Universe because they are different dimensions of different densities, the Higher Universe overlaps the Lower Universe. Thus, it is easy to move from one dimension to another during the Mid-Confluence and Confluence Age.

During the Mid-Confluence, the weaker souls were living in the Real World as they were dropping into the Lower Universe. The more powerful Mid-Confluence Aged gods had gone into the Real World so as to help them to stop falling any further, through helping them to remain pure. With just a thought, the Mid-Confluence Aged gods could go into the dimension of the Real World. Later, with just a thought, they could also bring themselves into the denser Real World of the Lower Universe, as the Real World of the people was dropping further down into the Lower Universe. The universe/world which they were in was based on a thought. Through that thought, they could bring themselves into the higher and lower dimensions because they were still spiritually powerful. However, thereafter, during the second half cycle, the denser Real World and Lower Universe were no longer being used due to a thought. This was so because souls are weak and so they are in a sunken state within the denser Real World in the Lower Universe. However, now, with just a thought, one can have the environment of the Higher Universe as one's environment or with just a thought one can be in the Indraloka which is beyond the present Corporeal World.

During the Mid-Confluence, those who lived in Swargaloka had wealth, freedom from diseases, etc. They could get anything they wanted and they had the ability to go into any of the dimensions. All it required was the thought to initiate it. They were spiritually powerful and so they had this ability. Those walking in, at the end of the cycle, will begin to acquire all these abilities.

In the Golden Age, all the QE Light energies, which are playing a role with the person to provide what the person wants, will resonate with the desires and thoughts of the person to provide what the person wants. Those walking in are walking into this scenario.

However, it should be noted that the spiritual strength of those walking in is still not powerful as yet, if they have not been using the BK knowledge to make spiritual efforts over a long duration of time. Some BKs, who had made serious spiritual efforts during the previous birth as a BK, can easily become powerful now because of the spiritual strength which they had accumulated in their previous birth. However, if one was only being introduced to the BK knowledge in this birth, it will take some time to become spiritually powerful. Further, those walking in are still in the process of settling for all the wrongs which they had done in the present and past births. Thus, often, it takes time for their thoughts to materialise.

In the Hindu scriptures, Swargaloka has been portrayed as the abode of the immortals because:

1. those who walked out of the Silver Age were still immortals and they were still using a heavenly loka after the world had begun dropping. Originally, the Swargaloka which they were using was not the one that is provided by the Third Chakra. Their Swargaloka was the one which was dropping from the Higher Universe to the Lower Universe as they were losing their divine world. For this reason too, Brahma and Vishnu were portrayed as residents of Swargaloka and yet also residents of Brahmaloka and Vaikuntha respectively.

2. those walking into the Golden Aged world, while using a heavenly loka, acquire the ability to remain in the soul conscious state and are attaining immortality which will be enjoyed by them in the Golden Age. Then, they walk into the Swargaloka (heavenly world) of the first half cycle, and they are using this heavenly world through the Crown Chakra and not through the Third Chakra.

3. the Confluence Aged souls use the Confluence Aged Subtle Region as Indraloka. These souls are becoming immortals and so they are immortals during their births in the Golden and Silver Ages.

Since Indraloka is experienced in the Confluence Auric Field, which connects the physical body to the Angelic Body that is beyond the Corporeal World, the vices can be used in the lower regions of Indraloka. The lower auric fields are also part of the Confluence Auric Field. Thus, when one is in Indraloka, one is capable of using the vices. Though one can use the vices in the Indraloka which is in section of the Confluence Auric Field that is within the Corporeal World, one cannot use the vices when one is beyond the present Corporeal World because the Angelic World is a pure world.

One is not completely way beyond the Corporeal World when one uses the vices; only the energies which are anchored within the Angelic Body are beyond the Corporeal World (since they constantly remain in the Angelic Body). The rest of one's energies are in the physical body and Confluence Auric Field (attempting to move beyond the Corporeal World). The vices can be among these energies which are in the physical body and Confluence Auric Field.

In the Lower Universe, non-Confluence Aged souls use a Swargaloka that is provided in the higher section within the Second Field. The Second Field provides the physical world through the wave-particle duality aspect. Thus, Swargaloka is like the highest heaven in the physical realm. In Swargaloka, one will be able to easily experience bliss because the pure energies from the First Field are coming into Swargaloka.

In the second half cycle, when souls use the third auric field, they are in Swargaloka and not in Indraloka. The word 'Indraloka' can only be used to refer:

1. to the lokas that had been used by the Mid-Confluence Aged gods (where the Mid-Confluence Aged gods had played the role of Indra), and

2. to the lokas that are used by the Confluence Aged souls (where God Himself is Indra, the King of the gods, i.e. King of the angelic beings who

are in the Angelic World).

Actually, it is only the Confluence Aged Subtle Region which can be referred to as Indraloka because God Himself is there as the King of the deity souls.

Chapter 33: Maharloka, Janaloka and Tapoloka

Lokas are realms where one's consciousness is in. As the Kundalini rises, the consciousness (from the core of the soul) of those walking in can be in one of the seven lokas, since the loka is provided by the chakra based on where their Kundalini resides. Those walking in also have some of the energies of the soul anchored within the Angelic Body which is in the Angelic World. Thus, as the Kundalini rises, it is as if the Kundalini and consciousness of the person rises to meet the energies of the soul which are anchored in the Angelic Body. In the ancient Hindu texts, this has also been portrayed as Shakti (Kundalini) rising to meet Shiva (the energies of the soul that are anchored in the Angelic Body). When they meet, the consciousness of the person is completely in the Angelic World and Brahmapuri will transform into the Golden Aged world for those walking in. It should be noted that as the Kundalini and consciousness rises, it is as if one is getting closer and closer to one's Angelic Self

One reason why the person remains in the Confluence Age, even if he is not making spiritual efforts, is that some of the energies of the soul are entangled in the Angelic Body. These energies are pure and divine like the energies of God Shiva, since they are close to God. Thus, they are like Shiva in the residence of God, i.e. in the Angelic World.

Once the Kundalini begins to rise, for the walking in process, it does not drop unless the person stops using the BK knowledge and so the person is no longer walking in. The Kundalini also drops after rising:

1. if it had temporarily risen for experiences,

2. if a person was having a weak stage, or

3. for providing something as per the World Drama.

If they did not continue making spiritual efforts, they might continue to use the lower lokas.

At the end of the cycle, when the Golden Aged world gets materialised, the souls who are using Maharloka, Janaloka or Tapoloka, due to a weak stage, will begin to use the Seventh Chakra and Vaikuntha. Then, they will walk into the new world and constantly remain in the higher Vaikuntha-loka.

In the Hindu scriptures, Maharloka, Janaloka and Tapoloka have been portrayed as Munilokas. This reflects how the Mid-Confluence Aged gods, those walking in and those in the Lower Universe could use these lokas for spiritual living. These are lokas of enlightened yogis who are in a higher spiritual stage.

Those using Maharloka, Janaloka and Tapoloka will be good at using knowledge and making spiritual efforts. If one has made more spiritual efforts, one uses a higher loka. Those who use these higher lokas acquire greater spiritual abilities than those who use the lower lokas.

Those in these three higher lokas can easily move around into all the other lokas, including Vaikuntha (the heavenly spiritual loka which is beyond Brahmaloka). They can easily move from one loka to another with just a thought.

In the myths, the fast movements of a subtle person, from loka to loka or from place to place, often reflect the swift movements of the soul's energies in the subtle dimensions. This reflects how, when in the aura, the energies of the soul fly from one scene to another or from one loka to another, very quickly.

When you keep making spiritual efforts and begin to use the higher chakras, you begin to create thoughts which are in these higher lokas. From there the frequencies of your thoughts easily influence everything else in the universe, consequently you get what you want. Your thoughts are also materialised through the higher chakras. Actually, all the chakras work together to fulfil your thoughts because they will all be serving the soul who is in the pure state. Even the Kundalini serves the soul who is in the pure state; hence even the Kundalini assists to fulfil your desires.

Those who are using these higher lokas can use all the specialities and Siddhis which are provided by the chakras that also provide these lokas. For example, when using Janaloka, one can use all the specialities and Siddhis which are provided by the Fifth Chakra, and so one:

1. is creative.

2. can easily know the past, present and future.

3. will have wisdom, and the ability to easily understand and explain knowledge well.

4. can be free from diseases and the body would not age so rapidly during old age.

5. has powerful abilities to create subtle dimensions to reside in.

6. can easily experience visions in the lokas.

In the Hindu scriptures, the sons of Brahma have been portrayed as residing in Janaloka. This symbolically signifies that those in Janaloka can play a great role in the creation process. Thus, they can easily acquire what they want.

Those walking in, who use Tapoloka, will be able to use all the specialities and Siddhis of the Sixth Chakra and so one:

1. can easily establish one's link to God and attain a powerful stage.

2. can easily become soul conscious or aware that one is the soul.

3. is intuitive.

4. has wisdom and a good understanding of knowledge.

5. can easily adopt different subtle bodies at will. The QE Light creates whatever kind of body one wants or needs in the auric field and this becomes one's subtle body in the loka which one is in.

6. plays a role with God for the creation, sustenance and destruction processes while walking into the Golden Aged world. Thus, if one wants something, the QE Light and quantum energies decode information (the destructive process) and then encode other information (the creation process) so as to fulfil one's desires. The QE Light and quantum energies do this because God fulfils the desires of those walking in.

Those walking in should only use these lokas for entertainment purposes during spiritual effort making. They should be more concerned about being in the Angelic World unless they prefer entertainment instead of spiritual strength.

Chapter 34: Brahmaloka

The word 'Brahmaloka' has been used to refer to different lokas. Thus, Brahmaloka has been depicted through different ways, in the Hindu scriptures, for example:

1. Brahmaloka is associated to the Spiritual Sky.

2. Brahmaloka is associated to Satyaloka and so Brahmaloka is portrayed as the highest loka within the material sky.

The Spiritual Sky is discussed in greater detail in Chapter 50. Among other things, the Spiritual Sky consists of the Vaikuntha-lokas, Confluence Aged Subtle Region etc. When Brahmaloka is associated to the Spiritual Sky, it concerns one of the following:

1. how the Seventh Chakra (Brahmaloka) connects one, who is on the religious path or spiritual path, to the Vaikuntha regions in the Lower Universe, during the second half cycle.

2. what is happening through the Seventh Chakra (Brahmaloka) during the Confluence Age, at the end of the cycle.

When Brahmaloka is associated to the material sky and Satyaloka, it is the 7th auric field which is being referred to since it is in the highest division within the Unified Field that provides the Real World. The material sky is what exists in the sky of the world stage.

It is the First Field and the Second Field (collectively called the 'Unified Field') which are basically involved with providing the Real World. Thus, it is as if our universe consists of what is happening in the Unified Field. Since Brahmaloka is at the very top section in the Unified Field, it can be said that Brahmaloka is at the very edge of our universe. Actually, there are many universes overlapping in this Unified Field so as to provide the universe (or Real World) which we live in. The 'universe', which we live in, involves everything that we can see in our visible universe. There are also other such universes which are invisible because the QE Light and quantum energies provide our Real World in stages where each universe will be denser than the one above it. There are also other universes provided by other Real World Quantum Dimensions. Even in these, there are numerous universes provided in stages. When one uses one of these other higher universes via Brahmaloka, it is as if one can live as Brahma (in Brahmaloka) in these higher universes.

Brahmaloka connects BKs to Brahmapuri because they do not go into the dimensions in the Higher Universe. Where those walking in are concerned:

1. Brahmaloka can connect them to the Confluence Aged Subtle Region, which is above the Corporeal World, when their spiritual stage is good, or

2. through the Seventh Chakra, they can enjoy residing in Brahmaloka in the Higher Universe (within the Corporeal World) when they are in a weaker stage.

Since different souls will have their consciousness at different levels in the Higher Universe (as they are walking in) it can seem like there are numerous Brahmalokas which exist along the way to Brahmapuri. This was also a reason why so many different Brahmalokas have been mentioned in the Hindu scriptures. From this angle it can be said that Brahmaloka is the subtle abode of the secondary level Brahma since those who use a Brahmaloka within the Corporeal World do not have a high spiritual stage. When those walking in have a high spiritual stage, Brahmaloka connects them to Brahmapuri which is in the Angelic World (beyond the Corporeal World). This involves a higher level Brahma.

There are many kinds of Brahmaloka. The Confluence Aged Brahmapuri is also a Brahmaloka. However, it is not the same as the Brahmaloka that is used by those in the Lower Universe or in the Higher Universe. Be that as it may, it should be remembered that, as the walking in process continues, Brahmaloka is getting uplifted into Brahmapuri.

Since those walking in are using their Brahmaloka in the space of Vaikuntha, within the Corporeal World or in Brahmapuri which is above the Corporeal World, Brahmaloka has been associated to Vaikuntha in the Hindu scriptures. While using Brahmaloka, those walking in can use all the specialities and Siddhis that are provided by the Seventh Chakra (which can also be seen as Brahmaloka) such as the ability to:

1. easily understand the Truth.

2. experience the true state of one's being. Thus, those walking in experience themselves as the soul using the body.

3. easily remain in the detached state.

4. remain in the divine state.

5. keep one's consciousness pure and enjoy a pure spiritual stage.

6. experience supreme bliss.

7. get whatever one wants.

If one's Kundalini is in the Seventh Chakra, one can easily use the higher lokas which are beyond the 7th auric field. At the end of the cycle, when the Golden Aged world materialises, the bodies (of all those whose Kundalini has risen to the Seventh Chakra) will be transforming into the perfect state as they begin to live in Dwarka. The QE Light and quantum energies will stop providing the body in the Lower Universe and will begin to provide the Golden Aged physical body in the same space as Brahmapuri (in Satyaloka). This is explained further in Chapter 44: Golden Aged Vaikuntha, Brahmaloka, Satyaloka and Dwarka.

In the Holographic Universe, the 2D SWD is above Brahmaloka. Thus, one is close to the 2D SWD when one is in Brahmaloka.

In the second half cycle, as one uses the higher dimensions, one also uses the energies deeper within the soul. Thus, when one uses Brahmaloka, one is also using energies which are closer to the World

Drama within the soul. One is the god self or Brahma, at that moment. Those in the second half cycle can actually begin the journey inward and then move upwards, or they can keep going deeper within. They can reach Brahmaloka either way.

Actually, the god self can be divided into two. The deepest one is normally not used as the god self. When one becomes the god self, one is only using energies (from the god self) which are higher up and one is not becoming the god self who is automatically doing everything as per the World Drama.

Where those walking in are concerned, the souls are already playing the role of Brahma since the whole soul is transforming into the divine godly state. Those walking in have to concentrate on journeying upwards, after having gone within, because they have to establish their link to God. When their link to God is established, they can use Brahmapuri through Brahmaloka.

Further, Confluence Aged souls do not act as the god self. They have to be instruments of God. This means that they allow God to move them through their link to God. This is similar to how a puppet is moved by strings. Though one is 'Brahma', one is only Brahma (the instrument of God). Through trying to go within to become the god self, you might only end up meeting all your past births there who had tried to remain in an emerged state as the god self. You will not get anything great by meeting them there. However, by meeting God and staying linked to Him, you can get a lot of benefits.

Those walking in are also not involved with trying to become the god self because they have to use God for the walking in process. So instead of trying to go deeper within the soul, they have to move upwards to establish their link to God. If their stage is weak, they may not end up in Brahmapuri; they may be in the Higher Universe. This means their Brahmaloka would be near the 2D SWD. So they can easily play the role of the creator (Brahma) from Brahmaloka in order to get what they want.

Even the QE Light and quantum energies act as Brahma. In fact, it can be said that it is the Ocean of QE Light which is really Brahma in the Corporeal World because it initiates the creative processes based on what exists in the World Drama. There has to be an initiation from the 'light' before the dark quantum forces act.

Anyway, once you begin to use the 7th auric field, you will be in the world of Brahma where the QE Light and quantum energies play the role of Brahma and create what you want.

No-one becomes a permanent resident in Brahmaloka in the second half cycle. It is only those who walk in who will begin to use Brahmaloka permanently because they would be constantly using the Seventh Chakra just before the Golden Aged world materialises (since the Kundalini permanently resides in the Crown Chakra). Even the Mid-Confluence Aged gods were permanently using Brahmaloka before their Kundalini began to drop into the lower lokas. For this reason too they had been referred to as Brahma in the Hindu scriptures. It should be noted that the space in the Crown Chakra can also be seen as Brahmaloka.

When the soul leaves the body to take another birth, the soul leaves the body through the Crown Chakra. At the end of the cycle, when all souls are taken back to the Soul World, the soul also leaves the body through the Seventh Chakra to go back to the Soul World with God.

Figure 3 portrays where the lokas are situated in the Lower Universe.

Figure 4 depicts the position of the lokas in the Higher Universe.

Chapter 35: Usage of Specialities and Siddhis in Lokas

As those walking in use each higher chakra, a new auric field is created in the Higher Universe and they can use the Siddhis and specialities through using that chakra and its auric field. As each higher auric field is created through a higher chakra, those walking in get more and more Siddhis and specialities.

Activation of the chakras helps the soul to attain the Siddhis, specialities and to use different lokas which are provided by the different chakras. Actually, it can be said that the seven chakras are also lokas because the lokas are experienced through the chakras and the lokas extend from the space in the chakras to the various dimensions in the Holographic Universe. One can have an experience while in the region of the chakra itself, if one has not gone into the auric field. In spite of this, normally, experiences are had in the auric fields where special lokas are provided reflecting the specialities of the chakras. Since the Siddhis and specialities, which are provided by a chakra, are also used in the auric field and loka, it can be said that:

1. through the use of Janaloka one can produce children via the power of yoga after having walked into the Golden Aged world.

2. through the use of Tapoloka, one can easily live a simple yogi life and be able to follow the BK Maryadas very easily and comfortably. Further, one's past lives can be easily experienced and so, their bad karma can be easily burnt through the power of yoga with God.

While in the lokas, since you are using the chakras efficiently, you will find that you can control everything that is in the loka, especially the elements that are entangled with the loka. If you do not like something that you see in the environment of your subtle dimension, you can change it or remove it. If you see a vision in the auric field or loka, you can change what is in that vision. However, BKs are not involved with changing what is in the subtle region or visions. Their only aim is to stay linked to God.

If those walking in are using the higher chakras (from the 4th chakra upwards), they can easily remain as detached observers. The higher the chakra which one uses, the greater the ability to watch everything as a detached observer. This is a speciality that is used through the higher chakras.

Often, as the chakras are opening to function better, especially for using the lokas, those walking in may experience "Siddhis" or powers. Thus, as you go into the higher lokas you are served accordingly. For example, those walking in, while they are in Brahmaloka, will get whatever they want because the QE Light and quantum energies create whatever is wished for. However, while in that dimension, you will not want anything. You will be happily enjoying the blissful state and you will understand that this is what life was meant to be for, i.e. for enjoying bliss and happiness. You will be in the truthful state and so you will be like this.

The loka, which you are in, reflects the state which you are in and the kind of experiences you can have. Whatever is experienced through the lokas also affect what the person is enjoying in the physical realm. Thus, living in a loka is like living on earth with those specialities and Siddhis that the chakras provide. While using the lokas, especially the higher lokas, one can create one's own reality, through using thoughts, visualisations, intentions and desires.

Those walking in will have their Kundalini rising from the Root Chakra to the Crown Chakra because one's consciousness will be in the Crown Chakra while one lives in the Golden Aged world. As the Kundalini rises, one can use all the Siddhis and specialities that are provided by the chakras because the chakras are being activated to function properly. One can use these Siddhis and specialities during experiences, in lokas, and/or in real life. These Siddhis and specialities are being developed due to the walking in process. Those walking in can enjoy the Siddhis and specialities because they are walking into a world where the people are served well.

If you are walking in, but you are more of a BK using the BK Maryadas, then, your Siddhis will not be developing because the BK knowledge is not for developing Siddhis. There will not be any need for BKs to have Siddhis because God does the magical wonders. BKs do not use the Siddhis though they can use the specialities.

Just because you don't have a certain speciality does not mean that your chakras are not functioning well. Specialities are often given to a person as per the World Drama. So you will find that some BKs can explain knowledge well while others are unable to. Those who cannot explain knowledge well might have other specialities. Different people have different specialities. However, you can make attempts to develop the specialities which you want, if you don't have them. Sometimes, specialities develop as you keep doing something. For example, even though you are not able to explain knowledge well, if you constantly keep explaining knowledge while having your link to God, the relevant chakras will get activated to help you to give good explanations.

Usually, even the Siddhis are provided as per the World Drama. However, one can make attempts to develop these; though, this is not advisable because people are currently capable of using the vices. In the first half cycle, people were not capable of using the vices. Thus, they were naturally imbued with magical abilities. They had magical abilities because all the chakras were functioning perfectly and so they had the ability to use all the Siddhis. It was also as if they were magically creating the environment which they lived in. Thus, leaves etc. did not rot. It was as if the leaves etc. just kept getting recreated again and again. The QE Light and quantum energies served them well. The leaves etc. also did not rot quickly because everything was suffused with longevity since they were healthy. Further, nothing really rots in the world of the first half cycle because the people were living in the denser 3D SWD. There was not much rubbish visible in the denser 3D SWD, as it would have been visible in the Real World which the Golden Aged people did not really use. Living in the denser 3D SWD was like living in a magical loka. Magic was done through the unity which humans have with everything else in the Corporeal World.

Everything in the Real World has a QE Light form or a product of the QE Light. There is unity or oneness in everything in the Real World through all the QE Light in the Corporeal World. Even the creation of the chakras was initiated by the QE Light, and these chakras consist of QE Light and quantum energies which are flowing from one dimension to another. The chakras have a QE Light form in the Higher Universe and a dark quantum form in the Lower Universe. Since the dark quantum energies are the other half of the QE Light, there is 'oneness' in everything in the universe. It is as if we are also one with everything else in the Corporeal World because the energies of the soul are entangled with the QE Light energies:

1. which play a role as the Kundalini.

2. which have the imprints of the 2D SWD.

3. which form the QE Light Mind in the brain of the person.

Actually, it is as if we are also entangled with the chakras etc. because we live our lives through using them. It was also through using the chakras that the people of the first half cycle were living a life like they were the creators of their environment. They played this role of the 'creator' along with the QE Light.

In the second half cycle, we have given different identities to everything without understanding the connections between everything in the universe. Through this, we have actually separated and alienated ourselves from the QE Light of the Corporeal World. This has also prevented us from having magical abilities. However, this has also happened as per the World Drama because impure people should not be involved with magically creating the environment as the people, in the first half cycle, were. Those walking in are acquiring this ability. However, they should not try to use this now. They will be naturally using it after having walked in. Until then, it is best to turn to God and visualisations.

Actually, even after walking in, the Siddhis are not to be used intentionally by those walking in. They will be naturally and automatically used to help sustain the world in the perfect state, in the Golden Age, after walking in. In the perfect world, you will also be getting whatever you want automatically. For this reason too, there will be no need to think of using the Siddhis.

The Mid-Confluence Aged people had given a lot of importance to using the seven chakras and seven lokas because they were making sure that they could continue doing magic. If they were losing the ability to do magic, they would be involved with developing their Siddhis. However, those walking in should not be involved with trying to develop and use the Siddhis. These Siddhis will develop naturally because these souls are walking in.

Chapter 36: Vaikuntha

Above Brahmaloka/Satyaloka is the 2D SWD; and above the 2D SWD is Vaikuntha. The Vaikuntha-lokas are provided by the pure QE Light energies. There are no dark quantum energies within the dimensions in Vaikuntha and one also cannot use the vices if one wants to use the Vaikuntha-lokas. Vaikuntha only exists if the energies of the soul are using the Vaikuntha-lokas in the space beyond the 2D SWD. Despite this general rule, in the Hindu scriptures, the word Vaikuntha or Vaikuntha-loka has been used to refer to many different kinds of heavenly lokas such as:

1. the Confluence Aged Subtle Region and Soul World.

2. the higher dimensions, in the Higher Universe and in the space of the Confluence Aged Subtle Region, which are used by those walking into the Golden Aged world.

3. the subtle Vaikuntha dimension that exists in the Golden Aged world.

4. the higher dimensions in the Lower Universe which exist beyond the 2D SWD. Each spiritual or religious group will have their own Vaikuntha.

5. the Mid-Confluence Aged subtle dimensions.

6. the Vaikuntha in which the memories etc. of the past births, who play a role in the afterlife, exist.

Sometimes, all the above have also been referred to by other names. In the Hindu scriptures, since God has also been portrayed as Vishnu, Vaikuntha was also used to describe God's residence in the Confluence Aged Subtle Region and in the Soul World. However, I do not refer to these as Vaikuntha because I use the BK names for these.

I refer to the Vaikuntha, which those walking in use, as the Golden Aged Vaikuntha. All those walking in use this Vaikuntha in the Higher Universe and Confluence Aged Subtle Region. There are various levels to the Golden Aged Vaikuntha because those walking in begin to use the lower chakras before beginning to use the higher chakras.

The QE Light provides the Golden Aged QE Light bodies through the seven chakras which are in the body. These QE Light bodies have a subtle Vaikuntha form in the subtle Golden Aged Vaikuntha dimension because each QE Light body, which is provided by a chakra, consists of QE Light bodies of various densities. The less dense ones are in subtle Golden Aged Vaikuntha dimension. As the seven QE Light bodies (of the seven chakras) materialise the physical body, the materialising body will also have a subtle Vaikuntha form because there are two aspects to the body: the real form and the subtle Vaikuntha form. Thus, those walking in are already using the Golden Aged Vaikuntha, though they are not in the true Golden Aged Vaikuntha because all the seven Golden Aged QE Light bodies have not been completely created as yet. When these seven Golden Aged QE Light bodies are completely created, those walking in will be in the true Golden Aged Vaikuntha. When all the seven Golden Aged QE Light bodies are completely created, those walking in will also be having their physical bodies provided in the Golden Aged world and not in the Kaliyug world. Since the Golden Aged body is created through the seven chakras, the seven chakras and their lokas are gateways to the Golden Aged Vaikuntha.

Those walking in can be seen as using Vaikuntha through all their chakras because everything is changing for them as their world is getting transformed into the Golden Aged world. Thus, even though they are living in the old world, since their bodies are in the Kaliyug world, they are in Vaikuntha because the Kaliyug world is in the process of being transformed into the Golden Aged world for them. Those walking in should have the faith that this is happening.

All seven chakras can also be seen as the gateway to the Golden Aged Vaikuntha because as the Kundalini rises, the consciousness (from the core of the soul) is rising into a higher Vaikuntha-loka. This is so because the Kundalini is rising due to the soul being taken into the Golden Aged world. So the energies of the soul are being given a Golden Aged subtle residence. However, the seven lokas are not considered as Vaikuntha if one wants to use the Siddhis and specialities intentionally, instead of just enjoying the Siddhis and specialities when they are provided as per the World Drama.

The chakras in the bodies and their lokas can also be considered as gateways to the Golden Aged Vaikuntha because those walking in begin to use the Golden Aged Vaikuntha-loka as their subtle dimension from the time they start the walking in process. Since they are already walking into the Golden Aged Vaikuntha, all the subtle lokas which they use can be considered as Vaikuntha-lokas. However, the 3rd to 7th chakras and their lokas are only the gateways to the lower Vaikuntha dimensions.

Just as the Confluence Aged Subtle Region can be seen as beginning from the lower auric fields but its true place is in the Angelic World which is beyond the Corporeal World, even the lower auric fields which are used by those walking in are Vaikuntha. However, the true Vaikuntha involve those Vaikuntha-lokas which are used via the higher chakras that are above the physical body, especially those in the Confluence Aged Subtle Region. These can properly be referred to as Vaikuntha since they are higher up and only QE Light energies exist in these higher dimensions.

Those walking in can use many Vaikuntha-lokas within the Golden Aged Vaikuntha, depending on their beliefs, desires etc. This is so because one's Vaikuntha-loka is experienced within one's own auric field which exists in the space of the Golden Aged Vaikuntha. It should be noted that each QE Light body has its own auric field. This means that those QE Light bodies which are in the Golden Aged Vaikuntha will have their own auric fields in the Golden Aged Vaikuntha. Since there are seven QE Light bodies produced by the seven chakras, there are seven auric fields. However, each of these seven auric fields consists of many auric fields, some of which are in the subtle Golden Aged Vaikuntha.

Don't try to live with others in your loka. They may not be in Vaikuntha. If you tried to live in the same loka as them, your aura might merge with theirs and you might get pulled into their lower loka unless you were so spiritually powerful that you were able to bring them into Vaikuntha. If they were not walking in, they will not be in the same Vaikuntha as you. Further, in the merged state, their unhappiness etc. can influence you, and this would not feel good. In addition, they may not want to be in the same loka as you, and this may give you a bad experience.

In the Hindu scriptures, Vaikuntha has been portrayed as the home of Lakshmi and Narayan because this represents the true Golden Aged Vaikuntha. The Golden Aged world is the true heavenly world and so its spiritual Vaikuntha dimension is the true heavenly dimension, i.e. the true Golden Aged Vaikuntha exists in the true Golden Aged world. Those walking in are in the process of walking into the true Golden Aged Vaikuntha. Their Vaikuntha has not transformed into the true Golden Aged Vaikuntha state as yet, though it will transform into the true Golden Aged Vaikuntha one day. Even so, it can be said that the spiritual realm that is used by those walking into the Golden Aged world is also a Vaikuntha-loka.

From the time of the Mid-Confluence, the word 'Vaikuntha' has been used to refer to all heavenly dimensions whether it is associated to the Golden Aged world or not. Thus, in the second half cycle, Vaikuntha is the QE Light lokas within the Cosmic Field and SWL (in the Lower Universe). This Vaikuntha is used through the chakras which are above the physical body and one goes into this Vaikuntha through Brahmaloka. Since even those who are not deity souls can benefit through using the practices in this book, I have used the word Vaikuntha to refer to all heavenly dimensions whether they are associated to the Golden Aged world or not.

Based on what has been left behind by the ancient people in the Hindu scriptures, it can be said that Vaikuntha even includes the various lokas used through belief systems. Each belief system will have its own pure QE Light dimension in the Cosmic Field or SWL which can be used as the

Vaikuntha-loka of that belief system. No-one can use these Vaikunthas, which have been created through belief systems, unless they accept the teachings of that belief system. However, these are different from the Vaikuntha of those walking into the Golden Aged world. The Vaikuntha of those walking in involves transformation of the world into the Golden Aged world whereas all others are just heavenly dimensions.

The QE Light energies which provide Vaikuntha can also be seen as Vaikuntha. These energies connect the energies of the soul, which are in Vaikuntha, to everything in the universe and so it allows the soul to live through using Vaikuntha. These QE Light energies also provide a heavenly environment for the energies of the soul in Vaikuntha. Further, in the second half cycle, it is easy to remain in the virtuous state while in Vaikuntha because the pure QE Light energies which exist there will influence one to remain pure. Though these QE Light energies are part of Vaikuntha, these QE Light energies are only playing a role with, and for, the energies of the soul in Vaikuntha. Vaikuntha will not exist if the energies of the soul were not in Vaikuntha.

Anyway, since Vaikuntha is provided by the QE Light energies, the QE Light was also portrayed as Vaikuntha in the Hindu scriptures. Thus, in the Mahabharata (Book 12: Santi Parva, Section CCCXLIII), Lord Krishna says "I till the Earth, assuming the form of a large plough-share of black iron. And because my complexion is black, therefore am I called by the name of Krishna. I have united the Earth with Water, Space with Mind, and Wind with Light. Therefore am I called Vaikuntha."

In the above quote, the dark complexion of Krishna reflects the dark quantum energies which play a huge role for materialising everything in the Real World, including the "large plough-share of black iron"; and, Vaikuntha represents the QE Light. The above quote is also attempting to reflect how the QE Light plays a significant role through its connections for what has to exist in the world. The above quote further reflects how the Mid-Confluence Aged gods gave a lot of importance to the QE Light and quantum energies because these played a role with them for the 'creation' of the universe which they lived in. Actually, the

QE Light plays its role as Vaikuntha because they provide the world based on the state of the energies of the soul.

More on the Vaikuntha-lokas are discussed in the subsequent chapters of this book.

Chapter 37: Brahmajyoti

In the Hindu scriptures, Brahmajyoti refers to:

1. the effulgence from the QE Light source.

2. God's effulgence.

Even the QE Light source, including the energies which vibrate out from it, is 'Sat' (Sanskrit word meaning 'existence'). It exists eternally for providing our universe. Its powerful light radiates out as the QE Light Ocean and this is its effulgence. From there, its light flows into the dimensions above the 2D SWD, where they are still in the pure, powerful state for the creation processes. One will not be able to see the QE Light source because it is too powerful to be seen. One will only be able to perceive its brilliant radiance or effulgence. Through this effulgence, our universes are created. Everything is created through the light of its effulgence because the QE Light initiates the creation process. Thus, it can be said that this effulgence is universal. However, it can be felt in the space above the 2D SWD because the energies of the effulgence are in the QE Light Ocean, Shore of the QE Light Ocean and Cosmic Field. All these can be seen as being part of Brahmajyoti; though it is the QE Light Ocean which is the most brilliant part of the effulgence.

The seven lokas, which are provided by the seven chakras and auric fields, are within the Unified Field. Thus, they are within the material realm where the quantum energies also exist. Quantum energies do not exist in the higher dimensions such as the Cosmic Field and SWL. Thus, those higher dimensions are spiritual realms since the QE Light are the spiritual aspect of the quantum energies. However, it is more accurate to refer to these as 'spiritual realms' only when the energies of the souls and/or Supreme Soul are within them since it is the energies of the soul and Supreme Soul which can most accurately be described as being spiritual energies.

Through the light from the QE Light's effulgence, the Vaikuntha-lokas and other lokas are created for those on the spiritual path. Thus, within Brahmajyoti, there are Vaikuntha-lokas which are enjoyed by those walking into the Golden Aged world as their environment is rising up to go into Brahmapuri. These Vaikuntha-lokas are pleasant dimensions to be in. One should not try to have an experience in the dimension of Brahmajyoti (outside the auric fields) because one will be exposed to the powerful forces which are there. It will not feel comfortable.

When you, the soul, are exposed to powerful QE Light energies, without being given protection to tolerate it, you will be thrown off-balance, feel weakened and have a spinning sensation (as if all your energies are spinning).

One can enjoy a Vaikuntha-loka that is within the higher auric fields (which are within the space of Brahmajyoti) because the pure fine energies from Brahmajyoti will be providing a heavenly environment in these lokas. Even God's vibrations which are within Brahmajyoti will flow into the loka to energise the energies of the soul and environment in the loka.

God is also 'Sat' (Sanskrit word which also means 'Truth'). One only experiences the Truth when exposed to His effulgence. However, God's effulgence (Brahmajyoti) is very powerful. So one will not be able to tolerate it if one was exposed to the whole strength of it. As a result, during the Confluence Age, God gives us a protection so that we can see and experience God through our link to God. God is just a point and we cannot see a point. However, we can discern God's effulgence or we can see an enlarged vision of God. Though we glimpse God's effulgence, we do not experience the whole strength of it because we are being given protection. We only experience the full strength of God's effulgence on Judgement Day. If a soul was in a weak stage and it was exposed to God's effulgence, which those in Shankerpuri are exposed to, they will not be able to tolerate it. They will feel a burning sensation as they would on Judgement Day, but it would not be so bad because the effulgence which those in Shankerpuri are exposed to is not really that powerful. It is still quite tolerable. God's effulgence is absorbed and sent into the world in tolerable amounts until the world is completely transformed. Thus, those walking in and others do not suffer as the world becomes purer. They can only easily enjoy the pure stage and feel good.

The more powerful you become, the greater your ability to tolerate more powerful energies. This is why you will be exposed to more of God's energies in Shankerpuri.

When BKs are in a powerful stage, their consciousness is in the Angelic World. Thus, most of God's energies which are emitted from them are sent into the QE Light source and QE Light Ocean because these are the closest to the Angelic World. The QE Light energies will be able to tolerate God's powerful energies because the QE Light energies are also powerful energies. However, God's energies which are sent through the Confluence Aged souls are only small amounts that can be tolerated by Mankind. It can only make others feel good. As a result, the QE Light source and QE Light Ocean will only be transformed very slowly.

God's effulgence is received and reflected into the world by the Confluence Aged souls because it is only God's effulgence which can create the Golden Aged world for us. God's effulgence is also being radiated into the space of Brahmajyoti, in the Corporeal World, from Goloka.

Goloka consists of God and the powerful Confluence Aged souls who are God's cows for providing the milk (God's energies) for:

1. transforming the World into the Golden Aged world, and

2. providing sustenance during the walking in process.

Thus, it can be said that it is those who are in the Confluence Aged Shankerpuri who are in Goloka. Goloka is above Vaikuntha since Shankerpuri is above:

1. Vishnupuri (where the Golden Aged spiritual realm called Vaikuntha or Vishnupuri exist), and

2. Brahmapuri (where the Golden Aged Real World will exist and where the subtle Golden Aged Vaikuntha exists for those walking in).

It can be said that Brahmajyoti exists in the Higher Universe, above the 2D SWD and just beneath the White Hole which provides the entrance to the Confluence Aged Subtle Region that is beyond the Corporeal World. The Brahmajyoti here consists of:

1. QE Light energies (which have been energised by God's energies that are flowing into the space of Brahmajyoti from the Confluence Aged Subtle Region), and

2. God's vibrations (which are being sent into the Corporeal World via the Confluence Aged souls).

Since God's effulgence is sent to the QE Light, the effulgence of the QE Light source becomes more powerful and becomes capable of creating the Golden Aged world for us. As this happens, the space which consists of Brahmajyoti gets uplifted into the Confluence Aged Subtle Region because it is transforming into a divine (less dense) dimension. Since it is becoming less dense, it will keep moving into a higher space; from the Lower Universe it moves into the Higher Universe and then it keeps moving higher up until it exists in the Confluence Aged Subtle Region so as to provide the Golden Aged Real World in the space of Brahmapuri. As Brahmajyoti is brought up, even the Golden Aged Unified Field is elevated since the QE Light is providing QE Light energies to the Unified Field. So the Golden Aged Real World will materialise in the space of Brahmapuri.

It is only when the QE Light source is completely transformed that it initiates the materialisation of the Golden Aged Real World. It becomes completely transformed when the deity souls are completely transformed.

Brahmajyoti is part of the Spiritual Sky since it consists of the vibrations of God and the pure spiritual QE Light from the QE Light source, both of which are in the higher dimension (in the space of the sky in the world stage).

Since the QE Light effulgence is a brilliant radiance, it cannot be tolerated when we are too close to it. This is why people do not use a loka/dimension in the QE Light Ocean during the second half cycle. Those walking in can use a Vaikuntha-loka in the space of the QE Light Ocean because God's energies protect us. So we will be able to tolerate the QE Light effulgence while enjoying a more powerful loka. We will not feel blinded by the strength of the QE Light energies in the QE Light Ocean. Those energies will only provide us with a heavenly loka where we can experience greater bliss.

However, those walking in are only in Brahmajyoti if their spiritual stage is not good (since they do not have a good link to God). Since their link is bad, they are not able to go beyond into the Angelic World.

Actually, the true Golden Aged Vaikuntha is in the space where the Confluence Aged Subtle Region exists and that is where the Golden Aged world materialises. So if one is in the space of the QE Light dimensions, above the 2D SWD, and has not gone into the Confluence Aged Subtle Region, one has not progressed into the space of the true Golden Aged Vaikuntha. It is only at the very end, as the world is about to be materialised, that all the QE Light dimensions, which are above the 2D SWD, will get up-lifted into the space of the Confluence Aged Subtle Region. Until then, if one is only in the space of Brahmajyoti, one's stage is not that strong; and when the stage weakens, one's intellect will fall back into the physical body.

However, what's so good about Brahmajyoti is that, even if one's spiritual stage is not that good, one can still easily enjoy a heavenly loka in the space of Brahmajyoti, even though the most heavenly experience and environment would be in the Vaikuntha which overlaps the Confluence Aged Subtle Region beyond the present Corporeal World. As the energies of the soul are moving up to go beyond the present Corporeal World, those walking in can have their consciousness in the Vaikuntha dimensions within Brahmajyoti (even if they are not making serious spiritual efforts). These experiences would also be heavenly because the environment in the Vaikuntha dimensions in Brahmajyoti consists of less dense, pure, heavenly energies. Since they are having QE Light bodies created in the Higher Universe, those walking in will find it very easy to use one of the Vaikuntha dimensions in Brahmajyoti because their QE Light bodies are created through energies which are from Brahmajyoti. Then, through greater spiritual effort making, they can utilise the Vaikuntha dimensions which exist beyond the present Corporeal World, in the space where the Confluence Aged Subtle Region exists.

Chapter 38: Confluence Aged Prana

Prana means 'energies'. Confluence Aged Prana refers to:

1. The energies accumulated within the depths of the soul, as the soul's energies are energised by God's effulgence, during the Confluence Age. Hereafter, this will be referred to as the 'Deity Soul's Confluence Aged Prana'.

2. The energies that accumulate within the QE Light source, as God's effulgence is sent into the Corporeal World so as to transform the world into the Golden Aged world, during the Confluence Age. Hereafter, this will be referred to as the 'QE Light's Confluence Aged Prana'.

3. God's energies which are being sent into the Corporeal World through the Confluence Aged spiritual effort makers. Hereafter, this will be referred to as 'God's Confluence Aged Prana'.

I refer to the accumulation of energies within the souls and QE Light source as Confluence Aged Prana because this accumulation is only taking place due to what is happening through the Confluence Age. It accumulates due to energies being exposed to God's effulgence and this accumulation of energies will finally transform the world into the Golden Aged world. Thus, it fulfils what God has come into the Corporeal World for. Confluence Aged Prana gives spiritual strength and so, since it accumulates within the soul and QE Light source, it strengthens until they transform into the divine state.

When deity souls accumulate spiritual strength, as they keep absorbing God's energies through their link to God (during the Confluence Age), they accumulate Deity Soul's Confluence Aged Prana. Since the soul is only exposed to a little of God's effulgence, when it is linked to God, only a little of its energies are permanently transformed to remain in the transformed state. These permanently transformed energies are Deity Soul's Confluence Aged Prana. The rest of the energies of the soul are only exposed to a minute fraction of God's energies which are vibrating out from the spot where God's effulgence hits. Thus, the rest of the soul is only being temporarily transformed into the pure divine state. Though a spot in the soul is exposed to God's powerful effulgence, the soul does not feel the burning sensation because it is just a very minuscule spot. This is why it takes many years for the soul to transform into the completely pure divine state. As the soul is hit by God's effulgence, it is also being given protection not to feel any pain because all the rest of the energies of the soul are being exposed to God's energies which help it to experience bliss instead. The rest of the energies of the soul are not being exposed to God's effulgence; it can be said that they are being exposed to God's Confluence Aged Prana. The completely transformed energies accumulate within the Deity Self. So the Deity Self becomes more and more powerful. As it becomes more powerful, it ascends to a higher level within the soul. By the time the Golden Aged world materialises, it would have ascended to the highest level and so it can be used as the Conscious Self in the Golden Aged world. The Deity Self cannot be used as the Conscious Self in the old world since the old world is an impure world; though, during the Confluence Age, we can constantly keep emerging the energies of the Deity Self to the surface and this will be like becoming the Deity Self.

As the BKs absorb God's energies into themselves, God's energies are also automatically flowing out from them into the world and their environment. Sometimes, BKs intentionally absorb and send God's energies into the world for world transformation. I am referring to God's energies, which are flowing out or sent out through the BKs, as God's Confluence Aged Prana because:

1. God's energies are received, by the QE Light and others, in an indirect way and not in the direct way as Confluence Aged souls are receiving it through their link to God.

2. only a little of God's energies are being sent out and not the whole of God's effulgence.

The words "God's Confluence Aged Prana" reflect that souls and the whole world are not exposed to all of God's effulgence when they receive God's energies through the BKs; they only receive a little. Though one will not be able to tolerate God's effulgence, one will be able to tolerate God's Confluence Aged Prana because this involves tolerable amounts of God's energies.

God's energies will be influencing all the energies, which are close to it, to vibrate at similar frequencies. One might prefer to say that these transformed energies are also Confluence Aged Prana because this transformation only takes place during the Confluence Age when energies can be exposed to God's energies directly. However, this transformation is a temporary one because the soul is not being exposed to all of God's effulgence. So I do not refer to these temporarily transformed energies as Confluence Aged Prana. I am just stating that these energies have God's Confluence Aged Prana because God's energies are within them. Through the words God's Confluence Aged Prana, I am referring to God's energies and not to the temporarily transformed energies.

God's energies empower the Corporeal World so that the world transforms into the perfect state. As God's Confluence Aged Prana are sent to the QE Light source, Ocean of QE Light, and all other QE Light and quantum energies in the Corporeal World, these energies become empowered. They get filled with God's Confluence Aged Prana. In addition to this, as BKs intentionally reflect God's effulgence (which has hit a spot within the soul) into the world, a greater amount of God's energies are sent out. It will be as if God's effulgence is being sent into the world. It will only be like this is the soul is in a powerful stage. If the soul is in a weak state, what is being sent out is like God's Confluence Aged Prana. Along with God's effulgence, God's Confluence Aged Prana is also sent into the world because God's energies vibrate outwards and do not remain in a spot. When God's energies are sent out, it helps the QE Light source to accumulate QE Light's Confluence Aged Prana. Actually, God's effulgence, which is sent to the QE Light, is not as powerful as it was when it hit the energies of the soul because after God's effulgence had hit a spot in the soul, God's energies vibrate out from there. However, this is not significant because the state of the QE Light is dependent on the state of the deity souls. So when the deity souls transform, the QE Light source will likewise transform. Be that as it may, when we send God's energies into the world, the QE Light does accumulate a little QE Light's Confluence Aged Prana instantly; through this way it accumulates QE Light's Confluence Aged Prana slowly.

As we keep sending God's energies to the world, the QE Light source is accumulating spiritual strength as its QE Light's Confluence Aged Prana accumulates. As this accumulation keeps taking place over a long duration of time, in the QE Light source, a time will come when the accumulated QE Light's Confluence Aged Prana is so powerful within it that the QE Light source transforms into the divine state. When this happens, divine QE Light is sent into the QE Light Ocean and other dimensions. Since they will then consist of lighter energies, they ascend into the Higher Universe where the new universe will exist. As these QE Light dimensions are being empowered and as they ascend, those walking into the Golden Aged world can take benefits:

1. from the Confluence Aged Prana which is within the QE Light dimensions.

2. through being uplifted along with the QE Light Ocean, and other dimensions, as they get uplifted.

God's energies, which are sent from Brahmapuri, reach both (the Higher Universe and the Lower Universe) since the Lower Universe has to be transformed and uplifted. Thus, there is God's Confluence Aged Prana in both these universes. Since the Vaikuntha-lokas are nearer to the Angelic World, those who are in Vaikuntha will be exposed to a lot of God's Confluence Aged Prana. The Golden Aged Vaikuntha dimension, which is used by those walking in, contains the most amount of God's Confluence Aged Prana because God is assisting them for the walking in process.

God's Confluence Aged Prana is also flowing into the Corporeal World (Higher Universe and Lower Universe) through all the auric fields because the Confluence Aged souls are utilising auric fields in the Lower Universe and Higher Universe; God's energies flow out of these auric fields into the Higher Universe (through higher auric field) and Lower Universe (through the Etheric Field). It should be noted that the Etheric Field is connected to the higher auric fields; so God's energies from the higher auric fields flow into the Etheric Field before flowing out into the Lower Universe.

Further, since the QE Light's Confluence Aged Prana is accumulating in the QE Light source, it is as if it is accumulating in both, the Lower Universe and the Higher Universe, because the QE Light source empowers both.

It is when the 900, 000 Confluence Aged souls are ready for world transformation, by having accumulated a lot of Deity Soul's Confluence Aged Prana, that the QE Light source would have also accumulated sufficient QE Light's Confluence Aged Prana to transform into the divine state. The state of the QE Light source is a reflection of the state which the deity souls are in. Thus, even if we do not intentionally send God's energies to the world, the QE Light will be accumulating energies as the deity souls accumulate energies. This happens because God's energies will be naturally flowing out into the universe through the Confluence Aged deity souls who have a link to God. So God's energies are taking care of it, even though we are not aware that the QE Light source is being transformed as we transform.

From 1936, the QE Light source and all other QE Light energies (collectively referred to as the Cosmic Consciousness) were receiving God's energies. So the QE Light source was accumulating QE Light's Confluence Aged Prana; and God's Confluence Aged Prana, which is in the Cosmic Consciousness, can be utilised by those who are connecting themselves to the Cosmic Consciousness.

In the first half cycle, the whole world was sustained by the energies that were naturally flowing out of the deities who were living at that time. This kept the world in the perfect divine state. Even the QE Light source and QE Light Ocean were sustained through this way, during the first half cycle. When the deities lost their pure state, at the end of the Silver Age, even the QE Light source and QE Light Ocean lost its divine state. So the QE Light Ocean fell into the Quantum World. Though the QE Light source and QE Light Ocean lost their divine state, they do not use the vices like the human souls. Thus, the QE Light source and QE Light Ocean remained very powerful due to their pure state. They remained powerful similarly to how the core of the soul remained powerful. However, the QE Light was like an ocean whereas human souls were not. Thus, the QE Light had greater power than the soul. When the Mid-Confluence Aged gods became aware of all these, they began practices through which:

1. souls could easily remain pure by being surrounded by the pure QE Light energies in the higher dimensions.

2. weak souls could become empowered by the pure QE Light energies from the QE Light Ocean (which people began to refer to as the Cosmic Consciousness).

These practices had been continued and so, until now, people try their best to get connected to the Cosmic Consciousness so as to get energised. As a consequence, after the Confluence Age began, souls could get exposed to God's energies through being exposed to God's Confluence Aged Prana which have been sent into the Cosmic Consciousness. However, it is when one has the intention to be exposed to God's energies in the Cosmic Consciousness that they are exposed to God's Confluence Aged Prana. This is so because people only get what they want. They have a right to choose what they want. If one has the intention of getting exposed to the Confluence Aged Prana which is in the Cosmic Consciousness, one easily becomes pure and through that one easily gets what one wants via visualisations. Even if one had the desire to be exposed to God's energies which are in the Cosmic Consciousness, without being aware of what is happening through the

Confluence Age, they get exposed to God's Confluence Aged Prana in the Cosmic Consciousness because their desire was to be exposed to God's energies in the Cosmic Consciousness. Further, since God's Confluence Aged Prana is increasing in the universe, people will find it easier to become pure and remain in the pure state, even if they had no intention of getting God's help to remain pure. God's Confluence Aged Prana will only make them feel good since it influences them to become pure. If they are exposed to the energies which are coming from the QE Light Ocean, they will also be influenced by the QE Light's Confluence Aged Prana that is accumulating within the QE Light source since the QE Light is exposed to God's energies. For all these reasons, God got associated with the Cosmic Consciousness from the time of the Mid-Confluence. The Cosmic Consciousness was also given a lot of importance from those ancient days because, at the end of the cycle, there will be many deity souls who will be relying on absorbing God's Confluence Aged Prana, from the Cosmic Consciousness, instead of receiving God's energies through their own link to God.

There are 330 million deity souls who will be brought into the Confluence Age, at the end of the cycle. Most of them will not be powerful spiritual effort makers; thus, many of them will be dependent on God's Confluence Aged Prana to remain in the Confluence Age.

The Confluence Aged souls who are continuously making serious spiritual efforts, through using the BK knowledge, are like 'Adam' getting created through their own Confluence Aged spiritual effort-making. Those who are absorbing God's Confluence Aged Prana, to remain in the Confluence Age, are like Eve because they are dependent on the creation of Adam for their own creation. Despite what has been just said, it is Brahma Baba who is Adam and all other Confluence Aged souls are like Eve because all the others are using Brahma Baba's Confluence Auric Field to get their own perfect self created through the Confluence Age. Brahma Baba's Confluence Auric Field is also part of his body. Thus, it is as if the body of Adam is used to create the bodies of Eve.

BKs would say that Brahma Baba is Adam because his body was used to give the BK knowledge which all the rest use for becoming perfect. It is also said that each BK is getting his/her own Adam created through spiritual effort making and this enables the soul to take births in the first half cycle. It gives them a right to have a perfect body in the new world.

God's energies are sent into the Corporeal World by BKs, so as to transform the world into the Golden Aged world. These energies will also transform the bodies and souls of all those who are walking into the Golden Aged world.

God's energies which are in the Corporeal World, now, are like an Ocean of Nectar. Since BKs have become spiritually more powerful through many years of spiritual effort making, they are able to reflect more of God's energies into the Corporeal World. Those walking in can use these to easily attain a good stage, even if they were not making serious spiritual efforts. Having attained that high stage, they can do visualisations etc. which can help them to get what they want.

Non-Confluence Aged souls can also go into the Cosmic Consciousness and enjoy the benefits of these Godly energies which are in the Cosmic Consciousness. They will enjoy the pure state and will be able to use the higher lokas and dimensions in the Lower Universe. Through this, they can also achieve what they want via visualisations etc. Non-deity souls can even become the Deeper Self and experience themselves as the soul because the soul has been empowered through God's Confluence Aged Prana.

The Cycle of Time keeps repeating and so, from the Golden Age onwards, the deity souls slowly lose the spiritual strength which they acquired through the previous Confluence Age, though they are not aware that this is happening. Then, at the beginning of the next Copper Age, the energies of the souls and the QE Light and quantum energies transform into the ordinary form again. The QE Light energies also get weaker and weaker as the human souls get weaker and weaker.

Energies cannot be destroyed or created. However, they can be transformed from one form to another. Thus, at the end of the Silver Age, powerful pure divine energies transform into the ordinary state and then, they can also transform into the impure state.

By the end of the cycle, as people keep yielding to the vices, most of the QE Light energies and the energies of the soul would have been transformed into the impure state. A lot of the QE Light energies would be in the impure state because they are influenced by the impure state of the vices from the human souls. Though QE Light easily transforms into the impure state, in the lower dimensions, the QE Light Ocean always consists of pure energies because it is in a higher dimension which is far away from the impure people. However, as the impure energies get more powerful in the Second Field, the spiritual strength of the Cosmic Consciousness is actually getting weaker, though it is an ocean. However, before it gets completely weakened, the next Confluence Age begins and so it begins to get strengthened again. God's Confluence Aged Prana will be playing a great role through the Cosmic Consciousness again. God's energies will transform all impure ordinary energies back into the pure divine state. The deity souls and QE Light will be empowered to become pure and divine again. It is only God's energies which can uplift a weakened universe. No other energies can do this.

God is like a powerful Battery or Generator who has an ocean of energies to empower everything. Though God's energies are used to empower and rejuvenate the world, God will still remain all-powerful and omnipotent because He is an Ocean which cannot be drained out of its energies. Thus, an inexhaustible abundance of God's Confluence Aged Prana can be sent into the Corporeal World. The QE Light source and QE Light Ocean are more limited in nature even though the QE Light is also an ocean of energies. Thus, the QE Light will also have to be uplifted to become divine energies. As it transforms, the quantum energies also transform because they are the other half of the QE Light.

Though the Confluence Aged souls send God's energies into the environment around them and to the whole Corporeal World, it is only after the QE Light source transforms that the whole world gets transformed because the QE Light source provides the QE Light in the Corporeal World and the quantum energies are influenced by the state of the QE Light energies.

There will be no impure energies in the first half cycle. At the end of the cycle, though the world if filled with an abundance of impure energies, one can protect oneself from impure energies through establishing one's link to God or through absorbing God's Confluence Aged Prana into oneself. The soul and auric fields will get filled with God's light and this keeps one safe and spiritually powerful. One can stop all impure energies from influencing one through visualising that God's energies and God's Confluence Aged Prana are keeping one pure and so the impure energies are not able to influence one.

Despite all that which have been said, it should be noted that it is better to receive God's energies through one's own link to God and not through just relying on God's Confluence Aged Prana. One is exposed to more of God's energies through a very good link to God.

As you go into the higher dimensions, you are being purified through God's Confluence Aged Prana which exists there. However, not much spiritual power is received through just being exposed to God's Confluence Aged Prana. One needs to be exposed to God's powerful effulgence through one's own link to God to become spiritually powerful. Accordingly, to become spiritually powerful, you have to strengthen your link to God through mastering and applying the BK knowledge which you get in this book and/or in the BK centers.

Chapter 39: Sun Dynasty and Moon Dynasty

There are various groups of people who have been classified as the Sun Dynasty and Moon Dynasty. Three significant classifications are:

1. The Sun Dynasty and Moon Dynasty which exists in the first half cycle.

2. The division of the deity clan into the Sun Dynasty and Moon Dynasty, during the Mid-Confluence and at the end of the cycle.

3. The mortal or human Sun Dynasty and Moon Dynasty which were created in the Copper Age.

In accordance with the BK knowledge, the people in the Golden Age belong to the Sun Dynasty. This reflects how the human souls, in the Golden Age, shine very brightly like the sun since they are spiritually very powerful. The people of the Silver Age belong to the Moon Dynasty since the souls, in the Silver Age, do not shine as brilliantly as the souls in the Golden Age. This is so because they are, spiritually, not as powerful as the Golden aged souls. Thus, the souls in the Silver Age are similar to the moon which does not shine as brilliantly as the sun.

Those walking in also belong to the Sun Dynasty because they are walking into the Golden Aged world. The fact that they belong to the Sun Dynasty is not a reflection of the spiritual strength of the soul. It just represents that they are beginning the Sun Dynasty clan of the Golden Age. They do not belong to the Sun Dynasty in the sense that they will take all their subsequent births in the Golden Age. Though I refer to them as the Sun Dynasty, their descendants in the Golden Age will not be referring to themselves as being of the Sun Dynasty.

The Copper Age began just before the end of the Mid-Confluence, when Brahma Baba's soul takes a mortal birth in a body which is like what mortals use during the second half cycle. However, the Copper Age can also be said to have begun around the middle of the Mid-Confluence because the Mid-Confluence overlaps the Silver Age and Copper Age. Even the whole Mid-Confluence can be considered as the 'beginning of the Copper Age' because, during the Mid-Confluence, there was a more divine replica of the World Drama that takes place during the Copper Age.

Actually, the minute a vice was used, the whole community lost their divine world. So they are no longer in the Silver Age. If they are not in the Silver Age, they are in the Copper Age. However, they still used the same bodies and so they can be considered as being in the Mid-Confluence and not really in the Copper Age.

Since the gods of the first half cycle acted as per the World Drama, a Sun Dynasty clan was created around the end of the Silver Age. These Sun Dynasty souls were supposed to do what was necessary during the Mid-Confluence. The people of this Sun Dynasty clan had transformed, to appear like a Sun Dynasty clan, around the middle of the Mid-Confluence. The creation of this group had actually begun the division of the gods into two groups though they still acted as one, in unity. Later, the Mid-Confluence Aged Moon Dynasty had also begun to play a role on the world stage, during the Mid-Confluence. I have categorised both these groups as the Mid-Confluence Aged Sun and Moon Dynasties, and I refer to them as the Mid-Confluence Aged gods.

The Mid-Confluence Aged gods had created the mortal/human Sun Dynasty and Moon Dynasty, when the spiritual strength of the souls had got weaker and the people were becoming mortals. The actual mortal clan began to exist just before the end of the Mid-Confluence, when Brahma Baba was born a mortal. All those born after that were all also mortals (belonging to the true mortal clan). However, what was being done during the Mid-Confluence is a replica of what will exist and/or be continued after the Mid-Confluence. Thus, some of the people were considered as the descendants of the Mid-Confluence Aged Sun Dynasty and Moon Dynasty gods, during the Mid-Confluence. As a consequence, the ones playing the role of Manu and Ikshvaku (for the human/mortal

Sun Dynasty) were portrayed as the descendants of the sun god Vivasvan; Manu being the son of Vivasvan, and Ikshvaku being the son of Manu. The human/mortal Moon Dynasty consisted of the descendants of the Mid-Confluence Aged Moon Dynasty gods (through the moon god and Budha). However, it was Vivasvan who was playing an active role (as the sun god) since it was the Mid-Confluence Aged Sun Dynasty which was supposed to play a significant role during the Mid-Confluence. Thus, in the Hindu myths, Vivasvan (the sun god) was also an ancestor of the Lunar Dynasty. This was reflected through the following:

1. Vivasvan was the father of Manu,

2. all humans descended from Manu, and

3. Ila (Manu's child) and Budha (son of the moon god) were the progenitors of the Lunar Dynasty clan.

In the Hindu myths, Vivasvan was associated with the dawn (which was used to represent the Confluence Age) because he was playing his role based on what happens during the Confluence Age. Vivasvan also represents more than the gods of the Mid-Confluence Aged Sun Dynasty, e.g. it also represents God playing His role with the Sun Dynasty souls during the Confluence Age. It is just a matter of from which angle one is looking at it.

Manu, Ikshvaku etc. were supposed to take care of what was happening on earth (in the denser Real World). Then, their descendants (who were born after Brahma Baba was born as a mortal) continued to classify themselves as the descendants of the Sun Dynasty until this day. In India, the descendants of the Sun Dynasty are also referred to as the descendants of the Solar Dynasty, Suryavansh or Suryavamsa. The descendants of the Moon Dynasty are referred to as the Lunar Dynasty, Somvansh, Chandravansh or Chandravamsa. The term vansh or vamsa refers to one's descent. I am not discussing these human/mortal dynasties in this book.

Since the deity clan got divided into two and the Mid-Confluence is connected to the Confluence Age, even at the end, it will be as if there are two deity clans which will finally unite as the Golden Aged world begins to materialise.

The Mid-Confluence Aged Moon Dynasty souls were referred to as the Moon Dynasty because, at the end of the cycle, those souls will play a significant role as BKs within the Confluence Age. They will be absorbing and reflecting God's energies into the world akin to how the Moon reflects the Sun's energies into the world. In the myths etc., the full moon day has been used to reflect the time when the BKs will begin to play their role in the Confluence Age, at the end of the cycle.

The Mid-Confluence Aged Sun Dynasty souls were termed as the Sun Dynasty because:

1. they (the souls) will be walking into the Golden Aged world, at the end of the cycle (after having taken their final birth in this cycle).

2. they were preparing the stage for the walking into the Golden Aged world process (though this walking in process only begins through the Confluence Age, at the end of the cycle).

Since the Sun Dynasty souls will be walking into the Golden Aged world, they were preparing the stage, from the time of the Mid-Confluence, for bringing in the next Golden Aged world. The Mid-Confluence Aged Sun Dynasty gods had also left behind structures, knowledge etc. that would help to bring in the 330 million souls into the Confluence Age, when the role of their afterlife begins to be used at the end of the cycle. This in turn would help to bring in the next Golden Aged world.

Not all deity souls will become powerful Confluence Aged souls, though all deity souls will have to be brought into the Confluence Age for world transformation to take place. There are two requirements for bringing them into the Golden Aged world:

1. the 900,000 most powerful souls will have to be ready for world

transformation to take place. These souls are being trained by the Moon Dynasty souls, via the Brahma Kumaris, now.

2. all deity souls will have to be brought into the Confluence Age. The Sun Dynasty souls will make sure that they are all brought in, around the end of the Confluence Age.

Neither the Sun Dynasty souls nor the Moon Dynasty souls will be able to re-create the Golden Aged world on their own because the 900,000 most powerful Confluence Aged souls have to be ready and all the deity souls will also have to be brought into the Confluence Age. It is when the Sun Dynasty and Moon Dynasty souls accept each other's role that the world will get transformed.

At the end of the cycle, those who belong to the Moon Dynasty are the true prophets. During the Mid-Confluence and at the end of the cycle, those who belong to the Sun Dynasty are the False Prophets. False Prophets are also prophets, i.e. they are also spiritual people. However, they explain what the ancient people had left behind. I play the role of the true prophet and the False Prophet because I explain the BK knowledge and also what has been left behind by the ancient people.

The Mid-Confluence Aged Sun Dynasty souls will bring in all the deity souls into the Confluence Age through what happens via the afterlife. One reason why the ancient Mid-Confluence Aged Sun Dynasty souls had built and left behind the ancient structures etc. was to attract the people's attention, at the end of the cycle, so that they can easily play their roles during their afterlife. The Mid-Confluence Aged Sun Dynasty souls would be playing a role during their afterlife, at the end of the cycle, as I am doing so now. Through their afterlife, those souls will be helping to explain what they had left behind and, at the same time, assisting those who have to walk into the Golden Aged world, as they walk in. All that which they had had left behind, such as the huge pyramids, scriptures, myths etc. will get explained during their afterlife, as I am explaining them now. Through what they do, those souls would also be helping to put God on the world stage, at the end of the cycle.

Since God came into the Corporeal World to get the Golden Aged world created, these aims which God came for, will be given importance to and the whole world will be prepared for it.

During the Mid-Confluence, the Sun Dynasty was also preparing the stage for the walking in process because, at the end of the cycle, many of their Sun Dynasty souls would be involved with absorbing the Confluence Aged Prana, from the Cosmic Consciousness, through bringing themselves into the higher QE Light dimensions. So the Mid-Confluence Aged Sun Dynasty souls had to initiate spiritual practices which these people could easily use to do this.

Many of those walking in will not be powerful Confluence Aged souls. They will be dependent on the Confluence Aged Prana to enjoy a blissful stage. These people would be familiar with the practices that had been left by the ancient people where one connects oneself to the Cosmic Consciousness and absorbs prana from there to empower themselves. Thus, when they come into the Confluence Age, they can easily absorb the Confluence Aged Prana from the Confluence Aged environment and from the higher dimensions in the Holographic Universe. The practices used by these people would be slightly different from the practices used by the BKs (since the BKs are mainly involved with absorbing God's energies through their link to God).

Since the souls who were part of the Mid-Confluence Aged Sun Dynasty play a role in their afterlife, the souls would have been influenced to keep doing something or other, in all their subsequent lives. Thus, the soul would have developed psychic abilities in many of their births. As a result, at the end, the Sun Dynasty souls would be able to sense that they have already entered the Golden Age or that the Golden Aged world has already begun. They will also have this developed ability, in their final birth now, if they had been influenced to use the practices that had been left behind by the Mid-Confluence Aged gods.

However, one has to properly understand one's experiences and act accordingly. When I was having the experiences where I could see the golden light of the Cosmic Consciousness, sometimes, it was as if I was observing a golden environment as an onlooker. This did not feel right. When I used the BK knowledge, I was within the pure divine world which is transforming into the Golden Aged world. This would feel right. In the experiences, where I was just as onlooker, I noticed that the powerful lights from the Cosmic Consciousness, which were emitted into our world, were golden but they were not divine like how they would be in the first half cycle. When I started to make spiritual efforts by using the BK knowledge, those light energies transformed into a beautiful divine state when my spiritual stage became very high. If my spiritual stage was not high, the golden light did not feel divine though it felt powerful and was golden in colour.

While in the higher subtle dimensions, make sure that you are part and parcel of the transforming Golden Aged world. Make sure that you are not an on-looker. An on-looker is not in the process of walking into the Golden Aged world. BKs who do not walk in will also feel that they are part and parcel of the transforming world because the world is being transformed due to their powerful stage.

God fulfils the desires of the Sun Dynasty souls, who are walking in, since they can enjoy walking into the Golden Aged world, if they wish to do that. God also assists them to get whatever they want because of the worship which they had done, during ancient times, to make sure that they become rich again at the end. This was also why the practices were begun where the Egyptian king was buried with his wealth for his afterlife.

The Sun Dynasty souls, during the Mid-Confluence, were wealthy. The World Drama gave them wealth, authority and everything else so that they can play their roles:

1. for their afterlife, and

2. since they had to create the new world for the second half cycle, during the Mid-Confluence.

Thus, as per the World Drama, they got the riches which they needed. These souls will also play a significant role during the walking in process, at the end of the cycle.

Even at the end, now, these souls will be given wealth, authority and everything else so that they can play their roles well on the world stage. This will happen as per the World Drama. Thus, they will find it very easy to become rich again, at the end of the cycle (now). As a result, those using the knowledge in this book, which I relate as a member of the Sun Dynasty, will easily become rich as they had during the Mid-Confluence.

Do not misuse the funds, which you receive through these practices, by using it for killing or harming people, etc. Be careful about the intent with which you use these practices. Your intent is reflected in your aura and so people will judge you and interact with you based on what they sense in your aura. Your intention also affects what you get through the Law of Karma. For example, if you wanted the money to harm someone etc., this is a bad intent and you will pay the consequences through the Law of Karma. If your intention was for taking care of your body so that you can remain involved with the services for the walking in process or/and your intention was to use the extra money for what you need to do during the walking in process, then, you will get good rewards through the Law of Karma.

In the Hindu myths, some of the sages were wealthy but they used the funds wisely; the gods and sages also married and had children. Similarly, the Sun Dynasty souls who walk into the Golden Aged world should use their money wisely, and they can get married and have children.

The Moon Dynasty souls (BKs) are also given money for doing world service. However, the Moon Dynasty souls have to use the money, which they have, as trustees because the money which they have is God's money. The wealth, which the Sun Dynasty souls have, can be considered as being their own. They do not have to use it as trustees.

However, if they did use it as trustees, they will accumulate a great spiritual income within the soul and this will help to make them spiritually very powerful (if they did not use it for some other benefit).

There are no hard and fast rules as to which Dynasty you belong to. I belong to both: the Sun Dynasty and the Moon Dynasty. There will also be some Mid-Confluence Aged Moon Dynasty souls (BKs) walking in, which was also why they began to play a role on the world stage during the Mid-Confluence. They will be actively living a life as BKs. Then, when the Golden Aged world materialises, they become part of the Sun Dynasty that walks into the Golden Aged world.

The Confluence Aged Moon Dynasty souls would be of the view that the most important knowledge is the BK knowledge. They will only use the practices in this book, for the walking in process, as something that is done for entertainment. They will only use it when they feel like trying something new during meditation experimenting, etc. However, many in the Sun Dynasty, who are involved with walking in, will prefer to use these practices instead of the BK practices, especially since the BKs have to follow strict Maryadas. These people might only give secondary importance to the BK knowledge, though some (like me) will also give a lot of importance to the BK knowledge.

Those of the Sun Dynasty who are using the BK knowledge will have their consciousness/intellect flying into Confluence Aged Subtle Region too. They can also use Vaikuntha in the Angelic World.

The memories of both, the Sun Dynasty souls and the Moon Dynasty souls, play a role at the end. However, these memories are used differently. Where the Moon Dynasty souls are concerned, it helps them with their spiritual effort making. Where the Sun Dynasty souls are concerned, it helps them with service to establish their return on the world stage; through this, God is also put on the world stage.

In the Srimad Bhagavatam, Canto 5, Chapter 19, Verse 20 (SB 5.19.20) it has been stated that after having taken many births, one will be able to mix with pure devotees. The words 'pure devotees' are actually a reference to the Confluence Aged souls. This verse is actually reflecting how the Sun Dynasty souls will finally meet the BKs (Moon Dynasty souls) at the end of the cycle. As reflected in this verse, at the end of the cycle, when it is time to enjoy the fruits of one's pious activities (for the afterlife) which were done in all of one's births from the Mid-Confluence until the end of the cycle, one will mix with the BKs or get associated with those who use the BK knowledge. Then, as reflected in the verse, one receives knowledge, begins to serve God and attains liberation. As per the World Drama, the Sun Dynasty souls will meet the BKs if they had done a lot of pious activity for the afterlife; this was also a reason why I had met the BKs. The Sun Dynasty souls are those who will be trying to understand what had been left behind by the ancient people while they are accumulating good karma through their walking in process, spiritual effort-making and world service, as I am doing now.

In the ancient Hindu Bhumandala model, the Sun and Moon Dynasties have been depicted through the positioning of the sun and moon. This was possible because Bhumandala represents the world stage. In the world stage, during dusk or dawn, sometimes the moon is in a higher position than the sun in the sky. This has been used in the Bhumandala model to reflect how the spiritual strength of those who belong to the Confluence Aged Moon Dynasty will, generally, be higher than the Sun Dynasty souls. The Moon Dynasty souls, who are spiritually more powerful during the Confluence Age, would have also been spiritually more powerful during the Mid-Confluence. Actually, the Confluence Aged souls can enjoy a higher spiritual strength than the souls in the Golden Age too, when the Confluence Aged souls are filled with God's energies (as they are when they enjoy the stage of Shanker in Shankerpuri).

It should be noted that the ancient people had often used the dusk to represent the Mid-Confluence and the dawn to represent the Confluence Age because:

1. the first half cycle was depicted as the Day and the second half cycle

was seen as the Night.

2. the Mid-Confluence is the time when the deity souls lose their heavenly, divine world (the day) and their world drops into the dark Quantum World in the Lower Universe, like how the sun goes out of sight at the horizon during dusk.

3. the Mid-Confluence is the time when the deity souls lose their brilliantly shiny state (which looks like a sun) since they lose their divine state, and this is like the disappearance of the sun at dusk.

4. the Confluence Age is the time when the deity souls regain their heavenly, divine, Golden Aged world (the day) and this is like the sun reappearing again, at dawn, so as to provide them with their heavenly, lighted up world. It is lighted up because their world is in the SWL, in the Higher Universe.

5. the Confluence Age is the time when the deity souls regain their brilliantly shiny state, i.e. the soul regains its state which looks like a sun.

Bhumandala represents the world stage that was presented by the Mid-Confluence Aged gods, where the Mid-Confluence Aged stage (during the dusk) is connected to the stage that exists at the end of the cycle as the world transforms, into the Golden Aged world, through the Confluence Age (during the dawn). They created this stage in a similar manner to how we can create a picture of something which we want materialised. Since they created this stage for the materialisation of their aims, they placed the moon higher than the sun. They did this because, generally, the spiritual strength of the Moon Dynasty souls was higher than the spiritual strength of the Sun Dynasty souls (during the Mid-Confluence and at the end of the cycle). A lot more was also reflected through the Bhumandala model; these will be dealt with in future books. More, on why the Mid-Confluence Aged gods had connected the Mid-Confluence to the Confluence Age, is explained in the following chapters.

When BKs who have a higher spiritual strength walk in, they will only be serving in the Golden Aged world and not really enjoying life as the members of the Sun Dynasty would be doing there. Just as the Sun Dynasty souls will be able to reacquire the wealth which they had during the Mid-Confluence, they will be able to take what they had received (in the old world) into the new world. This may also be a reason why the Sun Dynasty souls can walk in as rulers and rich people, while the BKs will generally walk in to serve. The BKs will, generally, walk into the Golden Aged kingdom which will exist around Delhi in Northern India.

Chapter 40: Mid-Confluence Aged Lokas

The auric fields, in which the lokas exist, are in the dimensions of the Holographic Universe. During the Mid-Confluence, since the world/loka was dropping, these auric fields and their lokas existed in various different Real World Quantum Dimensions within the Holographic Universe, and those Real World Quantum Dimensions provided the space for their Real World and other lokas. Each Real World Quantum Dimension provides a different universe at a different level. Thus, it was as if, at each stage during the drop, all these auric fields and their lokas were in a different universe. Their world was in that universe for so long as their world existed at that level during their fall.

Since their world was dropping from the Higher Universe to the Lower Universe, the Mid-Confluence Aged people were experiencing various kinds of universes before their world fell to where it was in the early Copper Age. One of these universes had also facilitated the existence of dinosaurs. For convenience, I am going to refer to this universe, which facilitates the existence of dinosaurs, as the 'Dino Universe'. Since Dino Universe was provided by a different set of QE Light and quantum dimensions (Real World Quantum Dimension) at a different level, it was different.

During the time when the dinosaurs lived, the gods were able to bring themselves into the Dino Universe with just a thought; for example, if they were flying in their craft (in their divine world), with just a thought that they are in the lower denser Real World, they and their craft would be in the lower denser Real World. If they had gone there, during the time when the Dino Universe provided the environment, they would continue flying in its dinosaur world. They would be in this loka for so long as they are there. They could stay in this dinosaur world for so long as they wished to remain there. With just a thought, they could have the environment of the divine world again. They were actually doing everything in the same space; the difference was that their environment was being provided by higher or lower frequencies. They did not permanently live in the land of the dinosaurs; they only remained there for short periods of time so as to survey the place, do research (which was done in their spacecraft), for entertainment, etc.

The denser Real World had actually evolved for Mankind even before human beings dropped to live in the denser Real World, i.e. before the denser Real World became their loka. It can also be said that, as per the World Drama, the denser Real World was being prepared for them, long before their world/loka finally dropped to merge into that denser Real World.

Everything that is happening in the Corporeal World may be happening in different lokas which are in different dimensions. However, they are all happening on the same world stage and this world stage is provided on earth. During the Mid-Confluence, some of the gods had gone to begin civilisations on other cosmic bodies in outer space but all of them had to come back to earth when the perfect Corporeal World transformed into an imperfect one during the Mid-Confluence. Thereafter, only earth remained habitable because only earth was meant to provide us with the world stage. In the Hindu scriptures, Bhuloka was also portrayed as a heavenly loka because everyone is supposed to be enjoying life on earth. There is only one earth but what exists on the surface of the earth can be different depending on:

1. whether we are in the Higher Universe or the Lower Universe.

2. which universe is providing the Real World for us.

Since different kinds of lokas can exist on the world stage:

1. one can be living in one of two lokas, both of which are completely different. For example, the Mid-Confluence Aged gods were sometimes in the situation where there were either in the world of the dinosaurs or in the heavenly world. In both of these worlds, a completely different kind of world existed for them.

2. one can be living in an environment where two lokas/universe merge and so one can see a bit of both in the environment.

During the Mid-Confluence, with time, the heavenly world which was lived in was slowly becoming part of the denser Real World that existed in the Lower Universe. One by one people, from the Higher Universe, were dropping into the denser Real World that had evolved in the Lower Universe. Where the spiritually weaker souls were concerned, it was no longer the situation where they are in the denser Real World of the Lower Universe because of a 'thought'. However, their fall could be temporarily stopped and/or they could be brought into a higher dimension through remaining virtuous/pure or through spiritual efforts.

When the Mid-Confluence Aged world was plummeting from the Higher Universe, it was actually merging into the denser Real World of the Lower Universe. The merged form could be one where:

1. the whole area, which the person occupied in the Higher Universe, dropped into the Lower Universe and it took over the space in the Lower Universe. Thus, it was as if the whole place was a divine place, as it was in the Higher Universe, however, their loka was actually in the Lower Universe and not in the Higher Universe. Dinosaurs could not go into such a place because it was a completely different universe, though within the realm of the denser Real World of the Lower Universe.

2. someone of the Higher Universe remained in the same place but was in the environment of the Lower Universe. For example, when a person plunged into the denser Real World of the Lower Universe to live among the dinosaurs, the person was completely in the environment which the dinosaurs were in. He no longer enjoyed anything of his former divine world. This means a person could even drop right into the place where the dinosaurs lived and he would have to create a new home for himself.

3. the whole area, which the person used in the Higher Universe, descended into the Lower Universe and it merged with the environment

that existed in the denser Real World. In this scenario, the environment became a mixture of two worlds. This means that the person might have still had his home or anything else which he was using in the Higher Universe. However, dinosaurs could also exist in his environment.

Since the people who dropped were capable of using the vices, the dinosaurs could become wild too. Thus, it was possible for people to be in a dangerous situation. So the Mid-Confluence Aged gods had exterminated the dinosaurs to make the world a safer place to live in. Since the royalty of that time took good care of their subjects, it was ensured that the dinosaurs were no longer extant. If the destructive event had occurred while the loka/universe was being used as the world stage, then, that event becomes part of our past and the evidences of that event will remain since the event took place on the world stage. During the extermination of the dinosaurs, the gods were in the Dino Universe (in their air-crafts). Since the people had not committed any sins as yet, no one was permanently staying in the dinosaur world, at that time. Since the gods were there to carry out the destructive process, the loka existed for Mankind when the dinosaurs died and so the dinosaur bones remained until now. We can also still see their bones because those dinosaurs had existed in the second half cycle.

As per the World Drama, we cannot be exposed to what existed in the first half cycle while we live in the second half cycle. Thus, what existed in the first half cycle was pulled deeper into the earth by earthquakes since that was part of our past on the world stage. What exists in the first half cycle can only emerge on the surface when the next Golden Aged world comes into existence. Until then, no-one can be exposed to it.

Actually, when we live in one dimension, nothing exists in the other dimension unless we begin to use that other dimension. So nothing exists in the Dino Universe or in the Higher Universe during the second half cycle. Similarly nothing exists in the Lower Universe during the first half cycle. At the beginning of the Golden Age, when people only live in the Higher Universe and no humans exist in the Lower Universe, whatever that was in the Lower Universe would be in a transformed state. Everything would have transformed into something beneficial for the world which exists in the Higher Universe.

In visions, I have seen that at the end, when the world is about to be transformed into the perfect world, there will be dinosaurs living on earth. Perhaps, we might get uplifted into the Dino Universe before we get uplifted into the space of Brahmapuri. Possibly, at that time, not many people would be living in the Lower Universe because:

1. most of them would be inhabiting the Higher Universe or they might be capable of bringing themselves into the Higher Universe.

2. many souls would have returned to the Soul World.

The frequencies which provide the world stage for us can change:

1. as per the World Drama.

2. based on the circumstances that exist in the environment.

3. based on our thoughts, beliefs and spiritual stage.

4. as our world drops or gets uplifted during the Mid-Confluence and Confluence Age respectively.

If the frequencies of our environment change, we will be in another dimension and so we will be able to see what is in the other dimension. If not, we will be in the dimension which is, generally, providing the environment for us. Though different frequencies provide different kinds of worlds for us, we will still be on the same world stage.

Since we are in the underworld, our environment is not pure, powerful and stable. So we can be taken into the past or something from some other universe can come into our environment. For example, in the lake called Loch Ness and in Lake Champlain, there have been instances when people have spotted sea monsters which are being called:

1. Loch Ness monster or Nessie. This is in Loch Ness, Scotland.

2. Champ or Champy. This is in Lake Champlain, North America (US/Canada).

These monsters come into our universe temporarily because of the different circumstances in the place, for example, something may be temporarily bringing about the relevant higher frequencies into those places which facilitate the existence of the sea monsters. So, in those areas when the sea monsters are seen, there is a temporary merging of two universes (our present universe and the universe which facilitates the existence of those sea monsters). For convenience, I am going to assume that the universe, which the sea monsters are in, is the Dino Universe. Since the QE Light and quantum energies provide us with whatever needs to exist on our world stage, as per the 2D SWD and Nature's 2D World Drama, these sea monsters have also been provided on the world stage. Nature's 2D World Drama includes the laws based on which the universe is provided. Therefore, since the frequencies are those which facilitate the existence of those sea monsters, the QE Light and quantum energies provide the sea monsters.

The animal souls constantly remain in the Corporeal World because:

1. they are in the Corporeal World to entertain us.

2. they become part of the world stage, as various kinds of animals.

3. they cannot be judged on Judgement Day for wrongs which they have done since their inborn vicious state is a reflection of Mankind's innate vicious state. This means they do not go back to the Soul World with us. Human souls have to be purified before going back to the Soul World. So they have to face Judgement Day.

The animal souls can be reborn as different animals. The animal souls just play their part when they are provided with a body, as per the 2D SWD and Nature's 2D World Drama. This is why the animal soul which has been given the body of the sea monster just plays its role, naturally.

This is similar to how the baby sea turtles rush towards the ocean after leaving the nest. The animal soul will know how to use the body of the sea monster because it gets the relevant information from Nature's 2D World Drama which is a storehouse of information for the animals, just as the 2D SWD is a storehouse of information for the human souls. An animal soul gets the relevant information based on the body which it uses. Thus, the animal soul will know how to live as a sea monster when it is given the sea monster's body. A sea monster can exist in those lakes through one of the following two ways:

1. as per the World Drama, an animal soul which has just left a body underwater (and so does not have a body as yet) can be temporarily given the sea monster's body to roam around in.

2. an existing animal can be transformed into the sea monster temporarily.

These sea monsters are not from another planet which is in our universe. They are temporarily in the same space as we are in because the frequencies emitted in the lakes are higher than the frequencies which the environment normally has. Its 'higher frequency environment' can be considered as being the Dino Universe because it has the frequencies which only exist in the Dino Universe. These high frequencies do not exist in the universe which we currently live in. Since the environment of Dino Universe has come into existence in the space where we live, we can see the sea monsters. However, these sea monsters can only exist for some time because those frequencies were only emitted for a while into the those areas.

Just as two different Real World Quantum Dimensions are temporarily providing an environment around Loch Ness and Lake Champlain, those walking in can also be provided an environment through two different Real World Quantum Dimensions. Just as the animal soul can exist in another universe while it is in the Kaliyug Real World, you can also use another universe or loka while in the Kaliyug Real World. It all depends on the influence through different frequencies, as per the World Drama.

Since the world stage can have different lokas for different people, different Real World Quantum Dimensions can be providing the environment of a person. Whichever Real World Quantum Dimension one's loka is in, the QE Light and quantum dimensions of that Real World Quantum Dimension will be providing one's environment in the Real World. Thus, though all the environments in the Real World are connected, each section in the Real World may be provided through a different set of QE Light and quantum dimensions (depending on the spiritual strength of the souls who live there, the frequencies of the vibrations which provide a place, etc). One can also have experiences in different lokas due to the wave particle duality aspect of the quantum energies through which the Real World is being materialised. As a consequence, when the Mid-Confluence Aged people began to permanently live in the denser Real World, they could also use another loka which was provided through different frequencies, for example:

1. If they lived in Vaikuntha-loka, they lived in a 'heaven' on earth. The Mid-Confluence Aged gods were still capable of living in a 'heaven' on earth due to their high spiritual strength. Others could also live in Vaikuntha if they remained virtuous/pure or if they were using the spiritual practices to remain pure and virtuous.

2. If they lived in one of the seven lokas, they enjoyed magical abilities in the denser Real World. Some of the Mid-Confluence Aged people were living in all sorts of magical lokas since they had the ability to use all the Siddhis of all the seven chakras.

3. If they were using the vices, they could also be living in one of the Talas as their lokas.

Though they were living in all those lokas, they were also living on earth. This was also why, in the Hindu scriptures, it has been portrayed that during ancient times all types of beings (gods, asuras, Kinnaras, Kimpurushas, Vidyadharas, Gandharvas, Nagas, etc.) had inhabited earth. The Mid-Confluence Aged human beings were also reflected in the myths and scriptures based on what they were doing etc. For example, since the Kinnaras were those who used crafts that could fly and/or horses on land, they were portrayed as half human and half animal, i.e. as half bird or half horse. They had looked half human in the crafts since only the top half of their body was visible when they were seated in their crafts. On land, the Kinnara included both, the man and horse, together because the person was using the horse. This half man and half animal concept was also used because the Mid-Confluence Aged people were involved with genetic engineering.

Kinnaras, Kimpurushas, Vidyadharas etc. were portrayed as living in Bhuvarloka, apart from living on earth, because:

1. they used their Second Chakra a lot, and

2. they flew around through using crafts or flying equipment (which were strapped to their bodies).

It should be noted that when one's Second Chakra is activated, one lives in an environment of higher frequencies where:

1. one can communicate with the plants, clouds, water, air, etc. and have developed subtle perceptions (like animals). This was also a reason why Kinnaras, Kimpurushas, etc. were portrayed as half animal.

2. magic can be done. This was why Vidyadharas were capable of doing magic.

Actually, during the first half of the Mid-Confluence, as their loka was dropping, the people had still retained their magical abilities because all their chakras were still functioning well. So they could create all kinds of lokas for themselves.

Inter alia, the Kimpurushas have also been portrayed as having the body of a lion and a human head, like the Sphinx, Purushamriga, etc. The Kimpurushas have been depicted as existing on earth as well as in Bhuvarloka because they are human beings who are using more than one loka, i.e. Bhuloka and Bhuvarloka. The half-lion half-human forms

358

such as the Kimpurushas, Sphinx, Purushamriga, Narasimha et alia are significant for the afterlife. However, I will only be explaining about them in subsequent books when I shed light on their 'Return'.

In this chapter and book, for convenience, I have just simplified the history because this book is not about the ancient history. A brief explanation is being given on how the ancient people had used the lokas because those who use the practices in this book may use different lokas; having a better understanding on the lokas will help them to comprehend the situation which they are in.

When the deities living at the end of the Silver Age had lost their divine world, they had tried to:

1. rebuild their perfect world at that time itself.

2. keep the people in the Higher Universe and/or higher dimensions through remaining pure and virtuous.

3. keep the weaker souls in the Higher Universe and/or higher dimensions through introducing them to spiritual practices.

With time, they began to realise that the Golden Aged world can only be lived in again at the end of the cycle, after God comes and re-creates the Golden Aged world. The people also got to know that the Mid-Confluence was spiritually connected to the Confluence Age. Thus, the Mid-Confluence Aged gods (who were the powerful rulers of the whole world) had begun developing spiritual systems through which they easily remained spiritually connected to the 'Confluence Age and Golden Aged world that gets created at the end of the cycle'. Through this, the ancient people could be kept in a higher dimension/loka because as they remembered their experiences that were encountered during the Confluence Age, they experienced the Confluence Aged stage again (even though it was the Mid-Confluence and they did not have a link to God). The recollection had improved their purity and spiritual stage. Even all the spiritual efforts to recollect the Confluence Aged experiences had improved their spiritual stage. Thus, though the people and their world were dropping into the lower dimensions, they could temporarily stop the falling process. These were also reasons why the seven lokas and other lokas such as Vaikuntha were established in an elaborate manner.

All the seven higher lokas (Bhuloka, Bhuvarloka, Swargaloka, Maharloka, Janaloka, Tapaloka and Brahmaloka/Satyaloka) and Vaikuntha would be used when these souls walk into the Golden Aged world at the end of the cycle. Consequently, importance had to be given to these lokas since:

1. through giving importance to all these lokas, they could get spiritually connected to all the lokas that were used during the Confluence Age, when these souls were walking into the Golden Aged world. They were able to spiritually get connected because they were recollecting the previous Confluence Age experiences which were had in these lokas.

2. they had to play a role in the afterlife, i.e. they had to remember the Mid-Confluence Aged memories during the next Confluence Age.

The Mid-Confluence Aged gods had given a lot of importance to lokas such as Vaikuntha-loka and Satyaloka/Brahmaloka because these get closely connected to the Confluence Aged Subtle Region at the end of the cycle. Thus, the Sun Dynasty souls were introduced to practices that involved the usage of these lokas during the Mid-Confluence.

Bhuloka was seen as a heavenly loka since:

1. what is in Bhuloka gets transformed into the perfect Golden Aged Bhuloka at the end of the cycle.

2. connections were being made, through worship practices, to make sure that the souls who were walking in can reacquire all the wealth which they had had during the Mid-Confluence.

When one begins to use the higher chakras, one begins to use higher frequencies. As a result, the vibrations in the environment begin to resonate at the higher frequencies which are emitted by the chakras. Thus, one lives in a different loka. The loka which one lives in depends on the frequencies which are providing the environment. If higher frequencies from the higher dimensions are providing one's environment, one is in a higher loka. The Mid-Confluence Aged gods lived in higher dimensions, since their world had not completely dropped into the lower dimensions. Hence, the frequencies in their loka/world/environment were higher than what it is in all the lokas that are used in Kaliyug. They would not have used a loka which had the frequencies which are as low as those in the Kaliyug Bhuloka. For this reason too, the ancient Bhuloka was portrayed as a heavenly loka. The frequencies in the Kaliyug Bhuloka can change based on the fact that the person is involved with the afterlife. This helps one to reacquire one's wealth.

The Mid-Confluence Aged gods had given a lot of importance to Tapoloka, Janaloka and Maharloka because these will be used when the Sun Dynasty souls play their roles during their afterlife to explain knowledge etc. These lokas were also given importance because they were being used during the Mid-Confluence to understand knowledge etc. Further, when their spiritual stage was lower, they were generally using these lokas and they were using them beneficially to leave what was necessary behind so that what was left behind can get explained during the next Confluence Age, through the afterlife; for example, those who played the role of Bhrigu were using Maharloka beneficially. They were considered as great saints and sages but not as gods at the time when their spiritual stage was low. If their stage was good, they were considered as being in a higher loka, e.g. in Brahmaloka as the god Brahma. The souls who had used Janaloka and Maharloka also had the ability to understand what was in the Holographic Universe, Subtle World Drama and World Drama deep within the soul. These were given a lot of value since these needed to be explained. Thus, even if a soul was having his or her consciousness in a higher chakra (if the Kundalini was in a higher chakra), the souls could and would use these lower chakras in order to understand what they could through using the specialities of the chakras.

When the Mid-Confluence Aged people kept losing their spiritual strength, they kept descending further down into the lower dimensions and their Kundalini was also dropping. At the beginning of the Mid-Confluence, the souls still had their consciousness at the Crown Chakra. After that, it plummeted to the Ajna Chakra and later to the Throat Chakra. While it was dropping, the gods understood a lot of the knowledge that was used at the end of the previous cycle and they were guided to do all that which they had done. By the middle of the Mid-Confluence, their consciousness had plunged further to the Heart Chakra. It was about this time that the practices for the afterlife were seriously begun. Thus, the heart began to be given importance during the afterlife practices in Egypt.

The fact that they had given importance to the heart and Heart Chakra would assist them to use the Heart Chakra again during their afterlife, at the end of the cycle. This means they would be able to easily use the higher chakras to have a higher spiritual stage while living, at the end of the cycle, due to what they had done during those ancient times. As a result, they can easily play their roles during their afterlife and also reacquire the wealth they had accumulated in order to play their roles well.

During the Mid-Confluence, as the Kundalini was dropping, the people's consciousness was dropping into the lower dimensions until their consciousness was in the realm of the denser Real World. During the second half phase of the Mid-Confluence, when people began to use Swargaloka/Indraloka (which exists in the top section of the Second Field) while they were thinking etc., they were finding it difficult to go into the lokas in the Higher Universe. Then, with time, they could no longer go into the Higher Universe. However, when their Kundalini was at the Heart Chakra, they could make spiritual efforts to use the higher auric fields while thinking etc. If they were involved with using the vices, they used even lower lokas. The more impure one was, the further down they were within the Quantum World. These lower lokas were reflected as the Talas that were under Bhuloka. However, since the Kundalini was supposed to be at the Heart Chakra, those who used lower lokas could be lifted into the higher lokas. This was like lifting their world/loka out of the deeper parts of the Garbhodaka Ocean. However, it is only at the end of the cycle that the earth can get lifted out of the Garbhodaka Ocean as the world transforms into the Golden Aged world. It took some time for:

1. the consciousness (awareness) of the people to drop from the denser 3D SWD to go into the denser Real World.

2. the Real World to fall from the Higher Universe to go into the Lower Universe.

3. the Real World to drop from the SWL to go into the Quantum World.

Since their Real World and consciousness were dropping, all the lokas which they using were also dropping over a long period of time. Therefore, the lokas which they were using were continuously changing. It was changing because different universes were involved with providing those lokas, at different levels of the fall. These changes were reflected in the Hindu scriptures, though almost nothing was written about the dinosaurs because the people writing the scriptures were more concerned about the purity of the world.

Often, what was left behind in the Hindu scriptures evidences an attempt to make the connections from the ancient times to the next Confluence Age. It had to be like this because those in India had to remain pure so as to maintain the purity of the world. So the history in the Hindu scriptures also, often, connects the Mid-Confluence to the next Confluence Age and to the previous Confluence Age. These connections were also to remind the people in India/Bharath of their divine history and future, since God descends in India/Bharath at the end of each cycle.

Since the ancient Hindus were involved with maintaining the purity of Bhuloka, they considered Bhuloka as a heavenly loka. When Bhuloka is constantly seen as a heavenly realm, it helps to keep Bhuloka heavenly. So the efforts of the Hindus to maintain the purity of the world/Bhuloka can be easily achieved through the spiritual yogic practices which were introduced in India for this purpose.

From the Copper Age, lokas also began to exist based on the belief-systems that were established. The Mid-Confluence Aged gods had also provided knowledge on these lokas which are used through the belief systems because the belief systems will help Man remain virtuous and this contributes to the purity of the world.

If one wants to give a good explanation, one has to consider the fact that different people are living in different lokas since their purity and spiritual strength is at different levels. Despite this, generalisations can be made to make the explanations easier and this is also what I am doing because, in this book, I am only briefly explaining about the lokas.

When the scriptures were written, generalised information were also provided in respect of the lokas that had been used during the Mid-Confluence. The explanations on these lokas were also adopted and modified for the worshipers of the second half cycle. While the subsequent generations were using the knowledge that they had inherited from the Mid-Confluence Aged gods, they added more to it based on the needs and circumstances of their time. Thus, the information on the lokas is a little confusing in the Hindu scriptures.

Further, at the end of the cycle, the lokas will keep changing as the world transforms into the Golden Aged world. Since the Mid-Confluence Aged people had begun the system for connecting the ancient lokas, myths etc. to the Confluence Age, what is in the scriptures can be even more confusing.

Chapter 41: Mid-Confluence Aged Vaikuntha

In the Sumerian myths, the Mid-Confluence Aged gods have been depicted as having come into our universe from elsewhere or that they were from heaven because the universe that was used by the people of the first half cycle was in the Higher Universe and not in the Lower Universe. In the Hindu scriptures, the heavenly realm has also been referred to as Vaikuntha. In truth, Vaikuntha is the heaven that had existed in the Higher Universe. This Vaikuntha began to sink at the end of the Silver Age. Since the people were still powerful, spiritually, they were considered as continuing to live in Vaikuntha. Thus, in the Hindu scriptures, the heavenly dimension that was used by the Mid-Confluence Aged gods was also referred to as Vaikuntha.

Though Vaikuntha refers to the spiritual heavenly dimension, the places that were used by the Mid-Confluence Aged gods on earth were also referred to as Vaikuntha because:

1. it was heavenly to live there.

2. Vaikuntha-loka was also used while the person was using the Real World.

In the original Mid-Confluence Aged Vaikuntha, there was just one piece of land and it was surrounded by water. The people there used aircrafts that were created through advanced technology. Since everything was in the perfect state in the first half cycle, these aircrafts were also in their perfect state.

As the Mid-Confluence progressed, Vaikuntha continued to drop into the Lower Universe; it began to exist in the mid-region between the Higher Universe and Lower Universe. Some were living in the Lower Universe while others were still able to live in the Higher Universe through remaining pure or through spiritual effort making. The deity souls who had come into the Corporeal World around the end of the Silver Age, and so had taken their first birth just before the divine world was lost, were enjoying their satopradhan phase at that time even though it was not the Golden Age. Thus, they could easily remain in the Higher Universe, to enjoy living in a more heavenly Vaikuntha-loka, for a while. Only some of the Mid-Confluence Aged people were still 'gods'. Many of the people were either:

1. becoming mortals who were dropping into the denser Real World of the second half cycle, or,

2. mortals living in the denser Real World of the second half cycle.

So in the Hindu scriptures, some were portrayed as living in lower dimensions while the more spiritually powerful gods were considered as living in Vaikuntha. These gods were living in a higher dimension while they were taking care of the world which had dropped into the lower dimensions.

When the Mid-Confluence Aged gods left their bodies, they were considered as continuing to live in the subtle realm of Vaikuntha-loka that was continued to be provided by the QE Light energies. This is also where they will be in when they play their roles in their afterlife, at the end of the cycle. They will be able to play their roles in the afterlife, at the end, because the soul would have come back into the Confluence Age, and so it will be capable of using the higher Vaikuntha-loka again.

At the end of the cycle, we will be able to use the subtle Mid-Confluence Aged Vaikuntha easily because it is connected to the subtle Golden Aged Vaikuntha which we use as we are walking in. These two Vaikuntha-lokas easily get connected to each other:

1. since they exist in the same higher space.

2. since similarly powerful spiritual energies are involved.

3. due to the worship that was done during ancient times.

4. since the Mid-Confluence and the Confluence Age are connected as per the World Drama.

It can be said that the pure QE Light energies which were serving the Mid-Confluence Aged gods were also Vaikuntha because those energies still remained pure for serving the Mid-Confluence Aged gods (since they left their bodies in the pure state). It is these energies which provide the higher auric field for the Mid-Confluence Aged birth (hereafter referred to as Ancient Past Birth Auric Field) in the subsequent births of the soul.

Since this Ancient Past Birth Auric Field is higher than the seven auric fields which a person uses, it is in Vaikuntha. This Ancient Past Birth Auric Field remains higher up while the soul continues to take births in the Underworld (the second half cycle).

The memories, of our life during the Mid-Confluence, are in the Ancient Past Birth Auric Field (Vaikuntha) in addition to being deep within the soul. The soul will find it very hard to have access to the information which is in the Ancient Past Birth Auric Field, before coming into the Confluence Age, because the aura of the person only occupies a small distance around the soul, i.e. it does not reach or overlap the Ancient Past Birth Auric Field which is higher up. The soul is not capable of using that higher region during the subsequent births due to its weaker spiritual strength.

The original subtle body of the past birth is actually in the soul and the memories of the past birth are originally also there, deeper down within the soul. If the soul does not have access to the Ancient Past Birth Auric Field, the soul is also not having access to the memories which are deeper down within the soul.

When I use the word 'memories' I am referring to all the memories of the past birth which are in the Memory Bank deep within the soul. These memories include the past birth's personality traits too. Since these are also there in the Ancient Past Birth Auric Field, it will be as if the past birth is there in this auric field.

During the Confluence Age, since the soul has access to the Ancient Past Birth Auric Field, while the energies of the soul are on its way to the Angelic World, it is as if the past births are continuing to play their role through the Ancient Past Birth Auric Field (Vaikuntha). When the soul is exposed to the memories:

1. the soul can adopt the role of the past birth, as per the World Drama, in order to play that role again. This can involve the usage of the subtle body of the past birth.

2. the memories of the past birth can take control and so the soul adopts that past birth's role. Even this can involve the soul using the subtle body of the past birth.

3. the soul can only use the memories which are in the Ancient Past Birth Auric Field and not use the subtle body or role of the past birth. This means the soul is only using the role of the Confluence Aged Spiritual Effort Maker while recollecting ancient memories.

4. some of the energies of the soul can use the subtle bodies of the past birth or past births while the majority of the energies are still used by the Confluence Aged Spiritual Effort Maker.

Since the soul can be involved with the afterlife of a past birth, though the soul only uses the memories and not the role or subtle body of that past birth, the afterlife of the Mid-Confluence Aged gods can just involve the usage of the memories of the Mid-Confluence Aged birth. The memories of the Mid-Confluence Aged birth continues to remain in Vaikuntha-loka since that was where they were during the Mid-Confluence.

The memories of the past birth are deeper down within the soul and in the Ancient Past Birth Auric Field, while the past birth is in an emerged state within the soul. This means that the subtle body of the past birth, in the Detailed World Drama, is in a state where it can play its role again; this is why the memories are there in the Ancient Past Birth Auric Field. As a consequence of this state, the past birth:

1. can easily emerge to the surface of the soul to play the role of the Conscious Self.

2. is not in a sunken state within the 2D SWD.

The past birth would be in the sunken state in the 2D SWD, if it is no longer involved with the World Drama that is taking place on earth. The past birth, which plays a role in the afterlife, will continue playing its role in the World Drama at the end of the cycle through Vaikuntha-loka. So it is not in a sunken state. It is higher up than the energies of the soul which are in an entangled state with the 2D SWD. As a consequence, the past birth is in Vaikuntha and not just in the 2D SWD as a past life. In Vaikuntha, it exists in the Ancient Past Birth Auric Field. This auric field is part of the person's aura, even though it is not connected to the aura which the person is actively using. The person will have the Ancient Past Birth Auric Field because the person's past birth is in an emerged state. In the Detailed World Drama within the soul, it will be as if the energies of the subtle body of the past birth exist from the Detailed World Drama to a higher region within the soul (depending on the emerged state of the past birth). This higher space which it uses, within the soul, is also Vaikuntha. In the Holographic Universe, it will be as if the energies of the past birth begin from the 2D SWD and continue into the higher dimension where Vaikuntha exists in the Holographic Universe. One can also have experiences from this angle. In this chapter, I am not giving explanations from this angle and from the angle where the past birth can look like a giant, especially if it was connected from the physical body to that higher space where Vaikuntha exists. It should be noted that if the past birth has taken control of the physical body, the aura of the past birth will be from the physical body because the past birth will be using the auric fields of the physical body (since it has taken over control of the physical body). Anyway, in this chapter, I am only explaining from the angle where the past birth is in a higher auric field. It should be noted that normally, in the second half cycle, the auric fields which one uses do not reach the 2D SWD unless one was having a very good stage. Even if it reached the 2D SWD, it cannot overlap the space of the Mid-Confluence Aged Vaikuntha since the energies of the soul are not as powerful as it was during the Mid-Confluence. So there will be an empty space, between the aura of the person and the Ancient Past Birth Auric Field of the soul, until the soul comes into the Confluence Age and begins to use the Confluence Auric Field. Even though the Ancient Past Birth Auric Field is higher up, one can also have an experience where the past births are in front of one because space does not really exist in the subtle dimensions. For convenience, in this book, I am not going to consider it from this angle either. I will only be looking at it from the viewpoint that the Ancient Past Birth Auric Field is higher up.

Since the Mid-Confluence Aged past birth is also in an emerged state within the soul, Vaikuntha does not just refer to the holographic realm that is provided by the QE Light and quantum energies, it also refers to the realm within the soul where the past birth exists in an emerged state, so as to play its role in the afterlife. In view of the fact that the World Drama deep within the soul is indestructible, this aspect of Vaikuntha exists eternally. It can also be said that Vaikuntha was not perishable because the Mid-Confluence Aged memories will be influencing the soul until the end of the cycle, from Vaikuntha. This was also why subsequent births were influenced to use the practices for the afterlife.

After the Mid-Confluence, there were subsequent births who also had to play a role in their afterlife, as the Mid-Confluence Aged births would be doing. These subsequent births would also get connected to the Golden Aged Vaikuntha that is used by those walking in because the auric fields which these subsequent births use will become part of the Ancient Past Birth Auric Field. Since the Confluence Age and the Mid-Confluence are connected through the Ancient Past Birth Auric Field, the memories of these subsequent births could also be used by those who are in the Golden Aged Vaikuntha-loka during the walking in process. Thus, during the Mid-Confluence and thereafter, practices were developed for others to play a role in their afterlife. One pre-requisite, in these practices, was that the person (who wishes to play a role in the afterlife) must be living a pure and virtuous life. There had to be this pre-requisite because one can only use the higher dimensions if one was pure. The pure state of the past lives which were in an emerged state would also assist the soul to become pure and remain pure in subsequent lives. This would also assist the soul during spiritual effort making in the Confluence Age.

During the Mid-Confluence, as the gods were developing the practices for the afterlife, the gods realised the importance of remaining in the higher Vaikuntha dimension for the afterlife. Thus, they began creating tall structures:

1. to depict that the powerful gods who used those tall structures lived in the higher Vaikuntha dimension that was way high up in the sky (in the world stage). This was an example for others to follow.

2. to portray that after the Mid-Confluence Aged gods leave the body, they remain in the Vaikuntha dimension, which was high up in the sky, so as to continuing playing their role in their afterlife.

3. to remind the people of the 'aim to remain in the higher Vaikuntha dimension'. When the attention, of all those involved with the afterlife, is turned to the tall structure, they remember the aim. This helps to fulfil the aim for which the tall structure was created. This is similar to how one can use things, as a reminder of one's aims, so as to enable one's aims to be materialised.

4. as a portrayal that the Mid-Confluence Aged people will get what they want since they are close to the 2D SWD, which is higher up in the universe (within the world stage). Vaikuntha is on top of the 2D SWD and the QE Light from the QE Light source has to pass the Vaikuntha dimension before it reaches the actual imprints in the 2D SWD. Thus, one's desires, aims etc. easily get fulfilled. Actually, being in a tall

structure does not bring one closer to the 2D SWD; it was just a symbolic representation that would help them to achieve what they desired. This is similar to how we can easily get what we want through living an imagined life where we easily acquire what we want and where we already are in possession of what we want because we are living in a higher loka.

When the ancient people prepared themselves for their afterlife, they had to make sure that they had wealth, subtle abilities and all relevant connections (or relationships) with others, in their final birth, so that they could successfully carry out world service for bringing in the Golden Aged world. This was also why valuables etc. were left in, and around, the huge pyramids where the mummified Egyptian kings were placed.

All the worship which was done by a past birth will be in the past birth's auric field, after he leaves his body. The worship which was done by his priest for him, after he left the body, will all be attached to this past birth's auric field since they concern him. All these worship will help to make sure that the soul will have wealth and prosperity, at the end of the cycle, because:

1. their worship gets fulfilled like normal, i.e. God fulfils the desires of all worshippers and so their desires get fulfilled since they had done the worship.

2. God easily sees their desires, worship etc. when these past births' auric fields merge into the Confluence Auric Field. So God fulfils them.

The ancient people did not succeed in building anything that was as high as the Vaikuntha dimension (heaven) in the sky, and this was also depicted through the Tower of Babel myth. However, whatever they had built were significant because these structures were somehow connected to the sun and stars in the sky, e.g. the entrance might be facing east where the sun rises. All these connections to the sky represented how the Mid-Confluence was connected to the Confluence

Age. They also reflected that:

1. at the end of the cycle, God's light will shine into the place where the Mid-Confluence Aged gods exist, during the afterlife, i.e. God's light shines into the Ancient Past Birth Auric Field which is the Vaikuntha dimension that has been represented by the structure.

2. God (represented by the sun) will fulfil their aims, for which they had done the worship, when God's light comes into their Vaikuntha dimension that is within the Confluence Auric Field.

3. the Confluence Aged deity souls (depicted as the stars in the sky) will be in a higher Vaikuntha than that which was used by the Mid-Confluence Aged people.

4. the Mid-Confluence Aged souls will be playing a role in higher dimensions, at the end, during their afterlife.

As influenced by the World Drama and by what had been left behind, many people at the beginning of the Copper Age were also linking themselves to the end of the cycle, through the worship practices which had been created for the afterlife. Even when these births emerge to play their role in their afterlife now, they use those dimensions/lokas which they had used during their lifetime. These dimensions would also be higher than the ones which Kaliyug people use because the spiritual strength of the soul was higher during the Copper Age. The auric field which these subsequent births are in will also become part of the Ancient Past Birth Auric Field because they had also done worship to get connected to this Ancient Past Birth Auric Field so that they get connected to the Confluence Age during their afterlife. This was also a reason why importance was given to the Mid-Confluence Aged gods and why they were treated like 'gods'.

Within the Ancient Past Birth Auric Field, the Mid-Confluence Aged god is in a higher dimension/loka and the rest of the births will be in lower lokas. The Mid-Confluence Aged god will be in the Mid-Confluence Aged Vaikuntha while the subsequent births will be in lower Vaikuntha-lokas.

Thus, the memories of the subsequent births will be below the memories of the Mid-Confluence Aged past birth.

No-one can become as spiritually powerful as the Mid-Confluence Aged gods because the spiritual strength of the human soul keeps dropping, with time, until the end of the Cycle. The new souls, who come into the Corporeal World later, will not be as powerful as the new souls who came before them. Thus, no-one can have an auric field higher than that of the Mid-Confluence Aged gods until souls come into the Confluence Age.

Despite what has been said, if a Mid-Confluence Aged soul was using lower auric fields during his life-time, he would not be in the Mid-Confluence Aged Vaikuntha. He would be using a loka which is lower than the Mid-Confluence Aged Vaikuntha. Be that as it may, it would not be as low as the lokas which current day people use outside the Confluence Age.

All the auric fields, of the past births that play a role in their afterlife at the end, will merge into the Confluence Auric Field when the Confluence Auric Field is used. The Confluence Auric Field connects the physical body to the Angelic Body in the Angelic World. So all auric fields have to become part of the Confluence Auric Field. When the Ancient Past Birth Auric Field merges into the Confluence Auric Field, it is uplifted into the Higher Universe.

Those who are influenced by the memories (afterlife) of their Mid-Confluence Aged past birth will easily use the section in Vaikuntha which has existed from the Mid-Confluence. This is so because the Mid-Confluence Aged Vaikuntha gets connected to the Golden Aged Vaikuntha of those who are walking into the Golden Aged world, at the end of the cycle. These souls will be very concerned about the walking in process because those past births had done bhakti (worship) to enter into the Golden Aged Vaikuntha-loka for playing their role, at the end, during their afterlife. However, the memories of those ancient past births cannot remain in an emerged state when the Golden Aged Real

World materialises in the higher dimension, beyond the present Corporeal World, where the Confluence Aged Brahmapuri is situated. Thus, the souls who walk into the materialised Golden Aged Real World will no longer be influenced by their past births' afterlife or memories. The Mid-Confluence Aged Vaikuntha will no longer exist because the Golden Aged real world is higher than the Mid-Confluence Aged Vaikuntha. For this same reason, the afterlife cannot continue into the materialised Golden Aged world. The afterlife also cannot exist in the new materialised Golden Aged world because everything is in the perfect state there. This means past lives have to be in their respective places in the World Drama deep within the soul and not in an emerged state. Nevertheless, since it is the same soul who lives this life and the ancient lives, it is as if those ancient births have walked in too. However, the soul will be using the present birth to walk in. Until then, the memories of those ancient births will influence these souls.

Past births also cannot come into the Confluence Aged Subtle Region which is beyond the Corporeal World. They can only emerge to play a role in:

1. Brahmapuri or Indraloka which is within the section of the Confluence Auric Field that is in the Corporeal World, and

2. Vaikuntha which is within the Corporeal World.

Since the Ancient Past Birth Auric Field becomes part of Indraloka during the Confluence Age and since the Mid-Confluence is connected to the Confluence Age, it was as if those ancient births were also in Indraloka since they will be in Indraloka during the Confluence Age. This was also a reason why they began to play the role of Indra, on the world stage, during those ancient days.

Though the Ancient Past Birth Auric Field has merged into the Confluence Auric Field, it is only when one makes spiritual efforts and uses one's higher auric fields, in the Confluence Auric Field, that one can easily be influenced by what exists in the Ancient Past Birth Auric Field.

Once one begins to use the higher chakras, the influence from the Ancient Past Birth Auric Field is stronger unless one has gone beyond the Corporeal World through spiritual effort making.

Since I had used the practices for the afterlife during my births which were taken after my Mid-Confluence Aged birth, my subsequent births have also emerged now to play their role in the afterlife. Since the past births' auric fields get connected to me via my Confluence Auric Field, the past births could easily play their role again. They emerged to play their role when I was hearing the murli since that is when my energies are moving up into the higher space in my Confluence Auric Field. Though I will always have a Confluence Auric Field, I only use the higher space in this Confluence Auric Field when I make spiritual efforts to go beyond the Corporeal World. When my stage is good enough, my energies would be going past my past births' auric fields before going beyond; so I get influenced by my past births' memories etc. just before my stage becomes very good.

I was aware that my past births were emerging because of my developed psychic abilities. Many might be influenced by the memories of their past births, even though they are not aware that they are being influenced by these ancient memories. These ancient memories can also influence one, as per the World Drama, even if one was not having an aura which overlaps the Ancient Past Birth Auric Field. However, in such circumstances, it would be easier to be influenced by the memories of the births taken after the Mid-Confluence, than the memories of the Mid-Confluence Aged god, because they are lower down.

Those who have past births in an emerged state in the Ancient Past Birth Auric Field, will be influenced by their memories if their chakras get activated and so their aura gets closer to the Ancient Past Birth Auric Field. They will be influenced to understand what the ancient people had left behind. Though these memories can influence non-Confluence Aged souls, it is when one comes into the Confluence Age that these memories get beneficially used because the Ancient Past

Birth Auric Field will come within the Confluence Auric Field and God will be guiding one based on what exists there.

The pure QE Light energies, which were part of the Mid-Confluence Aged Vaikuntha, served those gods by becoming the energies of the higher dimension in the Ancient Past Birth Auric Field. These QE Light energies, which were providing Vaikuntha during the Mid-Confluence, will connect the Mid-Confluence Aged Vaikuntha to the Golden Aged Vaikuntha that will exist at the end of the cycle. They will also connect all the Vaikuntha-lokas of all the past births who play a role in their afterlife, at the end of the cycle, because all QE Light act as one; and so they can play their role well together as per the 2D SWD and Nature's 2D World Drama.

In the Hindu scriptures, Vaikuntha was also reflected as the final destination of the souls who make spiritual efforts to attain moksha or liberation because when an ancient person is in Vaikuntha for his afterlife, after having left his body, he is in the state of moksha/liberation since he no longer has to do anything during his life-time for attaining moksha which is finally received at the end of the cycle. For this person, Vaikuntha represented the Soul World and the Mid-Confluence Aged Vaikuntha which successfully connects the person to the Confluence Age when souls make spiritual efforts to return to the Soul World.

Attaining Moksha, Mukti or Liberation involves freedom from ignorance, self-realisation and the release from the present cycle of rebirth where there is suffering. Liberation is enjoyed by all souls when they are in the Soul World since souls are in the pure state and are no longer using physical bodies to take births in an imperfect loka/world that is within the Corporeal World. Souls are in their most peaceful state, while in the Soul World with God, because they are in the liberated state.

Liberation in life (Jeevanmukti) is enjoyed in the first half cycle because the souls are in the pure, liberated state where they will not be able to suffer and use the vices though they are using bodies in the Corporeal

World. Jeevanmukti involves living the life while in the soul conscious state.

The ancient people, who had walked out of the heavenly world, did not appreciate the imperfect world which they were in after having lost their perfect world. Thus, they did not appreciate the births in the second half cycle, though they did see these births as great 'opportunities' to make spiritual/religious efforts for the afterlife. Hence, one of their aims was to go back to the Soul World so that the present cycle can come to an end. When this happens, they will also be playing their roles in the next Golden Aged world. Further, during the Confluence Age, one becomes free from ignorance and has self-realisation through spiritual effort making. Through this, the Confluence Aged souls are also in the process of being taken back to the Soul World since they are being purified through direct exposure to God's energies, similarly to how it is done on Judgement Day before souls journey back to the Soul World. Then, at the end of the Confluence Age, all souls are taken back to the Soul World. This is what the afterlife gets connected to, at the end. Thus, the afterlife was connected to moksha/liberation. Further, since the Mid-Confluence Aged Vaikuntha connects the ancient people to the Confluence Age, remaining in the Mid-Confluence Aged Vaikuntha (after leaving the body) involved remaining in the state of moksha/liberation since that person no longer has to do anything during his life-time for attaining moksha (which is finally received at the end of the cycle). It is only those who are in Vaikuntha who will successfully play their roles in the afterlife because it is the Mid-Confluence Aged Vaikuntha which is connected to the end of the cycle when souls return to the Soul World. So the ancient people had the aim of going to Vaikuntha after leaving the body.

After the Mid-Confluence, people had continued to use the practices for the afterlife with the hope of residing in Vaikuntha-loka, in their afterlife. Even for them, this was attaining moksha because this afterlife will finally get connected to what is happening through the Confluence Age. During the Mid-Confluence and thereafter, it was the goal of the people to play a role again, during their afterlife, so as to regain their divine kingdom which they had just lost. However, with time, when people lost the information about how the heavenly world was lost at the end of the Silver Age, people began to use the ancient practices with other aims, including attaining moksha at that time itself. Since the scriptures were only put into writing at a later date, the subsequent desires found their way into the scriptures.

Those who play a role in the afterlife will first emerge in Brahmapuri, which has been represented as a Brahmaloka in the Hindu scriptures, because they have to have God's blessings to emerge and actively play their role in the afterlife. God will enable them to emerge and play their roles if they have to do that, as per the World Drama. So the Mid-Confluence Aged Vaikuntha merges into the Confluence Auric Field instead of just becoming part of the Confluence Auric Field. If the Mid-Confluence Aged Vaikuntha does not merge into the Confluence Auric Field, the soul will not easily remember those ancient memories. When the Mid-Confluence Aged Vaikuntha merges into the Confluence Auric Field, the auric field of other past births, which are in the Ancient Past Birth Auric Field, can also merge into the Confluence Auric Field if these past births also have to play a role in the afterlife as per the World Drama. In addition to this, only those who are walking in can be involved with the afterlife of past births because only those walking in can use dimensions in the Higher Universe. BKs do not use dimensions in the Higher Universe. These are reasons why most BKs do not remember anything of their ancient past. In Brahmapuri, the soul (who is influenced by the afterlife of past births) will be meditating on God until the end of the cycle when the soul has to return to the Soul World. While the soul is meditating, God uses the soul and its ancient memories for world service. Thus, the Mid-Confluence Aged Vaikuntha and Ancient Past Birth Auric Field become significant because that is where the memories exist. Since the Mid-Confluence Aged Vaikuntha is in a merged state within the Confluence Auric Field, God can easily see these memories. When we allow God to use us for world service, we get a huge spiritual income through the Law of Karma and this income can be used to enjoy wealth and prosperity now, after we walk in, in our births in the next first half cycle and during the next Mid-Confluence.

Some past births do not have an afterlife. When their memories are in an emerged state, due to a trauma in their life, these memories are in Bhuvarloka. Only memories of those who have an afterlife are in Vaikuntha.

When the Mid-Confluence Aged Vaikuntha is connected to the Golden Aged Vaikuntha of those walking in, all the other seven lokas (provided by the seven chakras), which were used by those ancient people, also get connected. This means that the ancient past birth can easily emerge to play its role again.

The Golden Aged Vaikuntha-loka, which is used through contemplating on the BK knowledge, is discussed further in subsequent chapters.

Chapter 42: Usage of Seven Chakras/Lokas during the Walking In Process

The seven chakras/lokas are used by those walking in because:

1. the Kundalini rises for those walking in (since their Kundalini will have to be at the Seventh Chakra during the materialised Golden Age).

2. the QE Light bodies get created through all seven chakras for the materialisation of the perfect Golden Aged body.

3. those walking in will be using the Siddhis and specialities as the seven chakras get activated while the Kundalini rises.

The Kundalini of those walking in rises:

1. due to their spiritual effort making, and

2. since the Confluence Aged Gathering of Shanker (900,000 most powerful Confluence Aged souls for world transformation) is getting more powerful.

When the consciousness of those walking in is in one of the seven lokas, as their Kundalini rises, they will begin their spiritual effort making from that loka and also from Bhuloka since they still need to use their body for spiritual effort making. It should be noted that the physical body is still being provided through the usage of all the seven chakras, in the Lower Universe, until the Golden Aged body materialises. Thus, even though the chakras are playing a role for what needs to exist and be used in the Higher Universe, all seven chakras are still playing a role in the Lower Universe (to a certain extent involving the usage of the body). Since the physical body is in Bhuloka, those walking in actually begin their spiritual effort making there. However, since the Kundalini is providing a different loka for the consciousness of the soul, the energies of the soul used for the spiritual effort making can be using a higher loka.

Though the Kundalini slowly rises from the Root Chakra, those walking in begin their spiritual effort making from Indraloka and Bhuloka at the same time because when one receives the BK knowledge, one begins to use Indraloka as one's subtle loka while also using Bhuloka so as to use one's physical body. The Kundalini would easily remain in the Third Chakra as a result of this, though it is supposed to be rising from the Root Chakra. Though the Kundalini constantly remains at the Third Chakra, since the soul has been brought into Indraloka, the Kundalini is also gaining the ability to reside at a higher chakra/loka due to the soul's improved spiritual strength. It should be noted that the soul is in Indraloka due to God's assistance. If it did not have that assistance, it would not be residing in Indraloka; it would drop into a lower loka. Through gaining spiritual strength, via the Confluence Age, the soul is gaining the ability to reside in a higher loka during the first half cycle.

When the Kundalini is in the Third Chakra/loka, for those walking in, higher frequencies are emitted from the chakras. So the environment which they live in is a heavenly environment, i.e. they would be living in Swargaloka, though this Swargaloka would be in the same space as the Kaliyug Real World. It will be as if they are living in heaven on earth even though their environment co-exists with other kinds of lokas within the Real World. In addition to this, those walking in will be in Indraloka because they are Confluence Aged souls. So they are in both: Swargaloka and Indraloka. In Indraloka, they will be able to experience God's unconditional love through the 6th and 4th chakras. When they make spiritual efforts to a greater extent, they would be able to experience God's unconditional love to a greater extent because they would be using the higher chakras instead of the lower chakras. If they were not making much spiritual efforts, the spiritual effort makers can be easily influenced by the vices since they are still using lower auric fields. This is also a reason why, in the myths, the Devas were portrayed as being capable of being influenced by the vices. However, all this changes after the walking in process is over.

At the end, if those walking in are in one of the lower lokas due to a weak stage, they will be automatically uplifted into Brahmaloka since they are walking into the materialised Golden Aged world. Thereafter, they will not use a lower loka.

In the first half cycle, the Kundalini of the people will constantly be at the Seventh Chakra and their consciousness will never drop into the Real World. They will also never experience unhappiness. This is the true heaven on earth. This is what you will also be enjoying after walking in. This is more than money's worth because you cannot use money to create such a world for yourself. The only way to enjoy such a world in this birth itself is through the walking in process.

The rising of the Kundalini is actually enabling one to walk in because as one's Kundalini keeps rising to a higher chakra, one is given a more heavenly loka until one finally walks in. Since the Kundalini is rising and bringing the consciousness from the Root Chakra to the Seventh Chakra for the walking in process, the seven chakras/lokas become gateways to the Golden Aged Vaikuntha.

While the Kundalini of those walking in rises upwards from the Root Chakra to the Seventh Chakra, the Golden Aged QE Light bodies also get created from the 7th to the first auric fields. As all these are happening, you are getting lifted into the higher dimensions in the Higher Universe until you are lifted into the Vaikuntha which exists in the space of the Confluence Aged Subtle Region. When you keep seeing yourself as getting lifted into the higher dimensions, you are actually getting lifted since this 'lifting process' has already begun for the walking in process. Your consciousness is also getting lifted up into the higher chakras, slowly, as you walk in. Thus, constantly visualising yourself as using the higher dimensions in the Higher Universe will lift your consciousness up from the lower chakras to the higher chakras.

Just as your body is getting lifted up through the creation of the Golden

Aged QE Light bodies and auric fields, even the dimensions in the Holographic Universe are getting lifted up as the dimensions get created in the Higher Universe for the Golden Aged QE Light bodies to exist in. Everything gets lifted up through being empowered by God's energies.

In a dream, I saw God as a tree with numerous branches. Each of those branches was like a Helping Hand for helping Mankind. One of those branches was the Helping Hand which allows the Confluence Aged souls to go into the Higher Universe from the Lower Universe. As each person received the BK knowledge, it was as if the person received a Helping Hand from here and the person continues to use the Helping Hand as his/her own for remaining in the Higher Universe. I understood this dream as I was getting up. God's energies are like a Helping Hand that brings one into Indraloka in the Higher Universe from the Lower Universe. As a result of this Helping Hand, all those who receive the BK knowledge will be able to go into the Higher Universe from the Lower Universe. Each soul is given a Helping Hand, as a right, since he has to be brought into the Higher Universe. Thus, each Confluence Aged soul can say, "God is mine". Those walking in also use this Helping Hand to use the lokas in the Higher Universe.

Since God has come to uplift the universe, we can take advantage of this and move along with it into the Higher Universe. As you are doing this, all the seven chakras get connected to the lokas in the Higher Universe.

If you were only in the Lower Universe, you would be using different lokas from those who are using the Higher Universe. Yet, there will be some similarities between the lokas of the Lower Universe and Higher Universe because the same seven chakras are used to go into the seven lokas (though they are in different universes). Further, these chakras also enable everyone to use specific specialities and Siddhis.

It is only the bodies of those who are walking in which will begin to exist in the Higher Universe after the materialisation of the Golden Aged world. At first, though their physical body remains in the Lower Universe, QE Light bodies are being created in the Higher Universe and this is actually the process through which their bodies get lifted up into the higher dimensions. Since the Golden Aged body is created through the seven chakras/lokas, these seven chakras/lokas are the gateways to become part of the materialising Golden Aged world.

By the time your final Golden Aged QE body and auric field are created through the First Chakra, all your chakras would have also been activated from the First Chakra to the Seventh Chakra. Then, you will be constantly enjoying bliss.

If you are walking in, there are two different sections in your Confluence Auric Field which you can use. One consists of the auric fields and lokas of the Golden Aged QE Light bodies which are being developed in the Higher Universe so that your body can transform into a perfect body as the Golden Aged world materialises. The other consists of the auric fields and lokas which are provided by the chakras, such as Indraloka/Swargaloka, Maharloka, Janaloka, Tapoloka and Brahmaloka.

Through the seven chakras/lokas, one uses lower dimensions in the Golden Aged Vaikuntha. This Golden Aged Vaikuntha is the subtle dimension whereas the Golden Aged QE Light bodies which are for the materialisation of the perfect Golden Aged bodies involve the provision of the real form; so the auric fields and lokas of the Golden Aged QE Light bodies are grouped together with the real form. This is similar to how the Etheric Field is the double of the physical body. It is better to use the Golden Aged Vaikuntha-loka instead of the auric fields and lokas of the Golden Aged QE Light bodies. Though the auric fields of the Golden Aged QE Light bodies are developing in the Confluence Auric Field, it is as if it is in a different dimension from that which is used by the soul:

1. for Confluence Aged purposes.

2. when it uses Vaikuntha-loka.

It should be noted that the Ancient Past Birth Auric Field merges into the Confluence Auric Field, yet it is also in a dimension of its own within

385

the Confluence Auric Field. The Ancient Past Birth Auric Field also only gets connected to the Golden Aged Vaikuntha. It is like this for the sake of world service and so:

1. those walking in might not be influenced by what is in the Ancient Past Birth Auric Field. Thus, they can continue living their own life as they wish.

2. what exists in the Ancient Past Birth Auric Field will not affect the development of the Golden Aged body through the Golden Aged QE Light bodies.

The Mid-Confluence Aged people had done a lot of worship to make sure that those who play a role in their afterlife, at the end, will become wealthy and prosperous so as to play their role well. Thus, when the Mid-Confluence Aged Vaikuntha gets connected to the Golden Aged Vaikuntha of those walking in, all the seven Mid-Confluence Aged lokas also get connected to the seven lokas that are the gateways to the Golden Aged Vaikuntha and so:

1. one will find it easy to get what one wants through the seven chakras/lokas.

2. one will also be able to reacquire the wealth and prosperity which one had during the Mid-Confluence.

3. one will easily find oneself in one of the higher lokas provided by the higher chakras.

There will be many, among those walking in, who would have learnt to use these higher lokas via the practices that were left behind. Thus, they will find it very easy to use these higher lokas even during the walking in process.

When using the lokas provided by the seven chakras, one could use the Mid-Confluence Aged lokas (to use the abilities which the ancient people had acquired) or use the lokas used by those walking in (to enjoy the heavenly environment in the Golden Aged Vaikuntha). During the Mid-Confluence if the soul was using the subtle higher lokas that were provided by the higher chakras, then the soul would be able to easily use those subtle higher lokas again now, if the memories of those past births are in an emerged state. However, you can also use the Golden Aged Vaikuntha-lokas provided by the chakras, unless you are using the lokas for magical abilities to manifest what you desire. The seven lokas which allow those walking in to use Siddhis and specialities are in different dimensions from those which have the Golden Aged Vaikuntha-lokas and the Mid-Confluence Aged lokas.

During the later phase of the walking in process, those walking in can use the seven chakras and their lokas to get whatever they want because the chakras will be functioning well. Though they have this ability, they will not use these magical abilities because, in their pure state, they will just enjoy the heavenly world which has been provided for them. However, their world will be such that they will be provided with whatever they wanted, e.g. if they desired food of a particular taste, they will get it. They will also have wealth if they wished to have that.

One will be getting wealth even if one was not using any of the other Siddhis that can be used via the activated chakras. One may not be receiving everything at the same time, when the chakras get activated, because one also receives as per the World Drama. Even the settling process may reduce what one gets. Watch it all as a detached observer.

The Mid-Confluence Aged people had given importance to Tapoloka, Janaloka and Maharloka because those who are influenced by the afterlife, and are using the knowledge acquired through the memories of the afterlife, use these lokas for explaining what had been done in ancient times. It is as if they are immortals because they can remember what had happened during the Mid-Confluence. 'Knowledge' will be their speciality as it is mine. Since the past births had acquired a right to play a role in their afterlife through remaining pure and virtuous, these souls will be able to easily use their ancient memories. Since these past births are in their pure state, the soul can easily make Confluence Aged spiritual efforts to go into Vaikuntha-loka and even into the Confluence Aged Subtle Regions through using the BK knowledge. When they use Brahmaloka and Tapoloka, they are also able to understand what is happening in the Holographic Universe (within the QE Light and quantum dimensions). Thus, some of those walking in can also understand what is happening in the Holographic Universe as they begin to employ various kinds of lokas.

Brahmaloka will also connect those walking in to Brahmapuri. So use the lokas which are the gateway to the Vaikuntha-lokas instead of the others. Through this, you can easily continue making spiritual efforts to become more powerful. A more powerful soul attains a higher status in the first half cycle. So don't just think of attaining wealth in this birth, think of becoming a royalty and receiving wealth in your births in the first half cycle as well.

Those walking in can go into Brahmapuri, which is beyond the present Corporeal World:

1. from Brahmaloka, i.e. via the Seventh Chakra.

2. through the Confluence Auric Field which connects them to the Angelic Body that is in the Angelic World.

Brahmaloka is connected directly to Brahmapuri because, as the intellect flies to link itself to God through the Sixth Chakra, some of the energies of the soul also flies through the Seventh Chakra (the space of which is also Brahmaloka) to leave the body and go into the Angelic World. The energies of the soul have to leave through the 7th chakra so as to bring one's consciousness into another realm. The Kundalini would also be at the Seventh Chakra because the Kundalini rises whenever our spiritual stage goes up.

As the Kundalini rises to go to the Seventh Chakra, some of the energies of the soul are also going through the activated chakras to go into the Confluence Auric Field. As each higher chakra gets activated, the energies of the soul go through that higher chakra to go into a higher space in the Confluence Auric Field. As this keeps happening, when higher chakras are utilised, the soul begins to use the higher auric fields until it finally begins to completely engage the Angelic Body which is beyond the Corporeal World. In addition, the Confluence Auric Field becomes more powerful because they get filled with more of God's energies. The energies of the soul that flies through the 6th and 7th chakras, and the energies of the soul which begins to use higher regions in the Confluence Auric Field, are all doing it at the same time and at the same pace. Thus, the energies of the soul reach the Angelic World and God in more than one way at the same time. When we have an experience of flying up, we just feel that we are flying up; we are not aware of how our energies are flying up and neither are we aware of how the Kundalini is also rising. This is similar to how we are not aware of what is happening in the body when we want to raise our hand. We are just aware that we are raising our hand. All Confluence Aged souls, including those walking in, go to the Angelic World and link themselves to God through this way when they make spiritual efforts. However, in addition to this, those walking in can use the lokas which are provided by the seven chakras in the body.

When those walking in use one of the higher lokas provided by the higher chakras in the body, they will have a lovely experience while in those lokas since they are in the Higher Universe. From these lokas, their consciousness can be taken into even higher lokas and also into the Angelic World which is beyond the present Corporeal World. They have to keep remembering God and get His assistance to go up into the higher dimensions. Once they begin to employ the Seventh Chakra, they can go into Brahmapuri or they can move into Brahmaloka which is in the Higher Universe. They become Brahma or Vishnu as they use the higher lokas, depending on whether they are in Vaikuntha, Brahmaloka or Brahmapuri.

Those walking in can play the role of Brahma (god self) well when they are using Brahmaloka (through the Seventh Chakra) instead of

Brahmapuri. This is due to the fact that their past births (especially the Mid-Confluence Aged gods) were playing the role of Brahma through the god self. Further, the god self initiates the 'creation' that will exist in the Real World because it all begins with what exists in the Detailed World Drama deep within the soul. Since the god self initiates or causes or begins the process for a 'creation', it can be said that the god self is Brahma 'the creator'. BKs only act as Brahma for world transformation through self-transformation. They do not play the role of Brahma for getting their personal desires fulfilled through the god self (Brahma). However, those who walk in can become the god self (Brahma) to get their desires fulfilled through visualisations.

If you were finding it difficult to connect yourself to Brahmapuri via Brahmaloka, you can always go into the pure divine dimensions of Vaikuntha-loka in Brahmajyoti from Brahmaloka. Then, as you keep making spiritual efforts, you go into the Angelic World. As you are enjoying these Vaikuntha dimensions, the energies of your soul are also flying up from Brahmaloka to Brahmapuri. Thus, those walking in could attempt to:

1. fly straight to the Angelic World through using their divine intellect, as BKs do, or

2. go into the Vaikuntha dimensions through their chakra and then move into the Angelic World via the higher Vaikuntha dimension in Brahmajyoti.

Brahmaloka connects to Brahmajyoti. It can also be said that Brahmaloka and Brahmajyoti are one and the same because:

1. Brahmaloka is the gateway to go into Brahmajyoti since Brahmaloka is the gateway to Vaikuntha and Vaikuntha is filled with Brahmajyoti.

2. Brahmajyoti consists of God's effulgence and the effulgence of the QE Light. These are also absorbed into Brahmaloka when the Seventh Chakra is activated. This is so because the Seventh Chakra absorbs some of the energies that are in the dimension which is above it.

Since Brahmaloka is the gateway to Vaikuntha, some of the energies from the higher Vaikuntha-loka can be absorbed into the lower Vaikuntha-loka. This is possible since auric fields and chakras absorb the energies which are near them. However, the Vaikuntha used through Brahmaloka will not be as powerful as the Vaikuntha in the higher dimensions.

BKs will not use the lokas in the Higher Universe to go into the Angelic World, even though their Confluence Auric Field is getting filled in the Higher Universe as their divine intellect flies to the Angelic World.

As the Golden Aged QE Light bodies are getting created and as the person's seven chakras are getting activated, the soul may have begun to use Vaikuntha-lokas in Brahmajyoti. The creation of all these Golden Aged QE Light bodies and the activation of all the chakras is a stepping stone to use the higher Vaikuntha-lokas in Brahmajyoti. When all the Golden Aged QE Light bodies are completely created and the Kundalini has reached the Crown Chakra, the soul will be using Vaikuntha-loka in the Confluence Aged Subtle Region.

There are a total of 330 million deity souls. Out of these 900,000 deity souls walk in and 900,000 become part of the Gathering of Shanker which helps to transform the world into the Golden Aged world. Some of those who walk in may also be part of the Gathering of Shanker. The remainder of the 330 million deity souls will be able to use the seven chakras/lokas for Siddhis and specialities just as those walking in can use them if they are not using the Golden Aged Vaikuntha through the seven chakras/lokas. They use the lokas in this way if they use the practices of the Sun Dynasty. If Confluence Aged souls, including those walking in, had used these practices during the Mid-Confluence, they would find it even easier to use the seven lokas for the usage of the Siddhis and specialities. If they only used the BK knowledge seriously, as BKs do, they by-pass these seven lokas and go straight into the Angelic World and they will not be using the Siddhis just as the BKs do not.

When deity souls take their births in the first half cycle, their consciousness will be at the Crown Chakra because they had already been completely purified on Judgement Day and/or during the Confluence Age. Before leaving the body to go back to the Soul World, if any of the remainder of the 330 million deity souls are in an area which has already been transformed into the Golden Aged world, their Kundalini would also be at the Seventh Chakra even though they are not one of those walking in to take care of the Golden Aged world. Thus, even if their Kundalini has only risen to the 3rd, 4th, 5th or 6th chakra, their Kundalini would be uplifted into the Seventh Chakra due to the purity of the place. This is different from how those walking in are assisted to have their Kundalini uplifted into the higher chakras even if they are not around those who are part and parcel of the Gathering of Shanker.

If you have the desire to walk in, then you must be one of those walking in. So do not sit and wonder if you are one of those walking in.

Chapter 43: QE Light Bodies and their Auric Fields for those Walking In

The QE Light Bodies and their auric fields are created through the chakras. There are numerous different QE Light bodies and auric fields which are provided by the seven chakras. All those QE Light bodies and auric fields which are provided through each chakra can be categorised as one QE Light body and auric field respectively, though they can also be considered as different QE Light bodies and auric fields based on the purposes for which they are provided.

The soul uses QE Light Bodies and auric fields for various purposes. Inter alia, for those walking in, the chakras are getting activated for:

1. the creation of auric fields, within the Confluence Auric Field, that are used for Confluence Aged purposes.

2. the creation of the Golden Aged Holographic Body (Golden Aged QE Light Body and its auric fields) which are for the creation of the Golden Aged physical body.

3. the usage of Siddhis and specialities. This also involves the creation and usage of QE Light bodies and auric fields in the Higher Universe.

4. the usage of the lower Vaikuntha-lokas. Even this involves the creation of QE Light bodies and auric fields in the Higher Universe so that Vaikuntha-loka can be used in the relevant auric field. As the Kundalini rises, a Vaikuntha-loka is created through each chakra for the consciousness of the soul to reside in. At the same time there is also a Vaikuntha-loka aspect to the Golden Aged QE Light bodies and auric fields.

All the above QE Light bodies and auric fields are created in the Higher Universe and they can be collectively referred to as the Higher Universe Holographic Body (consisting of the Higher Universe QE Light bodies and auric fields). During the walking in process one can use any of the Higher Universe QE Light bodies and auric fields.

The creation of auric fields which become part of the Confluence Auric Field also involves the creation of QE Light bodies first through the relevant chakras. As the Confluence Aged soul keeps making efforts, the higher chakras in the body get activated. As each higher chakra is activated, a QE Light body and its auric field are created in the Higher Universe. Thus, the person has an additional auric field which gets filled with the energies from the Confluence Aged Subtle Region (including God's energies since God resides in the Angelic World).

The environment in an auric field is provided by the dimension which it is in. Since the Confluence Auric Field is the aura of the Angelic Body, in the Angelic World, the energies which are in the Angelic World provide the environment in the Confluence Auric Field. When we adopt the Angelic Body, we adopt its aura as well and so the Confluence Auric Field stretches from the physical body to the Angelic Body which is beyond the Corporeal World. The Confluence Auric Field is actually another loka/dimension which has stretched into the Real World because our physical bodies are in the Real World. Despite this, the environment within the Confluence Auric Field is only being provided by the energies of the Angelic World because the QE Light body which provides the Confluence Auric Field is part and parcel of the Angelic Body that is beyond the Corporeal World. The Confluence Auric Field acts like a chakra to absorb the energies from the Angelic World so as to provide the environment within the Confluence Auric Field. Thus, it is as if the Confluence Aged Subtle Region is also within the Confluence Auric Field.

As each auric field gets created within the Confluence Auric Field, it acts like a chakra to absorb energies from the environment in the Confluence Auric Field. So the energies which provide an environment in each auric field are also from the Confluence Aged Subtle Region since the environment in the Confluence Auric Field is the same environment that is in the Confluence Aged Subtle Region.

God's energies also flow into our Confluence Auric Field via Brahma Baba's Confluence Auric Field which is used by God to keep us within the Confluence Age. So the auric fields which get created in our Confluence Auric Field also receive God's energies through this way.

The Confluence Auric Fields of all Confluence Aged souls are merged with Brahma Baba's Confluence Auric Field and this brings the BK Collective Consciousness into existence. When a person receives the BK knowledge and accepts it, the person's Confluence Auric Field will merge with Brahma Baba's Confluence Auric Field and so the person's consciousness becomes part and parcel of the BK Collective Consciousness. God's energies are also being emitted into this BK Collective Consciousness:

1. via the spiritual effort making of all the BKs, and

2. from Brahma Baba's Confluence Auric Field (since God uses Brahma Baba's Angelic Body). Since God uses Brahma Baba's Angelic Body and its Confluence Auric Field, it can be said that God's Consciousness is also part of the BK Collective Consciousness. Thus, the BK Collective Consciousness is actually a Godly Collective Consciousness. However, since I have already begun referring to it as the BK Collective Consciousness, I am continuing to refer to it as such.

Our Confluence Auric Field gets empowered with God's energies, even through the BK Collective Consciousness; each auric field that gets created within our Confluence Auric Field also gets empowered through it. You can find more information in Chapter 18 of my book titled "Holographic Universe: An Introduction" in respect of:

1. the BK Collective Consciousness, and

2. how Brahma Baba's Confluence Auric Field is used by God to keep us within the Confluence Age.

As more auric fields begin to exist in the Confluence Auric Field, more energy is absorbed from the Angelic World. When all 7 QE Light bodies and auric fields are created in the Higher Universe, through spiritual effort making, the soul enjoys a higher spiritual stage. Then, the divine intellect leaves the 7th auric field to establish the link to God who is in the Angelic World. At the same time, the energies of the soul adopt the Angelic Body completely since the soul and the whole Confluence Auric Field has become empowered with God's energies. In addition to these, those walking in also have other auric fields for the usage of Vaikuntha, for the usage of the Siddhis and specialities, and for the creation of the Golden Aged body. Since these are continuing to get created due to the walking in process, those walking in are being given more auric fields which can be filled with God's energies whether they are making spiritual efforts or not. Thus, those walking in will find it very easy to enjoy the pure and happy state without much spiritual effort making.

The chakras connect various dimensions in the Holographic Universe. They also connect the First Field to the Second Field for the creation and sustenance of the QE Light bodies and their auric fields. For Confluence Aged souls and those walking in, the chakras also connect the Higher Universe to the Lower Universe. Thus, those walking in can use:

1. the physical body in the Lower Universe, and

2. the QE Light bodies and auric fields in the Higher Universe.

Then, when the Golden Aged World is materialised, their physical body is provided through the new Golden Aged QE Light bodies and auric fields in the Higher Universe. Their physical body will no longer be provided through the QE Light bodies and auric fields in the Lower Universe. This means that their physical body gets uplifted into the Higher Universe.

The walking in process actually begins from the time the Golden Aged QE Light Bodies and auric fields begin to get created in the Higher Universe. When all the QE Light bodies of all the chakras are established (along with their relevant auric fields) then only can a person be given a perfect body in the Higher Universe. Through this process, those walking in get lifted out of the Bhuloka of the Lower Universe to go into the Bhuloka of the Higher Universe. The Bhuloka of the Higher Universe will be Dwarka or Satyaloka (Land of Truth) which exists in the same space as Brahmapuri. More explanations can be found on Dwarka and Satyaloka (Land of Truth) in Chapter 44: Golden Aged Vaikuntha, Brahmaloka, Satyaloka and Dwarka.

The QE Light bodies get created from the 7th auric field to the first auric field. When the first auric field is completely created, our bodies will begin to exist in the Golden Aged Real World and the environment around us is also uplifted into the Higher Universe. It is happening in the same space; yet, the world is up-lifted because the densities of the energies which provide the Golden Aged Real World will be very fine (less dense).

The Golden Aged QE Light Bodies and their auric fields are the new Golden Aged Holographic Body. There are two ways of creating the Golden Aged Holographic Body which provides the perfect Golden Aged body:

1. through the strengthening of the Gathering of Shanker in the Confluence Aged Subtle Region called Shankerpuri, and

2. through one's spiritual effort making which increases one's spiritual strength.

During the walking in process, based on how powerful the Gathering of Shanker is, one is getting lifted up from Bhuloka, in the Lower Universe, to go into the Bhuloka which will exist in the Angelic World. In addition to this, one's own spiritual effort making also lifts one up into the higher lokas so that one's Bhuloka will exist in the same space as Brahmapuri. All this happens since one's Golden Aged QE Light Bodies and auric fields are getting developed. As one gets lifted up (whether based on the gathering or based on one's own spiritual efforts), one uses lokas which are higher up since one begins to use higher auric fields. In addition to this, if one is making spiritual efforts to go into a high spiritual stage, one is also using a higher loka in a higher auric field, temporarily, during the experience.

If one manages to create all of one's Golden Aged QE Light bodies and auric fields for the walking in process through one's own spiritual effort making, then, one also belongs to the Gathering of Shanker and one has become ready for world transformation. However, all others (a total of 900,000 Confluence Aged souls) must also be ready for world transformation to take place. This is like a 'collective consciousness' requirement for creating the new world.

As the Golden Aged QE Light bodies and auric fields get developed, these auric fields will also get filled with God's energies. God's energies, within these auric fields, help to keep the energies, within these auric fields, in a pure and divine state until the new Golden Aged world materialises. This also helps one to easily experience happiness, the pure state, etc. Yet, one will find it very difficult to make spiritual efforts to establish one's link to God because the Golden Aged people do not have to make spiritual efforts. So their bodies do not provide the specialities which the people of the second half cycle have, through the brain and body, for spiritual effort making and worship. Similarly, even those walking in will not be able to make spiritual efforts if they used their Golden Aged Holographic Body. While using the Golden Aged Holographic Body, if you are in a BK centre, you will be exposed to God's energies which are being emitted through the other BKs but you will not be contributing much to fill the BK centre with God's energies. Your pure state will help others to attain the pure state but they will not be receiving much of God's vibrations through you. It is better to use the old physical body for spiritual effort making.

If your stage is very bad, you will find it easier to experience happiness through using the Golden Aged Holographic Body than through establishing your link to God because:

1. God and the Angelic Body are far away, since they are above the Corporeal World, whereas your Golden Aged Holographic Body is so

close to you.

2. the Golden Aged Holographic Body is your body now, even though it does not have a materialised real form; so you can easily use it, like how you can easily use your physical body.

3. you cannot experience unhappiness through the Golden Aged Holographic Body. No one should experience unhappiness in the first half cycle and so the bodies will not facilitate it.

You use the Angelic Body when you have your link to God. You have to make serious spiritual efforts to establish your link to God so that your intellect is energised to fly way beyond the Corporeal World. So you may find it difficult to completely use the Angelic Body and get your link to God. As a consequence, you will find it hard to experience happiness through this way. In contrast, you can easily use the Golden Aged Holographic Body because:

1. it overlaps your physical body even though it is in the Higher Universe.

2. you are in the process of walking into the Golden Aged world.

To use the Angelic Body you need to keep contemplating on the BK knowledge, the whole day. If not, you will be struggling to establish your link to God. If the vices are in an emerged state, you might have a fierce battle with them before becoming victorious to completely use the Angelic Body. You will not be battling fiercely with the vices if you were going to use the Golden Aged Holographic Body because the vices will not see you as a threat. They only see the BK spiritual effort making as a treat to their rule in the world. This is because the world is transforming due to the spiritual effort making of the BKs. Further, God will also be protecting you like a protective Mother. So the vices will quickly go away when you adopt the Golden Aged Holographic Body instead of becoming the Confluence Aged Spiritual Effort-Maker who uses the physical body to make spiritual efforts. However, you will not be able to adopt the Golden Aged Holographic Body if you are entertaining the vices. So put the vices aside if you want to adopt your Golden Aged Holographic Body.

Despite all that which has been just said, it is not advisable to use the Golden Aged Holographic Body because you will find it even more difficult (almost impossible) to establish your link to God once you have begun to use your Golden Aged Holographic Body. If you are using your Golden Aged Holographic Body and are finding it difficult to establish your own link to God, see yourself as the soul instead of seeing yourself as the Golden Aged self. Then, contemplate on the BK knowledge and see yourself as a Confluence Aged Spiritual Effort Maker. You are the Confluence Aged Spiritual Effort Maker when you begin making spiritual efforts through contemplating on the BK knowledge. It is only after you leave the Golden Aged Holographic Body, that you will be able to make spiritual efforts through becoming the Confluence Aged Spiritual Effort Maker.

If you want to easily establish your link to God via the walking in process, use the QE Light bodies and auric fields through which you use the Vaikuntha-lokas, etc. in the Higher Universe. Do not use the Golden Aged Holographic Body which is getting created for giving you a Golden Aged perfect physical body. During the walking in process:

1. as the Kundalini rises, the chakras are activated. Thus, QE Light bodies and auric fields are created by each chakra, where the Kundalini resides, for the usage of Vaikuntha-loka since the consciousness is at the chakra.

2. there is also a Vaikuntha-loka aspect to the Golden Aged QE Light bodies and auric fields.

All the above QE Light bodies and auric fields are also part of the Golden Aged Holographic Body. However, I prefer not to associate these with the Golden Aged Holographic Body because while in Vaikuntha-loka, even though one is like a 'divine god' of the first half cycle, those walking in can:

1. make spiritual efforts to link oneself to God, and

2. do world service for receiving a good spiritual income.

Within each auric field there are many auric fields. Each of these auric fields is emitted from the chakra to provide something specific. Some are involved with providing the physical body. All those involved with providing the physical body can be categorised as one auric field. This auric field is similar to a Golden Aged auric field which is emitted from a chakra for providing the Golden Aged physical body. The chakras also provide auric fields (Vaikuntha-lokas) for spiritual experiences. It can also be said that the aspect of the auric field which is used for experiences is Vaikuntha.

The chakras themselves can be used as lokas since energies of the soul can go and reside there. Thus, each chakra can be given a loka name. For instance, the Third Chakra itself can be referred to as Swargaloka and the auric field which is emitted from it is also Swargaloka. However, since those walking in use Vaikuntha-loka, Swargaloka is also Vaikuntha-loka. Through this way, the seven chakras/lokas are the gateway to Vaikuntha-loka.

In the Kaliyug world, all the 7 auric fields are involved with providing the old physical body and yet they also provide lokas which one can use for spiritual experiences. The Golden Aged QE Light bodies and auric fields are similar to the QE Light bodies and auric fields which materialise the old physical body. Vaikuntha-loka is similar to the loka which is used in an auric field during experiences. You will be able to make spiritual efforts while you use Vaikuntha because:

1. you are still within the QE Light body and auric fields which are providing the old physical body.

2. you are not involved with the usage of the new Golden Aged physical body nor are you using the Golden Aged QE Light bodies and auric fields which are involved with providing the Golden Aged physical body.

Those who use Vaikuntha-loka do not get caught up within the material aspects through which the Golden Aged physical body is provided. Thus, they can remain as spiritual effort makers even though they are in Vaikuntha-loka. If you use the Golden Aged QE Light Auric Fields you are trapped within the energies which are involved with providing the Golden Aged physical body. Thus, it is as if you are within the Golden Aged physical body. It should be noted that it is easier to go into the Vaikuntha from the Golden Aged QE Light Auric Fields than it is to go there from the old physical body. However, the problem is that if you go there from the Golden Aged QE Light Auric Fields, it will be as if you are using that as your body and not your old physical body. Hence, you will find it very difficult to make spiritual efforts since it is the old physical body which is designed for spiritual effort making.

The creation of the Golden Aged Holographic Body and the rising of the Kundalini through the seven chakras have been symbolically represented in the Bible through the myth where God creates a new world, including Adam and Eve, within 7 days. The '7 days' reflect the time which is taken:

1. to use the seven chakras for the creation of the new Golden Aged body.

2. for the Kundalini to rise along the seven chakras so that the consciousness of the soul can remain in the Crown Chakra.

The new Golden Aged world is created by the time all these seven chakras are used to complete the creation process.

In addition to experiencing the heavenly Vaikuntha-loka, one can also experience the development of the Siddhis as the auric fields develop during the walking in process. When you use the Siddhis, specific energies from the chakras are assisting you. These energies can also be seen as an auric field by itself. From the viewpoint that each auric field consists of different auric fields, even these energies which are involved with assisting to provide the Siddhis can be seen as another auric field. However, these energies can also be seen as just being involved with a different function.

When one is using specific Siddhis one is also using a higher loka (in addition to Bhuloka) and so a loka is also experienced in an auric field. It should be noted that a QE Light Body is created first and it is from this QE Light body that the auric field is emitted; though the auric field which is emitted from the QE Light body is also created by the energies from the chakra that created the QE Light body. The loka which is experienced in the auric field is also provided by the energies from the same chakra.

You can use more than one kind of loka at the same time. Thus, you can use Vaikuntha-loka at the same time as you use the Siddhis. However, since they are different auric fields and you must have a specific loka (auric field) in mind to have an experience in, select Vaikuntha and not the loka (auric field) which is used for the Siddhis. If you intentionally use the Siddhis, you might not be using Vaikuntha. If you are only concerned to use Vaikuntha, you will naturally use the Siddhis because they are also developing as you walk in.

BKs do not use the Siddhis because they have been told not to be concerned about developing them. However, those walking in can use the Siddhis.

Despite all that which has been said so far, it should be noted that it is the easiest to make spiritual efforts through using the Confluence Aged Spiritual Effort Maker Self because:

1. the Confluence Aged Spiritual Effort Maker only uses the old physical body which is very good for spiritual effort making.

2. the Vaikuntha-loka QE Light bodies and auric fields have the Golden Aged QE Light bodies and auric fields developing eventhough one is still using the old physical body and not the Golden Aged physical body.

Nevertheless, through using Vaikuntha, one is still capable of using the BK knowledge to make spiritual efforts and one can also get involved with Godly service instead of just happily living one's life. So from Vaikuntha, one can go into Goloka. One can also get involved with service in the material world, whether it is in the Kaliyug Real World or in the Golden Aged Real World which one walks into.

During experiences, those walking in can be given temporary QE Light subtle bodies to use. Thus, they can experience themselves as a subtle form. Temporary subtle QE Light bodies can also be created for the visions which they see or have an experience in. These are created in the Higher Universe, within the Confluence Auric Field. Thus, they can easily leave these to adopt the Angelic Body which is beyond the present Corporeal World (when their spiritual stage becomes higher).

Chapter 44: Golden Aged Vaikuntha, Brahmaloka, Satyaloka and Dwarka

There are many divisions in Vaikuntha. One of these is the Golden Aged Vaikuntha which is used for the walking in process. This Vaikuntha is established at the end of the cycle, when God establishes the new Golden Aged world through the Confluence Age. Since it has already begun to exist, those who want to begin the walking in process can do so now.

There are two kinds of dimensions in the Corporeal World:

1. the material dimensions for the existence of the physical world. These are not spiritual dimensions.

2. the spiritual dimensions. These are the subtle and metaphysical dimensions where the energies of the soul are in.

Vaikuntha is a subtle spiritual dimension within the Corporeal World. Generally, one uses Vaikuntha in one's higher auric fields which are beyond Satyaloka.

If the energies of the soul do not exist in Vaikuntha, the loka cannot be referred to as Vaikuntha. This is not how it is where the material dimensions are concerned. Further, though the energies in the material realms are also playing a role with, and for, the energies of the soul, the energies in the material realms are more involved with the materialisation process. This is so different from the situation where the QE Light energies, in the spiritual dimensions, play a role as if they are part and parcel of the energies of the soul.

In contrast to Vaikuntha, Satyaloka is generally the material realm. There are various aspects to Satyaloka, which includes the following:

1. the dimensions through which the Golden Aged Real World is materialised, and

2. the denser 3D SWD which the Golden Aged people use to live their lives.

Satyaloka is also the material dimension or world, in the Holographic Universe, where the Golden Aged body is getting created through the holographic form until the physical body materialises. In Satyaloka, the energies of the soul use a holographic form, similar to how the energies of the soul use a physical body. Thus, those walking in are in Satyaloka when they use the Golden Aged Holographic Body which is being created, though Satyaloka will not be completely divine now.

The chakras also provide a Satyaloka environment in one's 7th auric field where one experiences the Truth. Be that as it may, since one does not stay long in Satyaloka (as a result of experiences lasting for only a split second) one may not have completely understood everything about the Truth. One may have only experienced one aspect of the Truth.

The spiritual dimensions consist of less dense energies than the material dimensions. Thus, Vaikuntha is less dense than Satyaloka. As a result, it can be said that Vaikuntha will always be above Satyaloka. However, it should be noted that the energies of the soul (in Vaikuntha) are actually in the same space as the Holographic Universe and Real World. Thus, it is as if Vaikuntha and Satyaloka are in the same space.

In the first half cycle, people were not really living in the Real World, though they could have a body in the Real World. People did not attempt to use the Real World until the end of the Silver Age. Until then, they were living in the denser 3D SWD. Thus, they were living in the:

1. holographic Satyaloka (as their material realm), and

2. subtle Vaikuntha dimension (as their spiritual realm).

The BKs refer to both of the above as Vishnupuri.

As the god self, the Mid-Confluence Aged gods had acquired

information in respect of how the world transforms through the Holographic Universe. All that which the Mid-Confluence Aged gods had understood can now be used to have a better understanding on what is happening in the Holographic Universe as the world transforms into the Golden Aged world.

Those who teach the BK knowledge play the role of the true prophet as they explain how the world transforms into Vishnupuri. They explain based on the knowledge given in the BK murlis. Those who explain the knowledge left behind by the Mid-Confluence Aged gods play the role of the False Prophet as they explain how the world transforms into Vaikuntha, Satyaloka and Dwarka, all of which are just different aspects of the Golden Aged world. Since I play both roles (true prophet and False Prophet), I am explaining about Vishnupuri, Vaikuntha, Satyaloka and Dwarka.

When a soul has begun the walking in process, the person begins to get all the subtle forms which will provide the Golden Aged material form. The person will be living an ethereal life in the denser 3D SWD when the Land of Truth (Satyaloka) begins to exist in the Golden Age. The Golden Aged QE Light Body which is developing, during the walking in process, will become part of the denser 3D SWD (Satyaloka) when the Golden Aged world materialises.

Since the creation of the Golden Aged QE Light bodies and auric fields begin with the Seventh Chakra and Satyaloka, the new Golden Aged body is getting created in Satyaloka. As each subsequent lower Golden Aged QE Light body and auric field gets created, it is actually getting combined into the higher QE Light body and its auric field which exists in Satyaloka. Thus, the Golden Aged physical body is actually getting created in Satyaloka.

When one is in Satyaloka, one is in a truthful state and not capable of using the vices. However, it is not good to have one's consciousness in Satyaloka. It is better to have one's consciousness in Vaikuntha (which is used via Brahmaloka) because while using Brahmaloka, one can have a link to God. One cannot have a link to God through Satyaloka. From this point of view, Satyaloka is not as good as Brahmaloka because we need to use God now. If one looks at it from the view that one can link oneself to God via Brahmaloka but cannot link oneself to God via Satyaloka, it can be said that Brahmaloka is higher than Satyaloka because God's energies are more powerful than all other energies. However, from the point that one can use either Brahmaloka or Satyaloka through the Seventh Chakra, it can be said that both Brahmaloka and Satyaloka are at the same level. They can also be said to be at the same level because as one uses Brahmapuri (as Brahmaloka), one's Golden Aged Holographic Body is becoming more powerful until Satyaloka exists in the same space as Brahmapuri. Some of the denser dimensions of Satyaloka are part and parcel of the physical forms that will exist in the Golden Age. This is similar to how the Etheric Field is part and parcel of the physical body. However, the materialised Golden Aged Real World is Dwarka. Dwarka:

1. is where the materialised Golden Aged physical body exists.

2. begins to exist in the space beyond the present Corporeal World, when the Golden Aged world materialises.

3. is the less dense real world which one enjoys as an individual (Krishna) in the Golden Age.

However, the Golden Aged deities will not experience themselves as living in Dwarka because they will be living in Satyaloka which is the denser 3D SWD. The scenes in this 3D SWD are holographic with no solid objects because they are created through light (less dense) energies, like those which we see in visions, dreams, holographic images, etc. The people there speak through subtle communications. They can hear, just as how we can hear in visions. They hear through the sound of silence aspect.

The Golden Aged Holographic Body, which exists in Satyaloka, begins to get created in the Higher Universe during the walking in process. Thus,

Satyaloka is in the space of the Higher Universe, below Brahmapuri, before it gets lifted into the space beyond the present Corporeal World. When uplifted, Satyaloka overlaps Dwarka. However, during the whole walking in process, Satyaloka is below the space where Dwarka will exist and Vaikuntha is above Satyaloka. Even after materialisation, Vaikuntha would be higher than the Satyaloka which overlaps Dwarka.

Vaikuntha is a subtle spiritual loka which is empowered through combined energies. During the first half cycle, the combined energies of the deity souls, who are living in the Corporeal World, empower Vaikuntha. From there, what is in Satyaloka and Dwarka are influenced. However, during the walking in process, God's energies empower the subtle Vaikuntha-loka. Thus, during the walking in process, Vaikuntha is uplifted. Until it is completely uplifted, Vaikuntha includes all those QE Light dimensions in the SWL which are getting lifted to exist above the present Corporeal World. Then, during the first half cycle, Vaikuntha will be above the present Corporeal World.

Though the Golden Aged people live in Satyaloka, their consciousness will be in Vaikuntha. They live in Vaikuntha, and not really in Satyaloka, because they are soul conscious.

The BK knowledge teaches and trains one to remain in the soul conscious stage because this is the state which the souls will be in when they are living in the first half cycle. In the soul conscious state, one is virtuous and detached. Until one has completely walked in, one needs to constantly keep making spiritual efforts to remain soul conscious and virtuous, and practice remaining as a detached observer. It is through these practices that those who walk in will remain in Vaikuntha instead of going into Satyaloka.

Even if one was not making serious spiritual efforts, during the walking in process, one will definitely become soul conscious, virtuous and a detached observer. However, one will not become spiritually powerful if one depended on the walking in process to enjoy this state.

All those using the BK knowledge which has been given in this book, or in the BK centres, will be able to use the Confluence Aged Subtle Region. However, if you were more concerned about walking into the Golden Age, instead of using the Confluence Aged Subtle Region, you would be using Vaikuntha-loka in the Higher Universe or in the space of the Confluence Age Subtle Region which is beyond the present Corporeal World.

The seven chakras provide the gateways to use Vaikuntha during the walking in process. However, out of these seven chakras, those walking in will be mainly using the 3rd, 4th, 5th, 6th and 7th chakras to use Vaikuntha in the Higher Universe. For example, the Seventh Chakra provides the gateway to Vaikuntha in Brahmaloka (7th auric field).

One can also use the higher Vaikuntha-lokas in the Higher Universe through the chakras which are above the physical body. The 8th to 13th chakras are above the Seventh Chakra and the physical body. They are in the Confluence Auric Field, within the Higher Universe, of those walking in.

The Confluence Aged person is connected to Brahmapuri through Brahmaloka (the Seventh Chakra) since the seven chakras provide the physical body. The Seventh Chakra is the topmost chakra of the person and so the energies of the soul have to leave the Seventh Chakra to connect to Brahmapuri.

When those walking in have their Seventh Chakra in an activated state, they have a choice to go into Brahmapuri or Vaikuntha. They will use one of these based on their intentions. If they had the intent to go into Brahmapuri, they will go into Brahmapuri. If they intend to go into Vaikuntha, they will go into Vaikuntha. Sometimes, one will not be aware of which subtle region one is in. So long as you are making serious efforts, you will be going into the Confluence Aged Subtle Region. If you reduced your spiritual effort making, you might go into Vaikuntha.

Instead of flying straight to Brahmapuri, as BKs do, those walking in can use Brahmaloka/Vaikuntha in the 7th auric field. Then, from there, they can use the 8th to 13th chakras and their respective auric fields, in the Higher Universe, before going into Brahmapuri from the 13th auric field. They are in Vaikuntha-loka when they use lokas in the 8th to 13th auric fields.

People in the second half cycle cannot have an auric field in the QE Light Ocean (within the Depths of the SWL) because:

1. the QE Light Ocean is too powerful, and

2. the spiritual strength of the soul is low and so it cannot exist in the space of the QE Light Ocean.

However, during the walking in process, since God's energies empower the energies of the soul, the soul can use the 13th auric field within the dimension of the QE Light Ocean. With just a little spiritual effort, the energies of the soul can go past the 13th chakra to go into the 13th auric field. This has the highest and most divinised Vaikuntha in the Higher Universe. Through the usage of the 13th auric field, one can also easily go into the space beyond the Corporeal World. With just a little spiritual effort, they flow through the White Hole to go into the space where the Angelic World exists.

When the 8th to 13th chakras are activated, more auric fields are created and so more of God's energies get filled within the Confluence Auric Field of those walking in. Thus, all these auric fields enable the soul to have a very powerful Confluence Auric Field. As a result, the energies of the soul become powerful and so they rise to go beyond the Corporeal World. In the Vaikuntha which is beyond the present Corporeal World, the chakras in the Angelic Body will help them to use Vaikuntha-lokas in the space of the Angelic World. Since the energies of the soul are also in the Angelic Body, they can easily enjoy a powerful Confluence Aged stage too. Since those walking in have more auric fields than BKs, they can easily:

1. enjoy living a heavenly life.

2. have a high stage.

This is also a reason why they are in Vaikuntha-loka.

However, it should be noted that there is a difference between easily attaining a high stage through this way and using the Angelic Body through one's own spiritual effort making as BKs do. One does not earn a huge spiritual income if one uses the purity in Vaikuntha to easily attain a higher Confluence Aged stage. One should have made one's own efforts to enjoy a pure stage through which one begins to use a higher Confluence Aged stage. Though it is as if all the chakras have provided many gateways into Vaikuntha, it is God's energies which have actually opened the Gateway into Vaikuntha/Heaven. It should be noted that souls do not use the Golden Aged Vaikuntha until their Golden Aged Holographic Body begins to get created.

In the Angelic World, though both dimensions (Vaikuntha and the Confluence Aged Subtle Region) are in the same space, Vaikuntha is another dimension within that space. Vaikuntha is connected to the SWL which is below it whereas Brahmapuri is above the old Corporeal World. Through Vaikuntha, the SWL is getting lifted up into the region where the Confluence Aged Subtle Region exists. God's energies are coming from the Confluence Aged Subtle Region into Vaikuntha because Brahmapuri (which is also a Brahmaloka) is connected to the Vaikuntha which is above the present Corporeal World. Then, from Vaikuntha which is above the present Corporeal World, God's energies flow into the lower Vaikuntha dimensions.

When all your Golden Aged QE Light bodies have been created for getting a new perfect Golden Aged body, you would only be living in a Vaikuntha dimension in the space of the Confluence Aged Subtle Region, and not in the Higher Universe. You will also be able to use Satyaloka in the space of the Confluence Aged Subtle Region.

Satyaloka means Land of Truth and this is a description of the Golden

Aged world. However, Satyaloka has been associated with Brahmaloka because Satyaloka is created through:

1. Brahmaloka (as the Golden Aged body is created through the 7th auric field), and

2. Brahmapuri (another kind of Brahmaloka) since all those who play the role of Brahma, during the Confluence Age, use Brahmapuri.

The Seventh Chakra (Brahmaloka) is used to begin the creation of the Golden Aged body. This creation is taking place due to the role of Brahma being used during the Confluence Age. Finally, Satyaloka will exist in the same space as Brahmapuri since it is created through the Confluence Age, i.e. since the frequencies of the environment in Brahmapuri would be the same as the environment in Satyaloka that overlaps it. Until then, the subtle holographic Satyaloka is nourished through the Confluence Aged spiritual effort making.

Though Satyaloka will be in the same space as Brahmapuri when Satyaloka materialises, it is not in Brahmapuri now because the Real World is in the process of being lifted out of the Lower Universe to go into the same space as Brahmapuri. Until that happens, the Satyaloka of those walking in will be in the Higher Universe because that is where the Golden Aged Holographic Bodies are getting created to materialise the new body.

Vaikuntha is connected to the Satyaloka which is below it, during the walking in process. Through both, Satyaloka and Vaikuntha, the Real World and SWL are getting lifted into the same space as the Confluence Aged Subtle Region.

Vaikuntha is a spiritual or subtle dimension like the Confluence Aged Subtle Region. However, those who use Vaikuntha are in the process of getting lifted up along with their environment into the Higher Universe. Thus, there is a difference between Vaikuntha and the Confluence Aged subtle region called Vishnupuri.

As you keep getting lifted up into the higher Vaikuntha-lokas, your ability to do magical stuff improves because the QE Light and quantum energies etc. will serve you better and better. They serve you better because:

1. your spiritual strength and purity increases.

2. the higher chakras get activated as you get lifted up.

3. your Kundalini is rising.

4. the World Drama is such that those who are in the higher dimensions and/or in the Golden Age will get whatever they want.

5. God plays the role of the Mother for those who walk into the Golden Aged world. The QE Light flows along with whatever God is doing for these souls. When the QE Light initiates the moves, the quantum energies flow along to provide as initiated by the QE Light.

In the Hindu scriptures, Vaikuntha was portrayed as having trees which fulfils desires because those who are in the first half cycle, Mid-Confluence and walking in process, will have their desires fulfilled.

When one is not on the spiritual path, 'what one thinks' will not be happening in reality. As one begins to use the higher lokas, the chances that 'what one thinks is what is happening' becomes higher and higher.

In the Srimad Bhagavatam, Canto 2, Chapter 2, Text 27 (SB 2.2.27) it has been said that in Satyaloka there is no death, no bereavement, no pain nor any anxieties and no-one grows old. This description of Satyaloka is based on what exists in the first half cycle. These conditions will exist again when the new Golden Aged world is materialised. There is no sorrow etc. in Satyaloka because it is the Land of Truth (Satyaloka) which exists in the Golden Aged world. These conditions are similar to those in Vaikuntha because the Golden Aged Vaikuntha is the spiritual realm while Satyaloka is where the new perfect body is being materialised through the creation of new QE Light bodies and auric fields.

Through Satyaloka one is acquiring the ability to not be subjected to death, old age, disease nor to painful childbirth because Satyaloka is where one's Golden Aged Holographic Body is getting created. If one was using Brahmaloka, one would still be using the Holographic Body of the Kaliyug physical body. Thus, one is still subjected to death, old age, disease and painful childbirth. However, in accordance with the knowledge of the Brahma Kumaris, if one leaves the body while in remembrance of God, one passes the last test paper. So, one is not subjected to 'death'.

During the Mid-Confluence, the people who lived in the higher lokas were not capable of becoming diseased. Nor did they grow old. It was only when they used the vices, and were thus living in the lower lokas, that people began to be capable of becoming diseased and began to grow old quickly. This was so because the people who walked out of the Silver Age were still spiritually powerful and they were still using perfect bodies which only began to get affected badly when the people began to use the vices. During the second half cycle, the people are capable of having diseased bodies. However, they can keep themselves disease-free through meditation, worship etc. Those who walk into the Golden Aged world are acquiring the ability to have a disease-free body again. Until they get their perfect bodies, they can also use meditation and worship to remain disease-free. The higher the loka which one uses, the greater the ability to have a healthier body.

In the pure Corporeal World of the first half cycle, everything exists as 'one' because of the unity which all energies have. It is through this unity that the desires of the divine souls are satisfied, via the 2D SWD. While acting in a united manner, human souls do not lose their individuality in the first half cycle. It is as if the souls and the QE Light and quantum energies, together, enable the world to remain in a perfect state where nothing decays, becomes diseased or old. So Dwarka/Satyaloka will be true heaven on earth.

Though, in the Golden Aged world, there cannot be any suffering, diseases, misfortune, etc., those walking in are still settling for the wrongs which they have done. When they have completed their walking in process, they will not experience any disease, misfortune, suffering etc.

Though you are walking in, you may not be constantly remaining in Vaikuntha. You will have to keep making spiritual efforts to remain there. However, as you get more and more powerful, the time you spend in Vaikuntha will keep increasing and you will also find it easier and easier to go into Vaikuntha. Thus, those walking into the Golden Aged world will easily enjoy the divine state. When the Real World is about to transform into Dwarka, you will constantly remain in Vaikuntha as you walk into Dwarka. Dwarka and Satyaloka will have the heavenly Golden Aged spiritual realm called Vaikuntha or Vishnupuri.

When the Golden Aged world materialises, those walking in will use Vishnupuri/Vaikuntha, Satyaloka and Dwarka while the 900,000 most powerful Confluence Aged souls will be in Vishnupuri and Shankerpuri. As per the World Drama, through the Confluence Age, mortals get transformed into gods. So the Land of Truth (Satyaloka) will exist in the Golden Age. However, the 900,000 most powerful Confluence Aged souls will be like aliens in Dwarka because they will not have Golden Aged bodies.

During the Confluence Age, BKs use Vishnupuri to have an experience or vision of being a Golden Aged soul/person. The energies of the soul will be in an imaginary Vishnupuri which is within the Confluence Aged Subtle Region, during these experiences and visions. Even those walking in can have experiences or visions in the Confluence Aged Vishnupuri, if they were making spiritual efforts to go into the Confluence Aged Subtle Region.

Each person, involved with the walking in process, can also have his/her consciousness in an imaginary Vaikuntha of his/her own, based on his/her own desires. These imaginary Vaikunthas will be in their

Confluence Auric Field:

1. in the space of the Confluence Aged Vishnupuri if their spiritual stage was very high and in the space of Brahmapuri if their stage was not that high.

2. within the Higher Universe if their spiritual stage was not good enough to bring them into the space beyond the present Corporeal World.

While having an experience in the Confluence Aged Vishnupuri or in Vaikuntha, one uses QE Light bodies as subtle bodies. These QE Light bodies are not the Golden Aged QE Light bodies which are getting created, nor are they created based on them. These QE Light bodies are temporarily provided based on the QE Light Body which provides the physical body.

You use different subtle bodies in Satyaloka, Vaikuntha and in the Confluence Aged Subtle Regions. In experiences within Satyaloka, you will use QE Light bodies which are based on the new QE Light bodies which are being created for the walking in process.

BKs from the Confluence Aged Subtle Region can easily come into Satyaloka for the walking in process. Then, they will also find it difficult to go back into the Confluence Aged Subtle Region since they use the Golden Aged QE Light bodies and auric fields. However, BKs can go back into the Confluence Aged Subtle Region, if they keep using the BK knowledge constantly. Not everyone in Brahmapuri will be walking into the Golden Aged world; it is only those who are walking into the Golden Aged world from Brahmapuri who can also use Vaikuntha and Satyaloka.

Though Vaikuntha is a spiritual realm, the word 'Vaikuntha' can also be used to refer to the material realm similar to how the BKs use the word 'Vishnupuri' to refer to the spiritual and material realms in the Golden Age. It is the pure, divine QE Light energies (that can also be referred to as Vaikuntha) which provide the environment in Vaikuntha (the

Vaikuntha-loka), whether in the Higher Universe or in the same space where the Confluence Aged Subtle Region exists. Since the QE Light also provides 'light' in the Golden Aged Real World and since the QE Light is also used to provide the Real World, it is as if Vaikuntha also exists in the Real World.

The Confluence Aged Vishnupuri, where one has Golden Aged experiences and visions, is different from the Vishnupuri which exists in the first half cycle. In the Brahma Kumaris, the word 'Vishnupuri' is used to refer to all the Golden Aged dimensions (real, spiritual and holographic realms) of the first half cycle. Thus, Vishnupuri includes Dwarka, Satyaloka and Vaikuntha. BKs use these four words in a general way while referring to the Golden Aged world. Even the ancient people have used these words to refer to a heavenly world. However, based on what has been left behind by the ancient people, it can be said that these words (Dwarka, Satyaloka and Vaikuntha) have also been used to refer to different aspects of the heavenly world.

Actually, Vaikuntha is also Vishnupuri. Despite that, I am using the word 'Vaikuntha' differently so that the reader understands which aspect of Vishnupuri I am referring to. In my explanations, Vaikuntha also includes the less powerful lokas where souls are not making spiritual efforts to become part of the Gathering of Shanker (through which the world is transformed into the Golden Aged world). Those who are only in Vaikuntha, and not in Shankerpuri or in the Confluence Aged Vishnupuri, might be just enjoying life through the walking in process.

I have also used the word Vaikuntha for the subtle dimension which is used for the walking in process because our Mid-Confluence Aged past births can come into this Vaikuntha-loka (in the Confluence Auric Field which is within the Higher Universe) since Vaikuntha has not become a powerful dimension as yet. When Vaikuntha becomes powerful, past births will not be able to emerge to play their roles in their afterlife. They also cannot remain in an emerged state when our stage becomes more powerful and we go beyond the Corporeal World.

The following meditation guideline should be done while remaining relaxed and virtuous; at the same time visualise that you have your link to God:

1. See yourself living in the subtle Vaikuntha, in Dwarka (the Golden Aged Real World) or in Vishnupuri.

2. See yourself as a beautiful person with a perfect disease-free body in the Golden Aged world. See yourself moving around using that perfect disease free body. Enjoy living through that body.

3. Visualise the environment as being so pure and lovely in the Golden Aged realm.

4. Visualise everything and everyone else as also being in a pure divine state.

5. Visualise yourself as having everything that you want and need.

6. Visualise yourself getting everything with just a thought.

7. Visualise that your home is a golden palace decorated with rubies, diamonds, pearls etc. There is a throne in this palace for you to sit on. It is a golden throne which is beautifully decorated with all kinds of gems.

8. Visualise that there are also aircrafts in your garden which you can use to instantly go somewhere. With just a touch of a button, it will instantly bring you to the place where you want to go.

If you wish to be wealthy, then, during your meditation, visualise yourself as a wealthy person playing a significant role as a wealthy person in the Golden Aged world.

Chapter 45: Upliftment

Dwarka actually represents the land that is provided by the QE Light and quantum energies (Quantum Ocean) upon which the kingdoms of the Golden Aged world are created. This was why the Copper Aged Dwarka was built on lands that emerged from the waters. This Copper Aged Dwarka represented the new Golden Aged world which will be the land that is provided for through the Primordial Ocean. The Primordial Ocean has capital letters because it represents God and His energies. The Quantum Ocean is a primordial ocean (with no capital letters used) because it is involved with creating the world which people are living in, during the first and second half cycle.

During the Confluence Age, the Primordial Ocean also involves the QE Light and quantum energies playing their role along with the energies of God for the new Golden Aged creation. It is through this Primordial Ocean that Dwarka emerges

None of the kingdoms or capitals in the Golden Aged world will have the name 'Dwarka'. This is so because Dwarka represents the land that is provided through the Primordial Ocean upon which the scientists will build the new Golden Aged kingdoms. Krishna's first kingdom in the Golden Age will also not exist where the Copper Aged Dwarka was built. The Copper Aged Dwarka was just a symbolic representation and it was built in a strategic location for Copper Aged use. The myths involving Dwarka included a lot of symbolic representations and even the Mid-Confluence Aged history. These are not being explained here.

Dwarka is the materialised Golden Aged world. No-one sees Dwarka until it emerges from the QE Light and Quantum Ocean (Unified Field or Quantum Ocean) at the end of the walking in process. This involves the materialisation of the Golden Aged Real World from the QE Light and quantum energies because the Quantum Ocean provides the Real World. As Dwarka materialises, the Real World also gets lifted out of the Garbhodaka Ocean (Quantum World where the QE Ocean exists). So

Dwarka is also getting lifted out of the Garbhodaka Ocean.

In the Hindu scriptures, it has been portrayed that after the Night of Brahma, God (as the Boar) lifted the earth from the bottom of the primordial ocean which is also referred to as the Cosmic Ocean or Garbhodaka Ocean. It should be noted that God's energies, which plays the most significant part as the Primordial Ocean during the Confluence Age, are also in the Quantum World (energising the energies there). So it is as if the Primordial Ocean stretches from the Confluence Aged Subtle Region to go into the Quantum World where transformation is taking place for the upliftment of the world.

In the myth, after bringing the earth out of the ocean, he places it in its proper place. This 'proper place' is actually in the perfect orderly Golden Aged universe. This myth includes the Mid-Confluence Aged history and it also reflected how, at the end of the cycle, God lifts the earth:

1. out of the Quantum World (Garbhodaka Ocean) to bring it into the SWL.

2. out of the Quantum Ocean (primordial ocean) of the Lower Universe to bring it into the Higher Universe where the Golden Aged world exists.

As Bhuloka is getting lifted, those walking in are also getting lifted out of the Garbhodaka Ocean. It will be as if you and your world are moving from the Night into the light/day. This is also why the boar was portrayed as lifting Bhuloka out of the ocean, after the Night of Brahma, as the Day of Brahma begins. The Night represents the Quantum World, Lower Universe, old ordinary world and the second half cycle. The light/Day represents the SWL, Higher Universe, new divine world and the first half cycle. A new creation is actually taking place during the upliftment because the new world will not be the same as the old world; the dimension where the earth exists is also different.

At the end of each cycle, God comes into the Quantum World (Garbhodaka Ocean) in order to uplift the earth and use Brahma Baba (as Brahma). The lifting process continues after Brahma Baba began to be used.

When God came into the Corporeal World, in 1936, He had already given BKs the ability to move through the Higher Universe so as to enter the Angelic World which is beyond the Corporeal World. It can be said that God had already begun lifting the earth into the Higher Universe, from that time itself, because:

1. God had already given BKs the ability to use the space beyond the Corporeal World which would be the space where the new Golden Aged world exists.

2. the Higher Universe was already being used again.

The lifting process continues, thereafter:

1. because the Golden Aged world is created through the spiritual effort making of the BKs.

2. because of the walking in process.

The dimensions which provide the Real World will have to be lifted up too and this is where those walking in come into the picture, along with those who play the role of Brahma/Shanker. As the Golden Aged QE Light bodies and auric fields get created, it is as if the Real World is getting uplifted. However, the BKs have to be ready (spiritually powerful) for the upliftment to take place. Thus, the dimensions which provide the Real World are in the process of getting up-lifted into the space of Brahmapuri, where the Golden Aged Real World will exist. This was why I was able to get up-lifted into the Higher Universe during my experiences - to experience the various QE Light and quantum dimensions of the Higher Universe. The new universe was being created and I was enjoying what was being created during my experiences when I was seriously playing the role of 'Brahma' from 1996 to 2001.

In the second half cycle, the Real World is in the Garbhodaka Ocean (Quantum World). In the first half cycle, the Real World is above the

Garbhodaka Ocean. So Bhuloka has to get lifted up from within the ocean (Quantum World). As those walking in get lifted up, Bhuloka is also getting lifted up. Those walking in will become Vishnu after walking into the Golden Aged world. They are in the process of becoming Vishnu now. Thus, in the myths, Vishnu was portrayed as lifting Bhuloka out of the Garbhodaka Ocean. Since they are from the old world, where they are capable of using the vices, Vishnu was portrayed as an animal (the boar). The boar also reflected:

1. the specialities which they have during their spiritual effort making.

2. their combined state with God, since they have their link to God.

Actually, it is God who is lifting the world up. Without God, we would not be able to do it. So, actually, the boar represents God.

It should be noted that, in accordance with the BK knowledge, Vishnu is a combination of Lakshmi and Narayan (the Golden Aged married couple). Their combined forces help to sustain the Golden Aged world. Even those walking in will be helping to sustain the Golden Aged world, similarly to how Vishnu sustains the world; however, the world is sustained through their link to God. Though these people have walked in and are not making spiritual efforts, God's energies help to sustain the world through them because they are still Confluence Aged souls and not the deities who are born in the first half cycle. The fact that they are Confluence Aged souls means that they are still Confluence Aged spiritual effort makers. So God can still use, and assist, them even though they are not making spiritual efforts. God can still use them because they accepted God's assistance to come into the Confluence Age so as to walk in. When they leave their bodies, they still get God's assistance to go back to the Soul World.

What was happening during the Mid-Confluence was a shift from the Higher Universe to the Lower Universe. At the end of the cycle, through the Confluence Age, a shift occurs from the Lower Universe to the Higher Universe. During this shift, the whole SWL is lifted out of the

Quantum World as it is brought into the Higher Universe. The Real World dimension is also lifted out of the Quantum World and brought into the SWL in the Higher Universe. This is a long process and it will only get completed by the end of the Confluence Age.

The Higher Universe and Lower Universe are in the same space. However, since energies are getting more powerful in the Higher Universe and since more Golden Aged QE Light forms are getting created there, the Higher Universe is getting less dense with time. Thus, it is as if the Higher Universe is going higher and higher. Along with it, all the other dimensions in the Holographic Universe which are getting established in the Higher Universe are also getting lifted up. All these are getting established in Satyaloka, in the Higher Universe, before the Golden Aged Real World materialises as Dwarka in the same space as Brahmapuri. It can also be said that Dwarka is being lifted up since your Golden Aged QE Light Bodies and auric fields in Satyaloka are being lifted up.

When the Golden Aged dimensions have been uplifted into the Confluence Aged Subtle Region, part of the 3D SWD will overlap the Golden Aged Real World (in the space of Brahmapuri) while another part of it will be in the space of the Confluence Aged Vishnupuri. The denser part of Satyaloka (3D SWD) will be in Brahmapuri and the less dense part of it will be in Vishnupuri. Your physical body will be in Dwarka and your holographic body will be in Satyaloka, while your consciousness will be in Vaikuntha. Though the Golden Aged Real World (Dwarka) exists, or can exist, the Golden Aged people will be living in Satyaloka (3D SWD) that is in the space of Brahmapuri and Vishnupuri.

The people would not really be using the Real World which is in the space of Brahmapuri, though they can (with just a thought). When the Real World begins to materialise, in this higher region, the Corporeal World begins to expand. The new Golden Aged world will be in the region which is beyond the present Corporeal World because the Corporeal World will expand as a result of the Corporeal World transforming back into the perfect state. The new Corporeal World will include the space of Brahmapuri and Vishnupuri when the Golden Aged dimensions have been completely uplifted. The Higher Universe will then exist in the space of these Confluence Aged subtle regions. While walking in, based on how powerful the Gathering of Shanker is and based on your spiritual efforts, you will be getting lifted up from the Bhuloka, which exists in the Lower Universe, to go into the Bhuloka that will exist in the space of the Angelic World.

When you go up, you are actually taking Nature and your environment up with you, though you may not be aware of it. At first, you might just experience the walking in process through the good feelings which you experience and you might not be aware that Nature and the environment are also being brought up with you. However, with time, you might also have experiences where you are aware that you, your physical body, Nature and/or the environment around you are also being brought up into the higher dimension. It will be like this until you actually see the transformed world around you.

As you move up into the higher dimensions, you may be given a new place to stay in or you could continue staying in the place that you want to live in (which may be the place which you are currently living in). Do not worry about this. Just flow along with what is happening in the World Drama. As things are happening around you, watch it as a detached observer and continue living a blissful life.

If you are not interested in using the Confluence Aged subtle regions and you just want to lift yourself up into the Vaikuntha-lokas, don't think of lifting yourself up into any of the dimensions in the Second Field, First Field, Cosmic Field or in the SWL. Think of lifting yourself into Vaikuntha which is in the same space as the Confluence Aged Subtle Region. As you lift yourself up, you would actually be going through all the dimensions in the Second Field, First Field, Cosmic Field, and SWL (in the Higher Universe); but don't try to bring yourself up into those dimensions because the QE Light and quantum energies there are involved with providing what needs to exist in the Real World. Just think of lifting yourself up into Vaikuntha and you would be moving up through the various Vaikuntha-lokas.

Normally, we will not experience our Real World as rising into a higher dimension because it is all happening in the same space. Only the density of energies is changing. Based on density, it is as if our world is slowly getting uplifted as the spiritual strength of the deity souls keep increasing.

Currently (in 2016), some of the QE Light energies have gone up to provide the environment in Vaikuntha which exists in the same space as the Confluence Aged Subtle Region. However, the QE Light Ocean has not been uplifted as yet. It is still below Brahmapuri. Neither are there any quantum energies, currently, in the space of Brahmapuri or in the Higher Universe. Since the Real World has not materialised as yet, in the Higher Universe, one can only see the materialised Real World in the Lower Universe.

Since the Golden Aged Real World has not been materialised, we are only using the old body while the Golden Aged Holographic Body is getting more and more powerful. When the Golden Aged Holographic Body is completely created and has become very powerful, the Golden Aged Real Body will materialise. It will only become very powerful when the 900,000 most powerful BK souls are ready for world transformation. Then, the Golden Aged Real World will materialise in the space of the Confluence Aged Brahmapuri which will, then, become part of the Higher Universe. As this happens, you will use your Golden Aged Holographic Body to walk in. Until then, you are in the process of walking into the Golden Aged world as your Golden Aged Holographic Body develops.

Chapter 46: Confluence Aged use of Chakras, Auric Fields and Holographic Bodies

When deity souls receive the BK knowledge:

1. their Third Chakra is immediately activated and they begin to use Indraloka.

2. they get their link to God.

3. they begin to engage the Heart Chakra for spiritual living since 'love for God' is essential for establishing their link to God.

4. they begin to engage the Heart Chakra for using all the higher chakras for living their spiritual life.

5. they begin to use their Angelic Body, along with its Confluence Auric Field, as their Holographic Body.

6. they begin to use the Confluence Aged Spiritual Effort-maker's Holographic Body in the Higher Universe, even though they do not use lokas in the Higher Universe.

In accordance with the knowledge of the Brahma Kumaris, when God came into the Corporeal World in 1936, God created the Angelic Bodies in the Angelic World for all the deity souls since they have to be brought into the Confluence Age. Then, when deity souls are introduced to the BK knowledge, they are able to use their Angelic Body (which exists in the Angelic World) because some of the causal energies of the soul get anchored in the Angelic Body. So the deity soul begins to use the Angelic World.

BKs continue to use the Angelic Body, along with its Confluence Auric Field, if they continue having faith in the BK knowledge. As a consequence, the intellect of the deity soul can fly in its Confluence

Auric Field to go into the Angelic World which is beyond the Corporeal World. So they can employ all the Confluence Aged subtle regions: Brahmapuri, Vishnupuri and Shankerpuri. The Confluence Auric Field enables the Confluence Aged souls to use these Confluence Aged subtle regions which are beyond the Corporeal World.

The Angelic Body also has the seven main chakras as they exist in the physical body. The Confluence Auric Field is originally provided through the chakras in the Angelic Body which exists in Brahmapuri, beyond the Corporeal World. As soon as one receives the BK knowledge, all the auric fields (of the chakras in the physical body), except for those which provide the old physical body, become part of the Confluence Auric Field because this has become the aura of the Confluence Aged person. The Confluence Auric Field becomes their aura because they adopt the Angelic Body when they receive the BK knowledge. All their former auric fields become part of the Confluence Auric Field since they are part of their aura. Only the auric fields which provide the old physical body will not become part of the Confluence Auric Field because the old body is in the Lower Universe. The usage of the higher chakras will give BKs more auric fields within this Confluence Auric Field and so there is more space within the Confluence Auric Field which can be filled with God's energies. This is so because all these auric fields are in different dimensions though they occupy the same space as the Confluence Auric Field. Since there is more room for being filled with God's energies, one's Confluence Auric Field becomes more and more powerful as one keeps making spiritual efforts. The Confluence Auric Field can contain a lot of God's energies for the very reason that it is gigantic, since it is from the physical body to the Angelic Body in the Angelic World. However, the Confluence Auric Field only becomes more powerful as BKs keep making spiritual efforts. Those walking in are in this same situation because they have to come into the Confluence Age so as to walk in.

The Confluence Auric Field acts like a chakra to absorb energies from the Angelic World. Thus, the environment in the Confluence Auric Field is like that of the Angelic World. However there is a difference based on whether our stage is good or not. When our stage is very good, the higher section of the Confluence Auric Field is being used by the soul.

When our stage is very good, our aura expands into the higher subtle regions from Brahmapuri. It expands due to an experience being provided by God in the higher subtle regions or due to a higher auric field being created as a consequence of our spiritual effort making. It will be like this until the Gathering of Shanker is ready. Then, those who are part and parcel of this Gathering of Shanker will constantly have their aura reaching into Shankerpuri as if that is the natural state of their aura. The aura will not drop to a lower height. Normally, before the Gathering of Shanker is ready, the highest point of the aura will be in Brahmapuri since the Angelic Body is in Brahmapuri. The height of the aura will be taller than the Angelic Body because the aura surrounds the Angelic Body.

The higher auric fields which are in Shankerpuri and Vishnupuri have a more powerful environment because there is more of God's energies in these subtle regions, especially in Shankerpuri. Once these energies from Shankerpuri are absorbed by the highest auric field, the auric field which is below it will also absorb these energies from the highest auric field. As each lower auric field absorbs God's energies from the higher auric field, the whole Confluence Auric Field becomes very powerful. So one has a very powerful stage and environment, while in Shankerpuri. One also has a very powerful stage because one has a strong link to God and so one is absorbing a lot of energies directly from God, into the soul. From the soul, God's energies also flow into one's Confluence Auric Field. The higher the stage of the soul, the more of God's energies are absorbed into the soul and Confluence Auric Field. From the Confluence Auric Field, the energies flow into the environment. Thus, others are able to enjoy the benefit of this.

When our spiritual stage is bad, we are not using the higher part of the Confluence Auric Field. So the Confluence Auric Field is not energised to become powerful. As a result, the energies which are emitted from us are not that powerful. We receive and emit energies through the chakras and Confluence Auric Field, at the same time.

If one was not having a powerful link to God, one would not be having a powerful environment in one's Confluence Auric Field because one would be using the lower auric fields. The environment in the lower auric fields is provided from the lower dimensions which the auric fields are in. For example the third auric field is provided with an environment from the upper section of the Second Field. In addition to this, the energies from Brahmapuri (which is beyond the Corporeal World) are also flowing into the third auric field through Brahma Baba's Confluence Auric Field and through the BK Collective Consciousness. Since one is not using an auric field which is in the higher dimensions, one is not able to absorb energies from the higher dimensions directly into one's Confluence Auric Field. It is only when one uses the higher auric fields that the energies from the higher dimensions are able to flow into one's auric field so as to provide a less dense environment for the person. It is only when one has the stage of Shanker that the most powerful energies are filled within one's aura because there are a lot of God's energies in Shankerpuri.

If the BK's stage was not high, the energies of the soul would be hanging around in the Confluence Auric Field within the Corporeal World. These energies of the soul would not be going into the dimensions in the Angelic World, though the Confluence Auric Field connects the physical body (in the Lower Universe) to the Angelic Body (which is beyond the present Corporeal World) via the Higher Universe. However, they will be in the Confluence Aged Subtle Region even if the energies of the soul have not gone beyond the Corporeal World. They will be in Brahmapuri even though they are not making spiritual efforts. The environment, which they are in, is Brahmapuri because their Confluence Auric Field is getting filled with energies from the Angelic World (Brahmapuri) that is beyond the present Corporeal World. They will not be going out of Brahmapuri so as to see or use other universes which exists in the Holographic Universe. Only those walking in can go into other universes in the Holographic Universe.

Though BKs do not use the dimensions in the Higher Universe, other than Indraloka, they do use the auric fields in the Higher Universe. As they keep making spiritual efforts, all these auric fields get filled with God's vibrations. So they begin to live in a more and more powerful environment, which is less dense, since their aura provides the environment for them. Even though the BKs are provided with a less dense environment, they are not provided with a loka to walk into in the Higher Universe. Furthermore, no new body is being created in the Higher Universe for them during the transformation process.

BKs, who are not walking in, are only activating their relevant chakras and strengthening their Confluence Auric Fields through their spiritual effort making and they begin to use their Angelic Body to a greater and greater extent. Though the Angelic Body is already there in the Angelic World:

1. they only use it to a greater extent when their stage is high due to spiritual effort making.

2. their energies only begin to accumulate in this Angelic Body as the spiritual strength of the soul increases. Thus, it is as if one is getting closer and closer to one's Angelic Self. One is an Angelic Self when one uses the Angelic Body.

Since those walking in are also Confluence Aged souls, they can also use the Angelic Body to a greater extent to become the Angelic Self through spiritual effort making. Even so, those who walk in will also have their new Golden Aged Holographic Body created in the Higher Universe and they can also use lokas in the Higher Universe as their Kundalini rises. Thus, within their gigantic Confluence Auric Field, they will have additional auric fields in the Higher Universe. Since these auric fields are filled will God's energies, these assist them to remain in a good stage even if they are not making spiritual efforts.

Whichever subtle dimension the consciousness/awareness of the soul is in, that is where the soul resides. Thus, Confluence Aged souls reside in Brahmapuri since the energies of the soul are in an environment which is provided by the energies from the Angelic World. They reside in the Confluence Aged Subtle Region as either the Spiritual Effort-maker or as the Angelic Self. They do not leave the physical body to reside in the Angelic World. Only some of the energies of the soul flies up and enables the soul to reside in the Angelic World. From the moment the soul receives the BK knowledge, some of the energies of the soul stays permanently anchored within the Angelic Body, which is in the Angelic World, through the four lower chakras in the Angelic Body. Among these four chakras, the Heart Chakra plays the most significant role. Thus, all Confluence Aged souls have their permanent residence in the Confluence Aged Subtle Region which is beyond the Corporeal World. However, they still use their physical body which is in the Corporeal World. Though the Angelic Body is beyond the Corporeal World, it overlaps the physical body because space does not exist in the subtle region. As a consequence, the soul is in the physical body and also in the Angelic Body. However, these two bodies (physical and angelic) are two different bodies with two different subtle QE Light systems, in two different worlds, with chakras positioned in the same area within both.

The energies of the soul, which are anchored through the lower chakras of the Angelic Body, are not playing a role as the Conscious Self. They are just connecting the soul to the Angelic Body. Actually, we are also living a subtle life as the Angelic Self through using the Angelic Body in the Angelic World though we are not aware of this. The extent to which we use this Angelic Self and Angelic Body depends on the spiritual strength of the soul.

The Confluence Aged Holographic Body includes:

1. the QE Light body of the Angelic Body, and

2. Confluence Aged Spiritual Effort-maker's Holographic Body (hereafter referred to as the Spiritual Effort-maker's Holographic Body).

Thus, the Angelic Body is also part of the Confluence Aged Holographic Body. However, since the soul has the experience of being either the Spiritual Effort-maker or the Angelic Self, one can divide the Confluence Aged Holographic Body into two:

1. the Angelic Body. As the Angelic Self, the soul uses this Holographic Body.

2. the Spiritual Effort-maker's Holographic Body. This is used when one does not have a strong link to God and so one is in the Corporeal World while one makes spiritual efforts to go beyond the Corporeal World.

Since some of the energies of the soul are constantly anchored in the Angelic Body, the Angelic Body is constantly used as one's Holographic Body. However, one does not completely become the Angelic Self until one's spiritual stage is high. One becomes more and more like the Angelic Self as one keeps making spiritual efforts. In addition to the Angelic Body, one also uses the Spiritual Effort-maker's Holographic Body until one stops using the Spiritual Effort-maker's Holographic Body so as to only use the Angelic Body (as one's Holographic Body) during an experience. When one completely becomes the Angelic Self and is no longer the Confluence Aged Spiritual Effort-maker (during the split second experiences), one stops using the Spiritual Effort-maker's Holographic Body during the split second experiences and one only uses the Angelic Body (in addition to the physical body). At other times, since one is the Spiritual Effort-maker, one is using the Spiritual Effort-maker's Holographic Body while one also uses the Angelic Body and physical body. This Spiritual Effort-maker's Holographic Body, which is within the Corporeal World, is used as the Holographic Body while:

1. the spiritual stage is bad.

2. the soul is the Spiritual Effort-maker, i.e. the soul does not have an experience of being the Angelic Self.

The Spiritual Effort-maker's Holographic Body consists of the Confluence Aged QE Light bodies and their auric fields which exist in the

Higher Universe. However, the soul does not use the dimensions in the Higher Universe via these Confluence Aged QE Light bodies and auric fields. These Confluence Aged QE Light bodies and auric fields just give extra space for filling the aura with God's energies.

As our stage becomes good, our Conscious Self slowly begins to use the Angelic Body as its Holographic Body, to a greater extent, instead of using the Spiritual Effort-maker's Holographic Body within the Corporeal World. At the same time, the Confluence Auric Field continues to get filled with God's energies (as more auric fields get created through the higher chakras). As the higher chakras keep getting activated, the soul is moving out of the Corporeal World and is moving into the Angelic World. Thus, the Holographic Body, which the consciousness of the soul uses, changes. It changes because the consciousness leaves the Corporeal World to go into the Angelic World. The soul still continues to use the Confluence Aged Holographic Body, but it is using higher auric fields and so its consciousness is at a higher level. In addition to the Confluence Aged Holographic Body, the Holographic Body of the physical body is also used because we have to continue using the physical body. Thus, the Confluence Auric Field, which is part of the Confluence Aged Holographic Body, stays stretched from the physical body to the Angelic World.

In the second half cycle, the soul uses a physical body and its Holographic Body. This Holographic Body is used to act as the subtle Kaliyug self, in addition to it being used to provide the physical body. During the Confluence Age, two more Holographic Bodies are used; however, we stop using the physical body's Holographic Body to act as the subtle Kaliyug self. The physical body's Holographic Body is only utilised for the provision and sustenance of the old physical body.

Since the auric field is emitted from its QE Light body, the auric field is part of the QE Light body. Thus, all QE Light bodies and their auric fields, together, are the Holographic Body. However, the aura can also be used as the Holographic Body and if it is used in this way, those walking in would have the Higher Universe as their loka. Actually, one should not use the aura as one's Holographic Body; instead one should use the QE Light bodies as one's Holographic Body and the aura should provide the environment which we are in. When BKs make spiritual efforts, they always use the environment in the Confluence Auric Field as their Confluence Aged environment. It is only if the person tried to do something different, for example, tried to have an experience in the dimensions in the Corporeal World (which are involved with providing the Real World) that something odd happens such as using the Confluence Auric Field as one's Holographic Body. When the Confluence Auric Field is used as one's environment, both (QE Light bodies and their auric fields), together, can be said to be the Holographic Body because the higher auric fields help the soul to use higher dimensions in the Angelic World. It is as if one's Holographic Body becomes gigantic through the usage of the higher auric fields.

Since the Confluence Aged souls use the Confluence Auric Field and its QE Light bodies, they have a Confluence Aged Holographic Body. The Confluence Aged Spiritual Effort-maker resides in the Confluence Aged Subtle Region because the Confluence Auric Field is filled with God's energies and the energies from the Confluence Aged Subtle Region which exists beyond the Corporeal World.

The creation of the Spiritual Effort-maker's Holographic Body, in the Higher Universe, begins with the creation/upliftment of the third auric field into the Higher Universe and the usage of the Angelic Body. The uplifted third auric field is actually a new extra third auric field that has been created in the Higher Universe. BKs use this auric field, and they no longer use the third auric field in the Lower Universe, for spiritual experiences. So the third auric field in the Lower Universe will no longer exist for living purposes; though the Third Chakra continues to be used for using the body in the Lower Universe.

More and more QE Light Bodies and auric fields are created as a BK uses higher chakras. All these QE Light bodies and auric fields can all be categorised as the Confluence Aged Holographic Body which is used while living the Confluence Aged spiritual life. The Spiritual Effort-maker's Holographic Body gets more powerful as more and more Confluence Aged QE Light bodies and auric fields are created in the Higher Universe (as one keeps making spiritual efforts). Then, one begins to use the Angelic Body as even higher chakras and higher auric fields are used in the Angelic World.

Though all Confluence Aged souls use their Confluence Auric Field, the use of their Holographic Bodies depends on their spiritual stage: whether it is high or low. This is so because they use different chakras and auric fields to live their live while they are the Angelic Self and the Spiritual Effort-maker.

Though the Confluence Aged souls constantly use the Confluence Auric Field of the Angelic Body, it is as if the Angelic Body is separated from the Confluence Aged Spiritual Effort-maker when the higher auric fields, within the Confluence Auric Field, are not used. This is so because:

1. the auric fields, in the Confluence Auric Field, which are used by the Spiritual Effort-maker are those that are provided by the higher chakras within the Corporeal World.

2. the auric fields, in the Confluence Auric Field, which are used by the Angelic Self are those that are provided by the higher chakras of the Angelic Body within the Angelic World.

The Spiritual Effort-maker's Holographic Body is in the Higher Universe, though within the Corporeal World. The Angelic Body is in the Angelic World. Thus, it is as if the Angelic Self and the Spiritual Effort-maker have different, separate bodies. When one is a Spiritual Effort-maker, one uses both of these Holographic Bodies; thus, one might be able to see both of them, in visions. Their separated state, in visions, reflects that the soul is not completely using the Angelic Body which is beyond the Corporeal World. The more the auric fields in the Confluence Aged Holographic Body are filled with God's vibrations, the closer the soul is getting to his Angelic Self in the Angelic World.

As BKs are accumulating spiritual strength deep within the soul, their

Kundalini is getting lifted up (from the Root Chakra to go into the Crown Chakra). The higher their Kundalini, the easier it is for them to make spiritual efforts and to enjoy the blissful stage.

The Kundalini, of those in the Gathering of Shanker and all other Confluence Aged souls who are not walking in, only rises due to their own spiritual effort making. Their Kundalini does not rise just because the Gathering of Shanker is becoming more powerful. Only those walking in will have their Kundalini rising as the Gathering of Shanker becomes more powerful.

Through spiritual effort making, all Confluence Aged souls acquire the ability to have their Kundalini at the Crown Chakra by the end of the Confluence Age. This enables the soul to have its Kundalini at the Crown Chakra in all its births in the first half cycle. It is as if a Golden Aged Holographic Body is being created because as the soul becomes more pure and powerful, it develops the right to use a more divine Holographic Body. However, this Holographic Body will never have a material form in this birth itself because the souls are not using this Holographic Body to walk into the Golden Aged world. It is only those walking in who will have a Golden Aged Holographic Body in the Higher Universe for the walking in process. The bodies of Confluence Aged souls who are not walking in will remain in Bhuloka, in the Lower Universe, even after the Golden Aged world has been materialised.

As the Kundalini rises, the seat of the consciousness is also rising. The seat of the consciousness is different from the seat of the soul which is in the centre of the forehead.

As the seat of the consciousness rises, the soul is acquiring the ability to have the perfect Holographic Body in the first half cycle. Thus, as their Kundalini rises, due to their spiritual effort making, it is as if their Adam (first birth in the first half cycle) gets created. This is because the Holographic Body which they are entitled to use becomes more powerful through their spiritual effort making. The more powerful the soul becomes, the higher the Kundalini would have risen; thus, the more powerful its Holographic Body would be. However powerful the Holographic Body becomes by the end of the Confluence Age, through their spiritual effort making, their Holographic Body will be as powerful during their first birth in the first half cycle. This is so because through spiritual effort making, Confluence Aged souls are developing their right to a more powerful and divine Holographic Body.

All the 900,000 most powerful Confluence Aged souls will be using higher auric fields as their Kundalini rises to finally remain in the Crown Chakra. Since their Kundalini is rising to the Seventh Chakra due to their own spiritual effort making, they are gaining their ability to get a perfect Golden Aged body in their next birth at the beginning of the Golden Age. Their Adam is getting created through the QE Light bodies and auric fields which become part of the Confluence Auric Field, and not through QE Light bodies which are for transforming the present body into the Golden Aged body. They are not provided with the Golden Aged QE Light bodies, for transforming their present body into the perfect state, because it is not there in the World Drama for it to happen.

The Kundalini of all those in the Gathering of Shanker would have risen to the Seventh Chakra due to their own spiritual effort making. The other weaker deity souls might have their Kundalini at the lower chakras, if they are not walking in. Even though their Kundalini has not risen to the Seventh Chakra by the time the Golden Aged world materialises, they will have their consciousness in the Seventh Chakra during the first half cycle because the whole deity clan will be uplifted through the transformation process. However, since they had not made sufficient spiritual efforts to have a more powerful Holographic Body, they can only take births later, in the first half cycle, and not at the beginning of the first half cycle.

When the consciousness of the Confluence Aged souls is in one of the seven chakras, as their Kundalini rises due to their constant spiritual effort making, they will begin their spiritual effort making from Indraloka which is at that higher level and also from Bhuloka since they still need to use their physical body for spiritual effort making. Since the Kundalini is rising, the Indraloka which one resides in will become more and more powerful. Thus, one begins one's spiritual effort making from higher dimensions with time, though one also uses Bhuloka.

The higher chakras in the body are used for living the Confluence Aged spiritual life and the non-Confluence Aged spiritual life because the physical body (which is in the Lower Universe) is used for making spiritual efforts. However, the Confluence Aged souls have their Confluence Auric Field going into the Higher Universe and Angelic World. They would also be using chakras which exist beyond the Corporeal World. If they do not continue making spiritual efforts, after receiving the BK knowledge, they do not use the higher chakras for spiritual living.

When a person is first given the BK knowledge, the 3rd auric field is brought into the Higher Universe. As they keep making spiritual efforts, their higher activated chakras provide higher auric fields in the Higher Universe and Angelic World. This is in addition to the fact that all their chakras still exist in the Lower Universe because they are being used to provide and sustain the physical body.

Though BKs' use higher auric fields in the Higher Universe, these auric fields are only used as Indraloka and not as any other loka, similar to how those walking in do. BKs use Indraloka in the Higher Universe because they have been uplifted into the Higher Universe. This Indraloka can be in a higher or lower dimension (within the Higher Universe or Angelic World). Other than this, they do not use the other lokas in the Higher Universe. BKs fly straight up into the Confluence Aged Subtle Region. It will seem like they have to take the tunnel that exists between them and the entrance to the Angelic World. They do not see anything outside this tunnel. It should be noted that everything happens as per the World Drama. Thus, the BKs will not be able to use dimensions in the Higher Universe. The auric fields which exist there only provide the passageway for the energies of the soul to fly up to the Angelic World. If their stage becomes bad, their intellect will drop back into the body.

If you are moving up a dark tunnel before going into a lighted up region, you are experiencing the aspect where you begin your journey from the physical body which is in the Lower Universe. If you are already in a lighted up region, at the beginning of your experience, you may be experiencing the aspect where you begin your spiritual effort making from Indraloka or your consciousness/intellect is already in a higher dimension and you are continuing from there.

Since some of his energies had become anchored in his Angelic Body, Brahma Baba's aura transformed into the Confluence Auric field which connects his physical body (in the physical world) to his Angelic Body in the Angelic World. All BKs are in the Confluence Aged Subtle Region since their auras get merged with Brahma Baba's Confluence Auric Field. The entrance to the Angelic World is kept open, for all Confluence Aged souls, through Brahma Baba's Confluence Auric Field.

During the Confluence Age, one's Seventh Chakra (Brahmaloka) connects to Brahmapuri which is beyond the Corporeal World. The Seventh Chakra allows the energies of the soul to fly out of the body and out of the Corporeal World. Thus, when the energies of the soul leave from the Seventh Chakra (Brahmaloka), it flies into Brahmapuri. From the Seventh Chakra, the energies of the soul fly through a tunnel to reach Brahmapuri. At the same time the intellect also flies through the Sixth Chakra to link itself to God. They also ascend through the tunnel to go beyond the Corporeal World. As all these energies of the soul fly up through the tunnel, QE Light energies flow through the 7th to 13th chakras to provide the environment in the tunnel, for the energies of the soul to fly up in, until the energies of the soul reach the entrance to the Angelic World. The energies of the soul by-passes all the auric fields to reach Brahmapuri. As these energies of the soul fly up through this tunnel, other energies of the soul, which have gone into the Confluence Auric Field, will also go straight up into the Angelic World. They will all be flying up at the same time.

As each higher chakra gets activated, the energies of the soul would be flowing through the activated chakras to go into the Confluence Auric Field. From there all these energies of the soul will be flying up too. The Confluence Auric Field is also like a tunnel that provides the environment for us to fly up in.

As the BK makes spiritual efforts, the 4th, 5th, 6th and 7th chakras get activated. Then only do the energies of the soul leave the body to go beyond the Corporeal World. The intellect cannot go into the Angelic World until the Seventh Chakra gets activated because the entrance from the physical body to the Angelic World is through the Seventh Chakra (Brahmaloka).

BKs use the Seventh Chakra to use the higher part of the tunnel in order to leave the Corporeal World. Without the Seventh Chakra and the higher part of the tunnel, they will not be able to leave the Corporeal World. If the Seventh Chakra has not been activated, the intellect, having left through the Sixth Chakra, will be hanging around in the tunnel and will not be able to leave the tunnel to go beyond. Through more spiritual effort making, the energies of the soul leave the Seventh Chakra to go into Brahmapuri, then even the intellect flies beyond the Corporeal World.

God's energies can reach the soul through all the chakra in the bodies; though, often, the Ajna Chakra is the easiest way for energies to come to the soul and leave, during the Confluence Age, because the soul is seated in its seat in the centre of the forehead. When one receives God's energies through the 6th and 7th chakras, one has a strong link to God. When one does not have such a strong link to God, one is assisted by God's energies which are in one's Confluence Auric Field. When one receives God's energies only through one's Confluence Auric Field, one can be said to have a weak link to God. It can be said that when you only use your 3rd to 6th chakras, you have a weak link to God because you have not completely gone beyond the Corporeal World via the Seventh Chakra. However, you do have your link to God through Brahma Baba's Confluence Auric Field and the BK Collective Consciousness until you establish your strong link to God by going beyond the Corporeal World. It can also be said that you only establish your link to God when you have gone beyond.

Just see yourself as the Confluence Aged Spiritual Effort-Maker and you will be detaching yourself from the physical body to adopt a subtle body; this means that your consciousness/awareness will be within the subtle body, and not within the physical body, though you still use the physical body. Some people can have an experience or vision which reflects that this is happening. In addition, as you keep making spiritual efforts, the amount of God's energies (in your Confluence Auric Field and soul) increases. So the energies of your soul (which are in the aura) are empowered and less dense. As a consequence, they will rise up in the Confluence Auric Field until they go beyond the present Corporeal World and enter your Angelic Body which is beyond the present Corporeal World.

As you use more auric fields in the Confluence Auric Field, it is as if you are using your Angelic Body to a greater extent because the Confluence Auric Field is the aura of the Angelic Body. As you keep making spiritual efforts, more and more energies of your soul also flow into your Angelic Body until you completely become the Angelic Self.

Very fine QE Light energies, which are in the Angelic World, provide the Angelic Body. Thus, experiences would be very good while we use the Angelic Body. The Angelic Body consists of fine energies since these energies are close to God. The energies of the soul, which are in the Angelic Body, would also be lighter because they are closer to God. For this reason too, the experience would feel very blissful and light.

During experiences, most of the time, you might just feel that you (or your energies) are adopting your Angelic Body. It could feel as if the Angelic Body is replacing the physical body because your energies are flowing into the Angelic Body through all the chakras in the Angelic Body. The Angelic Body is not like the temporary subtle bodies which you use in experiences.

In the weak state, the four lower chakras in the Angelic Body are used. The soul is in Brahmapuri since it uses these lower chakras. When the soul uses the chakras which are above the region of the heart in the Angelic Body, the soul uses Shankerpuri and Vishnupuri. As one uses Shankerpuri and Vishnupuri, one's Confluence Auric Field expands higher up into those subtle regions. Shankerpuri is used through the 6th and 7th chakras in the Angelic Body. Vishnupuri is used through the 5th, 6th and 7th chakras in the Angelic Body. There are no higher dimensions beyond Shankerpuri which can be used through chakras which are above the Angelic Body.

The Confluence Aged souls who are in Shankerpuri are in a dimension which is spiritually higher because a lot of God's energies are within Shankerpuri. Further, the souls using Shankerpuri are also using more auric fields and so they are surrounded by more of God's energies. One enjoys the Confluence Aged subtle regions because God's energies are getting filled into one's auric fields.

As BKs keep making spiritual efforts to completely remain in the Angelic World, they begin to use higher chakras. The more they use the higher chakras, the higher their spiritual development and the easier it is for them to use one of the higher subtle regions like Shankerpuri and Vishnupuri.

Once the Kundalini has risen to the Seventh Chakra, BKs will easily remain in the Confluence Aged Subtle Region which is beyond the Corporeal World. This is so because their intellect can easily fly into Brahmapuri from Brahmaloka. The energies of the souls in the Confluence Auric Field are also rising up to go into the Angelic World. Then after they have gone into Brahmapuri, if the soul keeps making spiritual efforts, the higher chakras of the Angelic Body are used and so the soul has his consciousness in Vishnupuri or Shankerpuri. When these higher chakras remain activated due to the soul having acquired greater spiritual strength, they have the ability to easily and constantly remain in Shankerpuri. This is the state which the 900,000 most powerful Confluence Aged souls would be in when they are ready for world transformation. If those who walk in belong to this Gathering of Shanker, they will have the ability to easily and constantly remain in Vishnupuri/Vaikuntha or Shankerpuri until the Real World transforms into the Golden Aged Real World (Vishnupuri/Dwarka).

Actually, one can begin to use Vishnupuri and Shankerpuri from the beginning of one's spiritual life because the Kundalini rises temporarily and chakras get activated temporarily for an experience. This is different from how one, who has been long in the spiritual life, can easily go into Vishnupuri and Shankerpuri because their Kundalini has been slowly rising due to the higher spiritual strength of the soul and so the chakras remain activated permanently.

If one's higher chakras have not been activated permanently as yet, they will get activated temporarily for experiences. Then, one's Confluence Auric Field will get filled with God's energies as one uses Brahmapuri, Vishnupuri and Shankerpuri which are beyond the Corporeal World. At the same time, the soul is also receiving God's energies through its link to God. The minute one loses one's high stage, one's consciousness/awareness would be back in the Corporeal World. However, the consciousness/awareness would still be within the Confluence Auric Field and so one would still remain within the Confluence Age and Brahmapuri.

According to the BK knowledge, visions are for entertainment and they do not spiritually strengthen the soul. When a person watches a live show and they like the person who is performing, their aura can stretch and reach that person who is on the stage, even though their spiritual stage does not improve. Visions of being in Vishnupuri can be experienced in a similar way. Thus, during visions, one's higher auric fields might not be established. However, sometimes, we experience a vision because our spiritual strength is very high; though one need not experience a vision but can just have a blissful feeling since one is in the Confluence Aged Vishnupuri.

The Third Chakra can be used even if one is influenced by the vices.

Since Indraloka is initially used through the Third Chakra, one can use the vices while in this lower section of the Confluence Auric Field. The higher chakras and higher part of the Confluence Auric Field can only be used if one is pure.

Since the Confluence Aged souls are still capable of using the vices, they can use the vices if they have not properly established a link to God and so have not gone beyond the Corporeal World. They will use Brahmapuri/Indraloka in their Confluence Auric Field when they use the vices. However, they will not be beyond the Corporeal World. They can even be in one of the auric fields which are closer to the physical body.

Since Brahmapuri and Indraloka can be used through lower and higher chakras, it is as if they are divided into two as follows:

1. The lower division of Indraloka and Brahmapuri is within the Corporeal World (from the third auric field to the end of the Corporeal World, in the Higher Universe).

2. The higher division of Indraloka and Brahmapuri is beyond the Corporeal World, in the Angelic World.

One can use the vices in the lower division of Indraloka and Brahmapuri, which is within the Corporeal World, though one's energies are still within the Confluence Auric Field. One cannot use the vices in the higher division of Brahmapuri and Indraloka which is beyond the Corporeal World. In fact, one would also find it more difficult to indulge in the vices if one was using the higher chakras in the physical body.

Though the Confluence Aged soul's Indraloka has been brought into the Higher Universe and into the Angelic World, BKs are also using all the chakras and auric fields which are involved with providing and sustaining their physical body. Thus, their consciousness can get pulled by the body. When pulled in this way, one will find it easier to use the vices since one's consciousness comes into the body.

As the Kundalini rises and/or as the chakras get activated, BKs will develop certain specialities. For example, those who engage the Heart Chakra a lot will have a loving nature. If their 5th and 6th chakras are well developed, God can easily use them to give knowledge beautifully to others. Those whose Sixth Chakra has been activated will be able to practice severe disciplines like the Maryadas which are used by the members of the Brahma Kumaris. BKs also easily maintain their link to God through the 6th chakra. So they can remain blissful as they practice the Maryadas. The Seventh Chakra gives them the ability to stay connected to Brahmapuri and to remain in the Angelic World. BKs use the seven chakras to use specialities even while their consciousness (awareness) is in the Angelic World. While using these specialities they can be in one of the Confluence Aged subtle regions (Brahmapuri, Vishnupuri or Shankerpuri). Even those walking in are in this same situation if they are involved with spiritual effort making to become spiritually powerful instead of just enjoying the walking in process.

BKs are not involved with activating the chakras nor are they involved with trying to use the specialities that can be used via those chakras. All these happen as per the World Drama. It just happens, naturally, on its own. Sometimes, chakras are naturally and automatically activated to allow the souls to do something or live a specific lifestyle. For example, during spiritual effort making, those walking in and other Confluence Aged souls will naturally and automatically use the 6th and 7th Chakras so as to remain soul conscious.

The BKs, who are making spiritual efforts to act as instruments of God, are playing the role of Brahma for the creation of the new Golden Aged world. They are God's helpers or co-creators. However, they are not involved with developing magical abilities. It is God who does the magic since the new world is created through being energised by His energies. Thus, BKs are not involved with developing Siddhis.

For BKs, the chakras are, generally, only activated for spiritual effort making and not for keeping the physical body healthy etc. Thus, BKs can continue to suffer karmic accounts through their body. Once the karmic account is settled, the disease will disappear. It will disappear more quickly if the person keeps making a lot of spiritual efforts to burn away the karmic accounts through the power of yoga with God.

Actually, not all BKs are powerful spiritual effort makers though they are supposed to be. The BK knowledge is for powerful spiritual effort making. Thus, when making a reference to the BKs, I am referring to those who are actually making a lot of spiritual efforts as the BKs are supposed to do.

The following are meditation practices, based on the BK knowledge, which can be used at any time during the day or when one sits for meditation:

1. See yourself in the Confluence Aged Subtle Region, beyond the Corporeal World, absorbing God's light and sending it into the Corporeal World which is below you.

2. See the world below you transforming into the Golden Aged world through being exposed to God's energies which are being sent to it by you and all other Confluence Aged souls.

Chapter 47: Usage of Higher Lokas while Walking into the Golden Aged World

During the Mid-Confluence, the Mid-Confluence Aged gods had tried to remain in Vaikuntha even though everyone else was dropping into the lower dimensions. The fact that they had managed to remain in the higher dimension will help them at the end too because they will be in the auric field of their afterlife which exists as a higher Vaikuntha-loka until the end of the cycle. This helps the Sun Dynasty souls to remain in the higher Golden Aged Vaikuntha when they are in the process of walking into the Golden Aged world.

The ancient people had left behind meditation practices which the Sun Dynasty souls could use to absorb the Confluence Aged Prana that would be accumulating in the Cosmic Consciousness, at the end of the cycle. Since those walking in can use these Sun Dynasty meditation practices, they will be able to easily walk into the Golden Aged world by bringing their consciousness into the Cosmic Consciousness which is transforming through God's energies that are being sent to it via the Confluence Aged souls. Through connecting to or bringing themselves into the Cosmic Consciousness, they get influenced by the Confluence Aged Prana in the Cosmic Consciousness. This helps them to use even higher dimensions.

The Mid-Confluence Aged gods had also used dimensions, in the Holographic Universe, so as to understand how the Real World was being provided for. This will also help those souls, now, to use higher dimensions in the Holographic Universe so as to understand how the Golden Aged world is being provided for through the Holographic Universe. For all the above reasons, those walking in can use numerous kinds of higher lokas.

There are many different dimensions providing the Real World, in stages from the least dense to the most dense. Those walking in can be using any of these higher universes too while they are walking in. In addition, as the SWL is getting lifted out of the Quantum World to be brought into the space of the Angelic World, those walking in can use numerous lokas and universes all along the way until the SWL is lifted into Brahmapuri. Different sets of QE Light and quantum dimensions (Real World Quantum Dimensions) are capable of providing the Real World at each point during the upliftment of the world. Normally, a Real World is not being provided by all these other Real World Quantum Dimensions because a Real World Quantum Dimension provides the Kaliyug Real World. Those walking in should not be interested in using a Real World in a higher dimension. They should only be interested in remaining in the Confluence Aged Subtle Region, beyond the present Corporeal World. For spiritual effort making, they can just use the old physical body in the old Kaliyug Real World since that would be the best physical body for spiritual effort making. However, as Satyaloka is being uplifted, they will be able to use the dimensions in these other Real World Quantum Dimensions which are higher up. This is possible because, as Satyaloka is uplifted, they will begin to use the higher part of their Confluence Auric Field permanently unless their stage is so bad that they drop down to use lower dimensions.

Even during the Mid-Confluence, different sets of QE Light and quantum dimensions (Real World Quantum Dimensions) provided the world which was being lived in, at every point, as the world was quickly dropping during the Mid-Confluence. Due to the high spiritual strength of the Mid-Confluence Aged people, they had actually used Real Worlds at different levels. With just a thought, they could be in a different Real World, at a different level. Since the drop was very quick, during the Mid-Confluence, they could use many different lokas. The drop, thereafter, was not that quick. Thereafter, one set of QE Light and quantum dimension (Real World Quantum Dimension) provided the Real World for each generation. Thus, people continued to walk down the World Ladder while only using one different Real World, during each birth, as their spiritual strength reduced. It would seem as if many different Real Worlds are merged into the Kaliyug Real World since the spiritual strength of all the people are different. The consciousness of those walking in does not use any of these lower universes even though their old physical body is in the Kaliyug Real World.

The world is provided by the QE Light and quantum energies through vortices. Thus, as we use the higher lokas, the height of the vortices increases in order to take us into a higher dimension. The vortices spin to a higher height as we go into a higher dimension due to:

1. God's energies energising the QE Light and quantum energies (via the Confluence Age),

2. our more powerful spiritual stage, and/or

3. the walking in process.

Actually, the height increases because a different set of QE Light and quantum energies in the vortex, which are spinning to a higher height, provide the world for us. When our stage drops, the height of the vortices reduces unless it has gone up because of the walking in process. Even when the height of the vortices reduces, different sets of QE Light and quantum energies provide the environment for us.

Actually, the Higher Universe, Lower Universe and all dimensions in the Holographic Universe are all using the same space. Thus, even though we are getting lifted into a higher dimension, we will still be using the same space. However, we will feel that there is a difference in the environment. It will feel better when we are using the higher dimensions and this difference can easily be experienced via a spiritual experience. During experiences, we might also see the Higher Universe as being higher up (since the energies involved are lighter) and we might perceive the Lower Universe as being lower down (since it consists of denser energies).

When you are living in a higher universe, you are also in a world of your own. This is because the QE Light and quantum energies provide a loka for you there based on the circumstances which you are supposed to be in as per the World Drama etc. It should be noted that each of the higher universes are provided by many QE Light and quantum dimensions. You can have a loka in one of these QE Light and quantum dimensions or you can be in the lighter universe which they collectively provide. Thus, there are opportunities for various kinds of experiences.

As you are getting lifted up your environment is also becoming elevated. What is getting lifted is the environment of the new Golden Aged universe. It is getting raised aloft into the upper section of the Universe, through all the dimensions which exist on the way to the top. Thus, in experiences, if you look down, you will be able to see the old world as being way below you, depending on which higher dimension you are in. You begin to use a higher dimension as chakras open to allow you to reside in that dimension. Though you are in a higher dimension, you will still be able to interact with the others who are in the old world because your physical body is still being used in the old world. Others can also come into the higher dimension if they are involved with the practices for walking in. If not, though they see and interact with you, they are actually in the old world.

The SWL rises as those who are walking in become capable of using a higher loka in a higher auric field as if that is now their place of residence when they are not making spiritual efforts. So if their place of residence (if they are not making spiritual efforts) is in Tapoloka, that is an indication of where their environment has risen to. The physical body does not rise but the environment has become elevated because more than one dimension is being used in the same space.

During the walking in process, we begin to live in merged worlds (where the divine world co-exists with the Kaliyug world on earth) until the world completely transforms. In truth, until the Golden Aged world materialises, those walking in can enjoy the benefits of living in three worlds: Confluence Aged world, Higher Universe (new world) and Lower Universe (old world). Since your physical body is in the Lower Universe, your desires etc. are materialised in the Lower Universe. You will be able to enjoy this benefit, in the Lower Universe, until you have completely walked into the Golden Aged world.

The ancient people attributed a lot of importance to using the seven lokas because they were keen on using the specialities and Siddhis via the chakras. Those walking in are not intentionally developing the Siddhis. These are naturally getting developed since these souls are walking into the Golden Aged world.

One can get a lot of benefits through using the higher lokas because one's Siddhis (powers) are greatly developed through the usage of these lokas. One may be using a higher loka even though one does not have an experience of being in the higher loka.

All those who walk in can enjoy living a heavenly life from the time they start using Swargaloka in the third auric field. If these souls have not worked their way up higher than this, through their own spiritual effort making, then they will take their next birth in the Silver Age even though they will walk into the Golden Aged world. Those walking in may, actually, be using higher lokas due to the help from the Gathering of Shanker. However, based on their own spiritual efforts, they might not be entitled to be in this higher loka. It is better to make serious spiritual efforts so that one can take one's next birth in the Golden Age.

Those walking in (who do not want to be on the path to becoming spiritually powerful) can enjoy happiness easily and they can live a life of greater ease. They earn a lot of spiritual income for just becoming involved with the walking in process. If they wish, they can use this spiritual income to off-set their bad karmic accounts. Though they can effortlessly get over karmic accounts in this way, they will not become very powerful souls through doing this. One has a choice on whether they want to use their spiritual income to off-set karmic accounts. With just a thought that they want to off-set it, they can off-set it. I did this once because my health was getting progressively worse. So much of my spiritual income was used to off-set it that I decided that I was not going to do that anymore. Fortunately, my health has not been that bad ever since.

If those walking in were making spiritual efforts like a BK and got involved with world transformation through self-transformation, then, their spiritual income can be acquired through two sources:

1. the good karma done through the walking in process.

2. the Confluence Aged spiritual effort making.

During spiritual effort making, even though Confluence Aged souls are gaining the ability to use the higher Confluence Aged subtle regions for longer and longer durations, one's consciousness can suddenly drop if one's spiritual stage becomes very bad. Similarly, even those walking in can drop from the higher dimensions to a lower dimension when their spiritual stage is bad, even though one is gaining the ability to use the higher subtle dimensions. It is only after the walking in process is complete that one's spiritual stage cannot drop to a lower one.

Those walking in have:

1. the Golden Aged Holographic Body (Golden Aged QE Light Body and its auric fields), in the Higher Universe, which are for the creation of the Golden Aged body.

2. the QE Light bodies and auric fields which provide the Vaikuntha-lokas for them in the Higher Universe.

3. the QE Light bodies and auric fields in the Higher Universe for the usage of Siddhis and specialities.

4. the Confluence Aged Holographic Body which includes the Angelic Body, Spiritual Effort-maker's Holographic Body and Confluence Auric Field that are all used during the Confluence Age.

5. the QE light bodies and auric fields which provide the physical body in the Lower Universe.

Though those walking in cannot easily establish a link to God through using the Golden Aged Holographic Body, they can employ all the other

QE Light bodies and auric fields to establish a link to God. However, one becomes more powerful, spiritually, if one was making spiritual efforts to go straight into Brahmapuri instead of going into the lokas in the Higher Universe before going into Brahmapuri because one is using one's own spiritual efforts to establish one's link to God. If one was utilising Vaikuntha along with the seven lokas to go into Brahmapuri, one would have assistance from the environment to establish one's link to God. So one does not really do much spiritual effort making. However, instead of not making spiritual efforts at all, it would be better to make some spiritual efforts with the help of the walking in process. Further, life is for enjoying happiness. If one finds it difficult to enjoy bliss and happiness through seriously making efforts to establish one's link to God, one can easily enjoy happiness and bliss through the walking in process. Those walking into the Golden Aged world will not be having fierce battles against the vices because:

1. God acts as their Mother and so God protects them from the vices.

2. the walking in process does not require serious spiritual effort making and so the vices do not view this as a threat to their existence. The vices only see the BK's spiritual stage as a threat to their own existence and so they fiercely battle against the spiritual effort making of the BKs.

Thus, those walking in can easily lift themselves up into the lokas in the Higher Universe and then go into the Confluence Aged Subtle Region which is beyond the Corporeal World. One is being empowered by God's energies which are in the Confluence Auric Field as one uses these lokas and so, one can easily go beyond into the Confluence Aged Subtle Region. One should not see oneself as using specialities and Siddhis. Instead, one should just have the feeling that one was in Vaikuntha and one will surely be in them. Then, the pure divine environment and God's energies in the auric fields will influence one to attain a high spiritual stage quickly, though the person is not making much spiritual effort. As a consequence, it will be as if one's aura expands into the higher dimensions because the energies of the soul will flow outwards and then upwards as one goes into the higher QE

Light dimensions. One's aura will have to expand to allow the energies of the soul to travel into the higher dimensions. As one keeps doing this, one is developing the habit of using those higher dimensions; and so, as this happens:

1. one's chakras begin to remain activated,

2. one begins to constantly use the higher auric fields,

3. one's Kundalini will rise, and

4. one begins to use the seven chakras more efficiently.

One's aura can also be expanded through the visualisations where one sees oneself as being in the higher dimensions. One acquires the ability to use higher dimensions through such visualisations. Normally, the higher chakras are engaged to use the higher dimensions and so in an indirect manner you are activating your chakras.

When the 900,000 powerful BK souls are ready for world transformation, the QE Light Ocean transforms into the divine state and so it gets uplifted into the Higher Universe. After that, the new Golden Aged world materialises in the Higher Universe, in the space of Brahmapuri. As all this happens, those walking in acquire the ability to use the higher lokas which are in the same space as the Angelic World.

Through powerful spiritual effort making, those walking in can become part of the Gathering of Shanker; hence, they can also be in Goloka instead of being in Vaikuntha. If you are a powerful spiritual effort maker, then, it is as if you can travel around to go into so many lokas that exist all along the way right up to the highest loka (Goloka) and you will also be able to go into Goloka. There are great benefits in availing yourself of this highest Goloka because you will be becoming spiritually more powerful. Those walking in, who become spiritually more powerful, have a greater ability to get what they want, with just a thought. This is due to the fact that human souls are supposed to be involved with effecting and influencing what exists in their environment.

Though the walking in process includes employing the higher dimensions in the Higher Universe, not everyone, who is walking in, will be using the dimensions in the Higher Universe. Those who are not interested in using the dimensions in the Higher Universe, and who only want to fly straight into the Angelic World, will only be utilising the tunnel to go beyond into the Angelic World as all BKs do. Then, when it is time for the materialisation of the Golden Aged Real World in the space of Brahmapuri, they will walk in.

Even if you do not bother about deploying the seven lokas or Vaikuntha, and you prefer to just use the BK knowledge for self-transformation, you can still walk in (if you wish to walk in). There will be a lot of Confluence Aged souls who will be serving the royalty, after walking in. Many among these would not be interested in becoming rich or in using Vaikuntha or the other higher lokas which are employed by those walking in. For them, the walking in process is just for service and they will not aim to have status or wealth through the walking in process.

Below are some meditation commentaries which you can use during your spiritual effort making.

First Meditation Commentary:

Sit relaxed and begin your inward journey. Visualise God as an Ocean of Purity before you. You are absorbing God's energies and purifying yourself. As you keep doing this, your purity increases and you are ascending into a higher dimension until you are in Goloka/Shankerpuri.

Second Meditation Commentary:

See yourself in a pure divine golden dimension that has been provided by the pure divine QE Light. These QE Light energies are also in a blissful state because the dimension is full of God's energies. You are in Vaikuntha.

456

Chapter 48: Lokas used in the Lower Universe

Though only deity souls walk into the Golden Aged world, do not wonder if you are a deity soul or not. Have the thought that you are a deity soul and use the practices that have been suggested for the deity souls, in this book. Even if you are not walking into the Golden Aged world, you will benefit through using the practices in this book because you will begin to use the higher lokas in the Lower Universe and so you can get what you want. The visualisation practices and God will also help you to become enriched. To make sure that you get these benefits, get involved with spiritual effort making.

In the Lower Universe, when one is not making spiritual efforts or living a religious life, one's consciousness is normally in the body (which is in Bhuloka) and one normally engages the Root Chakra more than any of the other chakras. Though one is in Bhuloka, one's emotions come into the second auric field and one's thoughts come into the third auric field. Hence, while living their lives in the Lower Universe, people generally use the three lower chakras. While using these lower three chakras and their auric fields, one can be influenced by the vices.

When people are not on the spiritual or religious path, they can have experiences within the second auric field which is in the Second Field. It is through Bhuvarloka that one has astral experiences, experiences of what had happened in one's past birth, etc. The Second Chakra also helps one to socialise with others in the subtle dimension. One can become aware of someone's presence in the subtle dimension through this chakra. Those who are not on the religious or spiritual path and yet have powers, which they acquired from birth etc., are able to easily use Bhuvarloka.

Actually, one can have experiences through all three lower chakras and their auric fields. However, one faces limitations when one has an experience in the Etheric Field unless the Etheric Field is developed to expand for having experiences.

It was the Mid-Confluence Aged gods who had first introduced the knowledge about using chakras and heavenly lokas for spiritual and religious purposes so that these can be beneficially employed by the people in the second half cycle. Among all the chakras, it was the chakras in the physical body that were the most significant and so importance was only given to these. The soul's energies had to leave the Seventh Chakra in the body to use all other higher dimensions. Thus, as far as the person on the spiritual/religious path was concerned, the Seventh Chakra was the most significant. People had been able to utilise higher lokas through using these practices. These higher lokas are within the Corporeal World, though above the Real World, and one's experiences in them is blissful, especially if one is surrounded by the energies of the Cosmic Consciousness. Even the Sun Dynasty souls would have been influenced to use these higher lokas during the second half cycle. However, at the end of the cycle, the members of the Sun Dynasty will be involved with the walking in process.

When one uses any of the religious or spiritual knowledge, or/and the knowledge provided in this book to make spiritual efforts, one begins to engage the 3rd and 4th chakras to live a religious or spiritual life. After this, one begins to wield the higher 5th, 6th and 7th chakras to use less dense lokas while living. One can also enjoy all the other benefits of using those chakras. For example, through the command of the Root Chakra one can acquire qualities such as steadfastness, commitment and loyalty. Activation of the Root Chakra also helps one to have material wealth on earth.

If you are not on the spiritual path, what you think will not be what is happening. Through meditation, as you begin to avail yourself of the higher chakras and their lokas, there are higher chances that what you think is what is happening. If you are using a Vaikuntha-loka, what you think will surely be happening. It would be like this for so long as you are in a Vaikuntha-loka. However, you will not remain in Vaikuntha for long. Normally, you will only remain in Vaikuntha for split seconds, during experiences. However, as your chakras function better, you can go into Vaikuntha more frequently and remain there for a longer time.

Apart from the seven chakras, one also engages the chakras which are above the Seventh Chakra so as to use a heavenly Vaikuntha-loka. Vaikuntha is experienced in the auric fields which are higher than the 7th auric field. This Vaikuntha:

1. is not the same Vaikuntha which is used by those walking into the Golden Aged world.

2. has numerous divisions within the Lower Universe.

During experiences, each of the auric fields can be stretched to accommodate the experience. However, none of the auric fields can stretch to go beyond the Corporeal World. Only the Confluence Auric Field stays stretched beyond the Corporeal World. Thus, only the experiences in the Golden Aged Vaikuntha can be beyond the Corporeal World.

Each religious group or spiritual group is using a higher heavenly dimension of its own, which can be referred to as Vaikuntha or by any other name. This does not mean that they are walking into the Golden Aged world. If a deity soul was deploying the practices of one of these religions, the deity soul would be using these Vaikuntha-lokas, in the Lower Universe, until he receives the BK knowledge. Then, if he gets involved with the walking in process, he would be in a Vaikuntha in the Higher Universe or beyond the present Corporeal World.

There are no permanently existing lokas. Lokas get created based on one's desires, beliefs and as per the World Drama. Thus, there can be many different Vaikuntha-lokas. Each individual can have a loka of his own or the loka might be based on the same beliefs of a specific group of people. If you were using a loka based on only your beliefs, your loka would not be a powerful one unless you were spiritually powerful. So it might not be a Vaikuntha-loka. You can easily use a more powerful loka through joining a belief system. The beliefs of all believers unite for the existence of this loka. Even if the loka was based on the beliefs of only two people, the loka would be quite a powerful one because the 'combination of the energies of more than one soul' produces a tremendous amount of energies. So long as a person is having an experience in the loka, it will exist in aura of the person. When you use the loka, you will be bound by all the rules, practices, restrictions etc. of the belief system and its followers because the loka is employed through merged auras. When people do not like the practices of another, they can create their own belief system and so use a loka that is geared to their preferences. This was also a reason why so many religious groups got created during ancient times.

In the Hindu scriptures, lokas have been portrayed as planets because each loka is like a world of its own which exists higher up in the sky where the actual planets etc. are situated. It also reflects how you can experience yourself as being on a heavenly planet/loka where you are the ruler. This loka will be yours because your desires are satisfied in your loka. Each loka can also be referred to as a dimension.

If you were bringing into service the higher chakras and higher lokas, as is done when one is on the spiritual or religious path, the QE Light serves you better and they become aware of what is in your mind. This is so because the energies of the QE Light Ocean will play a role as the Cosmic Consciousness with the energies of the soul.

Since the QE Light Mind is like the Mind of the Cosmic Consciousness, what is in the mind of a human soul is sent to God. Whatever is in your mind goes into your QE Light Mind. Whatever is in your QE Light Mind is also there in the Mind of the Cosmic Consciousness. God becomes aware of what is in the Mind of the Cosmic Consciousness because He plays a role with the QE Light in order to serve the human souls in the Corporeal World. Thus, God becomes aware of your desire and it gets fulfilled. So you will be served well by God and the gods (QE Light and quantum energies) which are helping to materialise your desires. If you are not involved with meditation and worship, your thoughts etc. are weak and so the QE Light does not really become aware of what is in your mind, though they are assisting to help you use your body.

In the Lower Universe, the Vaikuntha-lokas are the higher QE Light dimensions in the Cosmic Field and SWL. These can also be seen as Vaikuntha dimensions because the QE Light energies in these dimensions are pure energies which are lighter (less dense) since these energies are higher up. Since they are pure and lighter energies, they are heavenly. Only souls who are in a pure state can have their consciousness in these dimensions. Though you are in the higher lokas, you can still influence your body from there because you are using both: the physical body in the Real World and the Holographic Body in the Holographic Universe.

It is better not to go into the lower lokas which are in the lower dark Quantum World since they are provided by the dark quantum energies. One should try to use and stay in the dimensions which are provided by the QE Light alone. Only the QE Light provides the environment in the Vaikuntha-lokas which are used in the Cosmic Field and SWL.

In the Lower Universe, bliss and the pure state can easily be experienced as soon as one attempts to make spiritual efforts. This is so because Swargaloka is close to the First Field. There are pure energies in the First Field which are being sent into the Second Field and also into Swargaloka. These energies help one to remain pure. However, since this loka is in the Second Field, one can be easily influenced by the vices. You cannot indulge the vices if you want to use the higher lokas.

Instead of just being influenced by the pure energies from the First Field, it would be better to be influenced by the Confluence Aged Prana which is in the higher dimensions. It is when the higher dimensions are transformed that the lower dimensions become pure. Until then, one needs to use the higher dimensions to get exposed to the Confluence Aged Prana. However, in those areas where there are BKs in their pure state, one is influenced by God's Confluence Aged Prana that exists in that environment. Thus, one can be influenced by Confluence Aged

Prana even while in the Real World.

Through using the practices in this book, one can easily engage the chakras and auric fields which are higher than the Seventh Chakra and 7th auric field because one becomes very powerful through being exposed to God's Confluence Aged Prana. God's energies, which accompany the BK knowledge, will also help your aura to get connected to dimensions where there is more of God's Confluence Aged Prana. Those using the BK knowledge are energised to become very powerful, since they are exposed to God's energies. So they command chakras and auric fields which are higher than those used by others in the Lower Universe.

If one was wielding the BK knowledge, though one was not a deity soul, one would easily come into Indraloka (in the Lower Universe). One only uses Indraloka if one was exposed to God's energies which are being emitted into the Corporeal World by the Confluence Aged souls. If not, one only uses Swargaloka. While using Indraloka, one can also use Vaikuntha because one is becoming powerfully energised through being exposed to God's Confluence Aged Prana. Those who are exposed to God's Confluence Aged Prana can use Vaikuntha through all their chakras because they become powerfully energised quickly. When these people constantly remember God, based on the BK knowledge, God becomes aware of their desires and fulfils them, even though they are not able to establish their link to God. Thus, while in Indraloka, they will be served by God and by the pure QE Light and quantum energies which act as gods. They will be served well; so they will be enjoying life and getting whatever they want.

Those applying the knowledge contained in this book can also use Brahmaloka to act as creators to get whatever they want; the pure QE Light and quantum energies will obey their commands to get it created for them. They can easily involve the Seventh Chakra to become the god self (Brahma) and so they can get what they want. However, when one is the god self, one would not want anything. So if you have a desire for something, you are not really the god self (Brahma). However, it does not really matter if you are the god self or not. Just have the faith that God will fulfil your visualisations and keep making spiritual efforts while doing the visualisations.

Actually, instead of remaining in Brahmaloka, one can move into Vaikuntha via the Seventh Chakra and Brahmaloka. Through using the higher Vaikuntha dimension, one will have better experiences and one will also be served better because:

1. one will be closer to the QE Light Ocean which is being divinised by God's energies that are being sent from the Confluence Aged Subtle Region.

2. one is closer to God's energies which are being sent there from the Confluence Aged Subtle Region.

Those exercising the practices in this book are capable of going into the highest dimension within Vaikuntha, in the Lower Universe, because they are being energised by God's Confluence Aged Prana. With God's help, the energies of the soul go past the 13th chakra to go into the 13th auric field which is a dimension in the QE Light Ocean. On one's own one cannot go into the space of the QE Light Ocean; though one can be energised by the energies which flow from there into the Holographic Body through the 13th chakra. Only devotees who are practising the BK knowledge, and are exposed to God's Confluence Aged Prana, can use the 13th auric field within the QE Light Ocean.

When God's vibrations transform the world into the Golden Aged world, this actually transforms what exists in the Lower Universe so that the world can be lifted into the Higher Universe. Thus, God's energies from the Confluence Aged Subtle Region come into the Vaikuntha which is in the Lower Universe since it is just below the Angelic World. As a result, the highest Vaikuntha dimension, in the Lower Universe, will be the most divinised Vaikuntha in the Lower Universe. It will be like a Golden Aged dimension because it is being divinised for the transformation of the old world into the new world. This is also where one's 13th auric field exists, in the region of the QE Light Ocean. One enjoys a Golden Aged loka, in this highest Vaikuntha dimension, while one's energies are in the 13th auric field.

From the QE Light Ocean, QE Light energies are flowing into the Shore of the QE Light Ocean and then into the Cosmic Field. The QE Light energies, in the Shore of the QE Light Ocean, are less dense and less powerful than those in the QE Light Ocean. The QE Light energies, in the Cosmic Field, are less dense and less powerful than those in the Shore of the QE Light Ocean. Normally, those having experiences beyond Brahmaloka can have experiences in lokas which are within the Cosmic Field or in the Shore of the QE Light Ocean. However, those mastering the practices in this book will be able to have lokas in the space of the QE Light Ocean itself because they are using lokas where God's energies exist. God's powerful energies will be providing a safe and blissful dimension for them in the region of the QE Light Ocean. The Vaikuntha-loka in the 13th auric field, which they will be in, will be very fine since it is filled with God's energies and pure divine energies from the QE Light Ocean.

Since these people (who are using the 13th auric field) are worshippers, they can continue deploying the worship practices which they had used before receiving this knowledge and/or they could also adopt other worship practices. The fact that these people also belief that the world is transforming into a Golden Aged world will help to bring about world transformation in an indirect manner.

The highest Vaikuntha dimension, in the Lower Universe, is also the place where these devotee souls (who have been influenced by God's Confluence Aged Prana) accumulate after leaving their bodies, if they have no more births to take in this cycle. They wait in this highest Vaikuntha dimension until God takes them back to the Soul World, at the end of the cycle. Their division in the Soul World will be just below that of the Deity Souls because they are devotees in the Deity Religion. This is also why they accumulate in the highest Vaikuntha dimension in the Lower Universe. They will be closest to the Angelic World, in the

Lower Universe.

Different religions have different divisions within the Soul World. If the devotee (who uses the BK knowledge and is exposed to God's Confluence Aged Prana) belongs to some other religious path, they will be in the highest space within the division of their religion in the Soul World. Normally, it will be the leaders of the other religions who will come and receive the BK knowledge and be influenced by God's Confluence Aged Prana. This is also a reason why they will be in the highest region within their religion's division. They are also in the highest space of their religion's division because they are spiritually more powerful than their followers.

The highest Vaikuntha that exists in the dimension of the QE Light Ocean is actually a heavenly dimension/loka. Any name can be given to it. Through mastering the practices in this book, all non-deity soul spiritual effort makers can go into a heavenly loka in this highest dimension in the Lower Universe:

1. during their spiritual effort making, and

2. after they leave their body.

During spiritual effort making, they will use one of many heavenly lokas until they reach this highest dimension/loka. If they have been making spiritual efforts for a long duration of time, they will easily go into this highest dimension. When they are in this highest heavenly dimension, during spiritual effort making, they can get whatever they want, including money, instantly.

While one is in the heavenly dimensions, one can use all the specialities and Siddhis that are attained through using the activated chakras. However, when one notices that one has these powers, it is better to only take note of it and not try to use them intentionally because if one is not careful, one might be overcome by the vices and end up being surrounded by the impure QE Light energies.

The same chakras are managed to provide the lokas in the Lower Universe or Higher Universe. Thus, the same Siddhis and specialities are used via these chakras in the Lower Universe or Higher Universe. For example, through using Tapoloka, whether in the Lower Universe or Higher Universe, you can easily understand knowledge because the Sixth Chakra, its QE Light body and auric field are meant to assist you with this (though all the other chakras are also generally used to assist the soul with all its activities). This is similar to how the various parts of the brain can be applied for specific functions though the whole brain is generally used while living.

If one is not walking in, one would be involved with providing world benefits through the Lower Universe. For example, as one constantly visualises oneself as being in the higher dimensions, it actually happens and one's aura will actually expand into the higher QE Light dimensions. Whether one uses a higher dimension in the Higher Universe or Lower Universe depends on what exists in the World Drama based on the person's role. If one was not a deity soul, one would be in a higher dimension in the Lower Universe. If one intends to be among the Confluence Aged Prana there, one would be and one would be able to absorb Confluence Aged Prana from there. As a result, pure and powerful QE Light energies, along with God's Confluence Aged Prana, are sent into the environment from one's aura. So others and the environment can also be influenced by these pure, powerful vibrations. Those who are trying to bring the pure QE Light energies from the higher dimensions into the lower dimensions are also involved with good karma. However, those who bring the Confluence Aged Prana into the lower dimensions through their aura are doing a greater good karma. One will reap the fruits of one's good karma through the Law of Karma. As one keeps bringing the Confluence Aged Prana into one's environment, one's spiritual abilities improve and one can easily help oneself to the higher chakras, auric fields and lokas. Thus, one can skilfully get what one want.

Through the meditations and visualisations for more money, one can get connected to others through the 2D SWD or through the aura so that one can receive help from others for financial benefits. Through one's aura, one gets connected to the people around one or with loved ones; whereas through the 2D SWD, one gets connected to all people on earth (whether one knows them or not). One's aura can also expand to anywhere in the world so as to get connected to others. This normally happens to people who know each other.

Even if you are not involved with walking into the Golden Aged world, you can become rich through absorbing and applying the contents of this book and getting involved with the service for world transformation. Since the World Drama cannot give you benefits in the first half cycle, you can get benefits in this birth itself or in your births in the next cycle. You can decide to use the benefits now or in subsequent births.

Even though you are not walking into the Golden Aged world, have the view that you are. This will help you to accomplish and live in a better environment etc. Do not sit and wonder if you are walking into the Golden Aged world. Have firm faith that you are walking into the Golden Aged world, and you will be.

I have only written this chapter for those who are curious about how it will be if they were not a deity soul. As I have said earlier, do not have doubts about whether you are a deity soul. Have faith that you are. Even if you were not, you will still be able to become spiritually powerful through using the practices in this book and so you can easily get what you want since you will be using the higher chakras and their lokas efficiently.

Chapter 49: Causal Ocean (Karana Ocean)

Numerous universes, each of which looks just like the universe which we live in, are provided through the 2D SWD during the creation of the visible universe (Real World). These universes are overlapping each other. Each of these universes is different because the density of each is different. These universes reflect the progression of the creation process for the materialisation of the Real World. During experiences, we can go into any of these universes. We can even go into one of these other universes through travelling at the speed of light or through the cosmic forces pulling us into one of these universes.

We can even use the different universes that are provided by all the different Real World Quantum Dimensions. Each of these Real World Quantum Dimensions is actually a universe since it is capable of providing a visible universe. All these dimensions/universes are also provided through the 2D SWD.

Since various universes are manifested based on what exists in the 2D SWD, it can be said that the 2D SWD is part and parcel of the Causal Ocean (Karana Ocean). Since the Nature's 2D World Drama have the Laws of Nature, based on which the universes are manifested, it can be said that Nature's 2D World Drama is also part and parcel of the Causal Ocean. Since the QE Light Ocean initiates what needs to be provided in the Real World, as per the 2D SWD and Nature's 2D World Drama, and the quantum energies materialise the Real World based on what has been initiated by the QE Light Ocean, it can be said that all four (QE Light Ocean, QE Ocean, 2D SWD and Nature's 2D World Drama) play a role together in the Causal Ocean. The 3D SWD can also be said to be part and parcel of the Karana Ocean because what exists in the Real World is based on what exists in the 3D SWD.

The QE Light is also creating stuff as co-creators with human souls. All human souls act based on what exists in the Detailed World Drama and Outlined World Drama within the soul. What is in the Outlined World Drama, in the human souls, influences what is in the 2D SWD and so it influences the QE Light in order to initiate the creation process. Thus, the human souls, Detailed World Dramas and Outlined World Dramas can also be said to be part of the Causal Ocean. Since they are all part of the Causal Ocean, their frequencies influence each other.

In the soul, when the visualisation is close to the Outlined World Drama, the visualisation influences the vibrations in the Outlined World Drama to resonate at similar frequencies. The nearer the visualisation is to the Outlined World Drama, the stronger the influence. If the visualisation is further away, it should be a strong visualisation. A strong visualisation is created through numerous visualisations, so it would have a strong impression, i.e. it would have a stronger vibration which can reach a further distance. As a consequence, what we visualise is part of the Outlined World Drama and this brings the visualisation into the Causal Ocean for materialisation. The vibrations in the Outlined World Drama will then influence the vibrations in the 2D SWD to resonate at similar frequencies since:

1. the Outlined World Drama is entangled with the 2D SWD, and

2. the Outlined World Drama and 2D SWD are both part of the Causal Ocean.

What is in the 2D SWD will influence the vibrations in the QE Light, which are providing the Real World, to vibrate at similar frequencies because they are also part of the Causal Ocean. Through all these, we can get what we visualise.

During the second half cycle, the QE Light is also creating stuff because it serves God. What humans request through worship etc. comes to the attention of the QE Light via the QE Light Mind. The QE Light transmits the request to God via the Mid-Element (element between the Soul World and Corporeal World) and the Brahm element (element in the

Soul World). God receives what has been transmitted to Him through these energies. Then, based on the request and based on what exists in the World Drama within God, God does something for the human souls. From all this, it can also be said that God, the World Drama within God, the Mid-Element and the Brahm element are all also part of the Causal Ocean during the second half cycle.

In the Hindu texts, the QE Light, God etc. have been portrayed as Vishnu playing a role for the creation process in the Causal Ocean, in respect of:

1. the creation and sustenance of the material world, and

2. the creation of the new Golden Aged world.

When the ancient Mid-Confluence Aged people were referring to the Causal Ocean, they were also referring to what happens through the Confluence Age because a new Golden Aged world is created through the Confluence Age. Where the walking in process and the Golden Aged world are concerned, God plays the most significant role for the creation process because the Golden Aged world cannot be created without God's help. So God plays the most significant role as the Causal Ocean.

However, God alone will not be able to get the new Golden Aged world created. The new Golden Aged world can only be created if the deity souls are ready for world transformation. This means they must have increased their spiritual strength through their link to God. Thus, it can be said that God and these deity souls play the most significant role in the Causal Ocean for the creation of the Golden Aged world.

However, the Golden Aged material world cannot be created without the QE Light and quantum energies playing their role. Thus, it can be pronounced that God, the deity souls and the QE Light and quantum energies together play the role of the Causal Ocean for the materialisation of the new Golden Aged world. It can be maintained that the QE Light source, QE Light Ocean, QE source, QE Ocean and all the other QE Light and/or quantum dimensions which are involved with materialising the Golden Aged Real World are all part and parcel of the Causal Ocean.

God's energies transform the QE Light into divine QE Light. Thus, all the QE Light energies which are beyond the Corporeal World remain divine all the time. All these divine QE Light also act as 'one' with the QE Light in the Corporeal World (though the divine QE Light is beyond the Corporeal World). Thus, the QE Light energies which are beyond the Corporeal World will influence the QE Light which exists in the Corporeal World. This also helps the world to transform as the Golden Aged world materialises.

The Golden Aged world is also created as per the World Drama within God, Detailed World Drama, Outlined World Drama, 2D SWD and 3D SWD. Thus, where the creation of the Golden Aged world is concerned, it can be said that the World Drama within God, Detailed World Drama, Outlined World Drama, 2D SWD and 3D SWD are all also part of the Causal Ocean. 'What consists of the Karana Ocean' is a matter of which angle one is looking at it from.

Based on what exists in the 2D SWD, the creation of the 3D SWD brings about the existence of the Real World. Thus, it can be stated that the Karana Ocean exists in the area of the SWD in the Holographic Universe. It is actually very difficult to put the Karana Ocean in a specific location. You can place it in a location based on what aspects of it you are giving importance to.

It can be said that the Real World is in the Causal Ocean because all the QE Light and quantum energies, in the Holographic Universe, are involved with the creation of the Real World which we live in. This creation process is taking place at every point in time. However, based on density, it can be asserted that the QE Light and quantum energies are higher up than the Real World. Thus, the Causal Ocean is higher up. Further, the QE Light energies which initiate the creation process based on the 2D SWD are also higher up. For this reason too, it can be said that the Causal Ocean is higher up in the Holographic Universe.

The QE Light Ocean is at the edge of the Corporeal World and the Confluence Aged Subtle Region is above the QE Light Ocean. It can be voiced that, at the end of the cycle, this whole area is like the Causal Ocean since the Golden Aged world is created through the energies that are sent down into the Corporeal World from the Angelic World.

The 2D SWD (as the Causal Ocean) is connected to everything in the Lower Universe and Higher Universe for the creation process. Thus, it can be said that the Causal Ocean overlaps both, the Higher Universe and Lower Universe. Since the 2D SWD overlaps both (the Higher Universe and Lower Universe), the World Drama deep within the soul also overlaps the Higher Universe and Lower Universe (since it is entangled to the 2D SWD). Thus, visualisations done through the Higher Universe can materialise in the Higher Universe and/or in the Lower Universe. However, the visualisations done in the Lower Universe can only materialise something in the Lower Universe.

Though the Higher Universe overlaps the Lower Universe, the Higher Universe is less dense and so it is as if everything that is in the Higher Universe is higher up and is part of Causal Ocean that creates the Golden Aged world. This is so since the new QE Light bodies and auric fields are being created in the Higher Universe for the creation of the new Golden Aged world. From this viewpoint, the energies creating the new Golden Aged QE Light bodies and auric fields can all be seen as being part of the Causal Ocean because these have begun the creation process which will finally lead to the materialisation of the new Golden Aged bodies.

It can also be maintained that below Brahmajyoti is the Causal Ocean or Viraja River (a word used in the Hindu scriptures). Among other things, the Viraja River reflects the 2D SWD which all deity souls are entangled to and to which each soul contributes a path (for each of their incarnation in the next cycle). Based on everything that has been contributed from the deity souls into the 2D SWD, including based on the spiritual efforts of the deity souls, the QE Light initiates the creation of what needs to exist. Even in this situation, the Causal Ocean includes more than the 2D SWD because the deity souls are co-creators.

Even while in Brahmaloka, one plays a role as part of the Causal Ocean and so one's daydreams/desires/visualisations can become a reality. However, at the end of the cycle, when one is walking into the Golden Aged world, this magical ability combined with what happens through the Karana Ocean creates magical wonders.

In this book I have explained quite a lot about how the QE Light plays a significant role for the creation process (as part of the Causal Ocean) and I have not explained much about how the quantum energies also play a significant role in the Real World (as part of the Causal Ocean); in this book, I have generally simplified the role of the quantum energies by stating that it materialises what the QE Light have initiated. The significant role of the quantum energies will be discussed in subsequent books.

Chapter 50: The Spiritual Sky (Paravyoma) and its Lokas

In the Hindu scriptures, it has been portrayed that there are innumerable spiritual planets/lokas/dimensions in the Spiritual Sky, i.e. beyond the material creations. These lokas include:

1. the subtle lokas used during the Confluence Age.

2. the lokas used during the walking in process.

3. the Soul World.

4. the subtle lokas used by souls, to reside in, just before they are taken back to the Soul World, at the end of the cycle.

5. the lokas used during the first half cycle.

6. the lokas used during the Mid-Confluence.

7. the subtle lokas used during the afterlife.

8. the subtle lokas which were provided for the worshipers of the second half cycle.

During the Confluence Age, there are three skies within the Spiritual Sky (one on top of the other) or the Spiritual Sky can be said to be divided into three as follows:

1. the dimensions within the sky region of the Corporeal World.

2. the Confluence Aged Subtle Region.

3. the Soul World.

The Confluence Aged Subtle Region and the Soul World can be said to be either a 'sky' or a space which is situated within the Spiritual Sky. The Confluence Aged Subtle Region is above the sky of the Corporeal World.

The Soul World is above the Confluence Aged Subtle Region. Actually, there is no space in the Confluence Aged Subtle Region and Soul World similar to how 'space' exists in the Real World. So one's energies can be anywhere and everywhere. Yet, there is a certain structure in the Confluence Aged Subtle Region and Soul World due to the strength of the energies.

During the Confluence Age, the Spiritual Sky (Paravyoma), which is above the 2D SWD, consists of the Confluence Aged subtle regions, Soul World, Mid-Confluence Aged Vaikuntha dimension, and all the dimensions in the 'Higher Universe and beyond the present Corporeal World' which are being used by those walking in. At the end of the cycle, all the higher dimensions in the Vaikuntha of the Lower Universe are also part of the Spiritual Sky because the Confluence Aged Prana is also getting filled in these higher dimensions within the Lower Universe so as to transform the old world into the new world.

The Spiritual Sky is also significant for all human souls, at the end of the cycle, because:

1. the whole Corporeal World is being transformed through what is happening in the Spiritual Sky.

2. all souls will be taken back to the Soul World at the end of the cycle. Having left their bodies, they will reside in the Spiritual Sky (within the Corporeal World) before being taken to the Soul World which is also part of the Spiritual Sky.

Since God only comes into the Corporeal World at the end of the cycle, it can be said that the Spiritual Sky is only significantly used at the end of the cycle. However, in the Hindu scriptures, the Spiritual Sky has been portrayed as being eternal because:

1. the Soul World will always exist beyond the Corporeal World, in the Spiritual Sky.

2. lokas always exist in the Spiritual Sky. Lokas existed in the space of

the Spiritual Sky during the first half cycle because the people lived in that region. Then, from the time of the Mid-Confluence, due to the role of the afterlife, the higher dimensions continued to exist in the Spiritual Sky. Finally, at the end of the cycle, the Confluence Aged subtle regions are created in the space of the Spiritual Sky. Thus, the space in the Spiritual Sky was continuously used, though lower lokas were used during the afterlife.

The Vaikuntha dimensions can only be said to be part of the Spiritual Sky if there are energies of the soul or Supreme Soul there because only the energies of the soul and Supreme Soul are 'spiritual' energies. However, it can also be asserted that the Vaikuntha dimensions are part of the Spiritual Sky because only the less dense pure spiritual QE Light energies exist there; no dark quantum energies exist there. It is based on density that it can be said that those higher lokas are higher up in the sky. The energies in the Vaikuntha-lokas are less dense than:

1. the energies in the Real World.

2. the QE Light and quantum energies in the Unified Field which provide the Real World.

At the end of the cycle, the Causal Ocean is part of the Spiritual Sky (Paravyoma) because:

1. the Confluence Aged Subtle Region exists beyond the Corporeal World and what is being done there is bringing about the creation of the new divine world via the QE Light. God resides in the Confluence Aged Subtle Region and so it is filled with God's spiritual energies for world transformation. Even the deity souls, who are involved with the creation of the Golden Aged world, live in the Confluence Aged Subtle Region; so that higher region is also filled with their spiritual energies.

2. the QE Light Ocean, which consists of the spiritual light of the quantum energies, is getting filled with God's Confluence Aged Prana for the creation of the new Golden Aged world.

The Spiritual Sky is the Kingdom of God because:

1. at the end of the cycle, God's Confluence Aged Kingdom exists in the Confluence Aged Subtle Region.

2. those walking into the Golden Aged world are using higher dimension in the Spiritual Sky until the Golden Aged world, which is God's Kingdom, is materialised.

3. during the second half cycle, the QE Light energies in the higher dimensions (Spiritual Sky) can be used to get one's messages to God. Even though God is in the Soul World, it is as if God is close to us because the QE Light is close to us.

4. the Spiritual Sky includes the Soul World which is where God constantly resides; and One's Home is One's Kingdom.

Further, during the Mid-Confluence, the Spiritual Sky was the higher dimensions where the kingdom of the gods was situated, since the more powerful souls were using higher dimensions while the world was dropping into the Lower Universe. This trend of seeing the higher dimensions as the Spiritual Sky continued and so, during the second half cycle, even the Vaikuntha of the Lower Universe was considered as being part of the Spiritual Sky. This trend was also begun as a result of the worship which was done to play a role in the afterlife. The Spiritual Sky was seen as continuing to exist because those who play a role in the afterlife were seen as travelling in the sky to the end of the cycle. This will be explained further in subsequent books.

Since the roles of the deity souls in the Confluence Age, first half cycle and the afterlife exist eternally within the soul, it can be said that the Spiritual Sky is eternal. It eternally exists in the region of the sky since the World Dramas that are within the souls are entangled with the 2D SWD. From this angle, even the 2D SWD can be seen as being part of the Spiritual Sky, though the Spiritual Sky is actually above the 2D SWD.

The energies of the soul (in the World Drama within the soul) are entangled to the 2D SWD via the Seventh Chakra and Brahmaloka. Thus, is it as if part of Brahmaloka is within the 2D SWD. Some of the energies of the soul are actually in the 2D SWD due to this entangled state; it is as if the light of the soul is combined with the light of the QE Light, upon which the impressions of the 2D SWD exist. Brahmaloka just provides the environment for the energies of the soul which are entangled with the 2D SWD. Actually, Brahmaloka is used for more than just this.

The 2D SWD is in the sky region, since it is above Brahmaloka. All souls are also connected to the whole universe via the 2D SWD. They are all also connected to each other, as a Collective Consciousness, through the 2D SWD. For these reasons too, the region where the 2D SWD is situated is like a Spiritual Sky. However, this is not what the Spiritual Sky actually refers to. It is the Confluence Aged Subtle Region, at the end of the cycle, and the Vaikuntha dimension which overlaps it which can be most accurately said to be the Spiritual Sky because this is where:

1. God's Confluence Aged Kingdom exists, and

2. God's Golden Aged Kingdom is being created. The kingdom which exists in the Golden Age is God's Kingdom because God gets it created; even though God does not rule there and it is the gods who rule there.

The Spiritual Sky is in the space of the sky of the world stage. It is where the World of Angels also exists. In the avyakt murli dated 17th October 1981, it has been said, "Always remain conscious of being the form of an avyakt angel who lives in the world of angels. You do not live on land, but in the sky. To be an angel means not only to be someone who is beyond this world of vice but also who is beyond the vision and attitude of vice. An angel is beyond all of those things. Angels constantly love the Father and the Father constantly loves them. Both are constantly absorbed in love for one another."

Whichever world exists in the region where the Angelic World exists, will be a World of Angels or Land of Angels. Thus, during the Confluence Age, all those who are in the Angelic World are angels. During the first half cycle, since the Real World will also exist in the space where the Angelic World exists now, the world in the first half cycle is also a World of Angels. The frequencies in that region are very high and only those who have similarly high frequencies live there, i.e. only those who have an angelic nature live there. Thus, it is only when BKs have reached a very high spiritual stage that they are in the Angelic World as the Angelic Self. When one is the Angelic Self, one is not capable of using the vices.

During the second half cycle, the Spiritual Sky, which is beyond the 2D SWD, consists of the Cosmic Field, Shore of the QE Light Ocean and the QE Light Ocean. However, the energies of the souls cannot go into the space of the QE Light Ocean, and they can only go into the Cosmic Field and Shore of the QE Light Ocean during the spilt second experiences. Thus, there is not really a Spiritual Sky during the second half cycle, apart from the Spiritual Sky that is used by those who are involved with the afterlife. It is only at the end of the cycle that there is the true Spiritual Sky at the top because:

1. God and the Confluence Aged souls constantly reside in the Confluence Aged Subtle Region which is in the Spiritual Sky,

2. God's spiritual energies constantly keep getting sent into the Higher Universe and Lower Universe to purify and strengthen the QE Light source and QE Light Ocean which exist just below the Confluence Aged Subtle Region, and

3. the walking in process is taking place.

During the Confluence Age, God's energies are being sent to the whole Corporeal World from the Angelic World. Notwithstanding this, the regions just below the Angelic World are in a more powerful state because they are so close to the Angelic World.

In the Hindu scriptures, Sadashiva/Sadasiva was also used to represent God. This was also a reason why Sadasiva was said to be another name for Shiva. When Sadasiva represents God, His abode called Kailasa are in three places:

1. Soul World.

2. Confluence Aged Subtle Region (during the Confluence Age only).

3. Mount Abu, India. This is His residence on earth during the Confluence Age because He uses Brahma Baba from there, since Brahma Baba was living there when he was alive and his body was buried there after he left his body.

Kailasa also depicts the powerful vortex which provides the White Hole entrance to the Angelic World. It can be said that this is the actual dividing line between the material and spiritual realms because the spiritual realms (Angelic World and Soul World) exist beyond the Corporeal World (material realm).

The vortex, which gives us the White Hole entrance to the Angelic World, provides us with this entrance from the border of Brahmaloka, i.e. from just below the 2D SWD. Even this lower level can be said to be between the material realm and the spiritual realm, due to this and the following reasons:

1. only QE Light dimensions exist above the 2D SWD, and

2. the dimensions which provide the Real World exist below the 2D SWD.

The 2D SWD separates the spiritual realm from the material realm because all that which is above the 2D SWD consists of dimensions where only QE Light exists. The 2D SWD is like a dividing line above which the quantum energies cannot go. The QE Light and quantum energies, which are involved with providing the material realm, exist below the 2D SWD. The 2D SWD is above the Unified Field that manifests the Real World (visible universe). Thus, the 2D SWD is above the visible universe. It can also be said to be at the top edge of the visible universe. Despite this, the 2D SWD can also be maintained to be everywhere in the Unified Field since its influence is everywhere in the Unified Field. However, it is through what exists in the impressions of the 2D SWD, which are within the QE Light around the top of the Unified Field, that the manifestation of the material world takes place. So the dividing line between the spiritual and material realms is around the top of the Unified Field. It can also be said to be just above the Unified Field.

The vortex, which gives us the White Hole entrance to the Angelic World, begins providing the passageway to the entrance from just above the material realm, i.e. from the border of Brahmaloka since Brahmaloka is part of the material realm. Since the beginning of this tunnel can only be used to go to the Angelic World, the space that it uses (just below the 2D SWD) can be seen as the Abode of Sadasiva too. Since even those walking in use this same tunnel and space, it can be conveyed that above this Abode of Sadasiva is the Vaikuntha which is within the Higher Universe. Where BKs are concerned, the tunnel which is from this Abode of Sadasiva by-passes all the Vaikuntha-lokas so that the Confluence Aged souls can fly straight up into the Angelic World.

During the Mid-Confluence and early Copper Age, many were keen on using the Abode of Sadasiva that existed near the 2D SWD because they wanted to reside at the space where the vortex (which provides the entrance to the Angelic World at the end of the cycle) begins. It was as if they were waiting there for the gateway to be opened so that they could play their role in their afterlife, at the end of the cycle. Through constantly residing there, they would be able to reside there in their afterlife too. This means that they would be able to play their role in the afterlife when the energies of the soul go up that vortex, during the next Confluence Age. Others were also keen on using the Abode of Sadasiva that existed near the 2D SWD (Akashic Records) because they were interested in:

1. getting what they wanted through their worship to God/Shiva,

2. doing magic,

3. knowing what existed in the Akashic Records,

4. knowing everything about the Holographic Universes, etc.,

5. having subtle experiences in that life itself and/or in subsequent births, especially in their final birth of this cycle, and/or

6. keen on giving explanations during the births in the afterlife based on the knowledge acquired in that and other lives.

Through their worship to God/Shiva and through using an Abode of Sadasiva in the region of the 2D SWD, they could easily do magic. When these people play a role in their afterlife, the soul can easily do magic during its final birth now. One can also use this dimension for doing magic, now.

Above the Abode of Sadasiva is the Vaikuntha-lokas. If one was using this abode in the Lower Universe, the Vaikuntha-lokas will be within the Lower Universe. If one was using it in the Higher Universe, the Vaikuntha-lokas will be in the Higher Universe.

During the first half cycle, the border between the spiritual and material realms would have been higher since the lokas used are higher up within the same space as the Confluence Aged Subtle Region. The Mid-Confluence Aged people would have experienced the border, between the spiritual and material realms, as being at various levels since their world was dropping.

In the Hindu scriptures, Sadasiva was also portrayed as residing at a higher level and his abode Kailasa was supposed to be partly spiritual and partly material. His abode was also described in this way because it was linked to the afterlife and vortex. This was why Sadasiva has also been portrayed as a devotee of the eternal Vishnu who represents 'God and/or the QE Light and quantum energies'. His abode was portrayed as existing at the border between the spiritual realm and material realm because:

1. the role of the afterlife exists in the World Drama of the soul and this is entangled with the 2D SWD. The 2D SWD is the border between the material and spiritual realms.

2. the Ancient Past Birth Auric Field exists in the higher regions of Vaikuntha, below the edge of the Corporeal World. This is near the border between the material world and spiritual world.

3. all the past births' auric fields, which become part of the Ancient Past Birth Auric Field, can exist anywhere from around the 2D SWD to near the auric field of the Mid-Confluence Aged god. Since they become part of the Ancient Past Birth Auric Field, they are also near the border of the material and spiritual realms. They are also near the border because they are near the 2D SWD.

On earth, Kailasa was represented by one of the Himalayan Mountains called Mount Kailash which is white because:

1. a vortex is v-shaped or mountain shaped. Mount Kailash represented the vortex which provides the White Hole entrance to the Confluence Aged Subtle Region.

2. the QE Light energies, which provide the vortex of the White Hole that is the entrance to the Confluence Aged Subtle Region, consist of white light energies.

The top of Mount Kailash was said to be Shiva's abode because:

1. God's Confluence Aged residence is in the Angelic World, on top of the vortex which provides the White Hole entrance.

2. mountain tops are closest to the sky and so it was the best place to represent God's place of residence in the Spiritual Sky.

3. the density of the dimensions in the higher region is lighter.

4. powerful Mid-Confluence Aged gods lived on top of Mount Kailash and they were also using higher lokas than all others at that time.

The more powerful Mid-Confluence Aged gods were seen as Shanker on earth during those ancient times because:

1. they lived on higher dimensions and places which were not accessible to the subjects.

2. they were the world rulers who were doing meditation to get God's help and guidance; and they were acting based on God's guidance to help Mankind.

3. they will be used by God at the end of the cycle, during their afterlife.

From the angle that the White Hole entrance to the Angelic World is the Abode of Sadasiva, it can be said that:

1. the QE Light, which provides the White Hole entrance to the Confluence Aged Subtle Region, is also Sadasiva.

2. below the Abode of Sadasiva is Brahmajyoti.

Brahmajyoti, which is above the 2D SWD, is part of the Spiritual Sky since:

1. the Vaikuntha dimensions of those walking in are here (when these souls are not having a high spiritual stage).

2. God's energies are sent into Brahmajyoti for world transformation to take place.

There will be four significant lokas in the Spiritual Sky as the world is about to transform into the Golden Aged world:

1. Goloka (Confluence Aged Subtle Region),

2. Mathura (Mathura loka),

3. Dwarka (Dwarka loka), and

4. Ayodhya (Ayodhya loka).

The ancient people had used names such as Madhura, Dwarka, Ayodhya, Goloka and Gokul to reflect:

1. what would happen at the end of the cycle.

2. what had happened during the Mid-Confluence.

At the beginning of the Copper Age, during the Copper Aged phase of the Mid-Confluence, the Moon Dynasty souls were playing a significant role on the world stage through city-states on earth called Mathura and Dwarka. The soul of Brahma Baba was playing a role as Krishna at that time. This was also why, in the Hindu myths, Krishna was portrayed as a descendent of the Moon Dynasty. The myths about Krishna etc. were also depicting what was being done, during the Mid-Confluence, by the Moon Dynasty souls who will become BKs at the end of the cycle. The myths connected that ancient time to the end of the cycle when the Golden Aged world is created.

Before Krishna, during the Silver Aged phase of the Mid-Confluence, the Sun Dynasty souls were playing a significant role through the city-state called Ayodhya. This was to connect them to the end of the cycle when the Sun Dynasty souls play a significant role with God (Rama) on the world stage. It is through the service done by the Sun Dynasty souls that all the deity souls (Sitas) are brought into the Confluence Age. This was also why, in the Hindu myths, Rama was a descendant of the Sun/Solar Dynasty. In this book, I am not explaining how the words Madhura, Dwarka, Ayodhya etc. were used in the myths so as to narrate the Mid-Confluence Aged history. I am only giving explanations to give a better understanding of what the situation is like as people walk into the Golden Aged world.

In the Hindu myths, Dwarka depicts the heavenly Golden Aged kingdom. It has been portrayed as the kingdom of Krishna. In accordance with the BK knowledge, Krishna is the prince of the Golden Age and Dwarka represents the newly created Golden Aged world. Memories of this knowledge emerged, during the Mid-Confluence, to influence the people to depict Dwarka as a heavenly realm.

In the Hindu myths, Ayodhya is the city of Rama and Rama existed during Tretayuga (Silver Age). According to the BK knowledge, Rama is the prince of the Silver Age. Memories of this knowledge (which had emerged during the Mid-Confluence) and the fact that the Mid-Confluence Aged Rama played his role during the Silver Aged phase of the Mid-Confluence were reasons why Ayodhya was associated to the Silver Aged kingdom.

At the end of the cycle, we will know whether we are going to take our next birth in the Golden Aged kingdom (Dwarka) or in the Silver Aged kingdom (Ayodhya). At that time, all those who will be born in the Golden Age can be said to have their consciousness in the subtle 'Dwarka loka' since their spiritual state is that which they will have when they take their first birth in the Golden Age; and all those who take their next birth in the Silver Age can be said to have their consciousness in the subtle 'Ayodhya loka' since their spiritual stage is that which they will have when they take their first birth in the Silver Age.

All those walking in, who will take their next birth in the Golden Age, will also have their consciousness in Dwarka loka since their spiritual strength is that which can be experienced in the Golden Aged loka. The knowledge used by the BKs (Moon Dynasty souls) will be mainly used by these people during spiritual effort making.

All those walking in, who take their next birth in the Silver Age, can be categorised in the 'Ayodhya loka' category since their spiritual strength is that which can be experienced in the Silver Aged loka. The spiritual knowledge developed by the Sun Dynasty souls will be heavily relied upon by these people.

From all that which has been just said, it can be declared that, during the walking in process, Dwarka loka would be a higher realm than

Ayodhya loka because the spiritual strength of the Golden Aged souls is higher than the spiritual strength of the Silver Aged souls. Actually, those walking in would be using one or more of the following four lokas:

1. Goloka. Powerful BKs, who belong to the Gathering of Shanker will be using this loka. This is the most powerful loka which a person can use. Those walking in, who belong to the Gathering of Shanker, will be using this subtle loka too. They will be those who have the intention to serve Krishna and not those who wish to enjoy life in the Golden Aged world while serving. They will take their next birth as one the 900,000 Golden Aged deities who will populate the Golden Aged world, at the beginning of the Golden Age.

2. Mathura. The scientists who walk in to create what needs to exist in the Golden Aged world will be using this loka. They will work also with those who will serve in Krishna's kingdom (the first kingdom). So they can be seen as being second after the 'Goloka' category. They also belong to the second highest category because God will be using them and they are not there to enjoy the Golden Aged life. Though they do not make spiritual efforts, they will be filled with God's energies since God is using them. The fact that they are filled with God's energies will help them to easily get guidance from God through their link to God. They will have a link to God because they are Confluence Aged souls, i.e. deity souls. However, no one makes spiritual efforts after walking in. They will just be enjoying their high spiritual stage while serving.

3. Dwarka loka. Those walking in, who take their next birth in the Golden Age, will be in this loka. They are not the powerful souls who will be using Goloka. The loka which they use will not be as powerful as that which is used by those in Goloka. Even though they did not succeed in becoming part of the Gathering of Shanker, they had made a lot of spiritual efforts. So they have claimed their rights to take their next birth in the Golden Age.

4. Ayodhya loka. Those walking in, who take their next birth in the Silver Age, will be using this loka. They are actually in the least powerful loka

among all those walking in. Their spiritual strength will not be as powerful as those in Dwarka loka. They would not have done much spiritual effort making for becoming part of the Gathering of Shanker, which was why they are in Ayodhya loka. Many among the Sun Dynasty souls would be in this category because they would be walking in to enjoy life there. However, some among the Sun Dynasty souls would also be taking births in the Golden Age; just as some of the weaker Moon Dynasty souls would only be taking their next birth in the Silver Age.

During the walking in process, the bliss enjoyed by those in the Vaikuntha of the Higher Universe is less than the bliss enjoyed by those in Ayodhya because Ayodhya only exists as the world is about to transform into the Golden Aged world. The bliss enjoyed by those in Dwarka loka is greater than that which is enjoyed by those in Ayodhya. Those who are in Goloka enjoy bliss to the highest extent.

Actually, the Confluence Aged Subtle Region is Goloka; and Goloka is a higher dimension than Vaikuntha because it is the place of residence of God, during the Confluence Age, after God comes into the Corporeal World. It can be said that all BKs are in Goloka. However, it is those in Shankerpuri who play the greatest role as the cows, in Goloka, to provide the world with God's energies (milk) that is nourishing.

Even those who serve Krishna can be seen as being in Goloka since they will be powerful Confluence Aged souls. During the Mid-Confluence and Copper Age, these souls were identified and so they lived in places which became known as Gokul/Gokula and Vrindavan.

Where the creation of the new Golden Aged world is concerned, the most important role is played by those who are in Goloka (since the new world is created through what is happening in Goloka). The next most important are the scientists because they create everything that needs to exist in a civilization/kingdom, once the new world has materialised. They will help to set-up beautiful Golden Aged kingdoms for the Golden Aged deities to live in. The scientists may not be spiritually powerful but they play a significant role. So Madhura is the next most significant loka in the Spiritual Sky.

There are various divisions to the sciences. Many would be walking in while using one of these divisions so as to establish the new Golden Aged kingdoms. They will be given wealth, as per the World Drama, to play their roles well. Even during the Mid-Confluence, the scientists were wealthy and they would have been able to reacquire their wealth during their afterlife. In the myths, the scientists were portrayed as residing in Madhura because:

1. the Mid-Confluence Aged scientists were given the city-state called Madhura to reside in.

2. Madhura represents the old world, at the end of the cycle. The scientists from Madhura (old world) will build the new kingdom in the Golden Aged world (Dwarka). Then, they will reside there while continuing to serve as per the World Drama. However, it can also be stated that as they build the new Golden Aged kingdom, they move from the old world (Madhura) to Dwarka.

At the beginning of the Golden Age, Krishna will be comfortable in the womb and he will be born without any problems since he is conceived and born in the perfect world. Despite this, the sciences will be used to make sure that he is safe and comfortable until he is born. So it will be as if Krishna is born in Madhura. Then, Madhura will not remain significant.

Further, since the scientists build Dwarka, it is as if the new born Golden Aged deities are born in Madhura that becomes Dwarka when the old world has completely been transformed into the Golden Aged world. This was also why Krishna was portrayed as having been born in Madhura. It should be noted that the whole earth does not get transformed, all at once. The places around the more powerful Confluence Aged gatherings will transform first. So it is as if the world transforms slowly as all the other places on earth also transform. The

Golden Aged deity children will only be born in those areas which have already been transformed and not in those areas which are in the process of being transformed. Madhura is also the next most important loka after Goloka because Krishna was born in Madhura (since he is taken care of by those who have knowledge of the sciences).

Before the world gets completely transformed into Dwarka, the BKs who walk in will be taking care of Krishna, i.e. those who have the knowledge of the sciences will hand over Krishna to the BKs so that they can take good care of him. So, in the myths, Krishna was portrayed as being taken to Gokul from Madhura before Dwarka was built. Gokul is the material realm which has the celestial Goloka as its counterpart. From this viewpoint, Goloka can be seen as being part of Vaikuntha. However, not all BKs walk in to serve Krishna. Further, Goloka is actually the Confluence Aged Subtle Region. Be that as it may, it would be more appropriate to say that Goloka consists of the souls in Shankerpuri (including God) and also those BKs who serve Krishna after having walked in. It can also be said that until the new born Golden Aged deities grow up and take over rule (after marriage), the Golden Aged deities are in Krishnaloka. Then, when they marry and take over rule in the Golden Aged world, their world is no longer Krishnaloka but Vaikuntha. This is so because, in accordance with the BK knowledge, the unmarried Golden Aged man is 'Krishna' and the married Golden Aged man is 'Narayan'; and Krishna does not rule the Golden Aged kingdom, it is Narayan who rules the Golden Aged kingdom along with his wife Lakshmi. Anyway, those walking in play the role of Narayan for rule in the new kingdom (until the Golden Aged deities take over) and so they are not in Krishnaloka, they are in Vaikuntha-loka. This is so because Krishnaloka is the loka of Krishna while Vaikuntha is the loka of Narayan. In the myths, Goloka was associated to Krishnaloka because:

1. God had been portrayed as Krishna in the Hindu scriptures. Goloka is the Confluence Aged Subtle Region where He resides for the creation of Krishnaloka (the new Golden Aged world where the Golden Aged Krishnas live). Krishnaloka is created through the Confluence Aged

Subtle Region (Goloka); and this Krishnaloka also exists in the same space as Goloka.

2. some of those in Goloka will take good care of Krishna. So they use two lokas in the same place. Since they are taking care of Krishna who is in Krishnaloka, it can be said that they are also in Krishnaloka, though they are actually in Goloka. Krishna was also portrayed as a descendant of the Moon Dynasty because the Moon Dynasty souls take care of Krishna.

Krishnaloka, Mathura loka, Dwarka, Ayodhya and all the other lokas used during the walking in process, will all be in the Spiritual Sky by the end of the Confluence Age.

During the Mid-Confluence and Confluence Age, the general trend is that the Sun Dynasty souls are the Kshatriyas and the Moon Dynasty souls are the Brahmins. Though the Mid-Confluence Aged gods were all world rulers and priest-kings, they had divided themselves up into the Sun Dynasty and Moon Dynasty clans. These two clans were working together in a united manner until the vices grabbed the throats of many in their clans. By the end of the cycle, the ancient system where the Brahmins and the Kshatriyas work together will be established again to bring in the Golden Aged world. The souls of both, Sun Dynasty and Moon Dynasty, will all be in the Spiritual Sky, living their spiritual lives, as they are transformed to take their next birth in the first half cycle.

At the end of this spiritual birth, in the Confluence Age, God will take you back to the Soul World. Later, you (the soul) will take births in Dwarka (the Golden Aged world) or in Ayodhya (the Silver Aged world). If your spiritual effort making is not good enough, you will take your first birth in Ayodhya. If you had made more spiritual efforts, you would be taking your next birth in the Golden Age. Notwithstanding this, use your Power of Thought beneficially. Your thoughts shape you into what you are. When you have the view that your first birth will be in the Golden Age, that is how it will be unless you are not making sufficient spiritual efforts. Through making spiritual efforts, you will be in the Spiritual Sky and it will be as if you are on your way back to the Soul World which is also in the Spiritual Sky.

Chapter 51: God Helps and Guides those who Walk into the Golden Aged World

God came into the Corporeal World so as to get the world transformed into the Golden Aged world. He has established the Brahma Kumaris to get the 900,000 souls ready for world transformation because He is the Creator of the new Golden Aged world. When it is time for people to walk into the Golden Aged world, God will assist those walking in. He will also facilitate the setting up of the new kingdoms in the new Golden Aged world. God will assist those walking in with the building of what needs to be built, the setting up of systems that will be used in the Golden Aged world, etc. However, it is only those who accept God's knowledge, which have been given through the Brahma Kumaris, who will be able to walk in because God has to give a Helping Hand to the deity souls. Thus, use the BK knowledge, which has been given in this book, for spiritual effort making so as to make sure that you are walking into the Golden Aged world.

Though the people in the first half cycle will not be remembering God, those who walk in will have to remember God so as to get uplifted into the higher Golden Aged world. On your own you will not be able to jump into a higher dimension that does not even exist in the Lower Universe.

The high frequencies of the vibrations are slowed down for creating what exists in the Real World. All this happens based on the laws which govern the creation process in the second half cycle. One plays the role of the creator when one is involved with this. However, where the creation of the Golden Aged world is concerned, the lower frequencies which exist in the Kaliyug world will have to resonate with God's energies, i.e. the QE Light is strengthened to vibrate at the same frequencies as God's. This in turn influences the QE Light and quantum energies, which provide the Golden Aged world, to vibrate at higher frequencies while providing the world stage for us. All energies are also directly influenced to vibrate at higher frequencies when they are exposed to God's Confluence Aged Prana. Such higher frequencies cannot be found anywhere in the Kaliyug world. The energies of the human soul will not be able to influence energies to vibrate at such high frequencies. Only God's energies can get this done for us.

During experiences, after the Confluence Age was established, the sound of OM can be heard in the universe because the energies of God are involved with the new creation process. The sound of OM (God's energies) can also be heard in the universe because God is assisting those walking in and everyone else while He is in the Corporeal World (since His energies are in the Corporeal World). Hearing the sound of OM, during experiences, is a reflection of God's involvement. What one hears is the sound of silence aspects of God and the human souls in the universe.

God's energies make a dimension more heavenly than the Golden Aged world. It can be said that it is God's energies which are the 'Vaikuntha' aspect of this heavenly dimension. One will not be able to experience this bliss (which they experience through being exposed to God's energies) anywhere else. God's energies are received through one's link to God and through using the higher dimensions.

Since the higher lokas are used through the higher chakra, one might only have an experience, in a higher dimension, after sometime. Until your higher chakras are activated properly, God will support you. He could help you by sending you His vibrations so as to uplift you or He could give you visions to develop your faith, as a result of which you could easily have experiences.

For some time, after a deity soul has taken its spiritual Confluence Aged birth, God assists to give experiences to the soul. Later, if the soul was not walking in, the soul would only have experiences if he makes spiritual efforts. Just remembering the earlier experiences would help the soul to have another experience.

If you were walking in, you will constantly have God's help to go into the higher dimensions. Just think of God when you want to lift yourself up into the higher dimension; and instantly, you will get God's aid to get lifted up. Keeping God in your mind will help to keep you in the pure dimensions. The more you keep lifting yourself into the higher dimensions, the greater the QE Light energies, quantum energies, World Drama and God will serve you to attain your desires.

When your stage is not good, or you have just come into the Confluence Age, your Confluence Auric Field would not have a lot of God's energies within it. As you gain spiritual strength, your Confluence Auric Field becomes more and more powerful since you will be using more auric fields. When your stage is good, your whole Confluence Auric Field would be filled with God's vibrations. Through this, you will be surrounded by more of God's energies.

Those walking into the Golden Age will have more auric fields than all others. These enable them to contain more of God's energies and so, they can easily remain in a blissful state and get what they want.

God gets to know of your desires, through your link to God and also through your Confluence Auric Field. However, you will have to communicate your desire to Him. If not, there is an implication that you do not want anything and that all is fine. You can visualise that God's energies, in you and your aura, are assisting to constantly bring you an abundance of wealth etc. During experiences, human souls will also be able to hear the sound of 'om' because creation takes place based on what the human souls want.

Absorb God's energies into yourself and your aura, and have the faith that God's energies are keeping you protected from the bad electromagnetic energies in the environment and from the vices of others. When you have this kind of visualisations, God's energies will be protecting you in these ways too.

Always keep remembering God because He will make sure that you are alright. He will give you a Helping Hand to lift you out of the hell-like dimensions and He will also give a Helping Hand to bring you out of the situation where the evil impure QE Light are waiting to serve you.

The Brahma Kumaris are for preparing the 900,000 most powerful souls for transforming the world into the Golden Aged world. There are strict Maryadas that are followed by BKs; this helps them to remain pure and powerful. Since the Brahma Kumaris are to prepare the powerful souls, BKs cannot ask for anything during the spiritual effort making unless they are asking for something that is needed for BK service. God flows along with this system which exists in the Brahma Kumaris, where BKs are concerned. Hence, this is reflected in God's murlis, etc. in the Brahma Kumaris.

However, where those involved with the walking in process are concerned, they do not have to follow the Maryadas. They are free to live as they like because they will be living a free life in the Golden Age. So God also flows along with this system which those walking in are supposed to use. The help which God gives to those walking in is based on this freedom which they are given.

Those walking in can have desires because they are involved with 'living' and not with service. However, they will get great benefits through using the money, which they get, for service. There were many times, while I was in a high stage, when I had wondered why I need money since I can live a happy life without any money. I would tell myself that I will be able to do a lot of world service with the money and that the money will help me to do better world service. Without the money, the service which I do may be limited. Then, the thought that I do not need the money goes away and I just enjoy the high spiritual stage with acceptance that I need to do service. God flows along with whatever I do because no-one is forced to do anything.

As a rich person, you can easily do service to bring the 330 million gods into the Confluence Age. All of them have to be brought into the Confluence Age for the creation of the Golden Aged world. However,

God also takes care of that. If He has to use someone to bring them in, He will use them when it is time for that to happen. As far as we are concerned, if we have the opportunity to be used for service, we have to grab it because we earn a huge spiritual income through the Law of Karma for getting involved with the service for world transformation. The returns are multi-million fold.

God can use people through so many different ways; for example, from 1996 to 2001, I was so spiritually charged that I was constantly going into the Higher Universe, when I was going back home from the BK center. I was often, perhaps always, having experiences when I was on my way back from the BK center, after having had amrit vela and listened to the murli in the early morning hours. It may be possible that I was having these experiences at that time because I was still having a good stage; however, my stage may have been dropping since I was concentrating on driving my car. This will also explain why I was going into the Higher Universe and not into the Angelic World. Those who are walking in will find it effortless to go into the Higher Universe, even though they are not powerful spiritual effort-makers, because of God's assistance. I am also walking in, so I found it easy to go into the Higher Universe. However, God probably gave those experiences based on my role. Perhaps, I needed to be given those experiences so that I can explain as I am doing now.

Further, from 1996, I was given visions on what had happened during the Mid-Confluence. With time, from around 2012, I was also being guided to write on the Holographic Universe.

Others will also be guided, given experiences and everything else which they need, based on their roles. As per the World Drama, people are given specialities based on the roles which they have to play. Through using these specialities and what God gives, they will be able to play their roles well.

God also gives what a person desires. However, often, what a person desires will be based on the person's role in the World Drama. Thus, some of those who walk into the Golden Aged world will appreciate having money and they will be using the money, which God gives them, for creating that which will be taken into the Golden Aged world, etc. Others will appreciate a good environment and so God will be assisting them to create a lovely environment to stay in, etc. Many will love taking care of children and so they will be taking care of the divine children in the Golden Aged world. Others will prefer to take care of the place, get involved with administration, etc. So God puts them in that kind of situation as they walk into the Golden Aged World. Whatever you want and need will be manifested with God's help.

People's thoughts, desires, goals etc. can be materialised in two ways:

1. through the QE Light and quantum energies materialising it. This is how desires are materialised in the first half cycle.

2. through God giving a hand to materialise it. God flows along with what is in the World Drama and bestows what you want. Those in the second half cycle should use God's support since they can be influenced by the vices.

The people in the first half cycle automatically get what they want, through the World Drama, without God's assistance. Those walking in can also enjoy this. However, if one was capable of being influenced by the vices, it would be better to turn to God to get one's desires materialised because if not, one may be influencing the QE light energies in an adverse manner. With a little extra effort and through using God, one can be successful in getting what one wants, e.g. through visualisations, etc.

Though the people of the first half cycle will not be involved with worship, those walking into the Golden Aged world can do worship to get what they want. When doing worship:

1. they can establish their link to God (through using the BK knowledge) and then subtly ask for what they want.

2. they can just pray to God while having what they want in their mind.

3. they can use one of the existing worship systems, mantra etc. to get their desires across to God.

The worship systems that were established by the ancient people had made sure that it was God who was worshipped. Thus, the belief was developed that God is everywhere, omnipresent and ubiquitous. As a consequence of this belief, whatever you use to represent God, during the worship, will surely be worship to God and so it is God who fulfils the desires of the worshippers. The Mid-Confluence Aged gods were also worshipped as gods and as ancestors. Worship to them is actually worship to God. So long as what was worshipped was seen as God, one will be worshipping God. Since the ancient people were rich and prosperous, worship to them would be like worshipping God for wealth and prosperity. It would be like what you worship is your aims which God fulfils. When you have the image of these ancient people in your mind or before you, when you worship, it is like you are keeping your aims in your mind or before you, during the worship; and so God fulfils these aims.

The practices used in the belief systems are such that they facilitate getting the desires of the believers sent to God. Brief explanations on this have been given in my book "Holographic Universe: An Introduction". More will be given in later books.

In addition to getting help from the practices of the belief system, one's own strong belief (which the person has, based on faith in the worship system) will also be there in the Inner Mind. Thus, the desires are sent across to God via the Cosmic Consciousness. Since God gets to know of what one wants even through this way, one's faith can help to make sure that God fulfils one's desires. If the worship system is inherently a powerful one, one's desires can be fulfilled through the system itself even if one's faith was not that strong.

God will help you whether you use worship or meditations (along with visualisations or subtle communications). However, through the meditations and your link to God, you can become spiritually powerful as well; whereas you do not become spiritually powerful through merely using worship. You could also draw or write your desires and aims:

1. in a book which is only kept for your communications with God.

2. on materials which can be stuck on a wall so that you can be constantly reminded of what you have requested from God. Have firm faith that God will fulfil those aims. Each time you see it, you will be communicating it to God. If each thought was a weak thought, it might not reach God. But as the impressions of the thoughts keep increasing within the soul, they become like intense and powerful thoughts which can surely reach God when you have your link to God or through the QE Light. It will be as if your thought becomes more and more powerful until it reaches God. It becomes more powerful because there are numerous other impressions which help to give it more strength.

If you draw or write your desires and aims while in a meditative state, you are focusing your mind on it for a long time while having a powerful stage. This makes sure that the message is sent to God and so it helps to materialise your aims.

When we are linked to God, God takes care of everything. The Kundalini is also raised naturally, without hurting the body of the person because of the presence of God's powerful energies. When the Kundalini rises on its own, as it does during the walking in process, it only flows along with God and so it helps the soul:

1. to have a perfect body.

2. to use the higher lokas via the higher auric fields.

3. to remain in the blissful state.

4. to use the specialities and Siddhis which are provided through the

chakras during the walking in process.

By acquiring the ability to easily go into the higher dimensions, you are actually securing the ability to maintain a high spiritual stage and also acquiring the ability to become the master of the QE Light and quantum energies. But this does not mean that you have to give them instructions. They will serve you based on what exists in your mind. Instead of trying to instruct the QE Light and quantum energies, instruct God and He will get it done for you.

When you want something, do not ask your own energies to get it done for you because they are 'limited' by nature; they cannot procure much for you and they will not be able to do it efficiently for you. Visualise that God is getting it done for you or have the view or understanding that God is getting it done for you. God is the most superior Force with the most superior and most powerful energies. He is the greatest Magician. Since His energies are all-powerful, they can do wonders. If we leave it to God who is omnipotent, He will do a better job and take care of everything. The most important thing which you need to do is to establish your yoga with Him. You can even have meditation sessions where you visualise receiving money with God's help. Your meditation and visualisations can be done:

1. when you sit in meditation.

2. as you are doing your daily activities, (through your spiritual effort-making throughout the day).

You can use the following meditation exercises to keep yourself entertained through visualisations.

Meditation Experimentation 1:

1. Relax and see yourself as the soul seated in the center of the forehead.

2. See God as a Point of White living light.

3. See God's energies bathing you.

4. See yourself enjoying happiness etc. while being bathed.

5. Keep visualising that God's golden white light is bathing you (the soul) and the body.

6. After a few minutes of bathing in this divine light, visualise a shower of monetary notes falling unto you along with the God's golden divine light.

7. Visualise that these notes add up to millions/billions of dollars.

8. Visualise the money falling on you like rain along with God's beautiful blissful light energies.

9. Enjoy your blissful feeling and have firm faith that you are receiving the money. Also have the faith and feeling that God has enriched you with money. Allow this feeling to sink into your system.

Meditation Experimentation 2:
1. Have the feeling that God loves you and that He is taking care of you while you walk into the Golden Aged world.

2. Have the feeling that you deserve this beautiful life.

Use God in other creative ways too, when carrying out all your daily activities, and God will fulfil your desires. Visualisations may materialise immediately or it may take some time because:

1. others may be involved and they may take their time to fulfil what is required of them.

2. it may take time for the resources to be gathered.

3. it may take time for relevant activities to be performed.

4. it all also depends on your karmic accounts and on when you are to receive it as per the World Drama.

If you have your link to God as you are about to sleep, you will sleep in God's Lap and then wake up while still having your link to God. There are great benefits in doing this because it will help to keep you spiritually powerful throughout the day. I will be discussing this further in future books.

We will only truly understand the benefits of using God as we keep making spiritual efforts. These benefits cannot be properly understood through just reading about it.

Chapter 52: Meditation Practices

To walk into the Golden Aged world, one has to ensure that one has that aim. Do not wonder if you are going to walk into the Golden Aged world. Have faith that you are going to walk into the Golden Aged world and you will. One should also have the view that the riches which one accumulates is:

1. for world service, and/or

2. for establishing the Golden Aged world and then for living in the Golden Aged world.

Having such accurate aims and views are crucial during the meditation practices which are meant to help one to walk into the Golden Aged world. They will enable one to get whatever they want through the walking in process. If not, you may just be getting what you want due to the practices which you are doing and might not be walking in. The meditation practices, by themselves, can help one to get what one wants. The powerful spiritual state which one attains, through the meditation practices, will help one to easily acquire what one wants with just a thought.

When you become spiritually more powerful, you will have to exercise greater care with your thoughts, desires etc. If you do not like the idea of doing something, which is bringing you money, you will find yourself in a situation where you do not have to do it. So your financial income might reduce. You have to make sure that your meditation practices include you keeping a close watch on your spiritual stage, thoughts, desires, believes etc. Then, your thoughts etc. will be beneficial and not detrimental.

Learn to do everything in a detached state so that you do not form a dislike for doing the activities that give you an income. This makes sure that you continue to get the income through that activity. Check if you have any adverse reactions, when you are compelled to do something for receiving money etc. because these reactions may hinder you from getting the money through those means. For example, if you need to do something to get the money, are you getting miserable when faced with having to do it? Are you wishing that you need not have to do it? All these reactions obstruct and prevent you from getting the opportunities for receiving money through that way because your reactions will affect what happens via the QE Light and 2D SWD.

When you watch everything as a detached observer, you will surely watch everything as if you are watching a drama. Impressions of what is happening to you in the Corporeal World are not left within the soul since they are impressions left on pure energies while you are in a detached state. As a consequence, if you are in a poor environment and struggling to make ends meet, impressions of these are not left within the soul. So they will not influence what the QE Light and quantum energies provide for you since they provide based on impressions that are in the soul. Since the only impressions which you are creating are those where you are visualising yourself as a rich person, it is these impressions which will influence what the QE Light and quantum energies provide you. Based on the Spiritual Laws and the Laws of Nature, this is how it will be.

If in reality you are not rich and you were living your life without being a detached observer, the impressions which are created within your mind (since you are seeing and experiencing what is happening) will unfavourably impact the success of your visualisations. You may not be receiving money in abundance even though you keep visualising that you are procuring money in profusion. Your day to day thoughts will be slowing down or even completely hindering the success of your visualisations. So while faced with a situation, where you do not have enough wealth, make sure you are watching it as a detached observer. What you see and experience in your day to day life and also your beliefs, thoughts, visualisations, emotions etc. shape the world which you live in. Keep having the feeling that you are indeed rich and visualise that God is constantly bestowing you with an abundance of wealth. If you desire a million dollars, have the feeling that you already have that while maintaining a pure, divine state. The problem is, when you are in that pure state, you might wonder why you want that money and you might wonder what you are going to use that money for. Tell yourself that it is for world service and for the walking in process.

Often, spiritual effort makers will not value pecuniary gains and so it will not bother them if their income has reduced. Hence, they will not be bothered if their thoughts are not right for bringing in an income. They will be only concerned about their spiritual income. They will often have the view that yogis are supposed to be poor like beggars, in order to avoid the sin of inordinate pride and greed for example. This will adversely affect the amount of finances which they receive. Actually, BKs should not be having any kind of negative thoughts since they are supposed to be detached observers. BKs are given the training to see themselves as the deities and royalty who live in the Golden Aged world. This training will help them to remain as detached observers. Those walking in should also use these practices.

Your spiritual endeavour should include learning to see everything as a game and to enjoy living the game. Do not allow your emotions to get involved with what you are watching. Keep experiencing happiness and bliss, and not unhappiness. When you experience unhappiness, you will not be playing the role of a co-creator with the pure QE Light and quantum energies. During your meditation practices, you should have a firm faith:

1. that you have a right to enjoy what you want and that the laws of the World Drama will allow you to enjoy it.

2. that God, QE Light and quantum energies will fulfil your desires because you are in the process of walking into the Golden Aged world.

Then, you will see God giving you a Helping Hand. The faith which you had would have taken your desires across to God and so your desires get fulfilled. Your faith and visualisation will help to keep you connected to God and to the pure divine QE Light and quantum energies. Thus, you will be connected to enormous powers which will help materialise your desires.

Everything in the universe is in the form of vibrations which are interconnected to each other through one way or another via the QE Light and 2D SWD. As a result, you can bring about changes, in your world, through changing your thoughts and reactions.

Properly done meditation practices increase one's ability to get whatever one wants (including wealth) with just a thought. However, sometimes, you have to keep visualising until what you want materialises. It may happen immediately, in a couple of days' time or maybe even years later. It can take some time if:

1. you are in a weak state,

2. your visualisations are weak, or

3. as per the World Drama, you are not supposed to get it quickly.

If your thoughts and visualisations are weak, the accumulation of these thoughts and visualisations, with constant practice, will create strong impressions within the soul. Until this strong impression is created, it will not materialise. So keep doing the visualisation until it materialises.

Your visualisation may also take a long time to materialise because it takes time for resources to come and for people to help you. There is also the question of whether you believe that you can get what you desire. Often, people, have very negative views about whether they can get what they want. These views which are silently inherent within them will prevent them from getting what they want.

If your desires and beliefs are not the same, your desires might not be fulfilled because what is being materialised might be based on your beliefs. So if you are of the view that you are actually a poor person, that is the state which you will be in. If you are of the view that the environment, which you are in, is not a good one, this would ensure that you do not have a good environment.

You should also not have conflicting visualisations and thoughts, e.g. doing visualisations for something and then thinking that something else would be better. Your visualisations, desires, thoughts etc. should all be reflecting the same aims.

If you were interested in getting monetary benefits, keep that as your aim as you use the practices in this book. If you wish something else, then preserve that in your mind. You can have many aims. Continue remembering all your aims until they materialise. For example, if you want a piece of land or house, see yourself as living in and enjoying that piece of land or house. You should live your life as if you are enjoying it now or/and you can visualise yourself as living exactly how you want to be. Live this imagined lifestyle for as long as you can, throughout the day, day after day. Sustain the visualisation for as long as you can (at least for 5 minutes at a time). If it is no longer entertaining, change the visualisation while maintaining the aims in the visualisations. Then, one day you will find that you are actually living that life in reality. This is also how one begins to live in the Golden Aged world. Actually, all it requires is just a thought (if one was spiritually powerful). As you get spiritually more powerful through spiritual effort making, your thoughts and visualisations materialise more quickly.

I have noticed that my spiritual stage becomes very high, in a Confluence Aged sense, very easily and quickly when I contemplate on what I have written in Chapter 18 of my book, "Holographic Universe: An Introduction". The part about the gigantic Confluence Auric Fields, especially, helps me to attain a high Confluence Aged stage forthwith. It is easy to attain a high meditative stage when you keep trying new meditation experiments. The BKs have come up with numerous meditation commentaries etc. for keeping themselves entertained during meditation. You can use those too. The environment in the Brahma Kumaris will also help you to easily enjoy a good high stage.

Some meditation and visualisation practices are provided below. These meditation practices can be done:

1. while you are seated in a relaxed manner for meditation,

2. while you are carrying out your daily activities,

3. while lying down,

4. just before sleep, and/or

5. just upon waking up.

If you decide to sit, while doing the meditation, then make sure that you are comfortably seated on a chair or in any kind of cross legged posture. You can sit in meditation at any time, during the day. Make sure that you are in a relaxed state at that time. If you learn to maintain a meditative state while doing your daily activities, you can do your visualisations no matter what you are doing. Just remember to remain in a relaxed state and think of God when you start your visualisation. This helps to get you linked to Him and it also helps to get your message across to Him.

Always begin your meditation through emerging the divine virtues from deep within or make sure that you are in a virtuous state. It will be easier to go within when you are in a virtuous state. It is very difficult to meditate if you are entertaining the vices. So when you sit in meditation, make sure that there are no vices in an emerged state in your mind. For example, if you are feeling angry, remove that anger from your mind. Push that which has made you angry, out of your mind and think of how fortunate you are to have finally found God or/and to walk into the Golden Aged world. This will help to remove that anger from your mind and to keep the virtues in an emerged state.

Don't think about how things keep going wrong. Don't think about how you hate something or someone. Think positive and use positive affirmations to train yourself to remain happy. Positive affirmations are like mantras during meditation. So while in meditation, keep repeating words (silently) such as "I am a blissful soul" etc. When silently repeating these positive affirmations, make sure that you believe it. Feel it (e.g. feel the bliss etc.) and it will be as if you are believing it. So it will be a reality.

When you keep using the virtues, and not the vices, you will find that you become a virtuous person, i.e. this becomes your nature. Then, you will find it even easier to begin your meditation. Always start your visualisations after making sure that you are not using the vices.

Do not shut the world out and go into a state where you are not aware of what is happening around you. Instead look at everything that is happening around you without letting it emerge any feelings within you. Notice what is happening without getting angry, annoyed or distressed. Remain in a meditative state no matter what is happening around you. Watching everything while in this detached state will make sure that bad impressions are not left within the soul. Do not remember the bad situations, at a later time, when you are not in a detached state because it might leave bad impressions within the soul.

Constantly keep a smile on your face. When you keep smiling, your brain will be releasing substances into the body to keep you happy. If you are experiencing love or some other virtues, have an appropriate expression on your face while continuing to smile.

Constantly try to keep yourself in a blissful stage with only the virtues and powers in an emerged state. Saturate the mind with bliss and you will easily have all kinds of wonderful experiences.

When doing visualisations for getting money, be careful about the intentions with which you are doing these visualisations because:

1. your intentions will be reflected in your aura and people will be able to sense it. Their interactions with you will then be based on what they can sense. If you do the visualisations because you want to use the money for world service (e.g. to help establish something for the Golden

Aged world, for bringing all the other 330 million deity souls into the Confluence Age, etc.) people will sense that you are angelic. If you do the visualisations based on greed, people will be scared to interact with you or they will be very careful while interacting with you.

2. your intentions will affect what you get through the Law of Karma. The act of making money is not bad if the intentions are good. If your intentions are good, you will get something good in return. If it is bad, you will get something bad in return.

During your visualisations, do not visualise harming or robbing someone for the sake of making your fortunes. This is bad karma and it has bad consequences. Just see money coming to you continuously without seeing it coming from any specific person. It is this kind of unharmful visualisation which easily materialises to become a reality. The best visualisation is to see the money coming from God.

When you do a visualisation, make sure that you have a clear picture of what you want in your mind. To materialise your visualisation, emotionalise your visualisation. For example, feel and see yourself as already having the money. Feel happy that you can now use the money for creating what will be taken into the Golden Aged world. Live it as you visualise. For example, visualise yourself as already being wealthy and prosperous. Have the feeling and firm faith that money is constantly coming to you effortlessly. If you believe that money flows to you effortlessly and you maintain this belief (consciously and subconsciously), you will be in a situation where money becomes easy to acquire.

You can use various kinds of meditation and visualisation practices:

1. to get what you want.

2. to walk into the Golden Aged world.

3. to increase your spiritual power.

4. to enjoy happiness, inner peace and tranquillity.

Keep your thoughts simple, during meditation, without being confused. If something is confusing you, contemplate on it with the thought that you should receive an understanding. Then, put it aside and keep your mind in a clear state. You will receive an understanding when it is time to receive it.

I am not going to repeat all the above preliminaries during the following meditation guidelines. So remember that you have to start while remaining relaxed etc.

First Meditation Guideline:

1. Remove all other thoughts from the mind and see yourself as the soul, seated in its seat in the center of your forehead, shining brilliantly and blissfully.

2. See God as a Point of Light (above you or before you). See His energies vibrating upon you. Experience the bliss, joy and other virtues which they empower you with.

3. Have a conversation with God. Tell Him whatever is in your heart.

Second Meditation Guideline:

1. Visualise how your QE Light bodies, for the walking in process, are being created through your own spiritual effort making.

2. Visualise that as these bodies get created, you begin to get lifted higher and higher until you are using the Vaikuntha in the Confluence Aged Subtle Region.

3. Visualise how the body then transforms into the perfect and beautiful Golden Aged physical body. See yourself using this body to live your life. Enjoy your visualisations.

Third Meditation Guideline:

1. Visualise that God is bringing you into the Higher Universe (in the

Holographic Universe).

2. Visualise that you are in the Higher Universe and have the faith that you are walking into the Golden Aged world.

3. See yourself as a soul or as the holographic being in the Holographic Universe. Observe how everything in the Holographic Universe is so willing and ready to serve you. See how they are waiting to fulfil your every desire.

NB: If you keep doing these practices, you will find yourself in a state where you will easily achieve what you want.

Everything in the Holographic Universe was meant to serve the human souls. Thus, when you visualise that you are in the higher dimensions, you will go into the higher dimensions. You must have the faith that you are going into the higher dimensions. If you have doubts about this, you will not be served by anything in the Holographic Universe. You do not have to issue commands like, "I order you. So lift me up". Everything in the Holographic Universe flows along based on your feelings and not on your verbal commands.

Keep yourself entertained during yoga, through variations in the practices. During the day, see yourself as moving around in higher dimensions within the Holographic Universe. Even though your body is still in the old world, see yourself as being in the Holographic World of the first half cycle.

When you are carrying out your daily activities, do them with the view that you are doing so in the higher dimensions. When you do this, you will feel as if you are doing them in the higher dimensions.

You can also remain entertained while seeing yourself floating up into a higher dimension. Make sure that you are experiencing bliss while you do this.

During your meditation and at other times, see the old world as being below you. See yourself and your environment in a higher dimension from that of the old world. When you do this, you will actually be in a higher dimension. This does not involve levitation of the body. It is a matter of lifting yourself into the higher dimensions in the Holographic Universe that is being created for the first half cycle. You will find that as you get lifted into the higher dimensions, you can attain a happy blissful stage more easily. The more you are involved with these practices, the easier it is for you to attain a happy blissful stage.

Chapter 53: Nature Serves in the Golden Aged World

Nature consists of the physical world and its phenomena, including the plants, oceans, seas, rivers, landscapes, mountains, rocks, animals and their behaviour, production and growth of young animals and plants, earth and products of the earth, the environment, stars, weather, the natural forces and processes which create and control what is happening in the universe, and everything else that is part and parcel of the physical world but excluding Mankind and what Mankind has created.

In the Golden Aged world, Nature serves the people. Since the people live their lives as if they are playing a game, they also sell what Nature provides similarly to how people do so in a game. Even those who are walking in will be able to take the benefits of the beautiful stuff which Nature provides for those who are walking into the Golden Aged world. Thus, they can gain financially in their game of life.

If you plan to sell something which Nature provides, visualise how Nature is providing what you need in abundance. For example, visualise your crops giving you an abundance of good tasty fruits, etc. Visualise yourself becoming rich through selling these. Visualise God helping you too so that you can take and use the bounty that Nature proffers. Visualise yourself as the divine soul, in the soul conscious state, enjoying all the benefits that Nature has to offer you. You can also visualise gold, gems etc. being washed ashore by the oceans. Visualise yourself collecting these and building a house for you to stay in. Visualise that gold, gems etc. just exist everywhere in your land. Visualise yourself taking those and creating what you want. When you keep having these kinds of visualisations, it will actually happen. Whatever you visualise will materialise. As you walk into the Golden Aged world, you are transforming into a master of the world (a god) and so bounteous Nature will serve you well.

Sell and use what Nature provides as part of the game. One should not make use of what Nature gives in order to satisfy one's greed.

One way of becoming wealthy is through getting gold easily from Nature. Gold can emerge from beneath the ground, from the oceans, etc. Even gold that appears magically can be used.

If you are involved with visualisations for receiving gold, consider that you are doing these visualisations for the benefit of Mankind on earth. As per the World Drama, gold will emerge from deep within the earth and the oceans will wash them ashore. Your visualisations will help you to receive some of this gold and so you need not toil so hard to dig gold out of the ground.

While I was writing this book, there were many times when I had wanted to change the title of the book because "Grow Rich" did not sound so spiritual. Fortunately, I did not. It is only when we collectively keep saying and thinking "Grow Rich" that the world is going to get enriched as it would be in the first half cycle. At least this book would help to remove a 'block' by influencing the spiritual people to not be ashamed of becoming rich etc.

There has to be unity among all the souls who are in the Corporeal World. Then only can we act as a single entity, a Collective Consciousness that sustains a perfectly enriched Corporeal World. There will be unity among the deity souls in the first half cycle. Through this unity, the deity souls would be able to sustain the perfect world which will serve them well. There can also be unity among the people now based on the understanding that we have to turn this planet into an enriched planet.

It is actually wrong to think that one is poor and that one is living in a poor world or poor environment because this helps to transform the world into the poor Kaliyug world. One is not poor so long as one is living a happy life.

There are a lot of actions which one can perform to transform this planet into a wonderfully entertaining place. For example, one could develop an amusement park which is filled with all sorts of birds etc. and see it metamorphose into a Golden Aged environment. The bodies of the birds etc. in heaven will be able to produce lovely sounds because of their perfect state and divine environment. In the heavenly world, the sounds produced by birds and everything else in Nature will sound very harmonious together. It will be as if they are singing various musical parts together. God tells us that these natural sounds would be music to us in Heaven. For example, God has said in His murlis (in the Brahma Kumaris):

1. "The wind will blow, the trees will sway, and the branches and twigs will move. Through this movement there will automatically be natural music playing... The creation, as your child, will play a variety of music for its world parents by moving its leaves. The rustle of the leaves from swaying trees will make different kinds of natural music."

2. "Just as these days they make artificial sound, in Heaven the birds' voices will become the variety of musical instruments. Like living toys, they will show you many varieties of displays. These days, people have learned how to produce talking toys of many forms. Over there also, the birds will entertain you at your signal with many varieties of beautiful voices and displays."

3. "Heaven will be very entertaining ... In Heaven, the music will not play to wake you up..., but there will be sweet music of bird songs to awaken you."

In one of the above quotations, the words "The creation, as your child", is a reference to how Nature's divine state is dependent on our divine state. When we attain our perfect state through practicing Brahma Kumaris Raja Yoga, Nature will also attain its perfect state. This will happen at the end of this cycle, when BKs become so powerful that the Power of the Gathering will enable the new divine world to be created. We make spiritual efforts now to attain a perfect state and we will enjoy the perfect state in the heavenly world, which God is getting created for us. In that heavenly world, Nature will be sustained by our perfect state.

In another of the above quotations, the words 'the birds will entertain you at your signal' indicate how the deities would be able to communicate with the birds on a subtle level because of their soul conscious state.

When I was rearing fishes and birds, long ago, I noticed that those fishes and birds were able to subtly communicate their requests for food through pulling my attention to them. These animals were not in their perfect state and so they did not act like the animals which exist in the first half cycle.

Nature exists based on the laws that are provided through Nature's 2D World Drama. The Laws of Nature that are relevant for the second half cycle would merge to become part of the 2D SWD during the second half cycle and the Divine Laws of Nature, from Nature's 2D World Drama, merge to become part of the 2D SWD during the first half cycle. In accordance with the Divine Laws, the birds in the heavenly world are there to entertain us. The humans, animals, birds etc. of the heavenly world are not taught the Divine Laws and they are also not taught to obey the Divine Laws. They naturally act according to the Divine Laws. As are the human souls, so is everything else. So the melodious songs of the birds in Heaven would be entertaining us. With just a signal, given at thought level by the deities, the birds would break into tuneful melodies to entertain them and the harmony of their songs would be enchanting. Everything else in Heaven would also be entertaining since the world is in its idyllic, perfect state.

In the Golden Age, the people are actually enjoying the bird songs in the 3D SWD of the Holographic Universe in a unique way because one is also entertained by the sounds of silence of those sounds. This is also a reason why the songs will sound so beautiful. Sounds will not sound so beautiful if they are only heard in the Real World, like how we hear it.

In the Kaliyug world, the wealthy try to create a beautiful environment, which they can enjoy living in, through using their money. In the Golden Aged world, Nature naturally provides a perfect paradisal environment for the people to live in. Even those who walk into the Golden Aged world can enjoy living in a beautiful environment, naturally.

Actually, even if one was not involved with trying to acquire money, one is like a rich person in the Golden Aged world because one will not lack anything since Nature provides everything that one needs. It is only in the second half cycle that there will be poor people who lack food, shelter etc.

There are not many people in the Golden Aged world since most of the souls will be in the Soul World. So the people will not lack anything. Further, Nature etc. will provide sustenance like fruits etc. in abundance.

In experiences, when my spiritual stage was very high, I had seen Nature as being happy to see me. I saw them in a happy, blissful and peaceful state. I had these experiences even though I was not trying to have these kinds of experiences. Maybe God had given me those experiences because of the role which I have to play at the end (as I am doing now).

If your stage is high as you are being lifted up into the higher dimensions, Nature will be happy to see you too because they will be spiritually strengthened and lifted up through you. So establish your link to God instead of being dependent on the environment to be uplifted.

Through visualising yourself as being in the Nature that is in its perfect state, you can bring yourself into that environment. Thus, I have included meditation commentaries below which you could use during meditation so as to bring yourself into the Nature which is in its perfect state.

First Meditation Commentary:

1. Sit relaxed in a blissful state.

2. Visualise everything in Nature as being filled with pure perfect

energies.

3. Visualise the air, water and plants as being in the blissful state.

4. Visualise that they are happy to serve you and be close to you since your energies are helping them to remain in the perfect, divine state.

Second Meditation Commentary:

As you read the following, visualise that you are in the Golden Aged world and that you are just getting up after having taken a short nap under a tree:

As I open my eyes with such great happiness, peace and bliss, I hear sweet music of bird songs. I look up and see the birds entertaining me with beautiful songs and displays. Happiness wells up within me with such great intensity and my eyes delight in seeing such beautiful birds. The bird sounds are like a variety of musical instruments and the birds themselves have such great beauty. They are like living toys, showing me many varieties of displays. Along with them, the pleasant breeze which is a natural fan for me, is also entertaining me with music to my delight. The wind is blowing, the trees are swaying, the branches and twigs are moving, and these also produce natural music in harmony with the others, entertaining me into a delightfully blissful state. I get up and walk happily and blissfully to the river. The weather is like spring and Nature seems to be so happy to be with me. They are bubbling with bliss and feeling so joyful to be in my company. They are so beautiful, so pure, so fresh and so wonderful to be with. The fragrance of herbs that the river water brings provides natural fragrance for me. I put my hands into the clean, pure river water and fill my hands with some water from the river. The water is filled with minerals, goodness, bliss and supreme happiness. As I drink it, I can feel the cool water flowing within me. It is happy to serve me. The fruits, flowers, leaves, air, earth and everything else around me are also vibrant with life, at ease, warm, beautiful and in harmony. They are also so blissfully happy to be with me and to serve me. I experience such joy and glory. It feels so good because I am in paradise, the very essence of which is purity. I am completely happy, perfect, peaceful, blissful, joyful and pure with love in my heart which is unconditional. Nothing can disturb my happiness. At a distance, in a beautiful garden, I see others who are as beautiful as me. I walk towards them with movements that are full of grace, beauty and royalty...

NB: Some of the feelings felt by Nature and that of the deity were from the writer's own personal experiences in visions.

More Meditation Guidelines:

1. See yourself in Vaikuntha or Dwarka. See yourself as having a perfect disease-free body which is being nourished by food that gives the body everything that it needs. Visualise that all the people there are healthy and disease-free like you. Visualise that you and the others live long, as young people, in Vaikuntha/Dwarka because of the perfect state of the body.

2. Visualise Vaikuntha/Dwarka as being surrounded by water which is so nutritious that there are a lot of healthy life-forms in the water which are entertaining you.

3. Visualise that you can get whatever you want from that Ocean. Visualise that even gold is washed ashore from that Ocean.

4. Visualise that Vaikuntha/Dwarka is filled with gems, gold etc. Visualise that you can easily take these and use them as you want.

5. Visualise that your home is built with all these gems; and gold is adorning the walls. How beautiful they, and your home, look.

6. Visualise that there is a beautiful garden around your home which is filled with all sorts of lovely flowers and birds. These too serve you well. The whole place looks so gorgeous with unusual trees which provide you with lots of lovely stuff. There are lovely rivers and lakes there which are filled with pure drinking water. This water is as nutritious as milk and tastes like nectar. Words will not be able to express the splendour and heavenly beauty of the place.

7. Visualise that the beautiful birds and animals are entertaining you. They subtly know what you want them to do and they act accordingly.

Figure 1

Corporeal World and Holographic Universe during the **First Half Cycle**

A. Higher Universe:

1. QE Light source and white holes

2. Depths of the SWL

   Ocean of QE Light Energies or QE Light Ocean (Cosmic Consciousness)

3. Upper part in the Border of the SWL

   (Shore of the QE Light Ocean)

4. Cosmic Field

5. 2D SWD or 2D Subtle World Drama

   (part of the Akashic Records)

6. First Field } Quantum Ocean or Unified Field
   (Ocean of QE Light and Quantum Energies) that
   provides the 3D SWD (3D Subtle World Drama)
7. Second Field } which is the holographic form of the World Drama

8. Real World (the material world which we live in on earth)

(bracket annotation: dimensions wthin the Lower Part in the Border of the SWL)

B. Lower Universe:

1. Black Energy Field
   (between the SWL and the Quantum World,
   a dimension of the quantum energies around the edge of the Quantum World)

2. Border of the Quantum World
   (Shore of the QE Ocean)

3. Depths of the Quantum World

   (*Ocean of Quantum Energies* or QE Ocean)

   } Quantum World or Garbhodaka Ocean

A clearer picture of Figure 1 can be seen at the author's website at:
http://www.gbk-books.com/figure-1.html

Figure 2

Corporeal World and Holographic Universe during the **Second Half Cycle**

A. Higher Universe:

1. QE Light source and white holes

B. Lower Universe:

1. Depths of the SWL

   Ocean of QE Light Energies
   or QE Light Ocean (Cosmic Consciousness) } SWL

2. Border of the SWL
   (Shore of the QE Light Ocean)

3. Cosmic Field
   (in the border between the SWL and Quantum World,
   around the edge of the SWL)

4. 2D SWD or 2D Subtle World Drama

   (part of the Akashic Records)

5. First Field } Quantum Ocean or Unified Field
   (Ocean of QE Light and Quantum Energies) that
   provides the 3D SWD (3D Subtle World Drama)
6. Second Field } which is the holographic form of the World Drama

7. Real World

8. Black Energy Field

9. Lower Part in the Border of the Quantum World
   (Shore of the QE Ocean)

10. Depths of the Quantum World

    (*Ocean of Quantum Energies* or QE Ocean)

dimensions wthin the Upper Part
in the Border of the Quantum World

A clearer picture of Figure 2 can be seen at the author's website at:
http://www.gbk-books.com/figure-2.html

Figure 3

Dimensions in the Lower Universe (based on density)

Vaikuntha

1. Depths of the SWL or QE Light Ocean
   - 13th auric field

2. Border of the SWL
   - 11th and 12th auric fields

}SWL

3. Border between the SWL and Cosmic Field
   - 10th auric field can be said to be here

4. Cosmic Field
   - 8th , 9th and 10th auric fields

5. 2D SWD or 2D Subtle World Drama
   (Part of the Akashic Records and Karana Ocean)

Seven Heavenly Lokas

6. Satyaloka/Brahmaloka
   - Sahasrara Chakra & 7th Auric Field (in upper First Field)
   - Above Tapoloka until the top edge of the visible universe

7. Tapoloka
   - Third Eye Chakra & 6th Auric Field (in the middle of the First Field)
   - Above Milky Way Galaxy in the sky, where other galaxies are

8. Janaloka
   - Throat Chakra & 5th Auric Field (in lower First Field)
   - Above Maharloka, in the Milky Way Galaxy that is seen in the sky

9. Maharloka
   - Heart Chakra & 4th Auric Field
   (in the borders between First Field & Second Field)
   - Above Swargaloka & above Dhruva (pole star) in the sky

10. Svargaloka/Indraloka
    - Navel Chakra & 3rd Auric Field/Mental Plane (upper Second Field)
    - From sun to Dhruva (pole star) in the sky

11. Bhuvarloka
    - 2nd Chakra & 2nd Auric Field/Astral Plane (middle Second Field)
    - Atmospheric sphere (from earth to sun in the sky)

12. Bhuloka
    - Root Chakra & Etheric Field/1st Auric Field (lower Second Field)
    - Terrestrial sphere (Earth, physical body, etc.)

Upper Part in the Border of the Quantum World

13. Black Energy Field

14. Lower Part in the Border of the Quantum World

} Hell lokas are experienced here

15. Depths of the Quantum World

A clearer picture of Figure 3 can be seen at the author's website at:
http://www.gbk-books.com/figure-3.html

Figure 4

Dimensions during the Creation of the Golden Aged World

Spiritual Sky

Vaikuntha / Spiritual Sky / Paravyoma

1. Goloka

A. During the Confluence Age:

i. Confluence Aged Shankerpuri
(Consists of powerful Confluence Aged souls who are truly in Goloka. Their high spiritual stage transform the world into the Golden Aged world) - used through 6th & 7th chakras in Angelic Body

ii. Confluence Aged Vishnupuri
(Golden Aged 3D SWD, and subtle Vaikuntha of powerful Confluence Aged souls who are walking into the Golden Aged world, will overlap this space) - used through 5th, 6th & 7th chakras in Angelic Body

iii. Confluence Aged Brahmapuri
(Golden Aged Real World, & Golden Aged Vaikuntha for the weak Confluence Aged souls walking into the Golden Aged world, will overlap this space)

B. At the beginning of the Golden Age:

i. Goloka/Vrindavan
(This celestial/spiritual loka is used by Bks who walk in to serve Krishna, the first Golden Aged child born in the Golden Age)

ii. Gokul/Vrindavan
(This material loka is used by Bks who walk in to serve Krishna, the first Golden Aged child born in the Golden Age)

2. Madhura

3. Dwarka

4. Ayodhya

5. White Hole or Abode of Sadashiva
(Entrance to Angelic World. Abode of QE Light energies in White Hole)

6. Brahmajyoti
(Effulgence from the QE Light source energised by God's Effulgence)

7. 2D SWD or 2D Subtle World Drama
(Part of the Karana Ocean and Akashic Records)

8. Abode of Sadashiva
(Entrance to the tunnel that provides entrance to the Angelic World via White Hole)

9. Satyaloka/Brahmaloka (Sahasrara Chakra & 7th Auric Field)

10. Tapoloka (Third Eye Chakra & 6th Auric Field)

11. Janaloka (Throat Chakra & 5th Auric Field)

12. Maharloka (Heart Chakra & 4th Auric Field)

13. Svargaloka/Indraloka (Navel Chakra & 3rd Auric Field)

Higher Universe / Vaikuntha

A clearer picture of Figure 4 can be seen at the author's website at: http://www.gbk-books.com/figure-4.html

Other Books by Brahma Kumari Pari

1. Holographic Universe: An Introduction

NB: An eBook can be downloaded for free soon after the eBook has been published. So subscribe to Pari's Mailing List (at http://www.gbk-books.com/mailing-list.html) so that you will be informed when a new e-book has been published; as a consequence of which you will be able to download your free copy.

Lightning Source UK Ltd.
Milton Keynes UK
UKHW02f2131181217
314719UK00008B/1398/P

9 781548 064600